The Politics of Equality

COLUMBIA STUDIES IN CONTEMPORARY
AMERICAN HISTORY

William E. Leuchtenburg and Alan Brinkley,
General Editors

THE POLITICS OF EQUALITY

Hubert H. Humphrey and the
African American Freedom Struggle

Timothy N. Thurber

Columbia University Press   ◢◣   *New York*

Columbia University Press
New York   Chichester, West Sussex
Copyright © 1999 Columbia University Press
All rights reserved

Library of Congress Cataloging-in-Publication Data
Thurber, Timothy Nel.
    The politics of equality : Hubert H. Humphrey and the African
American freedom struggle / Timothy N. Thurber.
        p.   cm. — (Columbia studies in contemporary American history)
    Includes bibliographical references and index.
    ISBN 0-231-11046-4. — ISBN 0-231-11047-2.
    1. Humphrey, Hubert H. (Hubert Horatio), 1911–1978—Relations with
Afro-Americans. 2. Afro-Americans—Civil rights—History—20th
century. 3. Race discrimination—United States—History—20th
century. 4. United States—Race relations. I. Title. II. Series.
E840.8.H85T48   1998
973.923'092—dc21
                                                            98-36359
                                                            CIP

Casebound editions of Columbia University Press books are
printed on permanent and durable acid-free paper.

Printed in the United States of America

c 10 9 8 7 6 5 4 3 2 1
p 10 9 8 7 6 5 4 3 2 1

CONTENTS

ACKNOWLEDGMENTS

Completing this book would not have been possible without the generous financial support of several organizations. I would like to thank the Everett Dirksen Foundation, the John F. Kennedy Foundation, the Lyndon Baines Johnson Foundation, the Gerald R. Ford Foundation, the Minnesota Historical Society, and the University of North Carolina at Chapel Hill for making travel to numerous archives possible. I also want to extend my gratitude to the staff members of the archives I visited. Special thanks are in order for the friendly and helpful staff at the Minnesota Historical Society, who endured countless requests for materials and made thousands of copies in good humor.

Numerous friends have helped make this work possible. My brother Matt and his wife, Kristen, provided a place to stay and good company on my numerous research trips to the Humphrey papers. John Neumann and Ginny Read, Brad and Kim Gray, Margaret and David Kelliher, Ian Charpentier, and Margaret DeLapp all made sure that my time in the Twin Cities involved fun as well as work. I would also like to thank Larry Lorber, who helped arrange several oral history interviews.

Several former Humphrey friends and associates graciously took time from their busy schedules to share their thoughts and recollections with me. This work is stronger as a result of their insights and kindness.

I want to thank Kate Wittenberg, Susan Pensak, Alex Coolman, and the rest of the staff at Columbia University press for their help, patience, and guidance throughout the process of turning this manuscript into a book. They have been a delight to work with and have saved me from numerous errors.

I am indebted to several individuals who offered advice along the way. Steven Lawson, Steven Gillon, Bruce Schulman, Roger Lotchin, Peter Filene, and David Carter read all or part of the manuscript and made numerous helpful comments to help sharpen the analysis and clarify the prose. During my career as a graduate student at the University of North Carolina Peter Coclanis provided a great deal of good advice, encouragement, and friendship that helped make my time in Chapel Hill so enjoyable.

One could not ask for a better mentor than William E. Leuchtenburg. A source of inspiration, he has given generously of his time and strengthened this work by raising probing questions, pointing out foolish mistakes, sharing his encyclopedic knowledge of recent American history, and clarifying frequently sloppy prose. He cheerfully wrote letters of recommendation for me and, despite a busy schedule, returned my work, in a timely fashion, full of insightful suggestions for improvement. He has set a high standard of professionalism and collegiality that I can hope to emulate but never will equal.

Most important, there is Gretchen. She has been a source of love, understanding, and support and has patiently endured long periods of separation while I traveled or insisted on spending time in front of the computer rather than with her. This work is lovingly dedicated to her with deep gratitude for the years we have spent together and in eager anticipation of our future together.

The Politics of Equality

I

Air Force One touched down in Maryland shortly after noon on January 14, 1978. A casket containing the body of Senator Hubert H. Humphrey soon emerged from the jet to a nineteen-gun salute. The former vice president was headed for the Capitol, where he would lie in the Rotunda, a tribute normally reserved for a head of state, for the next twenty hours. Many in the crowd of three hundred people that greeted the arrival of the hearse and the Humphrey family at the Capitol were moved to tears as a U.S. Army band played "A Mighty Fortress is Our God" while military pallbearers slowly carried the casket up the steps.[1]

An estimated sixty thousand people braved the damp, chilly weather that had settled over Washington that weekend to pay their final respects. The queue of mourners lasted well past midnight and resumed the next morning. Many who came were African Americans who felt they had lost a friend. "He was a wonderful man, a great man," a black woman from Washington said. "He achieved so much, civil rights, that's number one." An African American teacher described Humphrey as "a great friend of our people," while an elderly black man, remembering how Humphrey had fought to change white attitudes about race, simply observed, "He was a good man." Another African American teacher who had grown up under segregation in Mississippi fondly recalled "how refreshing and encouraging" it was to hear Humphrey "saying that racial justice and equality are what the country is all about."[2]

Hundreds of Washington officials gathered in the Rotunda at eleven the next day for a memorial service. Lady Bird Johnson made a rare visit to

Washington to honor the man who had served so long with her husband. Even Humphrey's old nemesis, Richard Nixon, came. It was the first time Nixon had returned to Washington since resigning the presidency in 1974. President Jimmy Carter, the most prominent of a new type of southern Democrat who rejected the politics of hate and segregation, spoke eloquently of the profound influence Humphrey had upon him while growing up in Georgia. "In a time of impending social crisis thirty years ago, his was the first voice I ever heard, a lone voice, persistently demanding human rights for all Americans." Humphrey, the president continued, had "a clear voice, a strong voice, a passionate voice, which recruited others to join in a battle ... so that equal rights of black Americans could be gained."[3]

Humphrey's body was flown back to Minnesota that afternoon. When the hearse arrived at the state capitol, the three thousand people who had gathered despite frigid temperatures in the teens began singing "We Shall Overcome." Tens of thousands filed past the casket during the next several hours. "You have to take your hat off to him," a seventy-four-year-old African American woman from Chicago stated. "He dared to take a stand on civil rights. He was on the side of black people. That's why I came." Jesse Jackson, Coretta Scott King, and numerous other African American leaders attended Humphrey's funeral at St. Paul House of Hope Presbyterian Church. A black choir provided some of the music. That evening Humphrey was buried at Lakewood Cemetery in Minneapolis.[4]

The outpouring of grief over Humphrey's death was not limited to his home state or Washington, D.C. One thousand people, most of them African American, had met at Ebenezer Baptist Church in Atlanta the night Humphrey's body was flown to Washington. The original purpose of the gathering was to bestow upon Humphrey the Martin Luther King Jr. Humanitarian Award, but the senator's death the night before transformed the ceremony into a memorial service. Calling Humphrey "the most outspoken and courageous leader in the Senate," Coretta Scott King lamented that black Americans had "lost a great friend." Likewise, Ofield Dukes, who had worked with Humphrey on civil rights issues during the mid-1960s, described his ex-boss as "the best friend that black Americans ever had in the high echelons of government." John Lewis, the former head of SNCC, solemnly remarked that Humphrey had "demonstrated ... that one man, can, indeed, change the world." The final words fittingly belonged to Humphrey. In a prepared statement he noted:

> Today, life is better for most black Americans than it was for their parents or grandparents. Incomes are better, educational opportunities are

greater, health care has improved, political influence and representation has increased, and much more. . . . It is real progress, and we must not forget that it has occurred. But, we cannot be satisfied in measuring our progress solely by the distance we have come from the abominable conditions that existed in a period of gross injustice. . . . We are a long way from our goal of a society with equal opportunity and justice for all. In moving toward this goal, our focus today must be on jobs—decent jobs, good paying jobs, jobs with a challenge, jobs with a future.

Those in the audience undoubtedly agreed with Humphrey's emphasis on jobs as the key to racial equality, for King and many others were involved in an ongoing legislative battle in Washington to pass the Humphrey-Hawkins full employment bill, a measure intended to promote employment, including public service jobs as a last resort if necessary, as an alternative to welfare dependency and growing joblessness among segments of the African American population.[5]

Pundits commenting on Humphrey's civil rights legacy during those cold January days usually pointed to his 1948 speech at the Democratic convention urging his party to adopt a strong civil rights plank, his long crusade to eliminate segregation, which culminated in his leadership of the landmark 1964 Civil Rights Act through the Senate, and his efforts to promote equal voting rights for African Americans. These remained the lasting impressions that many Americans, both white and black, had of the ebullient politician from Minnesota. Because these issues are integral to any comprehensive understanding of Humphrey's involvement with racial matters, I have addressed them here. Nonetheless, such an emphasis fails to convey the complexity of Humphrey's commitment to racial justice. Anyone who had followed Humphrey's career closely knew that his remarks in Atlanta more accurately captured his thoughts about race relations in the United States. To be sure, segregation and the denial of equal political participation outraged Humphrey, but he saw economic inequality as the chief problem confronting African Americans. Indeed, while mayor of Minneapolis during the mid-1940s, he oversaw the adoption and implementation of the nation's first municipal Fair Employment Practices Commission (FEPC) law. During his early years in the Senate, he gave FEPC more attention than other civil rights legislation. He accorded voting rights and desegregation higher priority only after it had become clear that FEPC was going nowhere in Congress and when troubles intensified in the South regarding these two areas during the late 1950s and early 1960s. Humphrey joined the nation in condemning the brutality of Bull Connor's police dogs and fire hoses in 1963, but he was one of a few voices who also warned that structural changes in the economy threatened to undermine much of the progress African Americans had made since the end of World War II. "We can legislate civil rights until we fill the statute books, but until there are jobs which provide an opportunity for a man or woman to use their talents for constructive work, those rights will be in a sense only legal or theoretical rights," he observed that turbulent summer. "The radical transformation in the nature of the employment market means that only skilled workers will have any sustained and worthwhile employment." As vice president, he oversaw efforts to enforce civil rights laws, including the right to equal employment opportunity, and to provide summer jobs for ghetto youth. During the 1968 presidential race he sought to make a domestic Marshall Plan a central part of his campaign. Finally, after returning to the Senate in 1971, Humphrey regularly sponsored legislation to create a domestic development bank, which he believed would help promote economic growth in the nation's inner cities, and, more important, called upon the federal government to pursue a full employment policy. For Humphrey, fighting for racial equality involved far more than toppling Jim Crow.[6] And so issues of race, class, and politics at the national level form the backbone of this book.

Humphrey was not alone in linking economics and race, of course. Questions of jobs and economic power were integral to the modern African American freedom struggle. Labor leader A. Philip Randolph made jobs his central goal during his threatened march on Washington in 1941. The establishment of the federal FEPC dominated the legislative agenda of leading civil rights organizations such as the NAACP in the late 1940s and early 1950s. The March on Washington in 1963 was a rally for "Jobs and Freedom." Martin Luther King identified economic opportunity as his chief objective during the mid-1960s, when he centered his attention on the problems of the urban North. Likewise, Malcolm X and black power advocates urged African Americans to become economically self-sufficient. Urban League head Whitney Young regularly called for a domestic Marshall Plan during the 1960s, and Bayard Rustin endorsed full employment in his proposed freedom budget. Jobs comprised the heart of the demands of the Poor People's Campaign of 1968. That same year the Kerner Commission pointed to a lack of employment opportunity as a leading cause of the riots of the mid-1960s and urged the creation of one million public sector jobs as a way to prevent further violence.

By concentrating on how Humphrey wrestled with issues of economic opportunity for African Americans throughout his career, this work swims against the historiographical tide. Many historians have rightly observed that economic opportunity did indeed constitute the unfinished legacy of the Second Reconstruction, yet they have paid relatively little attention to how the state responded to demands for economic justice for blacks. Those interested in the politics of race have concentrated instead on voting rights and segregation, areas where there have been far more successes. To be sure, there are numerous works on the War on Poverty, but historians have focused largely on how the federal government helped end de jure discrimination in the South. They have looked at various presidential administrations, flashpoints such as Little Rock, Birmingham, and Selma, and legislative victories such as the 1964 Civil Rights Act and the Voting Rights Act of 1965. Relatively little attention, moreover, has been paid to questions of civil rights policy since the mid-1960s. The few historians who have explored civil rights policy issues at the federal level since then have provided much needed works on the origins and development of affirmative action, not economic policy. Scholars of the civil rights movement initially studied the activities of presidents, federal institutions, prominent black leaders such as Martin Luther King Jr., and national organizations such as the NAACP, the Urban League, SNCC, SCLC, and CORE. The vast majority of civil rights historians, however, have in recent years turned their focus away from the national stage altogether to concentrate on community studies that analyze the efforts of the heretofore anonymous but courageous black men and women who diligently fought for equality in countless place across the nation. This shift has resulted in a deeper and more accurate understanding of the black freedom struggle. We now appropriately recognize that it was primarily fought by "average" African Americans and their white allies, not famous black leaders such as King or politicians in Washington, D.C.[7]

Implicit in this shift are the assumptions that the full story of civil rights at the national level had been told by that first generation of scholars or that the role of the state was unimportant. But as the historian Hugh Davis Graham has noted, certain questions about race in modern America have demonstrated "an abiding importance and . . . generated a lasting controversy that was often not accorded them at the time." Graham's perceptive comment refers to the heated debate over affirmative action, but it can also be applied to the struggle over economic policy concerning African Americans. What the state did, and did not do, has had a profound effect on the economic fate of blacks since World War II. Aspects of this story, such as tax and spending policies for highways, home mortgages, or welfare and the War on Poverty, are well known. I hope to add to this literature by showing how issues that have received relatively little or no attention from historians but were of central concern to Humphrey, including FEPC, summer jobs for ghetto youth, a domestic Marshall Plan, and full employment, also help explain the outcomes of the last fifty years.

II

I also seek to contribute to the growing body of scholarship on the development of post–World War II liberalism. The travails of liberalism have attracted the attention of many scholars in recent years. Much of this literature contends that liberals sowed the seeds of their own destruction by advocating too timid a reform agenda, especially in the immediate aftermath of World War II. Had liberals only been bolder in seeking to tame the excesses of capitalism and promote racial equality, the basic argument goes, they would have won broad and lasting support among the public, cemented an alliance between working-class whites and African Americans, and taken the United States further down the road toward social democracy. Instead, liberals were allegedly too preoccupied with fighting communism and placating big business, and thus they thwarted a leftward thrust in American politics. However, as David Plotke has suggested, proponents of this interpretation underplay the depth of conservatism in American politics. They fail to see that the main alternatives to liberalism during the post–World War II era were not to be found on the left, but rather on the right. For a generation following World War II scholars followed Lionel Trilling's lead by assuming or asserting that conservatism was a marginal impulse in American public life. Recently, however, some historians have begun to acknowledge the depth of conservatism in post–World War II politics. Whereas many scholars have viewed liberalism as a steadily triumphant force dominating American politics during the twentieth century, I see reform efforts such as the New Deal or Great Society as aberrations resulting from peculiar historical developments. Contrary to critics who claim that liberals won only the easy battles in ending segregation and securing voting rights, I believe that liberals always had a difficult time advocating any type of civil rights reform. This was true in the late 1940s and early 1950s, when Humphrey found it impossible to amass a political coalition strong enough to move mild legislation to promote voting rights or create a civil rights commission through a recalcitrant Congress. He recalled the difficulties of those early days at a gathering of civil rights leaders at the Lyndon B. Johnson Library in 1972:

> We look back on [the late 1940s and 1950s] as the easy days of the civil rights struggle. But if we think a moment longer . . . these easy days were

not so easy. In the early 1950s, the number of U.S. Senators who were ac-
tively committed to passing the pending civil rights legislation could caucus in the rear corner of the Senate cloakroom. And I have the distinct
impression that the Senate establishment of those years was decidedly un-
enthusiastic about these bills. One might even say downright hostile. . . .
These were years of unrelieved frustration and failure.

Similarly, there were few significant legislative victories for Humphrey regarding racial matters after 1968. I do not mean to minimize liberalism's tri-
umphs, for indeed there were some significant gains, but rather to argue for
a more balanced explanation of its limits. There were other reasons in addition to flaws in liberals' civil rights vision or their occasional lack of political
courage holding back racial progress.[8]

Other scholars have located liberalism's troubles in the late 1960s. According to this view, liberalism took a politically disastrous turn after 1965
when it moved from a color-blind ideal based on equal opportunity to a
color-conscious policy of affirmative action rooted in a goal of equal results.
Had liberals maintained their original position, these scholars imply, the New
Deal coalition would have held together and much of the racial bitterness of
the past twenty-five years would have been avoided or minimized. Looking
at Humphrey's involvement with race casts doubt on this view as well. Only
under special circumstances resulting from the brutal crackdown on civil
rights demonstrators in 1963 and 1965 did the legislative logjam break. In retrospect the legislative victories of the mid-1960s stand more as isolated but
important gains, not signs of a deep and lasting commitment on the part of
whites to address social and economic troubles facing African Americans.
The New Deal coalition constituents who briefly supported civil rights legislation in 1964 and 1965 were unwilling to back more comprehensive efforts to ameliorate economic inequality. Thus, Humphrey's call for a domestic Marshall Plan in 1968 went unheeded, as did his efforts in the 1970s for a
national domestic development bank and full employment. Liberals such as
Humphrey were far more sympathetic to the plight of African Americans in
the rural South or the urban North than most whites in the New Deal coalition or most members of Congress. Conflict over crime, housing, and
schooling exacerbated already deep racial divisions and helped prevent
Humphrey from leading a class-based alliance of whites and blacks.[9]

Both camps looking to explain liberalism's demise thus posit too much
faith in liberals' ability to direct the flow of national politics and overestimate
the public's commitment to racial equality. They assume that had liberals
made the "right" choice, then the political history of the past fifty years

would have been markedly different. But leadership in a democratic society, as Garry Wills writes, involves more than "trumpeting one's own certitudes." It requires "sounding a specific call to a specific people capable of response."[10] Humphrey's career shows that liberals more often than not had to react to circumstances not of their own making and that they usually lacked the political strength to achieve their civil rights goals. As the historian Gary Gerstle has contended, liberals were not as dominant as their challengers on the right or left charged. This is not to suggest that liberals were powerless or to minimize Humphrey's shortcomings. There were flaws in many of his proposals to advance racial equality. He sometimes unnecessarily trimmed his civil rights views for political advantage for himself or his party. His poor administrative abilities contributed to the failure of two Great Society efforts he headed. Moreover, he placed too much faith in the public. Humphrey always trusted that whites would live up to their democratic ideals. Though he appropriately rejected the other extreme of thinking, that whites were racist to the core and would never change, there was a good deal more racism among whites than Humphrey acknowledged. He and other liberals did indeed contribute to their own political troubles. Nevertheless, broad social and political developments constituted severe constraints that sharply limited the possibilities for reform. Humphrey and other liberals faced fierce resistance from powerful forces determined to preserve the racial status quo.[11]

Humphrey's involvement with racial issues also sheds light not only on liberalism's troubled and tenuous political fortunes but also on its evolution during the post–World War II era. As the historian Alan Brinkley has outlined, liberalism underwent a significant transformation during this period. During the 1930s liberalism meant economic reform first and foremost. For New Deal liberals the chief problem confronting many Americans, both white and black, was economic. Liberals sought to use government to protect citizens from the vagaries of the market by implementing a rudimentary social welfare system and to promote economic prosperity for all by intervening in the economy through taxation and spending policies. This brand of liberalism exerted a powerful influence on Humphrey while he was growing up in South Dakota during the Depression and remained with him throughout his career. It shaped his thinking in a number of areas, including race. Starting in the 1940s, however, questions of individual and group rights moved onto the liberal agenda. By the late 1960s these concerns were paramount. Liberals eagerly embraced the rights revolution that saw previously marginalized groups, including African Americans, demand more forcefully than ever the chance to participate fully in American life. In fighting for an end to segregation and equal voting rights, Humphrey contributed to this shift in liberalism, yet he remained more concerned with promoting economic opportunity for African Americans. His involvement with race, especially after the mid-1960s, was to a considerable degree an unsuccessful attempt to blend these two strands of liberalism. Ironically, Humphrey's legislative successes during the 1960s helped cause his failures a decade later. Promoting greater individual rights for African Americans deepened racial animosity, which, in turn, limited Humphrey's ability to address economic problems confronting many blacks.[12]

Liberals faced two critical choices in the 1970s. The Democratic Party found itself in deep political trouble as white southerners and blue-collar whites in the North were voting for Republicans such as Richard Nixon or independents such as George Wallace. Race was not the only factor behind these seismic political shifts, but it clearly played a central role. Some Democrats argued that their party had to continue to advocate school busing and race-based polices, such as affirmative action, to remedy past injustices. White voters would simply have to be convinced of the merit of such approaches, they insisted. Humphrey offered a different prescription for the party's electoral misfortunes. He maintained that the Democrats could restore the New Deal coalition by concentrating on economic policies, such as full employment, that would apply to both whites and blacks alike. He favored the politics of class over the politics of race. There is good reason to doubt that the racial animosities that had intensified during the late 1960s and early 1970s could be swept aside as easily as Humphrey had assumed. Forming an alliance of working-class whites and African Americans would have been extremely difficult given the battles over busing, crime, housing, and education that embroiled many urban areas. The Democratic Party, though, never embraced such a political agenda. A new generation of Democrats had come to power. Having reached political maturity during the 1960s, they were determined to keep the battles of the rights revolution at the center of the Democratic agenda. This is not to intimate that Humphrey's call to return to class-based politics, which had numerous flaws, represented a superior moral or political alternative to race-based policies. It was a road not taken.[13]

The second choice confronting the Democratic Party involved how it would respond to the end of the post–World War II economic boom. By the 1970s high inflation and high unemployment had led to economic misery for numerous Americans, both white and black. As far as Humphrey was concerned, joblessness constituted the more pressing problem. "If price stability is to be gained at the price of seven million, eight million, ten million people being left unemployed, then that policy is politically and morally indefensible," he declared. "The test of a moral government is not only what it does for the majority, but how it responds to the needs of the minority." Humphrey's appeal for a return to New Deal liberalism fell largely on deaf ears, for, like their Republican counterparts, the vast majority of Democrats refused to tamper with the market in as dramatic a fashion as Humphrey wanted. Whereas Humphrey looked to the New Deal for inspiration, younger Democrats saw the solutions of the 1930s as largely irrelevant to modern problems. Though not unsympathetic to the plight of the jobless, they were more worried about inflation. Humphrey saw bureaucracy as beneficent, but the failures of the War on Poverty and other federal programs led many Democrats to doubt such a positive view of government. Politically, they wanted to pursue the votes of white, middle-class, suburban voters who were becoming hostile to government, rising taxes, and increasing prices. These voters, not the old coalition that had elected Franklin Roosevelt, constituted the new heart of a winning electoral majority. The suburbanization of American politics had begun, and with it a new set of issues dominated the national agenda.

Though Humphrey retained his New Deal faith in the primacy of economic equality and using the state to achieve his desired social and economic outcomes, his conception of what was necessary to reach his goals changed dramatically over his career. During his thirty years in public life he moved steadily toward greater governmental involvement in the economy. FEPC, with its command of "thou shalt not discriminate in hiring," was liberal for its day but ultimately too weak to address the economic problems facing African Americans. Humphrey belatedly realized this in the mid-1960s. Yet rather than embrace the emerging concept of group rights, he continued to seek expansion of individual opportunity. Like other liberals, Humphrey assumed that the economic system was fundamentally sound. Humphrey expected that a combination of economic growth and Great Society programs centered on reforming the individual would allow blacks to participate fully in the burgeoning economy. This strategy reduced black poverty and helped lead to the rise of a sizable African American middle class, but such an approach did little for blacks in the inner cities. Their plight worsened in the 1960s and 1970s as unemployment skyrocketed and social problems mushroomed. Convinced that the roots of the difficulties in the nation's inner cities lay in broad changes in the economy, Humphrey shifted his views substantially. The economy, he argued, had entered a new era in which old assumptions no longer applied. Humphrey now proposed to guarantee employment as a basic right of citizenship. Jobs would be created through greater reliance on European-style economic planning or, as a last resort, a public works jobs program. Whereas he had once concentrated on reforming the supply of labor, now he shifted his attention to the demand for labor. Joblessness, he concluded, was not the result of an individual's shortcomings, but rather structural flaws in the economy. Full employment was a far cry from FEPC.

A look at how Humphrey wrestled with questions of economic opportunity speaks powerfully to us today. He would welcome the growth of the black middle class, but he would not be surprised at the deplorable conditions in many of the nation's inner cities. Indeed, he foresaw much of what has transpired since his death in 1978. The continuation of economic trends begun in the late 1950s, he warned at the twilight of his career, would leave the United States with "a sizable segment of [its] population in danger of developing an alienated lifestyle—of becoming a class apart—separated from the mainstream . . . compelled to cut corners, and maintained by an inequitable and inadequate system of welfare." Humphrey would no doubt be disappointed in the nation's failure to confront these problems more vigorously than it has. Many pundits and politicians had written off Humphrey following his defeat in 1968 as emblematic of a stale liberalism that had grown irrelevant to the chief problems of the day. On the contrary, Humphrey's full employment bill, for all of its shortcomings, demonstrated that he was keenly aware of how economic trends had created deep problems for African Americans. He may not have found the right answer, but he was asking some important questions that need to be raised again. Humphrey had recognized that neither continued welfare dependency nor reliance on the invisible hand of the market would by themselves be sufficient to improve conditions in the ghetto.[14]

There is another aspect of Humphrey's career that resonates in the contemporary debate over race. Throughout his public life Humphrey remained deeply committed to integration and a vision of blacks and whites working together for a common goal of economic justice for all. He reminded whites and African Americans that their futures were inextricably intertwined. Attempts by whites to flee urban problems were ultimately futile, Humphrey realized, while African Americans who thought that blacks should avoid interracial alliances were also doomed to failure. His was not a call for the elimination of all differences into one ideal but rather an appeal for whites and blacks to recognize that they shared a common humanity and had a common interest in economic opportunity, safe streets, and stable families. Such a vision stands in sharp contrast to much of contemporary liberalism's focus on group identity and racial or cultural differences. Many liberals today equate integration with weakness and naïveté. They are quite right to be concerned about the possibility of certain interests being lost in broad coalitions. Humphrey's career shows how hard it was to build bridges between blacks and whites. Nevertheless, he knew that racial unity was a noble ideal worth fighting for. He understood that though liberals would have a difficult time achieving their aims, even when united, progressive politics was doomed to failure if liberals celebrated what divided them rather than their shared goals.

I

That the prairie of South Dakota had little in common with Harlem would
have been obvious to anyone who tuned to television station WNEW in
New York City at ten o'clock on the evening of June 1, 1964. During the
next hour, however, viewers with an abstract sense of the differences between these two places saw just how enormous that gap was thanks to a
documentary, "My Childhood," that depicted the early lives of Senator Hubert H. Humphrey of Minnesota and the noted African American author
James Baldwin. Neither man appeared on screen, but each described what
it was like to grow up in South Dakota and Harlem, respectively, as film
footage offered the audience a glimpse of those sharply contrasting locales.
Humphrey described life in the small town of Doland as "simply wonderful." He warmly recalled how his mother prepared breakfasts of oatmeal and
brown sugar and how his family often had big dinners with lots of company. Humphrey, moreover, spoke movingly of his generous and loving father.
In sharp contrast, Baldwin characterized his youth as "a nightmare" in
which he was surrounded by violent criminals, drug addicts, and alcoholics.
The son of a slave, his father was a "cruel" man who had once told Baldwin
that he was the ugliest child he had ever seen. On one occasion police officers had frisked, taunted, and knocked the author down for no apparent
reason other than his race. These and other experiences, Baldwin bitterly
observed, had transformed him into "an enraged human being." Many
viewers, no doubt, turned off their sets an hour later understandably wondering why a man with Humphrey's background was leading the Senate
fight for the strongest civil rights legislation since Reconstruction and

speaking out about the problems plaguing neighborhoods such as Baldwin's. What did Humphrey know about segregation or the economic difficulties of the inner city, and why did he care?[1]

II

Little about Humphrey's childhood prepared him to directly understand African American life. Born on May 27, 1911, Humphrey spent most of his youth in Doland, a village of six hundred people that mirrored countless other prairie towns of the Midwest. Living in Doland provided Humphrey with almost no opportunities to meet people of different races, ethnicities, or religions because nearly all of the town's residents were white Protestants of Scandinavian or German descent.[2]

Nevertheless, Humphrey learned several things growing up in this parochial setting that helped shape much of his broad-gauged views about human relations. As in other areas of Humphrey's life, his father exerted a particularly profound influence. The town druggist, Hubert Humphrey Sr. taught his children that human beings were basically good, that one needed to uncover the best in others, and, most important, that all people, no matter what their position, deserved respect. Having little use for claims of preferment based on social background, Humphrey Sr. shared the common midwestern belief in initiative and character as the measure of a person's worth and urged his children to treat others as individuals, not according to stereotypes. Humphrey Sr. often followed up his words with concrete deeds. He was one of a handful of Doland residents to vote for 1928 Democratic presidential candidate Al Smith, a Catholic, even though the Ku Klux Klan had burned a cross on the highest plot of land near the town that fall. Young Humphrey applied his father's creed of tolerance when a road construction crew, a few of whom were black, came to Doland. He sold newspapers to the workers, who let him sit on some of the equipment. Years later, Humphrey recounted how this episode "horrified" his mother but "pleased" his father.[3]

Religious instruction reinforced these teachings. Humphrey Sr. remained skeptical of organized religion for much of his early life, but he joined the church when Albert Hart, a liberal Methodist minister, came to Doland. Hart's emphasis on doing good works to improve the lot of others and the equality of all people before God appealed to Humphrey Sr., who imparted that lesson to his children. Humphrey recalled:

My early church experience really conditioned my attitude to civil rights and human rights. I could never understand how one could be a Christian and not have . . . a sacred regard for human rights or human dignity. When the Scripture tells us that God created man in his image it seems to me that this is one compelling reason above all others why there is spiritual equality among all people. . . . When the New Testament tells us that we are all one human family, I can't see how there is room for segregation, bigotry, or intolerance.

Humphrey found in Methodism a moral precept for individual behavior but also for governmental action on behalf of victims of injustice. Government, he thought, had an obligation to work for social justice "not by compulsion but in the spirit of understanding and love" that characterized Christianity.[4]

Humphrey's commitment to racial equality also arose out of a strong sense of compassion for the unfortunate. His father stressed empathy for the downtrodden and often canceled bills from farmers who lacked money. When the farm economy suffered in the late 1920s, however, the Humphrey family directly experienced the problems of the poor. Young Humphrey returned from school one day in 1927 and found his mother crying under a cottonwood tree. The family, Humphrey Sr. told his son, had to sell their house to pay their bills. The rural economy worsened over the next few years as wheat prices continued to drop. Banks closed. A close friend of the family committed suicide. Financial difficulties finally forced Humphrey Sr. to relocate his business to Huron, fifty miles south of Doland, in 1931. Life there was little better as dust storms, grasshoppers, falling commodity prices, and foreclosures plagued the region. Conditions became so difficult that in 1931 Humphrey had to drop out of the University of Minnesota, where he had enrolled in 1929, and return home to work in his father's store. After having a brief taste of city and academic life, he would remain in South Dakota for the next five years. His intense ambition for learning and experiencing the wider world had to be put on hold. Because farmers had little cash, Humphrey Sr. often extended liberal lines of credit or traded dry goods and animal vaccinations for food. He reminded his son to "respect" the struggling farmers because "what they spend in our store keeps us going." The Depression caused Humphrey to see the devastating effects of the lack of economic opportunity on individual and community life. Large impersonal forces over which one had little control, he concluded, could bring hardship to decent people. "I used to see my father sit at his desk with his head in his hands, a proud man, knowing that there were bills that we couldn't pay, taxes that were coming due, and we were literally on the verge of being thrown out of our little family business," Humphrey observed during congresssional hearings on unemployment in 1976. "I have never forgotten it."[5]

At the same time, the Depression deepened Humphrey's conviction that government could do something to alleviate suffering. Humphrey Sr.'s great passion was politics. Though he thought that railroads and large food processing corporations exploited small farmers, Humphrey Sr. never questioned the basic goodness of American institutions. Rather, he believed in extending economic opportunity and democracy to all. Humphrey Sr. adored Thomas Jefferson, Abraham Lincoln, William Jennings Bryan, and Woodrow Wilson. He made his son memorize the "Cross of Gold" speech and the Fourteen Points. It was no surprise, then, that the Humphrey family vigorously supported President Franklin D. Roosevelt. New Deal programs failed to restore farm prosperity, but Humphrey knew that they saved the farmers, and those tied to the farm economy like his father, from complete despair. In 1932 Humphrey Sr. took his son to meet FDR, who had stopped briefly in Huron to survey the devastation wrought by dust storms, drought, and falling prices. Roosevelt, Humphrey wrote three years later while visiting Washington, was "a super-man." Ultimately, the New Deal gave Humphrey faith that the problems of the nation could be addressed through existing political and economic institutions. He would be a liberal like his hero FDR, not a radical.[6]

Though Humphrey had come home from Minneapolis to help his father, he retained a strong urge to see what lay beyond the windswept South Dakota prairie. In 1936 he married Muriel Buck. The couple saved their money and talked of leaving South Dakota. That fall Humphrey Sr. won election to the state legislature. He wanted his son to assume full responsibility for the store, but Humphrey refused. "Dad, I don't want to peddle pills," he said. A year later, he and Muriel moved to Minneapolis, where he would complete his degree in political science at the University of Minnesota, a natural choice given his early experiences. Humphrey developed a special interest in political theory and American government, as liberal professors often pointed out the vast gulf between the nation's ideals of democracy and opportunity for all and the grim reality faced by many citizens. This reinforced what Humphrey's father had taught him as a child. Humphrey, meanwhile, eagerly debated current issues with his classmates and professors. In one class Humphrey rebutted a classmate who insisted that immigration to the United States should be restricted to northern Europeans by arguing that such a position contradicted the basic American tenet of equality of all people. The skinny young man with a sharp jaw and black hair that was already receding around the temples was making quite an impression on fellow students and professors alike.[7]

It was not until 1939, however, that Humphrey directly encountered the evils of racism. Elected to Phi Beta Kappa that spring, Humphrey, upon the advice of his mentor, decided to pursue a doctorate in political science. Because Muriel had given birth to a daughter, Humphrey desperately needed a way to make a living while in school. When Louisiana State University offered him a teaching fellowship, he and Muriel decided to move south. Baton Rouge was far removed from anything either of them had known in South Dakota. Humphrey saw segregation for the first time. "Why, it's uneconomic," he thought. The stark contrasts between the stately colonial mansions of the white elite and the dilapidated dwellings of the city's African American population made a strong impression upon him. When Humphrey visited the homes of white students, he often asked about race relations. Occasionally, he invited black students from a nearby school to his apartment. Humphrey drew several lessons about the complex relationship between whites and African Americans in the South from these encounters. Whites, he discovered, frequently developed close ties with individual blacks, often the black women who had raised them as young children. So strong was this bond that whites thought of that person as part of their family. This reinforced his belief that some good resided in everyone and led him to conclude that all southern whites did not hate all blacks. At the same time, Humphrey glimpsed the profound mistrust that blacks had for whites. African Americans, he learned, banded together to protect themselves from whites and harbored a deep suspicion of white authority figures such as bill collectors and the police.[8]

Humphrey's political thinking also matured at LSU. He wrote his master's thesis on the political philosophy of the New Deal. Though Humphrey did not specifically address issues of racial equality, he expressed beliefs about society, individual rights, and the role of government that would deeply influence his approach to civil rights matters throughout his life. The New Deal, Humphrey argued, had struck a balance between liberty and power as it attempted to meet the challenges of an urban industrial era. The dramatic economic changes of the previous fifty years meant that government could no longer simply provide a few basic rules for behavior while the scramble for wealth led to wide income disparities and produced much human suffering. Rather, Humphrey embraced the "positive liberty" of a benevolent state helping all citizens achieve happy meaningful lives. Whereas much of the American political tradition had characterized the state as hostile to freedom,

Humphrey saw government as an ally of average citizens. The New Deal properly added economic rights, such as an adequate standard of living, collective bargaining, health and leisure, and security against unemployment, illness, and old age, to the traditional rights of property and political participation. "First . . . there must be the right to creative work, to profitable and useful employment," he stressed. This was essential not just for individual well-being but also for the health of democracy. Roosevelt and his aides, Humphrey approvingly wrote, "[recognized] that [people] are not politically free when [they are] economically dependent." Therefore, it was appropriate for the state to ensure opportunity for individuals to develop their abilities to their full potential within the basic American framework of democracy and capitalism. The New Deal saw a just society as one that "[made] the common good available not only to a privileged class, but to all . . . so far as the capacity of each permits [him or her] to share it." Roosevelt, moreover, had astutely undertaken efforts, such as his fireside chats, to educate people regarding public matters. According to Humphrey, democracy "must be founded not on propaganda or regimentation, but on the steady growth of real understanding among the people and on real participation in discussion and plannning and in the execution of policies that affect their lives." Humphrey had no illusion that his goal of a freer, more democratic society would be reached quickly or easily. This was a long, slow process marked by trial and error. Failure might occur not only due to poorly conceived or implemented liberal efforts but also as a result of powerful opposition. America, Humphrey wrote, was "more conservative than courageous." Even a skillful politician such as FDR had to struggle mightily "against the essential conservatism of a highly developed business economy."[9]

Humphrey returned to Minneapolis in the summer of 1940 to complete his doctorate at the University of Minnesota. Economic troubles continued to plague the twenty-nine-year-old student and his family, however. Muriel could no longer work because she had to care for their daughter. Humphrey completed a year's coursework and teaching, but, with his wife pregnant again, poverty forced him to take a job with the Works Progress Administration. His student days were over. As director of the Twin Cities Workers' Education Program, Humphrey became exposed to people from a wide variety of nationalities and income levels. A year later, after having been deferred from military service, Humphrey became a regional director for training and reemployment for the War Manpower Commission. His new task was to establish vocational training across Minnesota for WPA workers and then channel them to wartime employment opportunities. Humphrey saw firsthand the economic suffering of both rural and urban Minnesotans, including that of the state's tiny black population. The *Minneapolis Spokesman*, the city's African American newspaper, noted that Humphrey was "instrumental and sometimes entirely responsible" for several black placements. Cecil Newman, the paper's editor, recalled years later that Humphrey had done some "finagling" to help African Americans find jobs. The young director was not patronizing toward blacks, the newspaperman remembered, and as a result he began to win the respect of African Americans in Minneapolis.[10]

By 1943 Humphrey was becoming well known in the city's liberal circles. His work with the WPA and the War Manpower Commission had brought him into contact with many labor leaders, an "invaluable experience" he wrote a former professor. Furthermore, his electrifying speaking style and thorough grasp of current events put him in demand on the lecture circuit. Humphrey, a friend later observed, "could make you want to rise off the ground and say, 'We'll follow you.' " Dozens of church and civic groups invited him to speak at night and on weekends, and the warm reception he received led him to think of running for public office. Several members of the city's liberal Farmer-Labor Party, who were searching for "new blood," urged him that spring to challenge Mayor Marvin Kline. Elective office had long held an interest for Humphrey, but lack of money and concern over the city's reputation as a stronghold of organized crime caused him to decline. Humphrey changed his mind, however, when the AFL's Central Labor Union promised financial support that April. Despite announcing his candidacy just nineteen days before the May nonpartisan primary, Humphrey surprised everyone by finishing second to Mayor Marvin Kline in a field of eight candidates. The general election runoff, which was just a month away, would be between Humphrey and the mayor. Race played a minor role in the campaign, but Humphrey spoke out for equality by blasting Kline for refusing to take a stand on a civil rights bill that had come before the recent session of the state legislature. Humphrey's support for the measure, occasional campaign stops in black neighborhoods, and fair treatment of blacks while working for the WPA won him much support among African Americans. The *Spokesman* was the only paper to endorse him. Blacks, Newman later observed, found Humphrey appealing because "he wasn't just another white man; he . . . seemed to have some heart and compassion." Kline triumphed in the June election by less than six thousand votes. Despite losing, Humphrey had established himself as a new and powerful force in city politics. Indeed, the *Minneapolis Star* noted that he had "come dashing out of nowhere to stage a colorful fighting campaign."[11]

Following the election Humphrey began to teach political science at a small college in St. Paul, and, to supplement his income and lay the ground-work for a future campaign, he continued to accept speaking offers from various organizations. His liberal views on human rights made him especially popular among Jewish and African American groups. During the next two years Humphrey frequently addressed organizations such as the United Hebrew Brotherhood, the Minnesota Jewish Council, and the local branches of B'nai B'rith and the National Association for the Advancement of Colored People (NAACP). He regularly stressed how religion compelled one to fight bigotry. At one Minneapolis synagogue Humphrey declared that all races and religions were equal before God and then related a "new" set of ten commandments that included "Thou shalt honor men for character and service alone, and dishonor none because of race, color, or previous condition of servitude." Maintaining that God saw all people as His children, Humphrey declared that racism violated the commandment forbidding bearing false witness against one's neighbor.[12]

Humphrey's speeches before such groups revealed the substantial influence of World War II on his racial views. Like many liberals, Humphrey thought that the war demonstrated the hypocrisy between the nation's ideals and the reality of unequal opportunity for many. These beliefs deepened in part as a result of letters from a Jewish friend who frequently wrote him from the battlefront in Europe. The Nazis had to be stopped, the friend asserted. Hitler's attempt to overrun Europe caused Humphrey to develop a new sense of urgency about civil rights. National unity was imperative if the United States were to defeat such a powerful enemy, he insisted. Indeed, Humphrey spoke to the NAACP on subjects such as "We're All Americans" and "Prejudice as a Threat to Democracy." Civil rights reforms such as the federal Fair Employment Practices Commission (FEPC), he also routinely stressed, were essential because the United States had to muster all of its resources and adhere to its democratic ideals.[13]

At the same time, Humphrey cooperated with liberal groups to combat prejudice in Minneapolis. When white supremacist and anti-Semite Gerald L. K. Smith applied for a permit to use the city's auditorium for a rally in 1944, Humphrey joined labor and civil rights organizations in opposition. Appearing before the City Council, he accused Smith of fostering intolerance that hurt the nation's war effort. The council denied Smith's request. A Jewish lawyer later congratulated Humphrey for giving Smith a justified "shellacking." Similarly, Humphrey worked to reduce appeals to racial and religious bigotry in Minnesota politics by helping the Minneapolis Round Table of Christians and Jews distribute a pamphlet, "Fair Play in Politics," during the 1944 elections.[14]

By 1945, then, Humphrey had a reputation among liberal groups in Minneapolis as a strong advocate for civil rights. Having narrowly lost the election two years earlier, he was eager to run for mayor again. Humphrey carefully cultivated the support of labor and business leaders. Crime, city finances, and planning for the postwar world were his chief issues, but, as the campaign would demonstrate, he was also determined to combat prejudice. Humphrey had been exposed to the issues of segregation, black poverty, and racial intolerance as a child and a young man, and he had now embarked on a political career during which he would continue to wrestle with them for the next thirty years.[15]

Race and Reform in Minneapolis

I

On the afternoon of March 20, 1945, two groups of teenage boys were playing baseball in a park in North Minneapolis. "Let's get the damn Jews!" one youth suddenly yelled. A melee ensued, leaving one Jewish boy severely hurt from being punched and kicked in the stomach. The irate parents of the victims reported the incident to the Jewish Community Relations Council, an organization that had been formed in 1938 to combat anti-Semitism in Minneapolis. The council promptly called the police, who promised to investigate. Two days later, more violence occurred when a group of teenagers broke a Jewish boy's nose. Claiming that there had been no fight at all, the chief of the Juvenile Division of the Minneapolis Police Department released the four suspects.[1]

Violence against Jewish youths in this neighborhood was nothing new, but shortly after these two incidents several rabbis and other leaders of the Jewish community called a mass meeting to discuss what could be done. A few days later, two thousand residents of North Minneapolis gathered at Lincoln Junior High School to express their indignation over the city's failure to do something about the attacks. Numerous children who had been set upon during the previous three years appeared before the crowd. "If the city of Minneapolis will not do its duty by providing adequate police protection," one angry rabbi declared afterward, "north side residents are prepared to organize their own guard."[2]

Occurring during the city's mayoral campaign, the meeting caught the attention of the two leading candidates for Minneapolis's highest office. Mayor Marvin Kline pledged the full support of the police to prevent future outbreaks. Kline's proposal, however, struck challenger Hubert Humphrey as inadequate. "This tragic display of intolerance requires more than the superficial treatment of additional police personnel," he asserted. "It requires a unified community program based on the recognition of the true ideals of democracy, wherein every person is accepted as a human being regardless of race, creed, or color." Humphrey cited a wartime correspondent who had recently warned that anti-Semitism in Minneapolis could turn violent and charged that Kline had been "woefully weak or callously unconcerned" about the problem. Humphrey went on to promise to convene a meeting of community leaders to inform them of the extent of prejudice, create a human rights council that would implement a program to promote better relations among all racial and ethnic groups, and instruct police officers on the magnitude of the problem and the prevention of further incidents.[3]

Though questions of city finances, crime, housing, and postwar economic development had occupied most of the candidates' attention, this was not the first time that candidate Humphrey had spoken out on racial issues. Equal treatment of all citizens, he regularly stressed, was fundamental in a democratic society. Insisting that government had "a duty and a responsibility" to guarantee equal employment opportunity, Humphrey proposed a municipal Fair Employment Practices Commission (FEPC) similar to the federal body that Franklin Roosevelt had established in 1941. Humphrey also pledged to involve more African Americans in city government. Blacks had been denied input in creating public policy for too long, he contended. These positions won Humphrey the enthusiastic endorsement of the *Minneapolis Spokesman*, the city's African American newspaper. Well aware that few city leaders had ever given much attention to African Americans' concerns, the paper praised Humphrey's "forthright ideas" and declared that he "has been a good friend and a courageous one who has spoken out when silence would have been more politic." Humphrey's stand on human rights also won him the support of Jews, many of whom were among his most generous financial backers.[4]

Thanks to his fierce determination to rid the city of organized crime, Humphrey trounced Kline by thirty-one thousand votes, the largest majority in city history, in the June election. Only thirty-four years old, he was about to become the leader of the sixteenth largest city in the United States after having lived there for less than five years. As friends crowded into Humphrey's apartment on election night to celebrate the happy news, the mayor-elect reaffirmed his commitment to appoint a community relations council and signaled his intention to educate the public about human rights. "I believe that it is part of the mayor's job to arouse concern in the minds of the people as to the city's future and the solution of the many problems ahead of us," the elated victor told the press.[5]

II

There was good reason to think that Humphrey's performance regarding racial matters could not match his lofty rhetoric. Minneapolis had an archaic city charter that lodged nearly all power in the City Council, a cumbersome and fiercely independent body of twenty-six members who controlled finances and most patronage jobs. Independent boards dealt with several other important issues. The mayor was thus largely a figurehead, responsible for little more than law enforcement. These limitations did not deter Humphrey. "Any office or position," he had insisted during the campaign, "can be one of importance or strength if the occupant has the initiative, the imagination, and the capacity to make it so." The energetic and confident Humphrey offered few specific plans, however, on how he would dramatically transform the nature of the mayor's office given such structural impediments.[6]

A far larger challenge loomed for the mayor-elect, however. Home to half a million people, Minneapolis was a remarkably homogeneous community. Yankee migrants founded the city in the mid-nineteenth century and turned it into the leading milling center for grain from the Midwest. Scandinavian and German immigrants flocked there in the late nineteenth and early twentieth centuries. Comprising just 1 percent of the city's population, the five thousand African American residents of Minneapolis constituted a small and isolated group. Though a demand for labor during World War I resulted in a 51 percent increase in the city's black population between 1910 and 1920, the vast majority of African Americans who left the South during the first wave of the Great Migration found better opportunities in cities such as Chicago, Detroit, Milwaukee, or Cleveland. The twenty-five thousand Jews in Minneapolis, many of whom had arrived from Eastern Europe during the early twentieth century, were the city's largest minority group, but even they were just 5 percent of the population.[7]

Like their counterparts in other northern cities, African Americans in Minneapolis faced severe social prejudice. Restrictive housing covenants helped isolate blacks largely in two neighborhoods north and east of downtown. Though Minnesota had outlawed discrimination by public service businesses in the late nineteenth century, none of the major hotels in Minneapolis allowed blacks to rent halls for dances or parties, and many would not accept them as guests. None of the city's finer restaurants served African

Americans, and some of the cheaper downtown lunch counters refused to wait on them for lengthy periods. Some doctors would not treat African American patients out of fear of getting a reputation as a "black doctor." White church members occasionally stopped blacks at the door and told them the locations of African American places of worship.[8]

Similarly, African Americans encountered enormous economic difficulties. A handful of blacks owned their own businesses, but those who did not usually struggled to find work. A 1926 study by the Urban League indicated that 145 of 192 employers surveyed would not hire African Americans. At places where they could find employment, such as the Minneapolis Athletic Club, jobs were often divided along racial lines with African Americans having no choice but to accept the lowest-paying and most menial positions. Blacks also labored on railroads or as janitors, porters, waiters, or domestics in the hotel and restaurant industries. Many unions, including those representing hotel and restaurant workers, excluded African Americans. During the mid-1920s the average annual earnings of a married black man in Minneapolis were $1,172, more than $1,000 below the federal poverty level of 1919. Not surprisingly, economic conditions for African Americans worsened during the Great Depression. Many of the handful who had industrial jobs were laid off, and several hotels replaced black waiters with white waitresses. Many black women lost their jobs as domestics and began to work in hotels. Several black-owned businesses closed. "There is little doubt," the Urban League reported in 1938, "that all social problems of disease, dependency, and delinquency are more severe among the colored group than in the general population." Though African Americans obtained a few WPA jobs, by 1939 more than 60 percent of the black population was on welfare, compared to 25 percent of whites. A handful of blacks looked to the Communist Party in the 1930s, but overall the vast majority of African Americans did not embrace the left. Economic prospects for African Americans did not improve until World War II, when, as in many other cities, labor shortages forced leading firms such as Northwest Airlines, International Harvester, and Honeywell, among others, to hire African Americans for the first time. By far the most hospitable place was the Twin Cities Ordinance Plant, which at one point employed more than one thousand African Americans at a wide variety of levels at wages as much as five times higher than what blacks were accustomed to earning. Despite these advances, however, many businesses and unions remained for whites only.[9]

Minneapolis blacks struggled to overcome these problems by forming several community organizations. They established local branches of the NAACP in 1912 and the Urban League in 1923. In 1924 the Phyllis Wheatley Settlement House opened its doors to foster a more vibrant community life. Blacks won a significant victory in the late 1930s when an African American union won an employment discrimination suit against a leading hotel, but overall African Americans found themselves at a tremendous social and economic disadvantage and with few allies. The white political leaders during the early twentieth century, one black labor leader bluntly recalled, "never [were] sensitive to the Negro problem because the Negro never had any voting power."[10]

Jews in Minneapolis also encountered prejudice. Populist leader Ignatius Donnelly had expressed anti-Semitic feelings during the nineteenth century. In 1919 editorials in the *Minneapolis Tribune* likened Jews to Bolsheviks, and a few years later scandal sheets proclaimed that "practically . . . every snake-faced gangster in the Twin Cities is a JEW" and charged "Jew thugs" with robberies, beatings, and bribery. Anonymous hate literature frequently appeared during the 1930s. One handbill listed Jews in the federal government and asked "Is Roosevelt a Jew?" Other leaflets charged Jews with driving the government into debt or told of Jewish plots to dominate the world's media, banking, and entertainment industries. Following the bloody truckers' strike of 1934, pamphlets circulated asking "Why, Rabbi Gordon, do you control the unions of Minneapolis?" Newspapers accused the governor during the 1938 campaign of being a tool of "Jew pigs," while the Republican Party alleged Jewish control of state government in a sixty-page pamphlet, "Are they Communists or Catspaws?" During World War II owners of rental properties openly advertised for Gentiles Only. One minister allegedly said from his pulpit, "The Jews should be wiped off the face of the earth." Jews frequently faced discriminatory service in downtown hotels and restaurants, while restrictive covenants helped lead to concentrations of the Jewish population on the north and south sides of town. Prominent civic organizations such as the Kiwanis, Rotary, and Lions Clubs forbade Jewish membership, and the local chapter of the American Automobile Association proudly told prospective members that it barred Jews. Rabid anti-Semite Gerald L. K. Smith, moreover, drew several hundred people to each of several rallies held during the early 1940s. This long and virulent history of anti-Semitism caused liberal journalist Carey McWilliams to label Minneapolis in a 1946 article "the capital of anti-Semitism in the United States." Though some Jews challenged McWilliams's conclusion, they nonetheless agreed that anti-Semitism was strong. Jews generally fared better than African Americans economically, but prejudice limited their economic opportunities too. Job advertisements occasionally asked for Gentiles Only. Because nearly all leading businesses would hire only Christians, some Jews went into business for themselves as grocers, butchers, or craftsmen, while others went into the apparel industry or worked for small shopkeepers. Many Jews, however, struggled to eke out a living by peddling.[11]

III

Humphrey reiterated his intention to confront these difficult problems when he delivered his inaugural address a month after his election. Pledging "to guard against the breakdown in human relations such as occurred in many localities after the last war," the new mayor called for a community relations program that "will . . . eradicate intolerance and discrimination wherever they may be found." He again proposed a local FEPC. "There are disturbing signs of disunity and intolerance which must command our attention," he warned. "Government can no longer ignore displays of bigotry, violence, and discrimination." The horrors of Nazi Germany had revealed that minority persecution represented "the first sign of social disintegration."[12]

A month after taking office, Humphrey met with representatives from more than a dozen human rights organizations to hammer out a plan for his human rights council. It is unclear where the idea originated, but it is quite possible Humphrey was attempting to copy similar bodies that had been created in several cities during World War II or an organization established by the governor of Minnesota in 1943. Developing a council in Minneapolis initially proved difficult. Groups such as the NAACP, the Urban League, the Round Table of Christians and Jews, and the Council of Jewish Women had tried to work together following the violence in North Minneapolis that spring, but cooperation had proved elusive because some organizations believed that others were taking too dominant a role. Though Humphrey hoped to smooth over tensions, the leaders soon found themselves at odds with the mayor. They expected that Humphrey's group would be comprised of leaders from existing organizations, but the mayor, thinking that few citizens would notice the council if such individuals were appointed, wanted his council to consist of prominent citizens not closely tied to such groups. Human rights organizations, he believed, could serve an important but secondary role by pointing out issues worthy of attention and providing links with the black and Jewish populations.[13]

Humphrey did not unveil his Mayor's Council on Human Relations until February 1946. The reasons for the delay are unclear, but his failure to move sooner upset human rights groups. Humphrey convinced Reverend Reuben Youngdahl to serve as chair. The brother of a leading state Republican,

Youngdahl was a progressive minister at Mount Olivet Lutheran, the city's largest church. He was thus just the type of person Humphrey needed to give the council instant credibility. Other members of the ten-person body included the vice-chair of the College of Education at the University of Minnesota, a representative from the Minneapolis public schools, an editor of the *Minneapolis Times*, a lawyer from the Minneapolis CIO who had been active in civil rights efforts since the 1930s, two other clergymen, and an attorney from General Mills. One African American and one Jew initially sat on the council. Humphrey's selection of council members, which occurred after consultations with business, labor, and civic organizations, indicated that he believed that minorities needed white allies.[14]

The council held its first meeting several days after Humphrey's announcement. Its self-defined tasks were "to assure all citizens the opportunity for full and equal participation in the affairs of [Minneapolis]" and "[enlarge] . . . that sound body of community opinion which respects the rights of all citizens, regardless of their race or creed or color." Lacking legal authority, the council would cooperate with existing human rights groups, advise city government, draft legislation, work for equal opportunity in housing, education, and employment, and create programs to educate the public about the evils of prejudice. Humphrey instructed members to foster ties with a broad range of community leaders who could co-sponsor activities and inform the public about the council. Public support was critical, Humphrey knew, not only for the council's success but also because city budgetary constraints meant that it, unlike similar bodies in other cities, had to depend solely upon private donations to fund its operating expenses and various activities.[15]

The council enjoyed a modicum of success in coordinating activities of various human rights groups. During the summer of 1946 it met with the Urban League, the NAACP, the Minnesota Jewish Council, and other groups to plan strategy regarding an upcoming appearance by Gerald L. K. Smith in Minneapolis. Nearly all thought that the best way to combat the right-wing extremist was to work with the press to deny him publicity. Leftists within the labor movement decided to denounce Smith publicly, however, and planned to picket outside the hall where Smith was to speak. Violence broke out the night of the meeting. Fearful that the incident would only build sympathy for Smith, the council and human rights groups quickly condemned both Smith and the "irresponsible pickets," whom they blamed for instigating the affair. Humphrey privately noted afterward, "Let us all pray that America may never fall into the hands of bigots, demagogues, and intolerant people whether they be Smiths or his violent adversaries." A year later, the council joined with the St. Paul Council on Human Relations to sponsor a joint exhibit at the Minnesota State Fair and cooperated with the University of Minnesota to conduct a seminar for educators, community organizations, and human rights groups.[16]

More commonly, the council developed its own broad range of promotional and outreach techniques to educate citizens about racial issues and minority concerns. During the spring of 1946 it distributed four thousand copies of "Outside the Home," a pamphlet describing the state law against discriminatory service, to hotel, restaurant, and retail organizations for their members. The council wrote letters to approximately five hundred companies that summer urging them to adopt a policy of nondiscrimination in employment, arranged for a Town Meeting in September that featured speakers such as Humphrey and leaders from black and Jewish groups discussing what government could do to promote better intergroup relations, and hung twenty-eight copies of a "Pledge for American Unity" in police stations, libraries, railway and bus terminals, and other public places. During the 1946 elections it obtained promises from more than one hundred candidates and organizations to refrain from using racial or ethnic slurs. The council, moreover, worked with a local theater company to produce a play, "Deep Are the Roots," and presented a skit, "Tolerance Can Be Taught," at the 1947 state convention of Minnesota teachers. It sponsored two radio series. One, *We Are Many People,* featured thirteen brief dramatic radio episodes that addressed topics such as restrictive covenants, job discrimination, and denial of service based on race. The other, *Neither Free Nor Equal*, was a six-part documentary that investigated the problems minorities encountered in areas such as employment and housing. Finally, Humphrey and council members participated in six thirty-minute radio broadcasts dramatizing cases that had been brought to the council's attention. The effects of such educational activities were difficult to measure. The council raised awareness of prejudice and sent the message that respected members of the community, including the mayor and other government officials, did not approve of it. African American and Jewish groups regularly expressed their support for these efforts. The Urban League indicated that programs such as *Neither Free Nor Equal* had "done much to help interpret conditions in the community." In many cases, however, educational activities fell short of desired goals. Many businesses simply ignored the council's letter regarding equal employment opportunity. Similarly, members privately acknowledged late in 1946 that additional techniques would have to be developed to persuade local businesses to treat all customers equally because "little use" had been made of "Outside the Home."[17]

The council also enjoyed mixed results as an advocate for legal reforms. During the summer of 1946 Humphrey and council members joined representatives from human rights groups to urge the City Council to withhold approval of a subdivision as long as the developers continued to block the purchase of a home by a Japanese American World War II veteran. "If someone brings a plat in here that says he won't sell to a Jew, or a Negro, or an Australian, we should say 'Brother, you're in the wrong school,'" Humphrey awkwardly contended at a hearing on the issue. Though the City Council adopted a resolution requesting real estate firms to eliminate restrictive covenants from developments, it approved the subdivision several months later without demanding a change regarding the veteran. Similarly, the City Council rejected the Council on Human Relations's call not to approve building permits on land covered by covenants. A year later, the legislative fortunes of the Council on Human Relations improved somewhat. It scored a tremendous victory in January by helping to convince the City Council to enact FEPC legislation. Likewise, Humphrey and the council joined forces that April to push for an ordinance prohibiting the publication of anonymous hate literature.[18]

African Americans found Humphrey and the council to be valuable allies on several occasions. When the Urban League informed the council of segregation in a public housing project, the council quickly investigated the allegation. The Housing Authority told the council's executive secretary that federal regulations demanded segregation, but the secretary, unsatisfied with that response, met with the five black families that had applied to live in the development. All wanted to live in integrated units. The secretary then went to Humphrey, who pledged to "stand behind [him] to the fullest." Buoyed by this promise of support, the secretary contacted the housing official, who agreed to integrate the project. The Urban League, Humphrey, and the council worked together to eliminate segregation at a veteran's housing project. Upon hearing that an apartment owner would not rent to an individual who had black friends, Humphrey convinced the owner to rent the unit without consideration of the race of a tenant's guests. Told that a bus driver had ordered a black man off a bus because he allegedly "smelled bad," Humphrey reminded the head of the public transportation department that all citizens should be treated equally. When several African American families let the council know about discrimination at a summer camp, it soon persuaded the camp to allow black guests.[19]

Direct lobbying rarely proved entirely successful. In the spring of 1946 two African Americans filed complaints with the council regarding discriminatory service by leading downtown hotels. Though the council met at least twice that spring with the Board of Directors of the Minneapolis Hotel Association to discuss the issue, most hotel operators refused to change their practices. When a traveling show with sixty African American members came to town that December, the council had to resort to subterfuge to secure accommodations for them. Working closely with the Urban League, the council booked numerous rooms in downtown hotels under Humphrey's name without telling managers the race of the guests. Some managers tried to backpedal when the members arrived by claiming that they could only accommodate a few people, while others indicated they would not have accepted the reservations had they known the guests were black. "I work Negroes, but I don't have to associate with them," one manager complained vehemently. "This is the last time that any will get rooms in this hotel." The recalcitrant managers backed down when the council stood firm. The council, however, rightly concluded that additional work was "definitely required" regarding the hotel issue. The limits of the council's power to effect long-term change were also evident in the summer of 1947, when a downtown bartender overcharged two African Americans and then spat in their glasses while two police officers present did nothing. Fearful that such incidents could provoke violence, the council sent one thousand leading citizens a letter stressing the importance of equal service. The council also requested the county attorney to take action for violation of state law and asked the City Council to consider revocation of the bar's liquor license for violation of local health codes, but neither suggestion was followed.[20]

The hotel and bar incidents reveal one of the main problems limiting the council's effectiveness—the lack of legal authority. It could only ask businesses to treat all customers equally. Sometimes the prestige of the mayor or council members proved sufficient, but businesses that adamantly refused to change had little to fear from the council. The victory in the case of the downtown hotels was a temporary, isolated achievement that resulted largely from clever trickery on the part of the council, not the beginning of a substantial change in hotel policy. Though service improved somewhat at a few establishments, by September 1948 the council was still searching for a policy that would lead to permanent changes by all hotels.[21]

Money constituted the council's other great problem. Six months into its existence, it had only $108 on hand and a projected deficit of $800. The council called upon Humphrey, who agreed to speak at a fund-raiser. "During the war Americans worked together and submerged their differences," Humphrey told the more than three hundred people who gathered at a downtown hotel. "Since then there has been an outbreak of all the pent-up frustrations, tensions, and prejudices. In some parts of the country, the Ku

Klux Klan is rising and there have been bitter race riots." The dinner proved to be an enormous success, and by year's end the council had more than $4,300. Lack of money continued to be a concern in 1947, however. Twice Humphrey failed to convince the City Council to make the Council on Human Relations eligible for public funds. Personality conflicts between two council members, meanwhile, prevented fund-raising efforts from getting off the ground. Humphrey turned to the Democratic National Committee in Washington, which helped persuade the IRS to classify contributions as tax deductible, but by October the council had bills of $3,800 and only $8 in its coffers. As the executive committee decided to terminate the council's three full-time staff members, Humphrey sent out more than seven hundred urgent requests for donations. If the budget could not be met, the mayor bluntly wrote, "it will almost necessitate closing shop." He occasionally followed up with phone calls. Humphrey's efforts began to bear fruit by spring. Dayton's, the city's largest department store, contributed $500, as did Minneapolis newspapers. These and other smaller donations meant that the council's survival was ensured. There is no evidence that the council's chronic financial troubles ever caused it to cancel or curtail any of its programs. On the contrary, the shortage of money stemmed in part from the myriad of activities it had undertaken. Still, it is clear that had the council enjoyed a more secure financial base it would have been able to undertake additional projects or devote more time to existing efforts.[22]

IV

The council's most ambitious, and most expensive, undertaking was the Community Self-Survey. L. Howard Bennett of the American Council on Race Relations told one council member of the technique in the spring of 1946, and the group, eager for ideas about how to confront such a daunting problem as racism, quickly agreed to do a survey. Developed by Dr. Charles Johnson, an eminent sociologist at Fisk University, the survey reflected the emerging belief among social scientists that environment, not biology, accounted for racial differences. In other respects, however, the survey represented a radical departure from standard social science practices. Instead of relying on a handful of academic experts, Johnson's method involved local citizen volunteers investigating aspects of minority life and offering solutions to the problems uncovered. Johnson believed that most citizens lacked experience with discrimination and minority concerns, and because they doubted there was a serious problem they could not be easily rallied to address it. Whereas many leading social scientists aspired to be value-neutral, Johnson openly expressed his goal of deepening citizens' sensitivity to racial matters. He also hoped to provide solid empirical evidence of racism to counter critics who might otherwise claim that outsiders knew nothing of local conditions or there was no problem at all. Assuming that most citizens would uphold democratic ideals when confronted with prejudice, Johnson expected that widespread knowledge of the problem as well as the force of public opinion would lead to change. Such an approach suited Humphrey's agenda perfectly. "Officials," he told a Minneapolis Town Meeting that had been devoted to explaining the survey, "can't do anything without the support of public will." In announcing plans for the project, Humphrey pointed out that informing whites about the problems of African Americans and Jews was more important than the actual findings. Lest some might think that the survey constituted nothing more than a hollow effort to allow whites to feel good, however, Humphrey added that it would also provide a basis for programs to promote equal opportunity for minorities.[23]

The survey proved to be a massive undertaking. Organizational difficulties led the council to delay it several times, but once these were overcome the council formed a sponsoring committee of more than two hundred leading citizens. Johnson and six other experts came to Minneapolis in November 1946 for three days of meetings with leaders from women's groups, human rights organizations, the business and labor community, and the council. To ensure that the project was not solely a white effort, the council met with officials from several racial and religious organizations to identify areas needing investigation. Those targeted included employment, housing, education, family life, public accommodations, health services, welfare and recreation, religion, and civic groups. Sociologists from Fisk and officials from the American Council on Race Relations trained the volunteer interviewers, who would investigate conditions among African Americans, Jews, Asian Americans, and Native Americans. Survey leaders estimated a need for three hundred volunteers, but, to their surprise, more than five hundred took part. Altogether, then, the survey involved more than eight hundred people. The scope of coverage and the number of people included made the Minneapolis survey far larger than those that had been done in three other cities.[24]

Fieldwork began in January 1947. For three months volunteers trudged through snow and battled the frigid temperatures of the harsh Minnesota winter to obtain information about minority life. They primarily conducted interviews, but questionnaires were sometimes used. Those who spoke with minority families inquired about living conditions, employment, schools, and treatment by the police. They also asked what the family wanted to see changed about these areas. Questions for employers and unions addressed types of jobs minorities held, performance, promotion, and whether the business or union was even open to minorities. To investigate public accommodations, the experiences of the local chapter of the Congress on Racial Equality (CORE) were used. Survey leaders sought information from 1,300 businesses, 300 labor unions, 350 real estate agents, 400 doctors, 75 hospitals and health agencies, 400 religious groups, and 2,200 educators. They obtained responses from more than 500 minority families, nearly all the health care facilities, and more than half the educators and doctors, but only 33 percent of real estate agents and 25 percent of businesses and labor groups.[25]

Respondents could falsify information, to be sure, but even allowing for an underreporting of discrimination the survey generated a rich portrait of minority life in Minneapolis. Predictably, it revealed that minorities encountered substantial social and economic disadvantages. The Housing Committee reported that shelter was marked by "a disproportion of overcrowding in substandard housing." The Industry-Labor Committee found that African Americans were "concentrated in non-manufacturing service jobs of the lower and less desirable levels," while the Social Welfare Agencies Committee pointed out that minorities' participation in case work agencies and social welfare institutions was "conspicuously low." The Health and Hospitals Committee revealed that some hospitals segregated patients by race or religion, with minorities having to pay higher rates for rooms, and that access to quality health care in general posed a serious problem. In nearly all the areas investigated African Americans fared worse than other minorities.[26]

Though Humphrey had little direct involvement in the survey, he remained committed to using its findings to launch a more ambitious human rights program. Midway through the undertaking he helped build support for the survey by speaking about its importance, and in the spring of 1948 he announced that the project represented "only a beginning." Humphrey ensured that the results received a high-profile airing in November 1948 by persuading noted NAACP lawyer Charles Hamilton Houston to speak at a two-day conference. Humphrey also addressed the gathering. Praising the committees for their hard work, he heartily endorsed the recommendations and urged the city to address the problems that had been uncovered. The mayor called upon religious groups to teach the majority population humility and respect for others, but he also asked business and labor groups to take the lead in this area because, he contended, they were responsible for many of the conditions found. Good employment prospects were vital to the overall health of minority communities, he intimated.[27]

V

Humphrey's commitment to equal economic opportunity went beyond rhetoric. Well aware that many African Americans across the North had long been denied high-paying jobs and fearing that blacks might lose gains enjoyed during the war years, liberals such as Humphrey believed that the state had to become involved in employer-employee relations if African Americans were to advance economically. His work with labor leaders during World War II, as well as his commitment to the principle of economic reform on behalf of the less fortunate, had made him sensitive to this issue, and thus in December 1945 Humphrey proposed legislation simply making discrimination by employers punishable by a fine. Though he had, for unknown reasons, retreated from his campaign pledge to create a municipal FEPC, by proposing any type of fair employment law Humphrey was part of an advance guard of northern liberals who had embraced equal employment opportunity following the demise of Franklin Roosevelt's federal FEPC, which southerners in Congress had killed earlier that year.[28]

Even Humphrey's mild plan initially met strong opposition. Many members of the City Council doubted the need for such a law, while others rightly noted that the mayor's proposal ignored discrimination by unions. Still others thought that Humphrey was rushing things. He fought back at a January hearing. "Ought we wait," Humphrey urgently testified, "until we see flagrant violations to pass such legislation?" The Ordinances and Legislation Subcommittee referred the bill to the city attorney for further review. Badly misjudging the political terrain, Humphrey had failed to lay the groundwork for his plan. Human rights groups had not yet developed a coordinated strategy, and the mayor had not yet appointed the Council on Human Relations. Following the setback, a friend wrote Humphrey that the hearing had demonstrated "the absolute immediate need of . . . your inter-racial council" and the need to amend the proposal to cover labor unions so as to minimize "difficult opposition" that would likely come from employers. Humphrey concurred and soon submitted a revised measure. The outlook for an equal employment law remained bleak, however, when the subcommittee took the matter up again a month later. The city attorney lobbied for a bill that would cover only firms with city contracts, while several aldermen expressed concern over how a fair employment law would be enforced. Humphrey failed to win any converts; the subcommittee rejected the proposal 3–2. Nevertheless, there was reason for hope; the aldermen ordered further study of the issue. "I have already learned that it takes a lot of patience to accomplish anything," Humphrey glumly wrote a friend. That success would not come as quickly or as easily as Humphrey had expected is not surprising. He was still a relative newcomer to Minneapolis politics, and though the young mayor had won an impressive electoral victory entrenched bureaucracies were not inclined to bend to his will.[29]

The Council on Human Relations, which Humphrey named in February 1946, provided a much needed boost to the struggle for equal employment opportunity. Most important, it significantly transformed the terms of the debate by drafting legislation creating a commission, modeled after the defunct federal FEPC, to investigate charges of discrimination. Given Humphrey's earlier failures, it was a surprising and audacious move, but the council's executive secretary was convinced that a commission was essential if the law were to be effective. It was also not an easy position for the council to take, given its precarious financial position, for several potential contributors subsequently withheld donations. Humphrey quickly joined the council's effort to build broad support for the new proposal. Organizations participating in the campaign included the Minnesota Jewish Council, the Urban League, the NAACP, the Council of Church Women, the Women's International League for Peace and Freedom, and several progressive labor unions. Throughout the year advocates sought to influence the City Council through testimony at public hearings and lobbying by prestigious individuals. The council argued that by opening up job opportunities an FEPC would eliminate "some of the sources of . . . unrest, poverty, disease, delinquency, and crime." To counter critics who claimed that an FEPC would be illegal, the council cited the general welfare clause of the city charter and prepared a cogent brief citing several New Deal-era Supreme Court cases that affirmed the right of the state to regulate a host of economic activities. Nonetheless, FEPC advocates faced an uphill battle because conservative members of the business community mounted a quiet but strong counteroffensive. The lack of progress, one member of the council noted in July, had left human rights groups "very much disappointed." Similarly, a frustrated Humphrey pointedly declared in October, "Some cities have had more courage than ours about passing such an act, and haven't had all the hairsplitting we've had over legal technicalities."[30]

Pro-FEPC forces had cause to celebrate six months later. Several businesses had urged Humphrey throughout the fall to delay consideration of the measure, but the mayor, the council, and human rights groups pressed ahead. On January 2, 1947, the Ordinances and Legislation Subcommittee recommended a compromise FEPC that would apply only to city departments under City Council control. The pro-FEPC coalition held firm to its demand for a broader law. When the City Council took up the issue on January 31, however, opposition came unexpectedly from several members of the council and the head of the survey, who objected not to FEPC per se but rather to the timing of its consideration. Enacting FEPC at that moment, they worried, would pass judgment on an issue that had yet to be investigated fully and thus undermine the effectiveness of the survey and the employment commission. Unpersuaded, the City Council approved the FEPC bill favored by the Council on Human Relations 21–3. Why the sudden transformation? Persistent lobbying by the council, human rights groups, and Humphrey, who insisted that FEPC was "vital" to his human rights program, had won a few converts. More important, pressure from several powerful labor leaders provided the extra leverage that FEPC proponents needed. Aldermen voting against FEPC, union chiefs had warned, would not receive labor's support in the upcoming elections. Given the hostility of many union members to African Americans and Jews, it is surprising that the City Council took the threat seriously. The victory, Humphrey proudly wrote a friend, represented "a milestone in our work." Though a major weakness of the law was its exclusion of domestic service workers, he still had good reason to be happy, for Minneapolis now had the strongest municipal equal employment opportunity law in the nation. The statute prohibited discrimination in hiring, firing, promotion, and compensation by all employers with more than two employees. It also forbade discrimination by labor unions. More important, it created the first municipal Fair Employment Practices Commission to investigate complaints of discrimination and promote equal opportunity. If the commission concluded that discrimination had occurred, it would refer the case to the city attorney for prosecution in municipal court. Penalties for violation of the law included a one-hundred dollar fine or ninety days in jail.[31]

As Jewish and African American organizations had requested, Humphrey ensured that the FEPC had a diverse membership. He appointed an African American attorney who was active in the Urban League, a vice president of the Minneapolis Central Labor Union, a lawyer who was co-chair of the local branch of the National Conference of Christians and Jews, a newspaper editor, and a corporate manager. Here again Humphrey revealed his faith in calm orderly progress and in the public's capacity for rational thinking. The commission, the mayor told the press when he announced his selections in May, was "no place for either zealots or hidebinders" because it would rely chiefly on consultation, persuasion, and education, not punishment, to obtain compliance.[32]

With the FEPC fight behind him Humphrey concentrated on his reelection campaign. Cecil Newman, editor of the *Spokesman*, suggested that Humphrey soft-pedal his civil rights activities. "I'd rather see you mayor, knowing how you feel, than to let some of these bigots start attacking you as a Negro-lover," Newman said. It is unclear if Newman was referring to any particular group, but he may have had in mind the ultraconservative Democratic Nationalist Party, which had been responsible for anti-Semitic literature at the University of Minnesota and threatening phone calls to Humphrey, Youngdahl, and other human rights leaders. "Well, you have to make up your mind about it," Humphrey replied. "I don't think it'll hurt. I don't care if it does hurt." To avoid civil rights matters, Humphrey thought, would compromise his effort to build a broad consensus for better relations between racial and ethnic groups. He thus told a radio audience during the campaign, "We must do everything in our power to learn the art of living together.... We threaten our prosperity, we destroy [our] sense of unity ... when we set one group against another or fail to appreciate the contribution that every group and individual can make to the general welfare." A month later, Humphrey proudly highlighted the work of the Council on Human Relations, the survey, and the enactment of FEPC. Once again, the *Spokesman* enthusiastically endorsed him. The mayor, the paper noted, was "willing to stick his neck out to practice what he preaches." As in 1945, human rights was not a prominent issue in the campaign, and Humphrey's stand did not hurt his candidacy. Sweeping every ward in the city, he defeated his hapless opponent by fifty thousand votes, thereby surpassing his record margin of victory two years earlier.[33]

The FEPC began its work shortly after the election. Like the Council on Human Relations, the commission saw its role as going beyond the resolution of individual complaints to include broad educational activities to prevent problems from arising. Hundreds of companies worked with it over a two-year period to remove questions related to race, religion, and ethnicity from their application forms. The commission produced and distributed a pamphlet outlining the law for more than four thousand businesses, unions, and community organizations. The FEPC's executive director appeared before more than forty business, civic, and labor groups to discuss the merits of equal employment opportunity. Other commission members met with more than one hundred organizations. Fair employment, FEPC officials routinely told their audiences, was the morally correct thing to do, but they added that it was also in the financial interest of everyone because helping minorities find well-paying jobs would improve productivity, translate into more purchasing power, and result in less government spending on health, law enforcement, and welfare programs. Increasing the status of African Americans would entail no cost to whites, commission members suggested.[34]

By pursuing such an approach, the FEPC helped eliminate a handful of employment barriers over the next two years. Within a few weeks of enactment of the law, an official from a drugstore cited it as the reason why the company had at last hired an African American for counter work. By August 1947 the commission had played a direct role in securing jobs for at least three African Americans. Similarly, the industrial secretary of the Urban League informed the commission that the league had settled several cases favorably "mainly because of the existence of [FEPC] legislation." The commission scored another significant victory in November 1948, when it persuaded the City Council to expand the scope of the statute by outlawing discrimination by employment agencies and banning questions dealing with race, religion, or ethnicity from all job applications at companies within the city.[35]

Though Humphrey rarely became involved in the FEPC's daily activities, he used the prestige of his office to aid its work on at least one important occasion. For several years the Urban League had unsuccessfully attempted to obtain jobs for blacks as salesclerks at downtown department stores. In 1947 forty civic groups, many of them women's organizations, formed the Joint Committee for Equal Opportunity and became involved in the Urban League's effort. The Joint Committee quickly launched a massive lobbying campaign in which it secured ten thousand signatures on petitions and sold twenty-six thousand stickers, bearing the statement "I would like to see racial and religious EQUALITY practiced in your entire employment policy," for customers to paste on their monthly credit statements. Store owners remained recalcitrant. By the spring of 1948 the Joint Committee and the Urban League had decided to ask the mayor for help. Humphrey gladly obliged. Hiring African American salesclerks was "more important than a thousand statements of principle," he wrote Donald Dayton, chief of the city's largest department store chain and head of the Minneapolis Retailers' Association. Whites, Humphrey added, felt "a strong sense of guilt" because they had "far too long avoided the responsibilities imposed by the plain implications of [their] Christian precepts." The combination of Humphrey and the alliance of civic groups proved impossible to resist as several stores, including Dayton's, agreed to hire black clerks. The resolution of this contentious issue marked a significant but largely symbolic advance, for by November 1948 three stores had employed only seven African Americans.[36]

African Americans and pro–civil rights groups could justly take pride in the outcome of the department store battle, but on this occasion and others the commission's value lay more in setting precedents than in achieving tangible gains for large numbers of minorities. The number of complaints filed with the FEPC cannot be the sole measure of the law's impact, for some businesses changed employment practices without having faced a charge of discrimination, but the FEPC's caseload does reveal the limits of its effectiveness. Between 1947 and 1949 the FEPC handled only 75 cases. This was a minuscule total when compared with the 827 cases brought to the Urban League in 1947 alone. The most popular type of case the FEPC dealt with involved an African American bringing a complaint against a private employer for refusal to hire. The commission dismissed 25 cases due to a lack of jurisdiction or a finding of nondiscrimination, while in 16 cases it deferred action pending further inquiry. In 28 cases it obtained a pledge to follow a nondiscriminatory policy in the future. In just 6 instances was the FEPC able to secure the job, promotion, or wage desired by the person making the complaint. All too aware of the slow pace of change, the *Spokesman* perceptively observed in 1949, "Neither the FEP commission nor the city will profit from the erroneous impression . . . that the FEP commission has settled the problem of racial and religious discrimination in employment."[37]

Several obstacles prevented the commission from making a significant impact for many minorities. It lacked a budget, office, or staff for several months after its creation. The FEPC did not even develop a standard criteria for disposition of cases until nearly a year after Humphrey had appointed the members. Even after these organizational problems had been overcome, deeper problems remained. Because commission members served on a part-time basis, they could not give the issue the sustained attention that it needed. The FEPC could not initiate proceedings; it became involved only after an individual or a human rights organization brought a case to its attention. Requiring minorities to initiate a complaint placed an extra burden on them—many lacked the financial resources to wait for the resolution of their case. Business or union leaders who discriminated, moreover, had little to fear. The FEPC could not force parties charged with discrimination to appear at a hearing to discuss the matter, and many took advantage of this loophole and ignored the commission's repeated requests for a meeting. When meetings did occur, the FEPC's lack of subpoena power meant that it had to take descriptions of employment practices at face value. Under such conditions, the FEPC candidly admitted to itself, proving discrimination was difficult, and thus it is not surprising that at no time during the Humphrey administration did the commission refer any organization to the city attorney for court proceedings.[38]

Humphrey greatly exaggerated the impact of the FEPC when, testifying before Congress in 1949, he claimed that it had led to "an amazing increase" in employment opportunities for African Americans and other minorities. Nevertheless, he recognized that economic inequality was beyond the abili-

ty of city government to address alone and thus urged Congress to reestab-
lish the federal FEPC and lobbied the Minnesota legislature to approve a
state commission.[39]

VI

Reform of the Minneapolis police department constituted the final item on
Humphrey's human rights agenda. Unlike many northern cities, Minneapolis had not experienced any substantial interracial violence following World
War I or during the early 1940s, but Humphrey knew that confrontation between African Americans and police officers had sparked the 1943 riot in
Harlem. Humphrey had more on his mind than municipal tranquillity, however. He was well aware that African Americans and Jews had often been
treated unfairly, or, as in the cases regarding the beatings of the Jewish children, had their concerns ignored by the department. Such policies,
Humphrey believed, could not be tolerated in a democratic society. Three
weeks after taking office he told a reporter from the *Spokesman* that police
officers needed to understand the wants, concerns, and frustrations of the
communities they patrolled.[40]

The new mayor witnessed firsthand the tensions between African Americans and the police force six weeks into his administration when several
plainclothes officers raided the Dreamland Cafe, a restaurant in an African
American neighborhood, late one August night. The officers, who did not
identify themselves, present their credentials, or explain the reasons for their
actions (they were looking for a murderer), blocked the entrances and began
to frisk male patrons for weapons and question all present. Restaurant patrons later reported that the officers used profane language. The officers did
not find their suspect, but they arrested two black women who refused to
give their names. One woman's husband immediately contacted *Spokesman*
editor Cecil Newman. The newspaperman called Humphrey, who told him
to get in touch with the officers involved. Newman then went downtown
to the city jail, where he found a police officer talking with the mayor by
phone. Claiming that the editor was trying to "intimidate" him, the head officer stormed out of the conference. Newman telephoned Humphrey again,
who came to City Hall in the middle of the night. The mayor apologized to
the women, and, following a heated discussion with the police, ordered the
pair released.[41]

The restaurant incident was not the only time Humphrey became involved in police-minority issues. Informed by Newman that officers regu-

larly stopped African American men on the street when they were with white women, Humphrey put a halt to the practice. Similarly, he suspended without pay two officers who had made anti-Semitic remarks. Though Humphrey refused to suspend the two officers who stood idle while a bartender overcharged and then spat in the glasses of two black men, the incident prompted him to send all members of the department a letter reminding them that denial of service based on race was a crime and outlining instructions on how to handle future incidents. When African American leaders expressed concern over a potential candidate for police chief, Humphrey reassured them that he would expect whoever received the job to be sensitive to issues of police-minority relations. The individual in question did not get the position, but it is unclear how important a factor minority concerns were in Humphrey's final decision. "There is no group in this city that has a monopoly either on decency or lawlessness," the mayor reminded the chief in a letter outlining yearly goals for the department. Officers needed to cultivate community goodwill in minority neighborhoods by becoming "acquainted with the leading citizens of the beat, and in particular, the social workers, the clergy, the school teachers, the businessmen, and those civic-minded citizens who . . . have gained the respect and confidence of their fellow citizens." Indeed, as far as Humphrey was concerned, police training regarding minority relations was "of prime importance."[42]

The Council on Human Relations also took a strong interest in this area. It decided soon after it had been established in the spring of 1946 to sponsor a police training program in the area of intergroup relations. Much to the delight of the Minnesota Jewish Council, Minneapolis was the first city to implement such a course, which had been developed by the American Council on Race Relations. Course instructor Joseph Kluchesky, former chief of the Milwaukee police department, met separately with Humphrey, several police officers, and leaders from Jewish and African American groups in April to discuss the need for such a program. Kluchesky returned a month later to conduct a ten-hour session for eighteen leaders in the police department. Detailed techniques of the course are unknown, but it sought to lessen prejudice among the officers by having them examine their attitudes toward minorities, learn about racial and ethnic stereotypes, and become aware of minority concerns. It also offered specific instructions on how to keep disturbances from escalating into race riots. "Law enforcement today is no longer a matter of the application of brute force," Humphrey announced during the sessions. "It must proceed from understanding." When the Council on Human Relations received reports of discriminatory treatment of African Americans three months later, however, it realized that the course had constituted only a first step. It invited Kluchesky back in September to give a two-hour session to be attended by all officers. The council followed this up by having two of its members participate in a series of two-hour discussions on intergroup tensions in police work that were part of a broader two-week training course given to groups of officers throughout the year. Officers and leaders from black and Jewish groups also met regularly to review matters of concern to each.[43]

The efforts by Humphrey and the council achieved some notable results. Relations between the police and minority communities improved as a result of the classes and closer contact between minority leaders and the department. There were no interracial conflagrations, and the administration's rhetoric and actions sent a clear message that old practices would no longer be tolerated. Nevertheless, isolated cases of discriminatory treatment, especially pertaining to African Americans, continued. Not surprisingly, customary habits proved hard to eliminate quickly. Recognizing the persistence of the problem, the Council on Human Relations decided in the fall of 1948 to expand the police training program to involve all officers in a sustained course.[44]

VII

Humphrey's programs to improve relations between racial and ethnic groups fell far short of his ambitious goals in a number of respects. The considerable limitations under which the FEPC operated meant that the vast majority of African Americans and Jews would continue to suffer economic discrimination. Minorities still faced housing problems as several neighborhoods remained hostile to their presence. Civic organizations and clubs made little progress in opening up their membership to Jews and African Americans. When a Jew became mayor in 1961, the Minneapolis Athletic Club did not send him a membership card, which it customarily did to all new mayors, until a reporter inquired about it. Clearly, prejudice persisted despite the educational efforts of the Mayor's Council on Human Relations and the FEPC.[45]

Nevertheless, these substantial shortcomings should not obscure what was accomplished, for the Humphrey administration achieved some notable results and set critical precedents in several areas. Many cities undertook civil rights reforms during the 1940s by creating bodies similar to the Mayor's Council on Human Relations, and numerous mayors worried about racial violence, yet in no city were reforms as broad as in Minneapolis. Recognizing the myriad of problems facing minority communities, Humphrey and his allies moved on several fronts at once. As a result, discriminatory service in many public places ended, a handful of job opportunities opened, and police officers began to treat minorities with more respect. The Community Self-Survey, moreover, had yielded a wealth of information on which new efforts to improve minority life could be based. Public awareness of discrimination was greater than ever. The Humphrey administration also had made the social and economic concerns of African Americans and Jews a legitimate object of governmental activity. Most important, Humphrey and his allies helped redefine the issue of prejudice. They successfully framed it as a problem to be solved rather than something taken for granted as an acceptable part of community life. These efforts were not enough to overcome the problems, of course, but they constituted essential first steps in a long and difficult struggle.

The dedication and hard work of many individuals led to these improvements, but Humphrey's energy and commitment to democratic values were critical. Many of the gains resulted directly from his efforts. There was nothing inevitable about the developments in Minneapolis during the late 1940s. Though World War II had brought race into public life in much of the United States, another mayor might have ignored racial issues or sought to placate African Americans and minorities simply through patronage or hollow rhetoric. Humphrey's successors took little interest in the FEPC or the Council on Human Relations, and as a result both languished until the 1960s.[46]

African Americans and Jews attested to the improved climate in the City of Lakes. During the 1947 campaign the *Spokesman* noted that "integration of the Negro community into the worthwhile progress of Minneapolis has been greater under Humphrey's administration . . . than at any other era." Similarly, the director of the Phyllis Wheatley House noted, "The mayor and his [Council on Human Relations] are really trying to do something and they're getting somewhere." In 1948 the Urban League cheerfully noted that thanks to the Mayor's Council on Human Relations and the FEPC, it no longer had to stand as "a voice in the wilderness." That same year the National Conference of Christians and Jews bestowed an award upon Minneapolis for improving race relations. Three years later, two hundred African Americans attending a union convention wrote the Council on Human Relations, "A few years ago our organization couldn't even think of holding a convention in your city because of the discrimination that existed." The group ate at downtown restaurants and stayed at hotels without any trouble.[47]

Humphrey's civil rights reforms established several patterns that would characterize his involvement with racial matters throughout his career and help to redefine liberalism in the post–World War II era. First, Humphrey embodied liberalism's new emphasis on pluralism. According to liberals, democracy involved the bargaining of various groups in society. Having been raised to see the United States largely in a positive light, Humphrey thought that the nation's democratic experiment would not be complete until African Americans and Jews were integrated into mainstream society and joined other groups in the search for power and influence. Humphrey's experiences in Baton Rouge and his work with the labor movement in the early 1940s exposed him to how African Americans and Jews had been pushed to the margins of society, but World War II deepened his sense of the injustice committed toward these groups. Humphrey did not practice an empty politics based only on symbolism and rhetoric, nor was his administration one in which a handful of well-meaning but uninformed whites attempted to dominate the reform agenda. On the contrary, Humphrey sought to change the conditions of life for African Americans and Jews and involved them at numerous points in the reform process. Pluralism also meant using government to establish a broad public consensus on public issues. Humphrey believed strongly in the power of education and had enormous faith in the basic goodness of most people. He recognized that legal reforms were necessary to achieve equality and shared the New Deal faith that government could improve conditions for the disadvantaged, but Humphrey remained skeptical about the efficacy of social reform programs lacking broad public support. His ambitious goal was a community in which all citizens willingly treated each other with dignity and enjoyed equal social and economic opportunity, not one in which the majority accepted minorities grudgingly under the threat of legal sanction. The educational efforts of the Community Self-Survey, the FEPC, and the Council on Human Relations, were thus necessary complements to legal reforms. They provided models for change that attempted to create shared community goals and remind the majority of how it had failed to live up to its ideals. They were not meaningless gestures deliberately constructed to give the appearance of change, empty attempts to make whites feel good, or ways to avoid a discussion of fundamental economic and social issues. As Garry Wills has argued, effective leadership demands more than government making rulings and expecting people to follow. Rather, law has to be combined with citizens' commitment to the ideals behind it.[48]

Humphrey's appeal to the public's conscience and his numerous references to the sense of guilt he assumed many whites felt reveal the deep in-

fluence of Gunnar Myrdal's *An American Dilemma*. Viewing relations between various groups within a context of morality, Humphrey thought that
the economic, political, and social injustices suffered by blacks and Jews
stemmed from the failure of the white majority to live up to its democratic
ideals. Concentrating on reforming individuals ignored the institutional aspects of discrimination, to be sure, but he nonetheless understood that the
difficulties in minority communities stemmed primarily from the failure of
the white majority, not minorities themselves. He thus rightly focused on
changing white behavior and attitudes. Like Myrdal, Humphrey considered
discrimination to be an anomaly, something practiced by a few bad people.
Most citizens were simply unaware of discrimination but would want to do
something about the problem once they learned of it. Humphrey appropriately concluded that a change in white attitudes and actions toward minorities was not impossible. This faith regarding the public reflected an important shift in liberal thought in the 1940s. Several developments since
World War I, including race riots, nationalism, and fundamentalist religion,
had led many liberals by the 1930s to see the public as irrational and intolerant. Reform, liberals contended, would have to focus on the supposedly
"safe" ground of economics and ignore social and cultural matters. But
World War II had brought social and cultural issues to the fore and commanded the attention of liberals such as Humphrey. Education had its limits, however. He overestimated the size of the reservoir of goodwill waiting
to be tapped, and, contrary to his assumptions, bigotry existed not only because of the practices of a few bad people and the ignorance of others. It also
stemmed from self-interest.[49]

Humphrey's commitment to racial equality signaled a second fundamental change in liberalism during the mid-1940s. Arguing that the needs of
blacks were largely the same as those of whites—relief, jobs, housing, and education—liberals during the New Deal era, to the extent that they thought
of race at all, had subsumed it to broader class interests. The economic concerns of the disadvantaged, both white and black, remained paramount as liberals focused on a redistributionist agenda that sought to reign in the power
of big business in favor of the disadvantaged. African Americans' concerns
overlapped with those of working-class whites in many respects, but, as a result of social issues raised during the war, liberals now realized that they were
not identical. The emergence of race as a leading issue among liberals in the
North during the 1940s, therefore, meant that the class-based economic reforms and redistributionist politics that had characterized liberalism during
the 1930s now had to compete with other concerns. Liberalism was thus un-
dergoing the beginnings of a shift toward a greater concern for individual

and group rights that would mushroom over the next twenty-five years and supplant economic reform at the center of liberals' agenda. By fighting for FEPC, Humphrey tried to keep alive the New Deal spirit of using government to open up economic opportunity for the disadvantaged. Indeed, he never lost sight of the importance of this issue. Nevertheless, by insisting on confronting discrimination and segregation in a wide array of settings, such as public accommodations and treatment by the police, not just the workplace, Humphrey was broadening the liberal agenda. These areas needed to be addressed, but doing so would dilute the emphasis on economics. Time would show that it was impossible to sustain a concerted fight in several areas at once.[50]

The numerous civil rights activities in Minneapolis caught the attention of the national media, with journalists touting Humphrey's human rights efforts as examples of enlightened progressive leadership. The FEPC had been "singularly successful," and Humphrey had made Minneapolis "soberly conscious" of its human relations program, one noted. Because of these and other reforms, reporters called Humphrey "the most interesting phenomenon in the liberal skies of the Northwest" and "the most extraordinary politician that Minnesota has produced in fifty years." Describing Humphrey as a "brash, young tornado," one journalist characterized his administration as "the most exhilarating in the city's political history, complete with more roller-coaster dips and turns than any other six administrations." The young mayor, many political observers agreed, was a rising star in the firmament of Democratic politics.[51]

2

Into the National Arena

I

The press was not alone in wondering what the young mayor of Minneapolis was doing to combat prejudice, for city leaders from across the country looked to Humphrey for guidance in dealing with racial tensions. Following a 1947 speech before the National Association of School Administrators in which he described the Self-Survey, Humphrey received more than 150 inquiries from communities across the country. He advised the Philadelphia Council on Human Relations about how to lobby for FEPC, met with the mayor and human rights groups in Kansas City about the formation of a council on human relations, and spoke to a pro-FEPC group in Los Angeles. In Omaha he addressed the annual dinner of the local branch of the Urban League and the meeting of the National Conference of Christians and Jews. He also urged city officials there to establish a council on human relations. "Our example is giving many other communities the inspiration and encouragement they need to go ahead with similar programs," Humphrey proudly wrote members of the Minneapolis council.[1]

Prominent liberal leaders keenly followed Humphrey's meteoric rise. He became a member of the National Committee on Segregation in the Nation's Capitol and the National Council for a Permanent FEPC, and in 1947 several New Deal liberals invited him to join Americans for Democratic Action (ADA). An organization comprised of intellectuals, former New Deal officials, union leaders, and politicians, ADA sought to be a liberal force in American politics that would extend the New Deal at home and oppose communism abroad. Its leaders included Eleanor Roosevelt and Franklin Roosevelt Jr., Walter Reuther of the United Auto Workers (UAW), the theologian Reinhold Niebuhr, and the NAACP's Walter White. Civil rights, members agreed, would be one of their chief emphases. World War II had deepened their conviction that civil rights constituted a vital next step in establishing social and economic justice. Humphrey, who initially became a member of ADA's organizing committee, was soon elected to the group's eight-member Executive Committee and eventually became a vice-chair.[2]

Humphrey also joined an effort to desegregate the American Bowling Congress (ABC). Claiming to be a private club, the ABC permitted only white males to join. Integration of this popular form of recreation, liberals expected, would help break down racism among blue-collar whites. The UAW had severed its ties with the ABC over the exclusionary policy in December 1946 and called a conference to discuss the matter in Chicago the following April. Noting that private appeals by the UAW had failed to change ABC rules, the thirty-six people who gathered in the Windy City decided that public pressure had to be mobilized by establishing protest groups in major cities and creating a national body to oversee strategy and coordinate local activities. Though he was unable to attend the Chicago meeting, Humphrey agreed in August to serve as co-chair of the National Committee for Fair Play in Bowling (NCFPB) with former women's golf champion Betty Hicks. Other members of the committee included former heavyweight boxing champion Joe Louis, Walter White, A. Philip Randolph, Walter Reuther, CIO President Philip Murray, and the Urban League's Lester Granger. The project appealed to Humphrey's sense of fairness, but he also welcomed the chance to establish closer ties to the politically powerful UAW. Clearly, the ambitious Humphrey saw civil rights as a way to make a name for himself in national political circles.[3]

Humphrey's approach to the ABC problem reflected his faith in orderly change and gentle persuasion. He and the Mayor's Council on Human Relations assembled a broad coalition that included representatives from the NAACP, CORE, the Urban League, and the Phyllis Wheatley House to attack discrimination in Minneapolis bowling alleys. "We must educate the bowlers on this problem, for only in acceptance of new rule changes by public opinion can they be made successful," Humphrey told the press. "Legislation is not enough." Pointing to the recent desegregation of major league baseball, he contended that it was "ridiculous" to keep African Americans out of the ABC. "I believe if people can learn to play together we can learn to understand people and work together," he said. "I think 95 percent of the people in Minneapolis will respond to this plea for a fair deal." Humphrey rejected calls to publicly use the term *"Un-American" Bowling Congress* and instead urged local chapters around the country to flood the ABC with polite resolutions calling upon it to change its bylaws. He did, however, ask the governor of Michigan to deny the ABC use of state-owned fairgrounds for a tournament. The governor refused. Meanwhile, the ABC would not alter its policies.[4]

These setbacks did not deter Humphrey and the NCFPB. Chapters in several northern cities brought attention to the ABC's discriminatory policy by holding integrated bowling tournaments during the spring of 1948. One thousand people participated in Detroit, the stronghold of the UAW. The ABC, meanwhile, unsuccessfully attempted to sabotage tournaments in Buffalo and Cleveland. Soon after some tournaments had ended, the ABC reluctantly agreed to Humphrey's request to let representatives from the NCFPB present a brief to its executive board at the ABC's annual convention in April. The organization refused to budge. Disappointed with this decision, Humphrey went ahead with plans for an integrated tournament in Minneapolis two weeks later. "It is very important to destroy by concrete action the myths and stereotypes . . . which are used to defend discrimination," he declared. Tournaments proved to be important symbolic gestures of racial harmony, but they had little immediate impact. The ABC did not integrate until 1950, when pending lawsuits in several northern states convinced the group's leaders to rescind their membership guidelines.[5]

Humphrey further increased his national profile as a staunch civil rights advocate during the summer of 1947, when he traveled to Washington to testify on behalf of ADA in support of FEPC legislation. The federal FEPC closed in 1945 because southerners in Congress had eliminated its funding, but civil rights groups such as the NAACP, well aware that African Americans stood to lose many of the gains they had experienced during the war, believed that a permanent FEPC would prevent further cutbacks and reduce discrimination in hiring. Humphrey carefully underscored the link between adequate employment and racial justice by warning of the "frustration" that resulted from people not being able to fully use their talents. A permanent FEPC would allow minorities to enjoy enhanced buying power and higher standards of living, while the rest of society would benefit from greater productivity and reduced governmental spending on welfare programs, public health, and crime fighting. Again revealing the influence of Gunnar Myrdal, Humphrey argued that Americans' consciences had "become corroded and encrusted with a bitter feeling of guilt" over the gap between the nation's ideal of equal opportunity and the limited options available to blacks and other groups. Increased contact between different races and ethnicities, he added, would lead to a breakdown of stereotypes and promote tolerance among all groups. Education and conciliation were necessary in employment

matters because mere "slapback enforcement [would] defeat its own purpose," Humphrey maintained. "The enemy that we must combat," he told
the legislators, "is not the self-interest of any group, but consists of ignorance
and apathy." Such excessive optimism about the power of education
notwithstanding, Humphrey rightly noted that the measure would not eliminate discrimination quickly and that an FEPC without any enforcement
provisions, which some conservatives were proposing, would represent "just
pious platitudes." But Humphrey did not stop there. Well aware that the race
issue had taken on international implications since World War II, the mayor
insisted that FEPC would help the United States resist the spread of Soviet
totalitarianism by creating an example of a truly democratic society. None of
these arguments proved effective, and the bill remained buried in committee
for the remainder of the session.[6]

II

Civil rights advocates received a needed boost in October 1947 when President Harry Truman's Committee on Civil Rights submitted its report, *To
Secure These Rights.* The group went well beyond its original charge and
found during its yearlong investigation that African Americans faced lynching, police brutality, and a lack of equal opportunity in employment, education, housing, and political participation. The committee offered a series of
recommendations that included eliminating segregation in the armed services, upgrading the civil rights office in the Justice Department to a full division, and enacting legislation to end lynching, create a civil rights commission, abolish the poll tax, guarantee voting rights, establish an FEPC, and
ban discrimination in interstate transportation. The federal government had
not taken such a strong position on behalf of African Americans since Reconstruction. Describing the report as "clear and courageous," Humphrey
enthusiastically declared that its program could be "the twentieth century
charter of freedom."[7]

Truman took another bold step on behalf of racial justice three months
later by calling for civil rights legislation dealing with voting, employment,
transportation, and lynching. The president believed that the measures were
necessary, but he was also faring poorly in public opinion polls and badly
needed all the support he could muster among African Americans if he were
to win reelection that November. Truman could not take the black vote for
granted because Thomas Dewey, the likely Republican nominee, was popular among African Americans as a result of his civil rights efforts as governor

of New York. Some Republicans in Congress, moreover, were pushing FEPC and anti–poll tax legislation in hopes of bringing African American voters back to the party of Lincoln. Truman also faced a challenge for black ballots from his left. Former vice president Henry Wallace, who had a strong record on racial matters, had announced his presidential candidacy as the head of the new Progressive Party and released a seventy-four-point domestic program that included demands for several civil rights measures. For Humphrey the president's civil rights message constituted "a call to action" that represented the "greatest chance we've ever had to realize our spoken ideals."[8]

The president's endorsement of civil rights legislation predictably outraged southern Democrats. One senator interpreted the president's action as a sign that "the orders of Joe Stalin [had] trickled down through his stooges right into our White House." Other southern Democrats accused Truman of "stabbing the South in the back" and "kissing the feet of minorities." Some congressman demanded that southern governors organize a "march on Washington" for a "showdown" with Truman, while others proposed that the eleven states of the former Confederacy back their own candidate for president, thereby denying Truman victory by throwing the election into the House of Representatives. Several days after Truman's message, southern governors adopted a resolution charging the administration with insulting the South and created a committee to persuade the president to back down. Southern congressmen warned that the party would face "serious consequences" if it included a strong civil rights plank in its platform. Later that month more than half of the 850 Arkansas Democrats attending the party's Jefferson-Jackson Day dinner in Little Rock left the hall when Truman's voice came on the loudspeaker system. Such protests worked brilliantly, for the president quickly shelved his civil rights program and began efforts to shore up his standing in the traditionally Democratic South.[9]

Though Humphrey proclaimed that "getting rid of the Southern die-hards" would aid the Democrats, privately he worried that defeat in 1948 for Truman and the Democrats meant the "possible disintegration of the whole social democratic block in this country." Humphrey reported no enthusiasm for the president in the Midwest, where Wallace forces and the Republicans were gaining strength. "We are getting so many broadsides from so many directions," he noted, "that although the ship is not sinking, at times it is listing badly." As despair over Truman mounted among Democrats across the country, Humphrey, ADA leaders, and several northern city bosses raised the possibility of drafting a new candidate. War hero Dwight Eisenhower looked like a winner to Humphrey and many others, but no one really knew if the general was a liberal. Eisenhower, moreover, routinely denied interest in the

Democratic nomination. Humphrey considered Supreme Court Justice
William Douglas an unexciting but acceptable second choice. About the best
liberals could expect, Humphrey believed, was to "lose with a good candidate" who would "help us hold our forces together and, particularly, help us
on the Congressional level."[10]

Failure to find an exciting liberal alternative to Truman led ADA liberals
to search for other ways to augment their power within the party. In mid-
March a handful of ADA members resolved to make a fight over civil rights.
Race constituted the perfect issue upon which to challenge the southerners
for control of the party, they believed, because the president's response to the
southern revolt indicated that civil rights proponents had lost their momentum. Several ADA leaders approached Humphrey a month later about organizing an effort to ensure that the Democrats took a strong position on civil
rights in their platform. Battling the southerners, they wrote the mayor, was
"absolutely essential" if northern and western Democratic congressional
candidates were to win in the fall. Even if they failed, liberals would score
political points among blacks for having made the attempt. If Truman were
the nominee, moreover, a victory by ADA would put the fledgling organization in a much stronger position to influence him.[11]

Humphrey had a high personal stake in this looming battle. His rapid ascent in Minneapolis and his significant role in drumming Communists out
of the state Democratic Farmer-Labor Party in 1947 had caused many party
leaders to urge him to challenge Senator Joseph Ball. Defeating Ball would
not be easy, because Minnesota was an overwhelmingly Republican state
even though it had voted for FDR four times. The GOP controlled the gov-
ernorship, both houses of the state legislature, eight of nine congressional
seats, and both Senate seats. No Democrat had ever won popular election to
the Senate. Nevertheless, in late April a confident Humphrey announced his
candidacy. As far as Minnesota politics was concerned, the civil rights convention fight carried more pitfalls than benefits for him. A loss at the Democratic convention would greatly embarrass Humphrey and thus hurt his
chances of winning the election, but victory would not necessarily be a boon
because civil rights was not of prime concern to the vast majority of Minnesota voters. Defeating the southerners would, however, improve
Humphrey's growing stature among national liberal leaders and make a contribution to an issue he cared deeply about, and thus he agreed to take a leading role in the effort.[12]

Humphrey quietly organized the ADA civil rights fight while campaigning in Minnesota that spring. He persuaded James Roosevelt, chair of the
California Democratic Party, and Chicago boss Jacob Arvey to serve as co-

sponsors. Their support gave the ADA undertaking greater respectability. Humphrey now turned to broadening his base by offering a blunt political argument. Northerners had to make their stand on civil rights "abundantly clear and with equal vigor" because the South was setting the agenda, he argued. "Any real concessions on this matter," Humphrey insisted, "would only serve to strengthen the political position both of our reactionary Republican opposition and the Communist-dominated Third Party movement." Two months later, however, Humphrey began to doubt whether he should have assumed a leading a role in the ADA struggle. Eager to placate the South, the Truman administration had offered no support to the liberals. When the southern revolt showed no signs of ending, Humphrey nervously wondered if he and the liberals were marching to their doom.[13]

The young mayor, however, decided to press ahead after consulting with several northern Democratic leaders. On July 5, with the convention just a week away, Humphrey held a press conference in Minneapolis to announce that fifty-three Democrats from twelve states had signed a statement pledging their efforts to write the Truman civil rights program into the party platform. Among those joining the effort were New York boss Ed Flynn, former New York governor Herbert Lehman, AFL president William Green, and Franklin Roosevelt Jr. The campaign also received the backing of several candidates for Congress who needed black votes in November. Racial justice was "in the worthiest tradition of our Party," they wrote. The Civil Rights Committee's report contained "fundamental principles . . . as old as our nation." With an eye toward growing tensions between the United States and the Soviet Union, they insisted that "neither imagined rights, private economic interests, nor cherished customs of any section of America can remain sacred if they jeopardize the position of our nation in world affairs."[14]

The liberals' declaration made life more difficult for the preliminary drafting committee of the Democratic platform when it assembled in Philadelphia two days later. Appointed in June by Democratic National Committee chair J. Howard McGrath, the seventeen-member committee reflected the divisions within the party. Humphrey led the liberal faction, while the former governors of Alabama and Texas headed the southern contingent. Liberals wanted a more specific civil rights statement than the party had issued in 1944; southerners demanded an affirmation of states' rights. Caught in the middle were Senator Francis Myers of Pennsylvania and McGrath, who, as spokesmen for the Truman administration, sought harmony by proposing a restatement of the 1944 civil rights plank. That document had vaguely recognized minorities' "right to live, develop, and vote equally with all citizens and share the rights guaranteed by [the] constitution" and asked Congress to "exert its full constitutional powers to protect those rights."[15]

The civil rights issue came to the fore on the second day of the committee's hearings. The NAACP's Walter White, testifying on behalf of twenty-one African American organizations, contended that the "day of reckoning had come" when the Democratic Party "must move forward or perish." Maintaining that northern black voters would play a pivotal role in the election, he labeled the 1944 plank "wholly unsatisfactory" and insisted that the platform include "nothing less than the full recommendations of the President's Committee on Civil Rights." Another civil rights advocate predicted that blacks would bolt to Henry Wallace if the Democrats equivocated on the race issue. Eager to avoid airing party disagreements in public, committee members listened silently. Formal courtesies only temporarily masked their differences. Following the hearings, Humphrey informed reporters that liberals would reject any attempt to placate the South by repeating the 1944 plank with added states' rights provisions. He did, though, hint at a compromise by commenting that liberals would not settle for less than an affirmation of the "high spots" of the Truman program. The committee made no headway. On the eve of the convention the Democratic Party stood more divided than at any point since the 1920s.[16]

III

With the civil rights dispute unresolved and Republican candidate Thomas Dewey looking like a sure bet to end the Democrats' sixteen-year control of the White House, delegates arrived in Philadelphia in a dejected mood. No Democratic faction had cause for celebration. Three days before the convention liberals' slim hopes that Eisenhower would rescue the party disappeared as the general again firmly declared that he would not be a candidate. Truman would be the nominee, but the president's forces had problems of their own because they could not generate any enthusiasm for their man. Southerners, meanwhile, talked of holding a rump convention and nominating a second Democratic candidate a week after the Philadelphia gathering if they failed to win the platform fight or nominate one of their own to replace Truman at the top of the ticket. Unlike previous conventions, there were no parades, bands, or excited crowds in the streets of Philadelphia. "We're going over Niagara Falls and we know it," one national committeeman dourly noted. "There's nothing we can do. Haven't even got a barrel." Hotel cancellations poured in from party officials and delegates certain of disaster in November. The Bellevue-Stratford, which served as Democratic headquarters, reported two hundred vacant rooms on the eve of the convention.[17]

Eager to break the civil rights impasse, platform drafting committee chair Myers selected five members to meet secretly throughout the weekend before the convention and work out a compromise. Liberals became incensed upon learning of the clandestine group. Noting that there was not a strong civil rights advocate among the five, an irate Humphrey charged that Myers's subcommittee was "stacked." He informed reporters that there would be "a minority report of at least one" if the civil rights plank were unsatisfactory and even forecast victory if the civil rights proponents took their fight to the convention floor. Large delegations from New York and other northern states, he predicted, would side with the liberals. Humphrey vowed to fight for inclusion of all ten elements of the Truman package, but he again revealed signs of a willingness to compromise by indicating that four, especially those addressing economic and political equality, was a minimum.[18]

Myers's group was still searching for a civil rights statement acceptable to all when the convention opened. The Pennsylvania senator emerged from a hotel suite at 3:30 on the morning of the second day of the convention to announce that a draft of the civil rights plank had been completed. It declared that the Democratic Party was "solely responsible" for advances in civil rights and then repeated much of the 1944 wording. "It doesn't suit," a platform drafting committee member from Alabama commented. Southerners from eleven states had drawn up a states' rights plank and announced their intention to take their case to the convention floor. Likewise, liberals were unhappy because the Myers plank contained no specific reference to Truman or his civil rights package. Humphrey, who had been up all night waiting for word from Myers's committee, immediately called a strategy conference of northern states. When that meeting ended shortly after four in the morning, he reported that several states were behind the liberals' effort to demand a stronger plank and promised to bring the issue before the convention if neither the full platform drafting committee nor the 108-member platform committee strengthened the Myers plank. Whatever these committees decided, a floor fight was certain. "If we lose, we will want a convention decision," said Humphrey. "If we win, the southerners will take it to the floor."[19]

Under pressure from both liberals and southerners, the platform drafting committee continued desperately to look for a way to unify the party. It beefed up the civil rights plank somewhat by declaring that the party "commits itself to continuing its effort to eradicate all racial, religious, and economic discrimination." To mollify the South, the committee floated the idea of restoring the two-thirds rule for this convention only or making concessions on the party's stand regarding federal control of tidelands oil. Humphrey, who had been meeting with dozens of people regarding civil rights, found the new language much better than the 1944 plank, but he reserved the right to come back and fight for even stronger provisions. Southerners, meanwhile, renewed talk of a walkout.[20]

All 108 members of the platform committee met on the second evening of the convention to resolve the thorny matter. The group first took up a southern plan to delete language dealing with congressional action and replace it with a states' rights provision. "I must say that to do that would be a complete repudiation of what the president has said." Humphrey countered. "It would be to tell the Republican Party and its friends, and those who haven't made up their minds that they are our friends yet, that we do not believe in the president's civil rights program." Humphrey continued to lobby the committee to strengthen the civil rights plank, even though he was under intense pressure from party leaders to accept the Myers proposal. Southerners' talk of a walkout, Humphrey believed, was just that because the South had threatened to bolt in years past but had never done so. Humphrey asked the committee to approve a plank that pledged congressional action to guarantee all citizens safety from lynching, equal employment opportunity, voting rights, and equal treatment in the armed forces. To placate the southerners he struck out the words "brutal crime" from the section on lynching. What remained, he asserted, represented "an irreducible minimum for a large number of people at [the] convention." A committee member asked if such pledges were already loosely worded in the 1944 plank. "If it is in there," Humphrey cleverly retorted, "let us say so in so many words, so that we can compete with the opposition platform and underwrite what we know to be in our hearts." When these arguments proved unpersuasive, Humphrey pointed out the party's hypocrisy in expressing sympathy for people in eastern Europe while the United States denied basic rights to citizens at home:

Listen. If we can say to two-hundred million Russians ... we don't like the way they are handling their countries ... if we can cry crocodile tears over Czechoslovakia, if we can rave and rant ... about Estonia, Lithuania ... then I ask you my good friends ... is there anyone in this room that says we cannot give to men, if you please, who have ancestry in this country longer than 99 percent of the whites—remember the next ship after the Mayflower was a slave ship—I say that you think we can guarantee to them in reasonably well spelled out terms a few simple things. ... There is only one aristocracy in this country and that is the aristocracy of skill.

Unmoved, the platform committee voted to retain the initial version of the civil rights plank.[21]

If the administration would not pledge action in four areas, Humphrey reasoned, perhaps it would commit to a specific statement on ending discrimination in the armed services. This matter struck him as the least controversial of the four he wanted. All Democrats could surely agree that African American servicemen deserved equal treatment because many had helped protect America from Hitler, he thought. Such a weak declaration, Humphrey privately confessed, would be primarily for political purposes. Believing that this was "one motion that can keep this party . . . in a unified status," Humphrey maintained that such language would at least allow the liberals to claim a partial victory. "It is the one thing," he told the committee, "on which I can go back to a lot of people who have been beating me over the head and say, 'Look, we have gotten a lot out of this convention. We have gotten a great deal out of this platform committee and we have got to have good common sense here.'" Seeing even this mild stand as a threat to party harmony, the committee rejected it. "This is a move to absolutely destroy the harmony . . . we are trying to build," Senator Scott Lucas of Illinois angrily responded. Humphrey attempted twice more to win approval of at least the armed forces provision, but to no avail. When the committee also voted down three states' rights planks, the Truman administration seemed to be firmly in control of the convention.[22]

The committee's rebuffs left Humphrey and the liberals at a crossroads. They could accept the administration's civil rights plank or make good on their promise to force a floor fight. Deciding that they had come too far to give up now, the ADA leaders and other civil rights proponents who had gathered at the University of Pennsylvania fraternity house that served as the group's convention headquarters quickly resolved to proceed with the floor fight. Few expected victory, but they agreed there was nothing to lose in going forward. Everyone expected Humphrey to lead the charge.[23]

At his hotel suite a few blocks away, however, Humphrey thought long and hard about whether he wanted to remain at the helm of what appeared to be a sinking ship. Drinking beers that had been on ice in the bathtub, numerous friends milled about and offered conflicting advice. Humphrey, who was exhausted from going for several days with minimal sleep, worried that persisting in the struggle would not only hurt civil rights and the ADA but also sink his political career. He had good reason to be concerned. The most powerful figures in the party, including the president, vice presidential nominee Alben Barkley, DNC chair McGrath, and David Niles, Truman's top civil rights aide, wanted a compromise. By challenging the president and

Democratic leaders, Humphrey was risking losing their help in his race against Ball. Even if Humphrey defeated his Republican opponent, Democratic officials could sentence him to obscurity in Washington for refusing to go along with their wishes at the convention. Humphrey turned to his father. A delegate from South Dakota, Hubert Humphrey Sr. advised his son to weigh carefully the consequences of a floor fight but to go ahead anyway. "This may tear the party apart," he said, "but . . . you can't run away from your conscience, son." Humphrey also talked to his wife, who urged him to press ahead. Finally, at five in the morning, he decided to deliver the speech on behalf of a minority civil rights plank that specifically demanded congressional action in four areas: voting, employment, lynching, and the armed services. Humphrey made up his mind only after a friend suggested that some of the anti-Truman sting be taken out of the minority plank through the addition of a sentence commending the president for his "courageous stand on the issue of civil rights."[24]

With Humphrey as their leader, civil rights advocates prepared for the looming battle. ADA members lined up the backing of Chicago's Jacob Arvey, New York's Ed Flynn, and Pennsylvania governor David Lawrence by arguing that failure to take a strong stand on civil rights would cause defections to Henry Wallace and hurt the party in the North. With only a few hours remaining before the platform debate, Humphrey dictated his speech to an aide while taking a shower. He then circulated a draft among ADA and union leaders, many of whom thought it needed to be strengthened. Humphrey concluded he had gone far enough, however. Meanwhile, Andrew Biemiller, a former congressman from Wisconsin, met with convention chair Sam Rayburn to ensure that the liberals would be heard and that a roll call would be taken on their plank. "Fat's in the fire," Rayburn commented. The southerners also contacted Rayburn to inform him of their states' rights minority planks, but because Biemiller had seen him first the southern proposals would be presented as amendments to the liberals' plank and thus debated first. This crucial procedural victory would give ADA more time to rally support.[25]

That afternoon delegates struggled to stay cool in the sweltering convention hall as they gathered in anticipation of the showdown. The southerners offered three states' rights minority reports. Biemiller then presented the liberals' plank, which amended the platform committee's civil rights statement by praising Truman by name and adding the following paragraph:

> We call upon Congress to support our President in guaranteeing these fundamental and basic American principles: The right of full and equal

political participation, the right of equal opportunity of employment, the
right of security of persons, and the right of equal treatment in the service and defense of our Nation.

Speeches on behalf of the southern reports followed as Philadelphia police
officers patrolled the aisles. One irate delegate from Tennessee predicted that
a rejection of states' rights meant "the dissolution of the Democratic Party in
the South." Another from Alabama asked the convention to acknowledge
"the right of local control over the rules involving our social order." The Truman administration attempted a last effort to dissuade ADA when Niles told
one liberal leader that they would receive less than fifty votes and "ruin the
chances of the best liberal product to come down the pike in years." As the
southerners spoke for thirty-five minutes, Humphrey nervously waited at
the rear of the platform. One Democratic mayor warned, "Don't do it. You're
gonna split the party." Flynn approached Humphrey and glanced at his
speech. "Hey, you kids, you know what you're doing," he commented. "This
is the only way we can win this election. You're gonna stir up the minorities,
and that's the only way we can win this election." To boost Humphrey's confidence, Flynn summoned the leaders of the Illinois, Pennsylvania, and New
Jersey delegations to the platform. All told Humphrey they would back the
liberals' plank. Even Senators Myers and Lucas promised their support.[26]

Suddenly, it was Humphrey's turn to speak. Wearing a bright yellow Truman button on the lapel of his dark suit, he began in a conciliatory manner.
Acknowledging that he was "dealing with a charged issue—with an issue
which has been confused by emotionalism on all sides," he told the crowd
that his respect for his opponents had increased "because of the sincerity, the
courtesy, and the forthrightness" they had displayed during the platform debates. All regions of the country shared in the nation's freedom and all were
guilty of "at least some of the infringements of that freedom."[27]

Nevertheless, he continued, there were very practical reasons for the Democratic Party to make definite pledges on behalf of civil rights. Franklin
Roosevelt had begun a march toward equality and Harry Truman had provided "a new emancipation proclamation." The party had to go forward if it
were "to maintain the trust and the confidence placed in it by the people of
all races and all sections of [the] country," Humphrey insisted. The international situation, moreover, demanded such a declaration. "[The] world is
being challenged by a world of slavery. For us to play our part effectively, we
must be in a morally sound position. . . . Our demands for democratic practices in other lands will be no more effective than the guarantee of those
practices in our own country," he declared.[28]

Humphrey ended on an idealistic note. Political advantage and international tensions were but secondary motivations for a forthright civil rights stand. To Humphrey the liberals' position represented nothing less than the fulfillment of America's democratic promise:

> There will be no hedging—no watering down—of the instruments of the civil rights program. To those who say that we are rushing this issue of civil rights—I say to them, we are 172 years late! To those who say that this bill of rights program is an infringement of states' rights, I say this—the time has arrived for the Democratic party to get out of the shadow of states' rights and walk forthrightly into the bright sunshine of human rights. People—human beings—this is the issue of the twentieth century. People . . . are looking to America for leadership and they're looking to America for examples. . . . Now is the time to recall those who were left on that path of American freedom. For all of us here . . . our land is now . . . the last best hope on earth. I know that we can—I know that we shall—begin here the fuller and richer realization of that hope—that promise of a land where all men are truly free and equal, and each man uses his freedom wisely and well. I ask my party—I ask the Democratic party—to march down the high road of progressive democracy.[29]

Though Humphrey's address lasted less than ten minutes (a rarity for him), no one who had heard it was left indifferent. He had been interrupted more than twenty times by applause from sympathetic liberals and a few shouts of disapproval from southerners. After he finished, delegates from a dozen northern states grabbed their state banners and marched down the center aisles in support. Someone called for music, but there was none because Rayburn had ordered the band to remain silent. Whistling instead, the delegates carried on for ten minutes as stunned southerners sat in utter disbelief. Watching the proceedings on television from the White House, Truman referred to Humphrey and the liberals as "crackpots."[30]

Rayburn soon called for order to begin voting. First up was a states' rights plank, which the delegates handily defeated 925–309. Then they rejected the other two southern reports by voice votes. Humphrey waited tensely as Rayburn called the roll on the liberal plank. Everyone could see that the outcome would be close. Prospects for approval initially appeared grim, as border states that had voted against the states' rights resolutions also opposed the liberal plank. Liberals grew more hopeful when Michigan, New York, and Pennsylvania sided with them. Humphrey's father rose to inform Rayburn that South Dakota cast its eight votes for the liberal report. When Wisconsin's twenty-four votes put the liberals over the top, Humphrey jumped to his feet, grinned, and clenched both fists high above his head. The minority plank won, 651½–582½. A disbelieving reporter turned to a colleague and said, "God! Can you imagine that?" The South, one columnist wrote, had "arrived at its second Appomatox." The convention proceeded to approve the amended platform by a voice vote. Only in 1932, when the Democrats had revised their platform to advocate repeal of Prohibition, had there been as dramatic a reversal in direction on the convention floor. At last the Democratic Party had taken an unequivocal stand for racial justice. Humphrey and the liberals dared to take on a president and the leaders of their party, and they had won an improbable victory.[31]

Predictably, the liberals' triumph outraged many southerners. Birmingham police commissioner Eugene "Bull" Connor climbed onto a chair and clamored for recognition so that he could announce a walkout by part of the Alabama delegation. Rayburn ignored him and instead quickly called a voice vote on a motion to recess. Delegates roared their approval for a two-hour break. "We'll be back tonight—and go out the first chance we get," vowed the seething chair of the Alabama delegation. "They can't keep us here." Shortly after eight, he made good on his promise. Announcing that half of his group could no longer participate in the convention, he grabbed the Alabama banner and marched out of the hall into a driving rainstorm. The entire Mississippi delegation, which had ripped their state flag from convention decorations, followed him as a mixture of cheers and boos ushered them out. Though Governor Strom Thurmond of South Carolina and Senator Richard Russell of Georgia were upset over the vote, they kept their delegations in the hall. The southern bolt had fallen far short of expectations. Once the walkout was complete, delegates nominated Truman and Barkley.[32]

The shocking developments in Philadelphia made Humphrey a liberal hero. The NAACP proclaimed, "We believe the victory . . . marks the greatest turning point for the South and for America which has occurred since the Civil War." Humphrey was now a household name to the sixty million people who listened to his address on radio and the ten million who watched on television. The mayor, one reporter commented, had "left his indelible mark" on the convention and was "one of the coming leaders of his party." The *Chicago Defender* observed that Humphrey personified the "firmness and courage" of northern liberals at the convention. When Humphrey returned home a cheering crowd of two thousand people awaited him at the train station. Some carried banners reading "Humphrey—Champion of Human Rights" or "Humphrey Fights for the People." The welcoming party included three Minneapolis African American leaders and dozens of black citizens.

As the mayor came into the station, a police band played and the crowd sang "For He's a Jolly Good Fellow." After Humphrey offered his thanks, five youths hoisted him onto their shoulders and carried him to a nearby car, which led an eighty-vehicle parade through downtown. The festivities ended at the Nicollet Hotel, where Humphrey recounted his role at the convention to five hundred people.[33]

Though some southerners thought further revolt against the Democratic Party would only hurt their region, others remained defiant. Six thousand delegates gathered in Birmingham just two days after the Democratic convention to organize the State's Rights Party. They unanimously selected Strom Thurmond as their presidential candidate, and Mississippi governor Fielding Wright, who had led the Magnolia State walkout in Philadelphia, as their vice presidential nominee. The southerners hoped that the former Confederate states would unite behind the new party's affirmation of segregation and force the election into the House of Representatives, where they expected to block the despised Truman. Because there were four major candidates for the Oval Office, most political observers continued to forecast a Republican victory. Without the South Truman appeared to have no chance.[34]

Thurmond's entry into the race did not alarm Humphrey. He continued to think that the liberal civil rights plank constituted good morals and good politics. Dismissing the State's Rights Party as "nothing more or less than a rebel noise," he argued that the southerners "were just blowing off steam." Truman had a long way to go, to be sure, if he were to beat Dewey, but Humphrey predicted that the convention had laid the foundation for victory in 1948 and beyond. "I . . . have never been convinced that our Party could survive as a powerful force if we continuously had to compromise and make peace with elements and persons who were not interested in progressive democracy," he wrote a fellow member of ADA. "The Democratic Party belongs to the liberal people, and it is about time we justly claimed that it was ours."[35]

IV

Humphrey turned his attention to his Senate race once the celebrations had ended. After crushing his Progressive opponent by an eight to one margin in the September DFL primary, he set his sights on Joseph Ball. Reporters from around the country closely followed the Minnesota race to see if the young mayor could continue his rapid ascent. Eager for revenge, the southern rebels gave money to Ball and sent ex-Louisiana governor Sam Jones to Minnesota to campaign for him. Humphrey, however, also reaped financial benefits from his Philadelphia speech as sizable contributions from around the country poured into his campaign war chest. Some members of the DFL attempted to persuade Humphrey to downplay his advocacy of racial justice. "The Democratic Party doesn't need people who believe in race or religious bigotry," he replied. "I'm glad those people are against me." Racial matters, however, only played a small part in a campaign dominated by foreign affairs, labor concerns, and farm policy.[36]

On election night Humphrey gathered with family and friends at his home in Minneapolis to await the returns. More and more friends and neighbors arrived as the evening wore on, and Muriel set up a smorgasbord to feed to growing throng. Early results pointed toward a Humphrey victory, but Truman's fate was not as easily discernible. Later that evening, with victory a near certainty, Humphrey went downtown to visit his campaign headquarters. "Hello, Senator," the exuberant crowd shouted when he arrived. Humphrey went on to trounce Ball by 243,000 votes. Humphrey's grueling schedule, in which he had visited every county in the state at least twice and had given eight to twelve speeches a day, paid off handsomely.[37]

By the following day it was clear that, contrary to almost all predictions, the president had won too. African Americans could rightly claim to have provided the margin of victory, because a substantial black vote for Truman in California, Illinois, and Ohio had enabled him to best Dewey in those pivotal states. The party's civil rights stand more than offset the loss of four Deep South states to Thurmond. Two days after the election Humphrey congratulated Truman for "the greatest personal triumph in the history of this country."[38]

The 1948 election, one historian has rightly observed, "legitimized the issue of civil rights" in American politics. Through organizing the ADA forces in the spring and leading them at the convention, Humphrey played an integral role in this development. By strengthening the civil rights plank the Democrats had taken a significant step in committing themselves to racial justice. Humphrey and ADA had taken a huge step forward in continuing their effort to redefine liberalism. FDR had largely ignored the civil rights issue, but henceforth no liberal on the national level could. The South, which had dominated the Democratic Party for decades, was now on the defensive over the sensitive issue of race. By fanning the flames of sectional discord, Humphrey and his allies had also unwittingly helped begin a monumental sea change in American politics. No one knew at the time, but the defection of several southern states to Thurmond initiated the slow drift of the South to the Republican Party over the next three decades.[39]

Political observers expected the senator-elect from Minnesota to continue his fight for racial justice in Washington. One columnist predicted that Humphrey would "bring . . . a clamorous voice for civil rights and social reforms to the Senate." Declaring that Humphrey's name was "anathema" among southerners, an Alabama paper gloomily forecast that he would "deal the South misery" in the new Congress by leading the battle for Truman's civil rights program. Humphrey, though, saw himself taking a secondary role. Amid a jubilant crowd at campaign headquarters on election night, reporters asked if he would push civil rights legislation when he arrived in Washington. Noting that he had a lot to learn about the workings of the Senate, Humphrey cautiously replied, "No. I won't push anything. But civil rights turned out to be the rallying point for all factions of the party, and I think it'll be included in the legislation of the 81st Congress. President Truman is in a beautiful position on that—he doesn't owe a thing to the southern bloc." Humphrey would soon learn whether his optimism was warranted.[40]

3

FEPC
Stalemate in the Senate

I

On the chilly, overcast morning of January 3, 1949, members of the Senate gathered for the opening of the eighty-first Congress. Shortly after the chaplain said a prayer, Minnesota Republican Ed Thye escorted Humphrey to the rostrum. Wearing a blue double-breasted suit, the thirty-seven-year-old Humphrey took the oath of office as his parents watched proudly from the gallery. He was a member of a new Democratic majority, for just two years after the electoral slaughter of 1946 the party had reestablished its dominance of Congress. Few first-term senators had ever received as much attention as Humphrey. Upon arriving in Washington, he found over seven hundred speaking invitations waiting for him. The *Chicago Defender* named him to its "honor roll of democracy" for his convention fight, and the Negro Newspaper Publisher's Association gave him an award. *Life* called him the "most dynamic new face on the national political scene." Just two weeks after he was sworn in, *Time* put him on its cover. Portraying Humphrey as a prairie cyclone, the magazine described the senator as "a hard-working, fast-talking fireball from the Midwest" and predicted that he would lead the battle for President Truman's civil rights programs.[1]

Senate leaders were not about to let a new colleague set the legislative agenda, however. Majority Leader Scott Lucas of Illinois was nominally in charge of the Senate, but the southern Democrats, under the command of Georgia Senator Richard Russell, were the true lords of the upper house. Remembering their defeat at Philadelphia all too well, they were hungry for revenge. Every new senator but Humphrey received temporary office space before the opening of the new Congress, and when committee assignments were handed out Democratic leaders placed him on the insignificant Post Office and Government Operations Committees. On one occasion Russell made sure Humphrey heard him wonder, "How in hell could the people of Minnesota elect a damn fool like that to the United States Senate?"[2]

Early indications suggested that Humphrey had lost none of his combative spirit. Upon becoming national chair of ADA soon after being sworn in, he affirmed his commitment to enact the civil rights provisions of the Democratic platform. Shortly thereafter he took a principled stand for equality on Capitol Hill. The first senator to employ an African American male as one of his chief assistants, Humphrey brought the aide to the Senate dining room for lunch. A black waiter warned him that doing so would cause trouble. "[He] is a friend and he's my guest and I don't give a damn whether they like it or not," Humphrey replied. "He has been in my home. Anyone good enough to come into my home is good enough for this ptomaine parlor." The two proceeded to have lunch without incident. In like manner, Humphrey audaciously predicted that Congress would enact the first civil rights legislation since 1875. "There are enough votes in Congress to adopt civil rights if they are honest," he commented. "I warn them, if they are not sincere and honest, they may have some trouble in the future."

Numerous developments had led Humphrey to think that the alliance of southern Democrats and northern Republicans, which blocked progressive legislation since the late 1930s, could be overcome. For the first time in history both major parties had promised to fight for civil rights legislation. Truman's civil rights program, which Humphrey claimed enjoyed the "overwhelming approval" of the public, as well as the myriad of civil rights activities in states and cities across the nation, had convinced Americans that discrimination was a serious problem. Racial oppression in the South, he believed, stemmed primarily from the lack of economic opportunity for many whites, but urbanization, industrialization and, to a lesser extent, the growth of labor unions had dramatically transformed the region during the early 1940s and would improve the economic standing of whites and blacks and help lessen prejudice. Civil rights would be a vital ingredient in the continued economic development of the South, he prophetically noted. Similarly, an upsurge in political participation by African Americans in the 1940s meant that whites could no longer cling to their old ways. Across the South, Humphrey contended, politicians who made overtly racist appeals were fading from view as "new liberal political leaders [were] emerging to take the place of the familiar stereotypes of the past." To Humphrey "the resurgence of southern liberalism [was] one of the most hopeful events on the current political scene." He clearly overestimated the extent and depth of liberalism

in the South in the late 1940s, but his optimism about the future of race relations in Dixie was in line with that of many liberals of the era and not completely unwarranted. Given the terrible history of race relations since Reconstruction and the successful challenges to the old racial caste order that
had been mounted by the NAACP and other civil rights groups during the
1940s, there was good reason to think things were improving, albeit too slowly, for blacks in many parts of the South.[3]

The liberals' victory at the Democratic convention, as well as the president's improbable triumph in the fall, had also created an air of anticipation
among African Americans. "The vaunted power of the white-supremacists .
.. has been struck a death blow," the *Chicago Defender* stated. "The new Democratic Party's triumph has set the stage for a new era in democratic developments and our cause has won fresh champions." African Americans celebrated when the president clearly affirmed his support for civil rights
legislation in his State of the Union address. Three weeks later, they cheered
again as Truman's inaugural was the first ever to be integrated.[4]

Before any civil rights legislation could be adopted, though, Humphrey
and other civil rights supporters had to challenge the infamous Senate Rule
XXII, the filibuster rule. Southern Democrats, led by parliamentary expert
Richard Russell, had shrewdly employed it to stonewall civil rights legislation since the 1930s. Created in 1917, Rule XXII required the assent of two-
thirds of those senators present and voting to halt debate on a bill. There was
no provision to allow a vote to stop debate on a motion to take up legislation. The only way to end that talkathon would be to wear the southerners
out. Two filibusters, therefore, would have to be broken to pass a civil rights
measure: one on the motion to consider, one on the legislation itself. Recognizing that overcoming two filibusters would require a rare near unanimity among nonsoutherners in the Senate, Humphrey and other liberals favored cloture by a simple majority. Cloture had been voted in just four of
nineteen cases since 1917, and all six attempts to halt filibusters related to civil
rights legislation had failed. A simple majority had not voted for cloture on
a civil rights bill until 1946. Not even this long history of failure deterred
Humphrey. "There are a sufficient number of Democrats and Republicans
who are supposedly pledged to stop any filibuster, and it's just a matter of
arithmetic," he brashly declared.[5]

Getting the parties to adhere to their platforms proved more difficult than
Humphrey had expected. When Lucas moved to make the cloture issue the
Senate's pending business, southern Democrats launched a filibuster. Humphrey wanted the majority leader to employ round-the-clock sessions for a
week to dramatize the issue for the public and build support for majority

cloture. "There are plenty of us young men in Congress who can talk and stay up all night," he had said before the fight began. Once again, Humphrey's naïveté about the operation of the Senate was evident, for Lucas, who did not regard reform of Rule XXII as a high priority, immediately rejected such a course as too dangerous to older senators. The filibuster would go on as long as the southerners desired. Well aware that the president and other Democratic leaders urgently wanted the Senate to consider legislation dealing with rent control, labor issues, and the Marshall Plan, Russell met with Lucas and extracted a high price for ending the talkathon. First, they modified the pending filibuster resolution to require a two-thirds vote of the entire Senate, not just of those present and voting, to close debate. Sixty-four senators were thus needed for cloture. More important, the southerners fortified their position by forbidding cloture on filibusters against future attempts to change Rule XXII. Because southerners could now also talk to death any effort to make cloture easier, the daunting requirement of sixty-four senators appeared permanent. Under the new plan Humphrey would need the support of nearly every other nonsouthern senator to end debate. The Senate passed the resolution 63–23 in March. Only eight Republicans and fifteen Democrats, including Humphrey, voted against it. Describing the compromise as a "reprehensible sell-out," he conceded that chances for enacting civil rights legislation were slim. The Senate, he charged shortly thereafter, had been seized by "a society of wolves."[6]

Humphrey nevertheless soon submitted legislation to create a Civil Rights Commission and make lynching a federal crime. The commission, he hoped, would pave the way for more controversial legislation, such as FEPC, by gathering facts about civil rights violations. Having decreased dramatically since its peak in the 1910s, lynching was far from the most important problem facing African Americans. Incidents of violence still occurred, though, and the bill struck Humphrey as appropriate, for an antilynching measure stood at the center of the NAACP's legislative efforts in the 1930s. "An advance is an advance, no matter how small," he argued. The bills were also in part politically inspired, for Humphrey wanted to test the sincerity of Republicans who claimed they voted against majority cloture out of reverence for Senate traditions and not because they were against civil rights. Humphrey even thought that some of his southern colleagues might support his lynching measure, because many whites across Dixie, while vigorously opposed to black political or economic rights, abhorred this brutal crime. Aid from the Republicans or the southern Democrats was not forthcoming, and both of Humphrey's measures stalled in committee.[7]

The stalemate in Congress understandably upset the NAACP and other civil rights groups. Worried that African Americans were losing many of the economic gains they had experienced during World War II, leading civil rights organizations centered their legislative efforts on FEPC. The president knew that civil rights legislation stood virtually no chance in the Senate, but, concluding that an effort had to be made to demonstrate his commitment to racial justice, he presented a package of four civil rights bills to the Senate in late April: anti–poll tax, antilynching, FEPC, and an omnibus bill that included provisions for establishing a civil rights commission, creating a civil rights division in the Justice Department, setting up a joint congressional committee on civil rights, strengthening voting rights, and forbidding discrimination in interstate transportation.[8]

Any effort to address the economic problems facing African Americans was desperately needed. Unemployment among whites stood at 3.5 percent in 1948, whereas among blacks it was 5.9 percent. Median income of white workers in 1947 was $1,980; black income was $863. Median income of white families was $3,157; black income was $1,614. African American college graduates earned a median income of $1,074; white college graduates received $2,046. Unsurprisingly, African Americans made up a minuscule proportion of the workforce in higher-paying jobs. Black men constituted just 2.8 percent of professional and semiprofessional workers, and 1.1 percent of proprietors and managers, but they comprised 60.2 percent of those involved in domestic service and 21 percent of the farm labor workforce. The rates were similarly low for African American women.[9]

Humphrey shared the NAACP's interest in FEPC. Acknowledging that a federal FEPC would not solve all the economic problems facing African Americans, he nonetheless insisted that economic opportunity was essential to the struggle for racial justice. Equal economic opportunity would reduce welfare and crime, promote more stable neighborhoods, lead to improvements in the physical well-being of African Americans, and result in greater revenues for businesses, he contended. Day-to-day contact between the races in the workplace, moreover, would help break down vicious stereotypes. FEPC would benefit whites too. Once again revealing the influence of Gunnar Myrdal, Humphrey observed, "Our conscience has become corroded and encrusted with bitter feelings of guilt because we profess a belief in justice and equality of opportunity, but we practice injustice far too often." Such appeals fell on deaf ears, for Lucas revealed later that month that FEPC and the other civil rights bills were being dropped to give more attention to Taft-Hartley, international trade, and NATO. To liberal activist Joseph Rauh the decision represented a "flat betrayal of the Democratic platform." Outraged over the move, Walter White and Roy Wilkins of the NAACP, as well as rep-

resentatives from several other liberal groups, met with Humphrey and administration officials in early June. Highlighting the worsening economic
plight of many African Americans, they once again urged the administration
and congressional leaders to give highest priority to employment legislation.
FEPC aroused more hostility than any other civil rights measure, yet they
maintained there was no better way for the president to show his support for
racial justice than by fighting for the bill that was most important to African
Americans. The Truman administration soon declared that it would center its
efforts on FEPC. Doing so, it hoped, would satisfy African American leaders
and embarrass the Republicans when they failed to muster enough votes to
halt the certain southern filibuster in the Senate. As the session wore on,
Humphrey realized that nothing would be done regarding FEPC or any
other civil rights measure. Truman refused to spend his dwindling political
capital in a bitter fight with Congress over racial matters, and few legislators
owed their election to the president. In addition, nearly two-thirds of the
public opposed FEPC. Reflecting the desire of many senators to go home,
Lucas announced in early October that he would delay FEPC, which had
reached the Senate calendar, until the following year.[10]

Though civil rights legislation had gone nowhere in Congress,
Humphrey continued to identify himself with the cause of racial justice by
fighting segregation in Washington. He joined a picket line at National Theater, wrote city recreation leaders of his concern over segregation in local
parks, lobbied hotel and theater owners to open their facilities to all, and testified before congressional committees that oversaw the District of Columbia. Like other liberals, he regarded unequal treatment of citizens in the nation's capital as especially offensive because it provided good material for
Soviet propaganda. Nothing changed immediately as a result of Humphrey's
protests, but they did help set the stage for desegregation a few years later.[11]

The struggle for civil rights, then, had proved much more difficult than
Humphrey had expected. He had misread the election results; there was no
groundswell of public support. He had also mistakenly taken the GOP at its
word; the majority of Republicans were not eager to act upon their platform
pledge. Unifying the nonsouthern Democrats was difficult too, for, other
than Humphrey and a handful of his northern colleagues, few members of
Congress were interested in civil rights. Rather than build on the gains made
at the Democratic convention, as so many observers had predicted,
Humphrey and other liberals had suffered a grave setback with the new filibuster rule. Defeat on the civil rights front represented but one problem for
Humphrey. Judging the new senator from Minnesota to be impulsive and arrogant, many colleagues simply did not like him. Humphrey had not helped

matters by embarrassing himself in hearings regarding the Taft-Hartley labor law and attacking the sanctity of the seniority system, the key to southerners' domination of the Senate. (Worse, in 1950 Humphrey had received a stinging rebuke from colleagues after he attacked Harry Byrd's Committee on Nonessential Federal Expenditures on the Senate floor when the powerful Virginia senator was visiting his sick mother. Soon thereafter, Humphrey and Senator Homer Capehart got into a scuffle after a tense radio debate.) Humphrey later recalled that his early years in Washington had left him "lonely, broke, and bitter."[12]

II

When the new congressional session opened, FEPC topped Humphrey's civil rights agenda. In mid-January he addressed four thousand delegates who had come to Washington to lobby for FEPC and other legislation as part of the National Emergency Civil Rights Mobilization. Two weeks later, he attended an FEPC rally in New York. The Republican-southern Democrat coalition had delivered a "Machiavellian body-blow" to the cause of racial justice when it had passed the new filibuster rule, but "the time for political politeness [was] over," Humphrey assured the crowd. FEPC still faced considerable obstacles, however. Contrary to his promise at the end of the previous session, Lucas did not give FEPC an early hearing. The House passed an FEPC bill in February, but a coalition of southern Democrats and Republicans stripped its enforcement provisions. The result was a toothless measure that only empowered the commission to investigate, educate, and recommend solutions to employment discrimination. Though southern Democrats threatened to filibuster any civil rights bill that came before the Senate, Humphrey vowed civil rights proponents would fight for a commission with enforcement powers. Truman and Lucas, worried that a talkathon would endanger an important foreign aid bill, again decided to postpone the civil rights fight. The NAACP's Roy Wilkins gloomily observed that FEPC backers were "shocked and dismayed" by the delay.[13]

The Senate finally began debating equal employment opportunity legislation in early May, but, because the president did little to rally support for the bill, the battle was confined largely to Capitol Hill. Richard Russell once again led the southern forces as they launched a filibuster when Lucas moved that the Senate take up the administration's proposal. According to the Georgia senator the FEPC bill was "a legislative monstrosity . . . which would destroy natural rights guaranteed every citizen by the Constitution." Describing it as a cheap bid for African American votes, he alleged that FEPC was communist-inspired and would violate property rights, limit entrepreneurship, inhibit economic growth, waste taxpayers' money, undermine the nation's foreign policy, take away the right to trial by jury, promote the mixing of the races, create a bureaucratic "thought police," and give minority groups preferred status over whites for employment and promotion. An FEPC, he claimed, "discriminates against the average, garden-variety American citizen, who cannot claim connection with a minority group." Instead of producing jobs for blacks, FEPC would lead only to the employment of thousands of lawyers who would "harass" businesses about minority hiring.[14]

Humphrey countered by arguing that the continuing migration of African Americans to the North and emerging economic trends meant that FEPC was essential. Unemployment among blacks, he pointed out, had soared 280 percent from July 1945 to April 1949, compared to a 176 percent jump for whites during the same period. African Americans also suffered worse than whites during a recession because most companies laid them off first. Employment discrimination, moreover, led to lower levels of health, housing, and education among blacks. The successes of state and local commissions demonstrated that the measure could have a positive impact, Humphrey contended. As for charges that FEPC was communist-inspired, he sarcastically replied, "I suppose we'll have to get rid of the American flag because it has red in it." Russell's claim that civil rights proponents secretly favored giving special treatment to blacks could not be dismissed so lightly. Asserting that he simply wanted to ensure that race was not a factor in employment, Humphrey firmly declared that racial quotas were "completely the opposite of the purpose of the bill." To Humphrey it was wrong to use race as a reason to hire or not to hire. The quota argument, he added, proved that the bill's opponents sought to "delude the American people" and were "guilty of political trickery." This accusation outraged Tom Connally of Texas, who shot up from his chair and invoked Rule XIX, which forbade a senator from impugning a colleague's motives. Humphrey was called to order and forced to take his seat. Silenced only temporarily, he went on to maintain that FEPC would not only rebut communist propaganda but, more important, improve the social fabric at home. "When adults . . . are deprived for long of useful work . . . solely because of their color," Humphrey warned, "they are . . . likely to become irresponsible and impatient with the social order in which they live." Humphrey remained convinced that FEPC would eventually triumph, however. "My faith in the ultimate outcome of this battle for a Federal FEPC law," he wrote, "rests on the conviction that the integrity of our position is so unimpeachable that a virile democracy like ours has no choice but to recognize the inexorable rightness of our position: discrimination . . . is incompatible with a democracy."[15]

Lucas called for a cloture vote two weeks later. FEPC advocates mustered only fifty-two votes, twelve shy of the needed total. Nineteen Democrats, including Humphrey, and thirty-three Republicans voted to halt debate, while twenty-six Democrats (including six nonsoutherners) and six Republicans voted against it. A dozen senators, nine of whom were Democrats, did not vote at all. Roy Wilkins astutely observed that liberal Democrats would have a difficult time blaming the Republicans for the outcome. "There seems to be more concern over a Senate rule than there is for the Golden Rule," Humphrey lamented. Fearful that African Americans would support the GOP in November, the administration scheduled another cloture vote for July and brought pressure on all Democrats to attend. As expected, the result was the same. Humphrey now conceded that the best that probably could be won was an FEPC without enforcement powers. There was not enough support in Congress for anything stronger, and Truman, who was beset by the Korean War and attacks from Senator Joseph McCarthy, lacked the popularity or the will to rally the public behind a strong equal employment law.[16]

III

As the eighty-second Congress convened in January 1951, there was no reason for Humphrey to think that the chances for civil rights had improved. Though the Democrats retained control of the legislative branch despite heavy losses in the fall elections, southerners had emerged even stronger than before. In the House southerners constituted a majority of the Democratic members, while in the Senate they were just one short of a majority. To make matters worse, the Democrats, under the sway of Russell, elected Ernest Mc-Farland of Arizona majority leader and Lyndon Johnson of Texas majority whip. Both opposed civil rights legislation and a liberalization of Rule XXII. Likewise, few Republicans had campaigned in support of racial justice. Weakened by the midterm elections, Truman offered only a tepid endorsement of civil rights legislation in his State of the Union address. It was thus no surprise when a resolution for majority cloture offered by Humphrey and other civil rights advocates in January failed miserably.[17]

With the likelihood of congressional action remote, Humphrey searched for other ways to advance the civil rights agenda. The Korean War, which had been raging since the previous June, seemed to provide an opportunity to get around the southern legislative blockade. A week after returning to Washing-

ton, Humphrey followed the lead of labor activist A. Philip Randolph and
urged Truman to create by executive order an agency to guarantee equal employment opportunity in defense plants. The NAACP applauded this strategy as an appropriate step until the logjam in the Senate could be broken. The
war constituted a "national emergency" that demanded full mobilization of
resources, Humphrey asserted. This argument, which civil rights advocates
had successfully employed during World War II to help convince Franklin
Roosevelt to create the federal FEPC, proved far less effective with Truman.
The president issued an executive order in February, but rather than establish an independent employment agency with enforcement powers he simply declared discrimination in war plants to be against government policy.
African American leaders such as Walter White bluntly informed the president that his executive order did not go far enough. Such appeals carried little weight at the White House because Truman, recalling the enormous trouble that Russell had caused the FEPC during World War II, was in no mood
to provoke a fight with southern Democrats.[18]

Humphrey, who had not introduced any civil rights legislation during the
session, dropped eight bills into the hopper a month later. They included
FEPC, antilynching, and anti–poll tax measures, as well as legislation to create a Civil Rights Commission, outlaw segregation in interstate transportation, guarantee voting rights, amend existing civil rights statutes, and
strengthen laws against involuntary servitude. Humphrey knew these bills
had no chance of being enacted that session, but he remained convinced that
orderly progress would occur eventually if he and other liberals kept putting
the issues before the Senate and the American public. A lack of adequate employment opportunity, Humphrey pointed out, helped result in the average
life span of African Americans being ten years less than that for whites and
three times as many black women dying in childbirth as whites. Implicitly
invoking the analysis of Myrdal once again, he proclaimed that Americans
were a democratic people who, though imperfect in living up to their ideals,
would eventually overcome their shortcomings. "The story of America,"
Humphrey boasted, "is one of an expanding democracy opening up new opportunities to more and more of our citizens."[19]

Truman finally moved on the civil rights front in December by creating
an eleven-person Committee on Government Contract Compliance. Lacking any enforcement powers, the group was purely an advisory board that
would oversee implementation of nondiscrimination policies in firms with
federal contracts. Southerners charged the president with political expediency, but Humphrey described the move as a "step in the right direction." He
made no secret, however, of his disappointment that it was not a revival of

FEPC and pledged to continue to fight for an employment commission with broader enforcement powers. Determined to keep FEPC alive, Humphrey announced that his Subcommittee on Labor and Labor-Management Relations would hold hearings on equal employment opportunity in the next session of Congress.[20]

IV

During the fall of 1951 some southern Democrats gave signs of plotting another rebellion against Truman. The president had not fought for civil rights legislation, but many still considered him too liberal on racial matters and worried about recent Supreme Court decisions against segregation in real estate, higher education, and some forms of transportation. In early November Senator Harry Byrd of Virginia denounced Truman for his civil rights activities and identified Humphrey as the "champion of this infamy, hypocrisy, and reprisal." The ADA civil rights plank had to be removed, Byrd announced. Several southern governors also declared their opposition to Truman. Some southerners hoped that Byrd would become a presidential candidate, while others spoke of voting for potential Republican nominee Dwight Eisenhower.[21]

Meanwhile, Humphrey pondered the role of civil rights in the Democratic Party. Liberals had accomplished little since their convention victory in 1948. No civil rights bill had even come to a vote in the Senate; simply raising the issue had made a repeat of the 1948 split possible. No one expected Truman, who had an approval rating of just 30 percent, to pull off another miracle. Sensing that the race issue meant trouble for the nation and his party, Humphrey concluded that liberals held a weak hand and had to offer an olive branch to the South.[22]

He did so that November in the form of a letter outlining his civil rights positions to twenty-two editors of leading southern newspapers. The idea had been suggested to him in February by a friend from Georgia, who noted that most white southerners had been exposed only to racist views and needed to hear firsthand the case for equality. Believing that there were racial moderates in the South with whom he might be able to find common ground, Humphrey drafted a clear but gentle overview of his civil rights positions. As he had in his 1948 convention speech, Humphrey opened by seeking to downplay sectional differences. He commended the several southern states and cities that had recently abolished the poll tax, passed antilynching and antimask laws, and made modest gains in health, housing, and community services for African Americans. Because racism also existed in the North, it was "wrong and unjust to single out any section of the country as the worst offender." To identify himself with the South, Humphrey recalled that he had lived there for a year while attending graduate school at Louisiana State University and regularly supported economic initiatives that benefited the area. Anti–civil rights forces had successfully linked civil rights with communism, but Humphrey again attempted to reverse the argument by claiming that improving the condition of African Americans would help the nation's foreign policy. "The day of white supremacy in the world is over," he wrote. "It was always immoral, and is today impossible." Developing countries in Asia and Africa wanted to ally themselves with the United States but would not do so if it continued the contradiction of upholding racist practices at home while defending democracy around the world. "We need their friendship if we are to avoid a war," Humphrey declared, "and we need their strength if we are to win a war." Military might alone was insufficient to counter the Soviet Union, because the "ruthless" leaders in the Kremlin exploited American weaknesses for their propaganda purposes. As a result, it was "particularly essential that we become in all respects 'one nation indivisible.' " Though Humphrey refrained from mentioning specific civil rights measures, he did outline his vision of how to ensure equal opportunity. The federal government had an obligation and right to "set standards or guideposts." But, Humphrey assured readers, progress would not come simply as a result of passing laws. Once laws were on the books, it was "the responsibility for spiritual, civic, and educational institutions, as well as individual leaders, to create observance and respect for these standards among the people." Unsurprisingly, the tone and substance of the letter differed little from what Humphrey had advocated as mayor of Minneapolis. He remained convinced that time, education, and understanding would lead to orderly progress. The letter, he observed later, reflected his hope that "calm reason and intelligent understanding" would replace "the deep emotionalism" generated by the race issue.[23]

Humphrey's attempt to bridge differences with white southerners flopped badly. A handful of southern liberals welcomed the move, but many other southerners denounced it. The *Tampa Tribune* blasted Humphrey as an "irrational and intemperate" demagogue, while the *Savannah Morning News* argued that he "might as well have . . . advocated the change in our Flag from the Stars and Stripes to the hammer and sickle." Civil rights advocates in the North, on the other hand, interpreted it as a sign that Humphrey would seek harmony with the South at the upcoming Democratic convention. Humphrey moved quickly to squelch such speculation by announcing that he would fight to strengthen the 1948 plank by adding a provision calling for the liberalization of the filibuster rule. "Let's be frank about it, and say some [legislative] things must wait," he told reporters. "But that doesn't mean that a party's political program should not make it clear what the party stands for."[24]

At the same time he was reassuring liberals, however, Humphrey continued to search for common ground with the South on civil rights legislation by revealing in November that he was willing to sit down with Congressman Brooks Hays of Arkansas. "Any agreement that we reached would probably go too far for some people and not far enough for others," Humphrey remarked. "But progress is better than the inaction of the past few years." Hays had developed the Arkansas Plan, which included elimination of segregation in the armed forces, a constitutional amendment outlawing the poll tax, antilynching legislation, and an FEPC without enforcement powers. Russell had indicated a willingness to accept parts of the Hays program. If the Georgia senator could support some of the plan, Humphrey reasoned, the rest of the southern Democrats in the Senate, and possibly local leaders across the South, would follow suit.[25]

Humphrey talked with Hays about a compromise, but he also knew that African American organizations still considered a strong FEPC their chief goal. Indeed, the NAACP kept the heat on Congress by holding a civil rights rally in which more than eight hundred people representing fifty-two organizations came to Washington. Humphrey joined Republican Irving Ives of New York to sponsor FEPC legislation shortly thereafter. They attempted to lessen the acrimony surrounding the bill by renaming it the "National Act Against Discrimination in Employment," but all the old arguments against FEPC resurfaced. Humphrey again found himself on the defensive, especially regarding southerners' patently false claim that the FEPC would have the power to sentence individuals to jail without a fair hearing. To allay fears of iron-handed enforcement by Washington bureaucrats, he repeatedly emphasized the bill's reliance on conciliation first and its assurances that only a judge could mete out punishment. "The club is there, all right," Humphrey pointed out, "but it is a pretty small club and can be used only as a last resort." To counter persistent charges of favoritism for minorities, he once more clearly indicated that he was against any type of racial quota or use of race in employment decisions. "The fact is that quotas would violate the law because they would make race, color, religion, national origin or ancestry a criterion for hiring and/or firing" he noted. "This is just what the bill is against." The Labor and Public Welfare Committee reported the legislation favorably to the Senate, but leaders refused to call it up before the end of the session.[26]

As FEPC stalled in Congress, Humphrey staked out a liberal position regarding the upcoming Democratic convention. "The Democratic Party," he told the ADA convention, "does not deserve to endure if it equivocates on the issue of civil rights." Speaking to the NAACP convention, he admitted to being under "terrific pressure" to compromise on the civil rights plank but vowed to be "no part of . . . a sell-out of other people's rights and privileges." Humphrey also met regularly with ADA and NAACP leaders to develop convention strategy and promoted an "area block" program under which states from the upper Midwest would work together to resist southern efforts to control the party. There were two main reasons, Humphrey believed, for the Democrats to go forward on civil rights. He considered "the moral issue" of equal opportunity in employment, voting, and other areas to be "very great and basic to the principle of the Democratic Party." Any Democrat who backpedaled on civil rights did not deserve to win the election, he asserted. But in this case good morals also constituted good politics, for Humphrey, like many liberals of the era, believed that African American votes could mean the margin of victory in large northern states. Five states (Illinois, Michigan, New York, Ohio, and California) accounted for 169 electoral votes, more than half the total needed for victory. The Democrats could lose the election if northern African Americans backed the GOP or stayed home. If a sizable number of white southerners voted Republican or formed a third party again, the Democrats had to win most of the large northern and western states, as they had in 1948, and with the immensely popular war hero Dwight Eisenhower as the likely Republican nominee the battle for these states would be fierce.[27]

Humphrey wanted his party to take a strong stand on civil rights and win the black vote, but he thought it could do so without sacrificing the South. Accordingly, he joined several southerners and northern liberals at a meeting that spring organized by Brooks Hays and Senator John Sparkman of Alabama. Liberal Herbert Lehman of New York demanded a civil rights plank that included support for an FEPC with enforcement powers and vowed to fight diligently for such wording, but Humphrey diplomatically expressed hope that a statement acceptable to both sides could be drafted. One senator suggested that Hays and Humphrey sit down and work out a compromise. Uncertain of how the civil rights issue would develop, Humphrey backed off. "I will not get into any kind of conference or any kind of drafting committee," he said, "that will embarrass me in case I decide to go before the convention to plead for an all-out 100 percent declaration on civil rights." The meeting ended amicably without an agreement on the civil rights plank.[28]

Humphrey's inclination to seek harmony had led him to discussions with Hays, but so did his interest in being president someday. Many liberals encouraged him to seek the nomination when Truman announced in March he would not run again. Thinking that he was not ready to be president and worried about damaging future prospects if he failed, a flattered Humphrey refused. He also feared that any rash action would jeopardize the modicum of respect he had finally won from Senate colleagues. "The first two years were tough ones and in many ways heartbreaking ones," he wrote a close friend on the eve of the 1952 Democratic convention. "I now believe that I have earned for myself a place of respect among my colleagues." By 1951 he had demonstrated a thorough knowledge of tax issues and had shown that he and the southerners could agree on foreign relations and farm policies. The ambitious Humphrey had his eye on the future, however, and he knew that winning the Democratic nomination required convincing the party that he was not a civil rights radical who wanted the federal government to run roughshod over the South. Just as the race issue prevented a southerner from winning the party's nomination, so too would it block someone who was regarded as too liberal. Humphrey thus viewed the 1952 convention as a chance to improve his growing standing within the party and position himself as one who could heal sectional divisions.[29]

The Democrats who gathered at the amphitheater on Chicago's south side in late July were anything but united. Southerners talked of reasserting their control of the party and northerners hoped to add to the civil rights plank a clause calling for majority cloture. To make matters worse, a bitter controversy arose shortly after the convention opened regarding the seating of the Texas and Mississippi delegations. Two groups from each state fought for the right to be seated. One represented the Dixiecrat, anti-Truman wing of the state parties, while the other was comprised of "loyalist" pro-Truman delegates. Both liberals and conservatives saw the dispute as a matter of paramount importance, for the outcome of this issue would set the tone of the convention. The party appeared headed for another showdown to rival that of Philadelphia.[30]

As the seating issue commanded center stage, Humphrey publicly sided with the liberals. Meeting with presidential candidates Estes Kefauver and Averill Harriman on successive days, he helped persuade them to join forces behind the "loyalists." He urged the Minnesota delegates to resist efforts to seat the anti-Truman groups. "These Dixiecrats are the same people who ganged up on Roosevelt, then his wife, then his children, then his dog Fala," Humphrey commented. The loyalists suffered a defeat, however, when the Credentials Committee voted to temporarily seat the anti-Truman delegations. Liberals then hatched plans to make all delegates sign a loyalty pledge requiring that they use all "honorable means" to place the party's nominees on their state ballots under the Democratic emblem and work for them in the fall. When the delegates adopted the loyalty pledge, liberals seemed in firm control of the convention.[31]

Their victory proved to be short-lived. DNC chair Frank McKinney and Senator Sparkman warned that several southern states were threatening to bolt the convention. Eager to have the South on board in what would be a difficult race against Republican nominee Dwight Eisenhower, the delegates quickly watered down the pledge so that it would apply only if it did not cause delegates to violate state laws or orders from state party leaders. The anti-Truman delegations were seated. Blasting McKinney for his role in this sudden turnaround, Humphrey charged that the move represented "the first dagger in the back of the New Deal–Fair Deal." When reporters questioned him about the final compromise, a surprised Humphrey claimed he had not been consulted and declared that there would be a floor fight if it represented a retreat. Liberals took heart, for their champion from 1948 appeared ready to lead them into battle once again. But all was not what it seemed. To be sure, Humphrey supported the loyalist forces from Texas and Mississippi. He thought it was wrong for states to attend the convention but put other candidates under the Democratic heading on the November ballot, as several southern states had done in 1948, yet he also wanted to keep the party together for the fall election. When liberals sought to force the loyalty pledge on the South, Humphrey grew concerned that their strategy would backfire, and thus despite his combative rhetoric he did not lead a floor fight to uphold the original pledge. The South had triumphed.[32]

Attention now turned to the civil rights plank. Representatives from liberal groups such as the Leadership Conference on Civil Rights (LCCR—an umbrella organization of over fifty groups interested in civil rights) demanded that the Democrats support an FEPC with enforcement provisions and, more important, restrictions on the right to filibuster in the Senate. The latter goal, the LCCR asserted, constituted "the primary requisite for a meaningful . . . plank." Southerners wanted as vague a statement as possible. As on the loyalty matter, Humphrey searched for a middle course while appearing to be fully behind the liberals. Before coming to Chicago he had denounced those who favored a soft civil rights plank as "nothing but a bunch of Republicans with a southern accent," yet when asked at the convention if he would lead a movement to include a plank calling for restrictions on Rule XXII, he carefully replied that he would "support" a call for tightening the filibuster rule. Other liberals talked of a floor fight if the plank did not contain the LCCR goals. Hoping to avoid such a development, Brooks Hays and John Sparkman arranged to meet with Humphrey. During an hour-long discussion over breakfast in Sparkman's hotel room, they acknowledged the political necessity of language committing the party to some type of civil rights action but indicated that southerners would never accept wording, such as "compulsory FEPC" or "enforceable," that would suggest federal action in racial matters. Likewise, they would reject any plank that included a call for the repeal of Rule XXII or used the words *cloture* or *filibuster.* Humphrey assured the pair that he would not lead a floor fight and expressed hope that an agreement could be reached. The civil rights plank adopted by the delegates reflected the prevailing spirit of harmony. The Democrats affirmed their support for legislation that assured the right to equal employment opportunity, personal security, and political participation as well as strengthened existing civil rights statutes and their enforcement. Unlike four years earlier, they did not explicitly urge Congress to guarantee those rights. In another section of the platform entitled "Improving Congressional Procedure," the party meekly called for allowing Congress to take legislative action "after reasonable debate without being blocked by a minority in either house." Contrary to claims by Humphrey and a few other liberals such as Walter White, the South had won its second victory in Chicago.[33]

Once the loyalty and platform fights were settled, delegates focused on choosing candidates. For the first time in twenty years there was no incumbent Democratic president seeking reelection. Because no one had emerged from the spring primaries as the clear favorite for the presidential nomination, many saw Governor Adlai Stevenson of Illinois as the ideal choice. Some northerners looked favorably upon Stevenson in part because he had established an FEPC in Illinois. Ironically, southerners thought he could be persuaded to go slow on civil rights. Efforts to draft the governor, which had been underway since the spring, continued as the convention opened. Some liberals, however, had become dismayed at the stress on harmony that dominated the proceedings and were not ready to fall into line behind Stevenson. On the last day of the convention several hundred delegates gathered at the Congress Hotel at three in the morning to launch an anti-Stevenson drive. But a battle did not occur. Serving as peacemaker, Humphrey told the crowd that Stevenson, whom he regarded as the best man to take on Eisenhower, was basically a liberal whom they ought to accept. He pointed out that a challenge would be futile because Stevenson's nomination was inevitable and liberals would be hurt if the South received credit for nominating the governor. The liberals aborted their rebellion, and Stevenson easily won the nomination that evening. The desire for unity was evident again when Stevenson selected Senator John Sparkman of Alabama as his running mate. Though he was fairly progressive on most issues, Sparkman had a weak civil rights record. Sparkman's nomination outraged the NAACP's Walter White and many other liberals, but Humphrey had a different view. Acknowledging differences with the Alabamian on civil rights, Humphrey nonetheless highlighted Sparkman's role in drafting the civil rights plank and commended him for courageously ousting the Dixiecrats from the Alabama Democratic Party even though he had backed Strom Thurmond in 1948. "I believe," Humphrey announced, "it's important that the voice of liberalism in the South be given a chance to be heard." On one level, Humphrey was being a loyal Democrat and accepting what could not be changed; Stevenson was not going to dump Sparkman. Humphrey's comments also carried a deeper significance, however. Sparkman certainly was not a strong advocate of civil rights, but he was more moderate than white supremacist politicians such as Thurmond. To Humphrey working with figures like Sparkman represented the only hope for breaking the southern stranglehold on civil rights legislation and achieving racial progress in the South.[34]

Civil rights played only a tiny role in the fall campaign as Eisenhower turned the issues of the Korean War, communism at home, and corruption in the federal government to his advantage. The former general courted the white South by refusing to back a federal FEPC and offering only a vague endorsement of equal rights. Stevenson, meanwhile, took inconsistent positions on civil rights. Eisenhower rolled to an easy victory on election day. Stevenson triumphed in only nine states, all of them in the South or in border areas, but the Democrats did not have a lock on Dixie. Eisenhower won Texas, Florida, Virginia, Tennessee, and Oklahoma. Blacks remained loyal to the Democrats, as Stevenson received 75 percent of the African American vote.[35]

V

Though World War II had helped bring the issues of segregation and the denial of voting rights to Humphrey's attention, he gave these matters relatively little attention during the Truman years. To be sure, Humphrey regularly introduced legislation to remedy these injustices and frequently spoke out against them, but during this period he focused most heavily on FEPC and economic concerns. His emphasis on FEPC was due in part to prodding by the NAACP and other pro–civil rights organizations that had put it atop their legislative agenda, but he was not blindly following their demands. He had fought for FEPC in Minneapolis. More important, Humphrey's New Deal roots convinced him that poverty remained African Americans' top problem. The inability of African Americans to participate fully in the economy, he feared, would result in social ills within black communities, retard economic growth overall, and further poison race relations. Employment discrimination offended Humphrey's belief that everyone deserved equal opportunity. What African Americans needed, in Humphrey's eyes, was the chance to compete on equal terms with whites. That meant promoting employment opportunity regardless of race. Government's proper role was to remove race consciousness from employment decisions. To Humphrey race consciousness was an artificial barrier that had retarded economic progress for African Americans as employers had followed a "whites only" hiring and promotion policy for decades. Given this tragic history, Humphrey concluded that the logical answer was to eliminate race consciousness from such matters, not use it to promote black hiring. Russell and the southern Democrats had directly challenged Humphrey on this issue several times, and he explicitly indicated that he wanted to remove race from consideration in employment issues. He expected that African Americans would advance economically if government could ensure that hiring and promotion decisions were color-blind. Progress would be slow, but he had no doubt that changes in law and white attitudes, coupled with gains by blacks in education, would lead to a narrowing of the economic gap between the races.

Within a few decades many liberals would favor a far different approach to economic equality, and Humphrey's advocacy of FEPC would look tame. But one must remember that his position was liberal for its day. Indeed, the idea that the federal government would intervene in hiring and promotion decisions by private companies at all struck most Americans as inappropriate. Similarly, there was little support for FEPC within national political circles. To have argued for a more comprehensive program to combat economic inequality, therefore, would have been equally fruitless. The nation and the Democratic Party, enamored by the economic boom that was occurring for most Americans and preoccupied with the emerging Cold War, were moving rightward, not leftward. The old New Deal crusades for economic justice no longer seemed to resonate in this new environment.[36]

To be sure, Humphrey's case for FEPC had its limitations. He was fundamentally wrong when he contended that the lack of court cases and hearings by local and state FEPCs in the North offered proof that equal employment opportunity could be promoted without tension; the lack of cases provided evidence that such bodies were largely ineffective. Moreover, a federal FEPC similar to the relatively weak body created during World War II would not achieve all that was needed to improve the economic situation among blacks. Humphrey recognized this, but by fighting for FEPC and pointing to increasing black unemployment he was raising an important issue that needed to be addressed. In 1950 black joblessness stood at 9 percent, roughly 33 percent higher than it had been two years earlier and almost double the white rate. World War II had resulted in significant economic gains for blacks, but, as one historian has pointed out, the late 1940s and early 1950s were far from a "golden age" for many African Americans. Rather, those years marked the beginning of an urban crisis that would not dominate public attention for nearly twenty more years. Humphrey would deepen his understanding of the connections between race and economics over time, but unlike most political leaders in the late 1940s he was aware of the nascent problem.[37]

Humphrey's regular search for accommodation with the South constitutes the second persistent theme of his involvement with civil rights during the Truman years. This was in part a political calculation. He thought the Democrats needed to retain the South to keep their hold on the White House and Congress. Humphrey also wanted to advance politically, and he knew that he had to have southern support to do so. The contrast of Humphrey's role in Philadelphia with his position in Chicago is striking. Whereas he had led the ADA charge for a strong civil rights plank in 1948, four years later he counseled against actions that would disrupt party unity. There was more to Humphrey's search for harmony than political expediency, however. Though the New Deal coalition had shown signs of cracking in the 1948 over racial issues, he believed that civil rights advances could be made without alienating the South. To Humphrey the South was not a monolithic bastion of seething racial hatred. Some southern politicians, he believed, were "reactionaries" who were Democrats "only by accident of birth and geography" and "ought to belong in the Republican party" for their opposition to civil rights and other New Deal-Fair Deal programs. At the same time, he saw a new, more liberal white South emerging, which, while not as progressive as he on civil rights, was at least willing to engage in discussion about racial matters. This new generation of politicians would have to lead the South out of its racist past. Agreement could be reached with these southern Democrats, he expected, which would result in racial justice for African Americans. Though Humphrey overstated the extent of liberalism in Dixie, events during the next thirty years would show that he was not wrong to believe that the white South would change.[38]

By 1952 Humphrey's initial optimism that the civil rights gains of the 1940s could be readily translated into legislative victories had given way to the hard realities of life in the Senate. Armed with the potent Rule XXII, southern Democrats bitterly resisted any bill, no matter how mild, that increased the federal government's efforts on behalf of African Americans. A few Republicans shared Humphrey's concern for racial justice, but overall the GOP offered little help. No civil rights bill, Humphrey rightly calculated, would become law until a sufficient number of Republicans decided to support it. With a new Republican president who had not given any sign of an interest in civil rights about to be inaugurated, Humphrey had to doubt whether the legislative stalemate would be broken anytime soon.

4

Desegregation, Voting Rights, and the Elusive Search for Consensus

I

To many observers Republican control of the executive and legislative branches for the first time in two decades signaled the dawn of a new political era. Democrats had occupied the White House for so long that none of the 48 Republicans in the Senate and only 9 of the 221 in the House had ever served under a Republican president. The first year of the new administration, one reporter predicted, would be full of "sweeping and sometimes sharp changes." African Americans had little reason to think that the transfer of power in Washington would mean anything for civil rights, however. The congressional alliance between the southern Democrats and the Republicans showed no sign of ending, and because the new president believed that discrimination lay beyond the reach of legislative solutions there would be little pressure on Congress from the Oval Office regarding racial issues.[1]

Though he doubted the chances for success, Humphrey pressed for majority cloture soon after the eighty-third Congress opened in January 1953. To get around the provision of Rule XXII that allowed for a filibuster on any attempt to change the rule, Humphrey and his allies cleverly argued that the Senate could draft new rules at the beginning of each Congress, before the Senate formally adopted its rules for that term. Allowing the old rules to automatically carry over from the previous session denied new members the chance to decide the rules under which they would operate, Humphrey contended. Most of Humphrey's colleagues agreed with Republican leader Robert Taft and the southern Democrats, who insisted that the Senate was a continuing body whose rules automatically carried over. Civil rights proponents suffered a crushing defeat, 70–21. The civil rights fight, Humphrey dejectedly observed, was off to "a gloomy start."[2]

Humphrey soon offered his customary package of civil rights legislation, yet rather than stress FEPC he highlighted his bill to create a civil rights commission. Similar to the Mayor's Council on Human Relations in Minneapolis, the commission would gather information about civil rights activities and violations, advise the president, and assist local agencies. Humphrey was well aware that emphasizing the commission measure would appear to be a weakening of his position, but, believing that the civil rights debate had become "too much involved in all sorts of emotional crosscurrents," he contended that a commission was needed to provide a clear factual record on which to base future legislation. The commission offered a way to challenge the Republicans' sincerity on civil rights, and, because it would have no powers of enforcement, Humphrey expected that even some southern Democrats might support it. The failure to pass FEPC during the previous three years had convinced him that civil rights proponents had to start small. "I am so distressed over the long stalemate that I am perfectly willing to be the compromiser," he candidly remarked. "I am willing to offer the olive branch and get this thing moving. It's better to go a foot than to fail to go a mile." The legislation went nowhere.[3]

Humphrey's focus on the commission did not mean that he had lost interest in FEPC. Rather, he had turned primary responsibility for the employment bill over to coauthor Irving Ives in hope that the New York Republican might be able to rally GOP support. Seeking to build an empirical case for FEPC, Humphrey's Subcommittee on Labor and Labor-Management Relations issued two reports in February, one on the effects of state and local FEPCs and the other on the economic status of African Americans. One-third of the American public and one-eighth of the black population, the first report pointed out, lived under state or local FEPC laws. Although it was impossible to establish a firm number of jobs created or areas opened up to minorities as a result of FEPC laws, the subcommittee concluded that they had been successful in improving economic opportunities for minorities. More revealing was the study regarding the economic status of African Americans. It noted some important gains but indicated that a large gap between the races remained in several areas. The average black unemployment rate from 1947 to 1951 was more than 50 percent greater than the white rate. Average family income for African Americans in 1950 was 54 percent of white income, down from 57 percent in 1945. In urban areas average black income was 58 percent of white income, down from 66 percent in 1945. Average schooling for blacks in 1950 was almost three years less that for whites. Few African Americans were professional or technical workers. These alarming figures, Humphrey maintained, urgently demonstrated the need for FEPC, but no one was less surprised than he when Congress failed to act on the matter.[4]

A year later, the outlook for civil rights gains remained grim. The administration rebuffed Humphrey's regular requests that it desegregate schools on military bases across the South, and he found few allies for his civil rights commission proposal. Humphrey supported FEPC legislation, though he thought that it had no chance of being enacted. Bringing pressure on Congress for FEPC, he hoped, would at least prod state and local governments to act and assure African Americans that liberal Democrats were trying. Testifying before the Senate Committee on Labor and Public Welfare, Humphrey pointed out that low wages and the lack of employment opportunities for blacks had "deleterious economic and social effects" and meant that "incentives for improvement . . . [were] nonexistent for vast numbers of workers." Opponents once again charged that FEPC meant hiring quotas. The goal, Humphrey countered, was "no more and no less than . . . equal opportunity for all." The committee reported the bill out favorably, but it never came to the Senate floor because leaders wanted to avoid a filibuster.[5]

All was not bad news for civil rights advocates, however, for in May the Supreme Court handed down a ruling that gave the cause of racial justice a much needed boost and took the civil rights debate in a new direction. In *Brown v. Board of Education*, the Court, which had been chipping away at Jim Crow laws for years, unanimously declared the separate-but-equal policy of public education in the South to be "inherently unequal" because it violated the Fourteenth Amendment and created attitudes of inferiority among African Americans. The Court did not mandate a specific plan for compliance. Well aware that the decision struck at the core of Dixie's social system, southern Democrats denounced it as unconstitutional and pledged to defend their section's customs. "Delighted" with the ruling, Humphrey remarked that it provided "further evidence to the world that the American system is a democratic one" and expressed hope that it would nudge Congress to pass civil rights legislation.[6]

Though the *Brown* decision widened the chasm between Humphrey and the southerners regarding civil rights, he took two steps that fall to promote party harmony. Knowing that the Democratic National Committee (DNC) was searching for ways to bridge sectional divisions, Humphrey brought Lyndon Johnson and Russell Long of Louisiana, whom Humphrey had met while a student at LSU, to Minnesota to campaign for him. In addition, he accepted DNC chair Stephen Mitchell's request to serve as a vice-chair of an eighty-two member committee to develop rules for the 1956 Democratic convention. Southerners were still smarting over the loyalty oath controversy at the 1952 convention, and Mitchell, who headed the committee, desperately wanted to heal sectional rifts before the next presidential election. Humphrey and his co-vice-chair, Governor John Battle of Virginia, met several times during the fall to hammer out an agreement. The committee proposed in December that the party scrap the loyalty oath and require that states sending delegates to the convention place the nominees on their ballots under the Democratic heading. Delegates would be under no obligation to support the nominees in the fall election. No legal means existed, Humphrey reasonably pointed out, to compel individuals to do so. The committee adopted the plan four months later. Encouraged by "the unanimity that [was] being developed toward erasing sectionalism," Humphrey stressed that the party should work for harmony and victory in the 1956 campaign. He expected that he could maintain his good standing among civil rights advocates while working to polish his image as a loyal Democrat, but such comments drew fire from civil rights leaders such as Walter White, who, worried that too many concessions had been made to the South, commented bitterly that the committee "presented the country with some of the oddest assortments of political bedfellows which the country [had] witnessed in recent years."[7]

African American leaders again clashed with Humphrey when the new Congress opened in January 1955. They wanted to challenge Rule XXII on the opening day of the new session, but Majority Leader Lyndon Johnson, eager to establish consensus in the Senate, persuaded Humphrey to lobby his allies to abandon their frontal assault. After much debate he convinced civil rights proponents to seek majority cloture by the more cumbersome and less rancorous route of working through the Senate Rules Committee. Believing that the only opportunity for reform had passed, angry NAACP leaders charged that Humphrey's fealty to Johnson had overridden his interest in civil rights. Walter White called the liberals' tactics "the greatest shock which advocates of civil rights legislation have received in many-a-day" and speculated that pro–civil rights Democrats had traded silence on the filibuster issue in return for favorable committee assignments. Liberals, he perceptively noted, were making all the sacrifices for the sake of Democratic unity. Humphrey denied the existence of a quid pro quo, but he did acknowledge that liberals had received better assignments than in the past. Contrary to White's hopes, moreover, Humphrey had not demanded that Johnson assure enactment of civil rights legislation in return for retreating on the filibuster fight.[8]

White and other observers rightly noted that by the mid-1950s Humphrey and Johnson had grown closer. The relationship served the needs of both men. The majority leader, who saw most liberals as hopelessly idealistic and naive in their use of power, viewed Humphrey as a practical politician who could serve as his link to northern Democrats. He also admired Humphrey's eloquence and intelligence. Besides a willingness to compromise to advance their goals, the pair shared a rural background and fond memories of the New Deal. Humphrey, meanwhile, had grown especially fond of the Texan while working with him on several issues during the previous two years. Flattered by Johnson's attention, Humphrey was impressed by the majority leader's knowledge of the legislative process and his ability to forge a consensus. Forming an alliance with Johnson would give Humphrey access to the centers of power in the Senate he lacked during his early years in Washington.[9]

More anxious than ever that Congress do something about civil rights, Humphrey urged Johnson to lead an effort for mild steps such as a constitutional amendment to outlaw the poll tax as well as legislation to create a civil rights commission and make lynching a federal crime. Still doubting that FEPC could be enacted, Humphrey indicated that he was "prepared to accept any one or two or three . . . bills so that we can get off dead center and begin to make some progress." He wrote a southern colleague, "I have a fear that unless we . . . begin doing something about civil rights we Democrats . . . will find ourselves in the minority during the 85th Congress." Turning a cold shoulder to such naked political appeals, the southerners remained firmly opposed to any civil rights legislation, while Johnson, wanting to avoid a filibuster, refused to challenge them on the issue. Humphrey received another rebuff from the southerners several weeks later regarding a school construction bill. Thinking that federal aid to education would be a popular program, Humphrey hoped the Democrats could "beat the Republicans to the jump on this issue," but in light of the *Brown* decision the NAACP called upon liberals to demand an antisegregation amendment. Worried that this would only lead to a filibuster and loss of the bill, he approached the southerners about a deal in which the Senate would approve a school measure without an antisegregation amendment and then pass a civil rights bill. "It would be bad politics . . . to vote against the amendment without having some kind of other areas of accomplishment in the field," he wrote Alabama senator Lister Hill, whose Committee on Labor and Public Welfare was responsible for the legislation. When liberals showed no signs of backing down on their fight for an antisegregation amendment, Humphrey privately called upon Adlai Stevenson to broker a settlement, but the former Democratic nominee declined Humphrey's invitation and the session ended without any action regarding school construction or civil rights.[10]

This lack of progress, as well as the shifting of the civil rights debate away from economic concerns, led NAACP leaders began to wonder just how much they could count on Humphrey. They supported Humphrey's commission measure, but they also worried that fighting too vigorously for it would be seen as "a move to water down FEPC." Concluding that African Americans needed to do something to speed up the elephantine pace of reform, Roy Wilkins suggested that black voters might back Republican candidates in 1956. "Even an outstanding liberal like Senator Humphrey is not as active in the civil rights fight as he has been in previous years," Wilkins told the press. "It may be that Senator Humphrey is being sacrificed on the altar of Democratic Party unity." Such comments stung Humphrey. Highlighting the many unsuccessful attempts he had made to pass FEPC, he angrily wrote Wilkins that he was "getting a little tired of having people who should be working in the same cause undermine those of us down here in Congress who have stood up throughout the years for the very things for which you are fighting." Humphrey continued, "We have got to work together on these matters. It does not help you or me to have a prominent leader such as yourself going around the country weakening my position or contesting my sincerity." Wilkins astutely replied that the southern Democrats had "been taking all and giving not an inch." Urging Humphrey to convince them that unity was a two-way street, he reported that increasing numbers of African Americans were blaming the Democrats for the "intolerable" lack of progress in Congress and would not hesitate to back Eisenhower. Humphrey agreed that the president's efforts to reduce segregation in Washington and the armed forces had won some black votes for the Republicans, but he remained hopeful that the southern Democrats would recognize this and allow a civil rights bill or two to become law.[11]

Developments that summer intensified Humphrey's fear that African Americans would turn to the GOP. Vice President Richard Nixon expressed strong support for equal employment opportunity and a top administration official urged banks and other lending institutions to provide credit to African Americans for new housing. At the same time, Senator James Eastland, a Mississippi Democrat, called for an investigation of the Supreme Court on grounds that the authorities it had cited in *Brown* had been influenced by Communist-front organizations. Five days after Eastland's demand, the Court rejected NAACP appeals to order complete desegregation by 1956 and instead ruled that desegregation would be accomplished gradually, "with all deliberate speed." Humphrey, who had anticipated a more detailed plan, voiced his disappointment with the Court, while Eastland called upon the South to "defy this monstrous proposition." Humphrey promptly warned the DNC leader that the party should not "underestimate the deep resentments of many of the leaders of the Negro community" over incendiary statements such as Eastland's. A month later, after the congressional session had ended yet again with no action on civil rights, he alarmingly wrote his party chief that the Democrats had "better quit kidding [themselves]" because the Eisenhower administration was "making headway" regarding civil rights.[12]

Meanwhile, racial tensions were escalating dramatically across the South. Thousands of African Americans were pressing for school desegregation and attempting to register to vote. Voting, many blacks had decided, offered a way to make white leaders respond to their needs. Determined to maintain their social, economic, and political control, whites responded with a campaign of "massive resistance." Four states adopted pupil placement laws, which allowed schools to group students according to "ability," as a way to circumvent *Brown*, and voting registrars employed a wide variety of cunning schemes to deny blacks' applications. White Citizens' Councils sprang up, especially in the Deep South, to launch a campaign of intimidation. Blacks who challenged the status quo were often fired, evicted, denied credit, forced out of business, or worse. In Mississippi four African Americans were killed by white men. The victims included teenager Emmett Till, who allegedly whistled at a white woman, and a minister who was shot in broad daylight on a courthouse lawn for urging defeat of a white supremacist politician. There were no arrests in two of the murders, and the individuals charged in the other two cases went free.[13]

Shocked by the violence in the Magnolia State, Humphrey pleaded with Democratic leaders to move on the legislative front. Enacting three civil rights bills (antilynching, a civil rights commission, and a constitutional amendment to outlaw the poll tax), he believed, would restore calm to the South, advance the cause of racial justice, and keep the Democratic Party in good standing among black voters. Humphrey conferred with Johnson, who indicated that he would only back an effort to eliminate the poll tax by a constitutional amendment, a plan the NAACP opposed. "I am very worried," Humphrey informed a liberal congressman after the meeting with Johnson, "but possibly a miracle will come and save us. I am afraid it will take at least a miracle." Humphrey lobbied Missouri senator Thomas Hennings, who chaired a subcommittee that dealt with civil rights, to hold hearings and move the three civil rights bills forward. He again took his case to the head of the DNC. Arguing that progress could be made without "being inflammatory or being unreasonable," Humphrey sounded an alarm. "Unless we take a firm forward step our party is going to suffer at the ballot box, and it should," he observed. "Our Republican friends know they are not going to get votes in the South, so they're pushing hard for votes in the North—and I think they are making progress in the cities."[14]

Humphrey's desperate search for party harmony and orderly progress across Dixie appeared even more futile that spring. Southern Democrats took the offensive in March by introducing the Southern Manifesto. Nineteen senators and eighty-two representatives signed the declaration, which criticized *Brown* as "a clear abuse of judicial power" and boldly asserted southerners' right to use "all lawful means" necessary to defy the ruling. Fearing that the manifesto would inflame white resistance across the South, Humphrey immediately talked of circulating a declaration affirming *Brown*. Plans for a counterdeclaration soon evaporated, though, because some pro–civil rights legislators considered it to be of little value. Humphrey denounced nullification, but, worried that desegregation would take place only after further turmoil and violence, he also called for calm and national unity. "If there is one plea that I make here today, it is that we continue to reason with one another, rather than be the victims of passion and emotion," he observed. "Nothing could be worse . . . than to have a conflict between the races . . . [or] for North and South to become divided." Such appeals fell on deaf ears as tensions escalated in Congress and across the South. Similarly, Humphrey's compromise antisegregation amendment to another school construction bill went nowhere.[15]

The worsening situation in the South and the chance to woo black voters frustrated with the Democrats prompted the Eisenhower administration to submit a civil rights package to the Senate in April. Drawn from Humphrey's bills, the legislation would create a civil rights commission, upgrade the civil rights section of the Justice Department to a full division, and authorize the attorney general to seek injunctions to prevent civil rights violations in general and voting rights abuses in particular. The administration's package marked three critical departures in the civil rights debate. First, having the executive branch behind a civil rights bill would likely prod some reluctant Republicans in Congress to back civil rights. Furthermore, relying on Justice Department intervention to seek preventive relief signaled a growing impatience with the customary model of forcing individuals to win lawsuits to receive their rights. By the mid-1950s it had become clear that this was an expensive and cumbersome process that was failing miserably across the South. The federal government, many civil rights supporters rightly perceived, had to keep whites from tying up legal challenges to Jim Crow indefinitely. Finally, the substance of the administration's legislation, combined with the emphasis on desegregation in the wake of *Brown*, meant that economic concerns such as FEPC had largely faded from view. Civil rights now primarily meant voting rights and desegregation.[16]

Though Humphrey initially branded the administration's legislation as "lip service by leap-year liberals," he quickly decided he could not oppose it simply because it carried a Republican label. The NAACP, after all, had placed voting rights atop its 1956 legislative agenda. Chances for a voting measure receded in May when the president announced that he favored only the bill's provisions to create a civil rights commission and a civil rights division in the Justice Department (the other two sections had been sneaked past Eisenhower by the attorney general). Moreover, the lengthy process of hearings and debate likely meant that the session would end without action in even these two areas. "I am discouraged, disappointed, and most unhappy with the failure of Congress to take positive action in the field of civil rights," Humphrey wrote Roy Wilkins. "The situation is deplorable."[17]

By summer, though, prospects for enacting a civil rights bill had brightened somewhat because both parties wanted to court black voters. Johnson assured Humphrey in late June that the Senate would approve at least one civil rights measure. The majority leader would not be specific, but he probably meant legislation to create a civil rights commission. The House upset Johnson's plans a few weeks later by passing the Eisenhower administration's legislation intact. Richard Russell promptly informed the majority leader that southerners would filibuster if it came before the Senate. With the end of the session just a few days away, Johnson, who intended to dispose of several other measures and did not want to exacerbate sectional conflict just prior to the Democratic convention, took Russell's threat seriously. When liberal Paul Douglas of Illinois tried to circumvent normal procedure and place the House-passed civil rights measure directly before the entire Senate, Johnson crushed him. Humphrey joined over seventy other senators to block Douglas's move. Taking up civil rights, Humphrey argued, would lead only to a filibuster that would doom other important legislation, such as Social Security reform. Though he was willing to acquiesce for now, Humphrey vowed to be "relentless and persevering" on behalf of civil rights and would tolerate "no further delay" when Congress reconvened in January. Some liberals again questioned Humphrey's commitment to civil rights. "Anyone can come to a funeral," the angry lobbyist of the UAW muttered as he watched Humphrey side with the majority. Convinced that an opportunity to pass civil rights legislation had been lost because their allies had deserted them, civil rights lobbyists berated Humphrey in the Senate cloakroom that night.[18]

As the parties prepared for the fall elections, therefore, Humphrey could take little comfort in the developments surrounding civil rights during

Eisenhower's first term. Economic issues had all but disappeared from debate, yet, as he had argued on numerous occasions, many blacks still suffered from job discrimination and poverty. Meanwhile, racial tensions across the South had escalated during the two years since the *Brown* decision. Tired of being told to be patient, African Americans were demanding their rights immediately. White southerners, on the other hand, had become even more determined to resist any type of change. As the conflict intensified, Humphrey stood trapped in the middle, desperately trying to find a compromise between forces he could not control.

II

Brown and the spread of "massive resistance" across the South meant that finding common ground regarding civil rights at the Democratic convention in Chicago would be more difficult than ever. Roy Wilkins demanded the party pledge "affirmative action to see that the Court's decision [would be] made effective." Believing that the Democrats had to abandon the idea that differences over civil rights could be papered over, ADA leaders urged liberal unity behind a specific promise for executive and legislative action regarding desegregation. Herbert Lehman openly advocated a showdown over the issue. Southerners, on the other hand, pointed out that Eisenhower had done better in Dixie than any Republican presidential candidate since Herbert Hoover and insisted that the Democrats shore up their traditional base by adopting a civil rights plank that ignored the desegregation issue altogether.[19]

Thinking that the Democrats had to keep the New Deal coalition together to have any chance of victory against an immensely popular president, Humphrey took a more cautious approach regarding the civil rights plank than many of his liberal friends. Because desegregation and FEPC were so controversial, he approached the chair of the Platform Committee about uniting the party around the question of voting rights. The NAACP had stressed voting rights legislation in the previous session of Congress, and across the South thousands of African Americans were attempting to register unsuccessfully. Giving blacks the ballot would represent a crucial step forward, Humphrey thought. He also expected southerners to have a difficult time opposing the franchise, because whereas the Constitution gave no explicit guidance regarding FEPC or school desegregation it clearly affirmed the right of all qualified citizens to vote.[20]

There was more than party harmony and a Democratic victory at stake for Humphrey in Chicago. He had worked that spring to help front-runner Adlai Stevenson in the Minnesota primary, and at a meeting a few weeks later the former Illinois governor told Humphrey that he was thinking seriously about him as a running mate. When Humphrey raised the issue of southern opposition, Stevenson instructed him to rally some southern supporters. Understanding that the second spot on the Democratic ticket would be his if he could do so, Humphrey persuaded several southern senators to lobby Stevenson on his behalf and impetuously announced a week before the convention opened that he was a candidate for the vice presidential slot.[21]

Knowing that many southerners still hated him for his role in splitting the party in 1948, Humphrey appealed for sectional harmony upon arriving in the Windy City. His plan to stress voting rights found little favor, however, and the desegregation issue quickly came to the fore in platform hearings. Humphrey attempted to shift the focus of the convention by urging delegates to avoid becoming too immersed in sectional squabbles and remember that all shared the goal of victory over Eisenhower. Northerners had to understand the southern position and be "patient" regarding desegregation. "We have got to be responsible because we have to represent forty-eight states in the union, and that is different than being a sort of sectional party," Humphrey declared on national television. "I am not going to be one badgered down to the fact that the only issue before us is civil rights." Such comments shocked Humphrey's liberal friends. Clarence Mitchell pointedly charged that Humphrey was more interested in furthering his political ambitions than advancing civil rights, and a delegation of irate African American leaders soon confronted him. Humphrey had assumed that liberals would back him for the vice presidential nomination, but the black leaders candidly told him that the liberal vote would not be his if he continued to take a weak stand regarding the civil rights plank. Attempting to shore up his base, Humphrey quickly announced that the Democrats ought to "persevere in seeking compliance with the Supreme Court rulings against desegregation."[22]

As they had in 1952, the Democrats attempted to downplay deep sectional divisions. The civil rights plank condemned discrimination and expressed support for the right to vote, equal employment opportunity, personal security, and access to public education. On the crucial issue of *Brown*, it vaguely endorsed all Supreme Court decisions as "the law of the land." The South had triumphed. "They sold us down the river in the interest of unity," an African American delegate lamented. The plank, Clarence Mitchell charged, represented "a complete sellout." Still seeking the vice presidential nomination, Humphrey fully supported the party line.[23]

Liberals were not ready to quit just yet, however. Led by Joe Rauh, Herbert Lehman, and Walter Reuther, they drafted a minority civil rights plank pledging the Democrats to carry out *Brown* and made plans for a floor fight. They anticipated that large northern states would start a stampede toward their plank, as in 1948. Robert Short, a delegate from Minnesota, prepared to bring the liberals' declaration before the convention. Humphrey refused to join the insurgents and even attempted to halt their effort by sending Rauh a note saying that he would consider it a "personal insult" if Short spoke to the convention. Short presented the liberals' proposal anyway. It flopped. Fearing a southern walkout, the delegates heartily approved the majority civil rights plank in a voice vote.[24]

Stevenson won the presidential nomination, and, in a surprise move, he let the convention pick his running mate. The chief candidates were Humphrey and Senators Estes Kefauver of Tennessee and John F. Kennedy of Massachusetts. UAW leaders informed Humphrey the morning of the vote that his weak stand on civil rights had led the union to decide to support Kefauver. The Tennessee senator emerged victorious several hours later. Humphrey finished a distant and disappointing third. He received negligible backing from the northern industrial delegations, and, despite approaching Johnson late into the night on the eve of the contest, not one vote from any of the former Confederate states. Most Democrats left Chicago hopeful they had found the winning combination, but for Humphrey the convention had been a disaster. He had not gained any southern friends and, worse, had alienated many of his liberal allies by flip-flopping on civil rights. Humphrey quickly recognized the damage that had been done. "I am sorry that I disappointed my friends," he wrote Rauh a few weeks after the convention. "I want to assure you . . . that when the next Congress convenes your friend Hubert Humphrey will start at the very beginning to press for the enactment of civil rights legislation.[25]

Eisenhower trounced Stevenson again that November. Building on his previous success in Dixie, the president triumphed in seven southern states, most of which were in the Upper South, and reduced the Democrats' 1952 margin of victory in four others. As Humphrey had feared, Eisenhower also scored impressive gains among African American voters. The president received 39 percent of the black vote, a substantial improvement over the 21 percent he had won four years earlier. The increase was especially significant in northern cities. Wilkins tried to reassure Humphrey that the black vote was a protest "against the Southern Democrats and their policies" rather than an endorsement of the GOP, but he also predicted that continued inaction by the Democrats would translate into Republican victories in 1958 and

1960. "How smart is Lyndon Johnson?" the NAACP leader asked. Alarmed by the returns, Humphrey told fellow Democrats that they were "digging [their] own graves" by failing to enact civil rights legislation.[26]

Congressional action was urgently needed not only to improve the Democrats' political standing but, more important, because "massive resistance" had escalated dramatically throughout the South in 1956. Six southern states passed resolutions of interposition denying the applicability of federal laws. When mob violence broke out as schools opened in Clinton, Tennessee, and Mansfield, Texas, Eisenhower weakly declared that there was nothing the federal government could do because these were "local problems." Thousands of African Americans continued to be purged from voter lists or subjected to threats, intimidation, and economic reprisals for attempting to register. Harassment of the NAACP increased dramatically; branch activity was halted completely in three states. The FBI reported in November that more than eight thousand African Americans had been removed from voter rolls in ten Louisiana parishes. The total soared to over eleven thousand a month later.[27]

III

Humphrey and several other liberals met shortly after the election and drafted a Democratic plan of action to respond to this worsening crisis. They pledged to sponsor legislation to implement the party's civil rights plank (voting, fair employment, personal security, and equal educational opportunity) and to seek majority rule in the Senate. "We Democrats have prepared this product of civil rights," Humphrey told Johnson, "and I don't want to see the Eisenhower Republicans putting their trade-mark on it." Even before the election Humphrey and Douglas had begun to round up allies on both sides of the aisle to challenge the filibuster rule. Fighting for civil rights without seeking a change in Rule XXII, Roy Wilkins had reminded liberals, was "meaningless." Few Republicans had been involved in previous attempts, but Humphrey and Douglas resolved to press ahead whether they had GOP assistance or not. "Surely every analysis of the vote on November 6th underlies the necessity for action," they wrote Democratic colleagues.[28]

Humphrey found himself in the thick of the battle for majority cloture. As in 1953, the civil rights proponents claimed that each new Senate had the right to make its own rules, while southerners again argued that the old rules carried over. The Senate killed the rules-change proposal by a 55–38 vote to table it. Though Rule XXII survived intact again, Humphrey, justifiably, felt "greatly encouraged" by the results. "We actually gained more votes than we had a right to expect, and surely many more than the opposition had anticipated," he confided to an ally. Civil rights proponents had increased their 1953 total by seventeen votes, with five Democrats and twelve Republicans joining their ranks. Three senators who were absent, moreover, went on record in favor of majority cloture, thus raising the total to forty-one. Because a shift of seven votes was all that was needed to amend Rule XXII, southern Democrats knew that they would have to be careful about using the filibuster during the coming civil rights fight. Thanks in large part to developments in the South and the November election, the legislative momentum was finally beginning to turn in Humphrey's direction. But civil rights proponents still faced some important constraints. The rules fight indicated that there was more interest in civil rights than ever before, but not enough to overcome a filibuster. The only option for Humphrey and his allies was to draft a bill that would avoid a filibuster and garner enough support from Republicans and western Democrats to pass it.[29]

Though Humphrey submitted FEPC and his other customary bills, his legislative strategy demonstrated how far the civil rights debate had moved away from economic issues. "We should concentrate . . . on the bill to protect the right to vote," he now argued. Anyone who belittled voting rights was "just playing to the galleries and being a demagogue" because the violence, threats, and coercion used against African Americans attempting to register in the South made federal action imperative. School desegregation, Humphrey privately insisted, had to be avoided because taking it up would destroy the consensus he hoped to build behind voting rights.[30]

Humphrey pressed Johnson to convince the southerners to accept at least some of his measures, but when they refused he concluded that liberal Democrats would have to support Eisenhower's package. Identical to the measure submitted the year before, the administration's legislation contained four provisions. Title I would create a civil rights commission. Title II would establish a civil rights division in the Justice Department. Title III authorized the attorney general to seek injunctions against a wide range of civil rights violations, and Title IV permitted the Justice Department to intervene in voting rights cases. This time the president clearly indicated that he favored all four sections. Humphrey welcomed the news, for the GOP finally appeared eager to cooperate on civil rights. Further evidence of the Republicans' willingness to back the measure came in June, when they joined northern Democrats in the House to pass it, and then a few weeks later, when most Senate Republicans sided with liberal Democrats on a key procedural vote to bring the House bill directly before the Senate instead of sending it to the

Judiciary Committee. Southerners knew that they could not count on their longtime allies. The question now was not whether a bill would be approved but rather what kind of measure.[31]

Deciding that a filibuster would be counterproductive given the Rule XXII vote in January, southern Democrats concluded that the best they could do was to weaken the bill as much as possible. While the Senate was debating whether to take up the legislation, Richard Russell fired the opening salvo by denouncing Title III as a punitive measure "cunningly designed to bring to bear the whole might of the Federal Government, including the armed forces if necessary, to force a co-mingling of white and Negro children in the South." Technically, he had a valid point, for an obscure clause in the measure invoked Reconstruction-era statutes that granted the president authority to use troops to uphold Federal court rulings. Title III, he added, would destroy the American system of rule by law and replace it with rule by bureaucrats because it allowed the Justice Department to bring desegregation suits on its own. Charging that the legislation was not simply a voting rights measure, as many civil rights proponents had claimed, Russell wondered if Eisenhower fully understood its implications and predicted that Title III would lead to violence across the South. Russell's strategy of concentrating on legal arguments instead of racism gave southerners the upper hand. Eisenhower confessed at a news conference in early July that there were aspects of his legislation that he "didn't completely understand," and, two weeks later, he fully retreated from Title III by stressing that what he really wanted was a voting rights bill. "One day Ike is for the bill, the next day he doesn't know what is in it, and the third day he backs off it," an exasperated Humphrey privately grumbled. "It is unbelievable." Civil rights proponents might have been able to withstand the president's wavering, but several senators, who thought they were supporting a voting measure, began to reevaluate their positions following the president's retreat.[32]

Meanwhile, Johnson moved to assuage southerners' fears. He had decided that a civil rights bill needed to be enacted to advance his presidential ambitions, keep the African American vote Democratic, and bridge sectional differences. The resulting legislation had to be strong enough for liberals to claim victory, yet weak enough for southerners to tell their constituents that they had blocked something much worse. The majority leader persuaded Democrat Clinton Anderson of New Mexico and Republican George Aiken of Vermont to co-sponsor an amendment deleting Title III. The attack on Title III raised trouble for Humphrey. Support for a voting bill appeared solid, but the NAACP foresaw that abandoning Title III would leave African Americans "virtually helpless" and warned that blacks would find it "impossible to forget and difficult to forgive" the removal of the provision. Conversely, Johnson indicated that the southerners would filibuster unless Title III were eliminated. In an attempt save Title III and to show that the civil rights proponents were not interested in using it to punish the South, Humphrey joined with Republican leader William Knowland of California to draft an amendment repealing the Reconstruction-era laws that the measure invoked. The Senate approved the amendment 90–0, but southerners still demanded that Title III be removed. The civil rights coalition appeared to be breaking apart over this matter as both Republicans and Democrats expressed concern over Title III's authorization for the Justice Department to become involved on its own initiative in a wide range of civil rights cases, including those pertaining to segregation in schools or other public places. Humphrey could go no further than this group wanted if he expected to pass a bill. Additional efforts by Humphrey to work out a compromise with the Republicans and Johnson to save a portion of Title III came to naught, and the Senate adopted the Anderson-Aiken amendment, 52–38, in late July. Humphrey would have to accept a voting measure or nothing at all.[33]

The southern Democrats next turned their fire on Title IV's failure to guarantee jury trials for those found in contempt of court for violating voting rights laws. Russell vowed that his team would use every means possible to defeat the bill if jury trials were not assured. Fearing that a jury trial clause would severely weaken the bill because any southern official charged with blocking an individual's attempt to register could count on acquittal before an all-white jury, liberals pointed out that the Constitution did not guarantee jury trials in all cases. Many legislators, however, found Russell's claim that the bill denied the basic American right to trial by jury easier to follow. Once again southerners had the edge in the critical battle for the middle groups of senators who did not feel strongly about civil rights one way or the other but wanted to do something about the burgeoning crisis in the South.[34]

Worried that the jury issue would doom the legislation, Humphrey had been searching for a solution to this problem since the spring. He turned to Carl Auerbach, a friend at the University of Wisconsin Law School who had published an article suggesting that jury trials should apply to criminal contempt cases but not to those involving civil contempt. In the former a judge usually sentenced the defendant to time in jail, but an individual found guilty of civil contempt could go free simply by following the judge's order to comply with the law. A judge using civil proceedings, Auerbach maintained, could uphold voting rights in several ways. Humphrey persuaded the professor to put his plan into legislative language, and Johnson soon convinced

Democrats Joseph O' Mahoney of Wyoming and Estes Kefauver of Tennessee to co-sponsor an amendment that distinguished between civil and criminal contempt in voting cases. Because of his close identification with civil rights, however, Humphrey had to publicly oppose the jury trial amendment. Following some deft parliamentary maneuvering by Johnson, the Senate approved the jury trial amendment, 51–42, in early August.[35]

Six days later, the Senate passed the weakened civil rights measure 71–18. Eisenhower signed it in September. The Civil Rights Act constituted a personal triumph for Humphrey, who restored some of his credibility among liberals during the debate. More important, it represented a significant symbolic victory for those fighting for racial justice because Congress had gone on record on behalf of African Americans' rights for the first time in eighty-two years. The vaunted Republican-southern Democrat coalition, which had blocked civil rights legislation for so long, had collapsed, at least temporarily, as liberals had finally accomplished the breakthrough they had been fighting for since 1949. The new law established a Civil Rights Commission (but for three years only), upgraded the civil rights section of the Justice Department to a full division, and strengthened voting rights somewhat. These were mild gains indeed, hardly sufficient to address the mounting desegregation and voter registration crises in the South. The southerners, moreover, had scored an important victory by keeping the federal government from becoming more involved in school desegregation. Though the measure was not as strong as Humphrey would have liked, he regarded it as the best that could be achieved under the circumstances and expected that the commission would be valuable in documenting civil rights violations and Title IV would translate into increased voter registration. "This is not the end of civil rights legislation," Humphrey confidently predicted. "It is only the beginning."[36]

IV

As legislators were putting the finishing touches on the civil rights bill, racial animosities flared in Little Rock, Arkansas, when eight African American students, backed by a federal court ruling, prepared to desegregate Central High School. On September 2 Governor Orval Faubus ordered nearly three hundred members of the Arkansas National Guard to block their entry into the building. Barricading a school with armed soldiers took "massive resistance" to a new and more dangerous level, for a state was now defying federal law with force. Commenting on the situation the following day, Eisenhower reiterated his longstanding beliefs that "you cannot change people's hearts merely by law" and that integration had to occur gradually. The troops turned the students away the next morning. Federal and state officials sought a way out of the impasse during the next ten days as Eisenhower played golf in Rhode Island. When he and Faubus met on September 14, the president believed he had convinced the governor not to obstruct the court order. At home in Minnesota, Humphrey viewed the events in Arkansas with alarm. Calling upon Eisenhower to go to Little Rock and "personally take those colored children by the hand and lead them into school, where they belong," he blasted the president's policy of sitting idle while segregationists flouted the Supreme Court as "almost unbelievable." The day after the Faubus–Eisenhower meeting Humphrey joined other liberal Democrats in issuing a statement charging that the president's leadership in the crisis had been a "disappointment." Anything short of allowing the African American students admission to the school, they added, would be a "defeat for law and order and the Constitution itself."[37]

Faubus announced on September 20 that he would remove the guard, but violence erupted three days later when the students entered the school through a side door. Prodded more by the governor's delays and his failure to maintain order after promising to do so than by a commitment to racial justice, Eisenhower quickly federalized ten thousand Arkansas National Guard troops and dispatched one thousand U.S. soldiers to Little Rock. The African American students, accompanied by troops, entered Central High on September 25. Humphrey supported Eisenhower's decision, but he thought that the president's long silence regarding *Brown* had caused tensions across the South to escalate and enabled the Soviets to use the incident to "[make] hay while the sun shines."[38]

Worried that the Little Rock episode represented a harbinger of things to come, Humphrey urgently appealed for restraint by both whites and African Americans. After denouncing the White Citizens' Councils for linking civil rights with communism, he then turned his attention to civil rights organizations:

[Despite] understandable grievances and frustrations, some spokesmen have . . . blanketed all southern opposition to desegregation as a conspiracy against the Constitution . . . equally ignoring on their side the varying degrees of opposition . . . and cooperation which may still exist. At times there almost seems to be a mutual determination to solidify differences, to freeze antagonisms, and to set up barricades against those compromises upon which progress usually depends. The result is that in this domestic cold war . . . we are increasingly getting little more than propaganda and counter-propaganda. Somewhere in the process, law . . . and respect for the process of persuasion upon which our law fundamentally depends—these are forgotten.

Humphrey saw "alarming signs" of a growing tyranny across the South in which whites who supported *Brown* were being silenced by those who used intimidation and force to preserve the status quo. Unless whites, African Americans, and the federal government could find common ground, he feared, "the white South . . . will be won over to compliance with the Constitution not by persuasion but by force."[39]

Though the attorney general had called for a "cooling off" period for civil rights during 1958, Humphrey sought orderly progress in the South by introducing measures that would make permanent the Civil Rights Commission, increase the number of FBI personnel investigating civil rights violations, and provide financial and technical support to school districts for desegregation. He also offered a slightly modified version of Title III and FEPC legislation. Black unemployment, he noted, stood at 7.7 percent between 1954 and 1957, compared to 3.5 percent for whites. During the recession of 1958 African American unemployment had soared to 14.5 percent. These disturbing economic developments largely went unnoticed because most civil rights proponents focused on the burgeoning crises of desegregation and voting rights in the South. Few of Humphrey's colleagues were eager to revisit the issue of civil rights just a year after the 1957 Civil Rights Act, and as a result his legislation remained buried in various committees.[40]

Another failure by Humphrey and his allies to amend Rule XXII several months later dimmed the prospects for civil rights legislation in 1959, yet as the session wore on leaders in both parties recognized that with an election just a year away they had to satisfy black voters somehow. Arguing that there were thousands of white southerners who would work for peaceful desegregation if the federal government offered guidance, Humphrey and the liberal Democrats introduced a plan by which Congress would affirm the Court's desegregation ruling, provide financial and technical assistance to desegregating school districts, and authorize the Department of Health, Education, and Welfare to create desegregation plans for districts that refused to do so. They also put Title III before the Senate. In contrast, the Eisenhower administration submitted more limited measures that would have Congress declare its support for *Brown*, extend the Civil Rights Commission for two years, make interfering with desegregation through the threat or use of force a crime, require states to maintain for three years records pertaining to federal elections, and create a permanent commission to fight employment discrimination in firms with government contracts. Humphrey blasted the president's plan for its failure to include Title III. "We could use a little preaching from the White House right now—preaching the gospel of desegregation," he complained.[41]

Humphrey's attention shifted from desegregation back to voting rights, however, when the Civil Rights Commission offered dramatic evidence of the denial of the franchise across Dixie. There were sixteen counties in the South where African Americans constituted the majority of the population, the commission pointed out in the report it issued that fall, yet not one black person was registered to vote. In forty-nine other counties blacks constituted the majority but under 5 percent who were old enough to vote had registered. In Louisiana individuals seeking to register had to interpret obscure clauses of the state Constitution such as "Prescription shall not run against the state in any civil matter." The voting provisions of the 1957 Civil Rights Act had failed, the commission bluntly declared. To remedy the deplorable situation it recommended that federal power be expanded through the appointment of federal registrars in troubled areas. The registrar's tasks would include administering state election laws, registering the disfranchised who were qualified to vote, and observing the polls during federal elections. Disturbed by the commission's report of the deteriorating situation in the South, Humphrey demanded that the administration, which had brought only three voting rights suits in two years, explain its "incredible and inexcusable" record in this area. He introduced legislation to implement the registrar plan soon after the report had been released. The end of the session was fast approaching, however, and because Congress had already voted to extend the Civil Rights Commission for two years few legislators were willing to consider anything else regarding racial matters. Humphrey demanded assurances from Johnson that the race problem would be addressed early in the next session. Eager to pass other important legislation before adjourning, Johnson agreed.[42]

The commission's troubling report and the upcoming presidential election prompted the Eisenhower administration to rethink its civil rights program. In addition to its previous proposals, it submitted legislation when Congress reconvened in January to use voting referees in the South. Unlike registrars, referees would not sign up new voters; they would merely watch the polling place to ensure that voting proceeded smoothly. Those who discriminated would be found in contempt of court. This was a far more limited approach than the registrar plan, but the administration predicted it stood a better chance of surviving judicial scrutiny.[43]

As he had promised, Johnson brought the civil rights issue before the Senate in February, when he tricked the southern Democrats by arranging for a Republican to present the administration's package as an amendment to an unrelated bill that was already being debated. Outraged at Johnson's sneaky maneuver, southern Democrats paralyzed the Senate with a filibuster. Members set up cots in their offices and prepared to wait out the talkathon, but the southerners did not wear down. They quit only after Russell and Johnson had worked out a deal to limit the bill to voting rights. In March the Republicans joined the southern Democrats to defeat an attempt by liberal Democrats to add Title III and other aspects of their civil rights program to the president's package. The Senate approved a measure based on the referee system 71–18 a month later. Humphrey missed the final vote, but he announced his support for the legislation. Like many civil rights leaders, however, he found the bill wanting. The 1960 Civil Rights Act "falls far short of my hopes and expectations, and cannot be heralded as any great triumph," Humphrey commented. He had "grave doubts" that the referee system would register many African Americans. It was a weak law, to be sure, but Humphrey's blunt criticisms undoubtedly also reflected worry that it was hardly sufficient to rally black voters that fall.[44]

Humphrey had good reason to be disappointed as he considered the state of race relations in 1960. To be sure, the 1957 and 1960 Civil Rights Acts were important breakthroughs, but they were far too limited to adequately address the problems facing most blacks. Though the Republican-southern Democrat coalition had been weakened, civil rights advocates on Capitol Hill still encountered stiff resistance in the Senate and found little cooperation from the White House. Humphrey could only hope that the 1960 election would bring a change of direction.

Humphrey was in a position to influence the national debate on race that spring, for in December he had declared that he was a candidate for the 1960 Democratic presidential nomination. Determined not to repeat his mistake of 1956, when he had soft-pedaled civil rights and wound up without the support either of liberals or of white southerners in his ill-conceived bid for the Democratic vice presidential nomination, Humphrey quickly staked a claim to being the pro–civil rights candidate by promising "to do everything in [his] power" to fight against the denial of voting rights and declaring that the Democrats could "go look someplace else" for a nominee if they expected him to compromise on civil rights. Such statements did nothing to improve his standing in the South. Indeed, a Florida senator observed that Massachusetts Senator John F. Kennedy was the favorite in Dixie because Humphrey had "gone all out in his approach to the civil rights question."[45]

Events across the South that spring brought a new dimension to the race issue. On February 1 four African Americans students vividly exposed the in-

justices of Jim Crow by staging a sit-in at a Woolworth's lunch counter in
Greensboro, North Carolina. By the end of the month tensions had risen
throughout Dixie as blacks in hundreds of other communities emulated their
courageous Greensboro counterparts. Comparable to efforts such as the 1955
bus boycott in Montgomery, Alabama, the sit-ins signaled the revival of mass
direct-action protest techniques and dramatically revealed the frustration
among African Americans over the tortoiselike pace of change in the South.
Eisenhower expressed sympathy for the students as long as they remained
peaceful, but he customarily stressed that the protests were best handled by
local officials. In contrast, Humphrey vigorously defended the students against
white southern leaders, who denounced them as lawbreakers. "Even if [the
sit-ins] are not legal, they are morally right," he commented, "and if statutory
law is in conflict with moral law, [the former] should be changed."[46]

The civil rights issue availed Humphrey little. Kennedy handily beat
Humphrey in the Wisconsin primary that April. The battleground then shifted to West Virginia, where Kennedy cruised to a victory of roughly twenty
percentage points. Broke, exhausted, and with no hope of winning the nomination, Humphrey withdrew from the race just hours after the West Virginia
results were announced.[47]

Two months later, Humphrey joined fellow Democrats in Los Angeles for
the party's convention. Southerners' attempts to water down the civil rights
plank failed miserably. Under the able leadership of Kennedy aide Chester
Bowles, the liberal-dominated Platform Committee drafted a broad statement in which the party endorsed the sit-ins, demanded that all school districts affected by *Brown* submit a desegregation plan by 1963, pledged technical and financial assistance to desegregating districts, promised equal
opportunity in federal institutions, housing programs, and federal contracts,
and called for FEPC, voting, and Title III legislation. It represented a remarkable victory for the liberals, who obtained virtually everything they had
sought. Though southerners filed a minority report that denounced the
plank as the climax of "a campaign of studied vilification," the delegates easily approved the committee's plank. To Humphrey the plank was "the best
statement on civil rights ever made by any political party in America." Civil
rights leaders heartily agreed.[48]

Delegates then turned to the nominations. Secretly working with Johnson, who had announced his candidacy just before the convention opened,
Humphrey endorsed Adlai Stevenson as part of an effort to deny Kennedy
the top spot on the ticket. The Massachusetts senator could not be derailed,
however, and the convention selected him on the first ballot. Kennedy then
shocked the nation by choosing Johnson as his running mate. Southerners,

who had mounted a strong anti-Humphrey drive following press speculation that Kennedy might pick the Minnesotan, were relieved. Doubting Johnson's commitment to racial justice, many liberals expressed their strong disapproval, but Humphrey, who had worked closely with Johnson on civil rights matters in the Senate and was eager for a show of party unity in what promised to be a difficult campaign, urged them to accept the Texan.[49]

Though Kennedy refused to make civil rights a major issue in the campaign, he knew he had to woo African American voters lest they back Vice President Richard Nixon, the Republican nominee. Accordingly, the Kennedy campaign selected Humphrey to chair its National Conference on Constitutional Rights and American Freedom, which was held in New York in early October. Humphrey accepted the assignment out of party loyalty and with the hope that the event might prod Kennedy, whose support of civil rights had been lukewarm at best, to move vigorously in this area. More than four hundred civil rights and liberal leaders participated in the two-day conference, which focused on executive, legislative, and state and local action and featured vivid testimony from numerous individuals struggling to achieve school desegregation and voting rights in the South. Humphrey again squarely placed the blame for much of the nation's racial difficulties on the White House by blasting the Justice Department, which had brought just six voting rights cases in three years, for "inexcusable incompetence or indifference" and accusing Eisenhower of "inexcusable inertia" on civil rights. "With Jack Kennedy in the White House, you will see such action by Congress and the rest of the federal government that you have never seen before," Humphrey vowed. The final report of the conference contained numerous recommendations, including a White House conference regarding school desegregation, legislation based on the civil rights plank within the first hundred days of a Kennedy administration, increased enforcement of voting rights by the Justice Department, equal employment opportunity in the federal government, and steps to prohibit discrimination in public housing and other federally assisted programs.[50]

Racial matters entered the campaign in a much more dramatic way two weeks later. Martin Luther King, head of the Southern Christian Leadership Conference (SCLC) and leader of numerous civil rights marches, including the 1955 Montgomery bus boycott, was arrested for violating probation in Atlanta and sentenced to four months hard labor. The jailing greatly troubled Humphrey. Not only did he consider it "a gross miscarriage of justice" but he also feared the political implications for the Democrats. Polls showed that the Kennedy-Nixon race was tight, especially in the black community. Worried that having a prominent African American leader arrested in a southern state could spell trouble for Kennedy among black voters in the North, Humphrey quickly wired Lyndon Johnson asking him to approach Richard Russell about resolving "this farce." It is unclear whether Humphrey's prodding moved Johnson to act. Kennedy eventually called King's wife, who was deeply concerned for her husband's safety, and expressed his sympathy shortly after the sentence had been announced. Robert Kennedy then telephoned the judge who had sentenced King and helped secure the civil rights leader's freedom. Humphrey was greatly relieved.[51]

Election day brought welcome news for Democrats. Humphrey soundly defeated his opponent by 235,000 votes. Kennedy, too, was victorious, but with less than half the popular vote. Indeed, his margin of victory over Nixon was a mere 118,500 ballots. Given such a narrow triumph, several groups could justly claim to have put Kennedy in the White House. Thanks in considerable part to Johnson, there was no revolt in Dixie as only three southern states went to Nixon. At the same time, roughly 70 percent of black voters cast ballots for Kennedy, many as a result of his efforts on behalf of King. African Americans provided critical support in helping the Democrats carry such pivotal states as Illinois, Pennsylvania, New Jersey, Michigan, and Texas. Black voters eagerly expected Kennedy to live up to his pledges for executive, moral, and legislative leadership on civil rights. On the other hand, white southerners hoped that Kennedy's rhetoric was only that.[52]

Whether Kennedy would move on civil rights quickly became a matter of doubt. Upon advice of his top aides, the president-elect failed to include civil rights on a list of domestic priorities he had drafted in December, and he did not mention the topic in his inaugural address. Similarly, he did not take sides in the effort to amend Rule XXII launched by Humphrey and other civil rights proponents in January. It is unlikely that Kennedy could have saved the advocates from another defeat, but his silence offered another clue as to how he felt about civil rights. Little in Kennedy's personal background had given him a strong commitment to racial equality, and the political scenario, he thought, was not conducive to a bold departure. He had barely won the election, and the Democrats had lost two seats in the Senate and twenty in the House. Southerners continued to dominate important congressional committees. Believing he would have to depend heavily on southern support to enact any of his legislative programs, Kennedy feared that a bitter fight for civil rights risked loss of other domestic, as well as foreign, initiatives. Finally, Kennedy declined to press the race issue because, having never been an insider while a senator, he was decidedly uncomfortable with personally lobbying members of Congress for their votes on such a sensitive matter.[53]

Kennedy worked instead to eliminate racial barriers through executive action. He assigned an African American to the press pool for his inauguration and invited many blacks to participate in the festivities. Within two months of taking office he named over forty blacks to important government posts. Kennedy included African Americans at White House social affairs and made his staff accessible to civil rights leaders. In March he established the President's Committee on Equal Employment Opportunity (PCEEO) to combat discrimination in firms with government contracts. Attorney General Robert Kennedy, meanwhile, vowed to defend civil rights laws vigorously. The aura of excitement and optimism that surrounded the early days of the New Frontier infected Humphrey. Noting that he was "tremendously pleased" by the president's actions and statements on civil rights, he reported "a new mood of action, a new awareness of leadership, [and] a new sense of dedication" concerning racial justice. To be sure, there had been a positive change from the complacency of the Eisenhower administration, but Humphrey's party loyalty and eagerness to please powerful people led him to exaggerate by asserting that the PCEEO represented "one of the greatest advances in civil rights since the Emancipation Proclamation," and that Kennedy had already provided "bold and decisive leadership" in this area.[54]

Though he did not abandon the struggle for civil rights legislation, Humphrey was not nearly as outspoken on this subject as before. Whereas he had usually submitted civil rights legislation in January, now he did not introduce any such measures until March. He and other liberal Democrats waited three additional weeks to sponsor Title III and legislation to force districts to draw up initial plans for desegregation by 1963. Civil rights groups, however, viewed legislation as "indispensable," for several Democratic platform proposals could only be met through Congressional action. Liberal Republicans were the first to offer civil rights bills in the new Congress, and Humphrey had to sign on as a co-sponsor lest he appear uncommitted to the issue. After a campaign during which Humphrey had promised significant legislative progress under Kennedy, the only accomplishment liberal Democrats in Congress could point to in 1961 was a two-year extension of the Civil Rights Commission. Humphrey had routinely lambasted Eisenhower for refusing to push civil rights despite considerable odds, but he said little regarding Kennedy's similar approach. Two factors accounted for Humphrey's relative silence. He believed that Kennedy's stress on executive action yielded meaningful gains that far outdistanced anything that Eisenhower had accomplished, and thus he was willing to give the new president a chance to see what could be done through such an approach. More important, Humphrey wanted to remain a loyal Democrat, and criticizing Kennedy for not backing civil rights legislation would hurt the party as well as damage his own chances for political advancement.[55]

This meager record gave African Americans good reason to wonder about the importance of civil rights to the Democratic Party. Exasperated by the federal government's temporizing over civil rights, the Congress of Racial Equality (CORE) launched the Freedom Rides in May. Two buses of student activists set out on a journey from Washington to New Orleans to demonstrate the persistence of segregation in southern bus terminals despite a recent Supreme Court decision requiring integrated facilities. When the students arrived in Anniston, Alabama, militant whites bombed one bus and mercilessly beat them with iron clubs, chains, and blackjacks as they attempted to flee the burning vehicle. The students escaped and made their way to Birmingham, where another mob brutally attacked them. A new group of students took over for the trip to Montgomery. There a mob of more than one thousand people set upon them and even knocked a Justice Department official unconscious for twenty-five minutes. When an angry crowd threatened a rally at a church in which Martin Luther King was defending the students, the president decided that he had seen enough and dispatched four hundred U.S. marshals, who restored order to Montgomery with tear gas and billy clubs. The students then went on to Mississippi, where they were arrested after Robert Kennedy worked out an agreement with state officials whereby the federal government would allow the students to be jailed in return for a guarantee that no violence would occur.[56]

Here, too, Humphrey followed the administration's cautious lead. He applauded the use of troops and thought the administration had acted "efficiently and courageously" in siding with the students against the arch segregationists. But Humphrey was hardly alone in taking this position. Even Senator Sam Ervin of North Carolina, a staunch opponent of racial equality, publicly condoned the use of marshals to quell the violence. When Robert Kennedy called for a "cooling off" period for civil rights activities in the South, Humphrey raised no objection. Once again, the contrast between Humphrey's rhetoric during the Eisenhower and Kennedy administrations was striking.[57]

The president demonstrated his first serious interest in civil rights legislation a year later by submitting a constitutional amendment to outlaw the poll tax and a measure to establish completion of the sixth grade as the sole literacy requirement to vote in federal elections. The Civil Rights Commission had recently issued its second report, which provided detailed accounts of the continued widespread use of ridiculous questions and discriminatory application of literacy tests to African Americans seeking to register to vote. In 129 counties in 10 southern states, the commission noted, less than 10 percent of eligible blacks were registered. One African American applicant had been rejected for misspellings by a registrar who had misspelled the word *misspellings*. African Americans with graduate and professional degrees were frequently denied registration. Such abuses appalled Kennedy, but the president also hoped to silence his liberal critics as the midterm elections neared and believed that chances for success in regard to voting rights were greater than in areas such as employment or desegregation because Congress had acted twice in the previous five years to remedy abuses at the ballot box.[58]

Though the president's limited legislative agenda troubled Humphrey, he continued to tailor his public efforts to fit Kennedy's agenda. He co-sponsored several measures dealing with school desegregation, government employment, and violence by public officials, but instead of fighting for them he trumpeted the administration's voting bill. Even this small step proved impossible because southern Democrats promptly launched a filibuster when Senate Majority Leader Mike Mansfield of Montana brought the Kennedy bill up for debate. Mansfield attempted to impose cloture twice in early May, but each time only forty-three senators supported halting the talkathon. Liberal Republicans denounced Kennedy for failing to lobby personally for his bill, and one pro–civil rights Democrat publicly blamed his party's leadership for the outcome. Though disappointed in the results, Humphrey refused to criticize the White House.[59]

Two seminal events later that year deepened Humphrey's conviction that Kennedy needed to move more vigorously to confront the worsening situation in the South. First, Martin Luther King led numerous peaceful marches in Albany, Georgia, during the summer to protest segregation. Thousands of African Americans were jailed after city leaders refused to yield. Humphrey joined nine other senators in asking the Justice Department to take "all possible steps" on behalf of those behind bars. Federal officials kept close watch on developments, but that was all they did. Little had changed in Albany by fall. Indeed, the protests would constitute one of King's greatest defeats. The second crisis developed at the University of Mississippi in September, when Governor Ross Barnett and university officials refused to obey a court ruling ordering the admission of James Meredith, an African American applicant. After several weeks of tense negotiations with Barnett had yielded no progress, the president dispatched several thousand marshals to the university to enroll Meredith. A hostile crowd pelted them with rocks, bottles, and other debris. Kennedy then federalized the state National Guard and ordered several thousand troops to the university. The forces restored order by using tear gas, but the violence led to two deaths and several hundred injuries. Meredith went to class accompanied by armed soldiers on October 1. Three days later, Humphrey joined Paul Douglas and Kenneth Keating, a New York Republican, in urging the president to take whatever action was necessary to ensure that the court's decision was followed. "I believe the time has come for substantive proposals to be brought before Congress," Humphrey confided to Joe Rauh. "I certainly am going to do whatever I can to urge a strong commitment by the President to make such proposals."[60]

V

The opening of a new Congress in January 1963 meant another attempt to amend Rule XXII. All too aware that the filibuster constituted an impregnable barrier to meaningful civil rights legislation, Humphrey again called for cloture by a constitutional majority or, at the very least, three-fifths of those present and voting. When the motion to consider a rules change came up, southern Democrats began a filibuster that dragged on for two weeks. Two cloture attempts failed. Rule XXII had survived unchanged. Though Humphrey privately blamed Johnson for the loss because the vice president, as leader of the Senate, had refused to make parliamentary rulings sympathetic to the reformers, he optimistically pointed out that because a majority of the Senate had voted to shut off debate in the second attempt civil rights advocates were "gaining ground and bound to win."[61]

At the same time, Humphrey and five other Democratic senators appealed to Kennedy to submit a more comprehensive civil rights package. Executive action was important, but it was time for "forthright action in the legislative field," if for no other reason than bolstering Democratic prospects in the 1964 elections. They asked Kennedy to back measures to make the Civil Rights Commission permanent and broaden its functions, end discriminatory job practices, address the problem of school desegregation, and remove the unfair application of literacy tests. Enactment of such a program, they contended, was clearly impossible without strong leadership by the president. Much to the liberals' relief, Kennedy sent a civil rights message to Congress in February. Citing economic, international, and moral reasons, the president emphatically stated that the country had to eliminate racial injustice. He asked for legislation that would increase black voter registration, expedite voting suits in the courts, allow completion of the sixth grade to stand as proof of literacy for federal elections, provide assistance to desegregating school districts, and extend the Civil Rights Commission for four years. It was the boldest set of proposals he had ever offered, yet African Americans rightly contended that Kennedy had ignored their most pressing problems. The president, Roy Wilkins pointed out, had failed to confront desegregation of public accommodations, had not gone far enough in dealing with school integration, and had neglected to address housing or employment issues. Though he too wished that the administration had taken a bolder stand, Humphrey vigorously defended Kennedy against criticism from Wilkins and pro–civil rights Republicans. Privately, however, he warned the DNC chair that continued Congressional inaction on civil rights would hurt the Democrats' chances in 1964.[62]

While politicians wrangled in Washington, a far more significant confrontation was brewing in Birmingham, Alabama. Martin Luther King launched a campaign of sit-ins, marches, and boycotts in early April, hoping that mass action in the most segregated city in America would lead to a crisis that would force the president to take more substantial action. Thus far, King believed, Kennedy had only moved the nation to accept "tokenism." King soon found himself in jail with hundreds of other black protesters. Tensions escalated two weeks later when he began to employ black children, some of them only six years old, in the marches. Police Chief Eugene "Bull" Connor decided that he had seen enough and brought the full force of the law to bear on the demonstrators. Officers wantonly beat the defenseless protesters, turned dogs on them, and blasted them with high-powered water cannons on May 3. Countless people across the nation were outraged at the graphic images and accounts of the horrible violence. King suddenly had the support of much of the country.[63]

Stunned by the violence in Birmingham, Humphrey denounced Connor for "the most shameful attacks" in American history. This "blotch on the face of America," he predicted, would set the nation back twenty years in its quest to woo allies in the developing world. More important, the dramatic events in Birmingham had created a "new climate" of awareness in the nation. Dismayed that violence was necessary to awaken white Americans to the plight of blacks, Humphrey nonetheless insisted that the time "was most definitely ripe" for meaningful action in Congress. "The choice [lay] between a quickened pace of reform or violence," he maintained.[64]

Humphrey met with the president, the attorney general, and a handful of other influential legislators and administration officials in June to plot a course of action. The civil rights issue could be resolved in the streets or in the courts, Humphrey bluntly told the president. After several discussions Kennedy decided to back a far more comprehensive legislative package than what he had offered in February, but division remained over just how far the administration should go. Many argued that the inclusion of FEPC and a cutoff of federal funds to programs that discriminated would doom the bill in Congress. In contrast, Humphrey urged Kennedy to embrace a broad agenda that included not only these two areas but also Title III, voting rights, school desegregation, and the desegregation of public accommodations. Furthermore, he recommended that Kennedy hold a series of meetings with a variety of leaders, including representatives from unions, religious organizations, businesses, and schools, among others, to build support for his legislation. The president had to be the moral leader on this matter and take advantage of the extraordinary and unprecedented outpouring of public concern over civil rights, Humphrey contended.[65]

Kennedy soon had both the bill he wanted and a ripe opportunity to introduce it. In late May Alabama governor George Wallace, who had vowed in his inaugural address to preserve "segregation forever," defiantly resolved to use state police to block desegregation of the University of Alabama. The governor backed down, though, when Justice Department officials confronted him on June 11 at the registration building on the Tuscaloosa campus. Kennedy gave a moving television speech to the nation that evening on the urgent need for civil rights legislation. Shortly after the address the president sought Humphrey's counsel as he put the finishing touches on his civil rights message to Congress. Contrary to what Humphrey and other liberals had hoped, the president backed off of FEPC. He did, however, submit a far-reaching program. In addition to the February proposals, he asked Congress for legislation that included desegregating public accommodations, empowering the federal government to withhold money from federal-supported programs that discriminated, authorizing the attorney general to initiate school desegregation suits (a scaled-down Title III), creating a community relations service, giving statutory authority to the PCEEO, and beefing up job training programs.[66]

The new Kennedy plan went well beyond anything he had ever offered, but could the president build a coalition of northern Democrats and Republicans to break the certain southern filibuster? Early evidence suggested that Kennedy, who had a poor record of persuading Congress to enact his programs, could not. Minority Leader Everett Dirksen of Illinois, whose support would be needed to win Republican votes for cloture, expressed doubts about the constitutionality of ordering the desegregation of public accommodations, the heart of Kennedy's package. Dissent also came from the left, as labor leaders informed Humphrey that they intended to fight for the inclusion of an FEPC provision. Such rumblings of discontent failed to discourage Humphrey. Old parliamentary delaying tactics would no longer work, he insisted, because the courageous African Americans of Birmingham and violence by city officials had moved the nation from "indifference . . . to concern and personal involvement" and created a new political environment that was as different from the old as "the age of space compared with the age of the covered wagon." Anticipating the unprecedented outpouring of public support for the Kennedy bill that did eventually materialize, Humphrey confidently predicted that more would be done for civil rights in the subsequent fifteen months than in the previous fifteen years.[67]

Though the desegregation crisis in the South had eclipsed economic concerns since the mid-1950s, Humphrey continued to regard the economic position of African Americans to be a far more serious, enduring, and national issue than segregation or voting rights. Blacks, especially those in urban areas, suffered enormous economic disadvantages. During the 1950s the proportion of African Americans among the urban jobless had risen from 18 to 28 percent. By 1959 blacks were three times as likely as the general population to be chronically unemployed. After a dramatic improvement during the 1940s, black income relative to white income had leveled off during the Eisenhower years, and, according to a Labor Department study that deeply troubled Humphrey, conditions for many blacks would worsen in the future. Unemployment in 1962 was 4.9 percent for whites and 11 percent for blacks, but Humphrey warned that this large disparity would increase because structural changes in the economy since World War II had created "a second industrial revolution" that threatened to pass African Americans by almost completely. Production jobs, which had been almost solely responsible for black economic gains, had declined by six hundred thousand since the 1940s. There were almost ten million more white-collar workers, yet African Americans were largely absent from this burgeoning sector of the labor market. One in eight white workers was a professional-technical worker; only one in twenty blacks was. One in seven whites worked as some type of manager; only one in forty African Americans did. Jobs in these areas were projected to grow by three million by 1970, while manufacturing would continue to diminish. African Americans' economic prospects were "very grim indeed" unless something were done to reverse these alarming trends, Humphrey asserted. "Until we come to grips with the problem of job discrimination and inequality of job opportunities, as well as the inequality of job training and education, we will be considering only partial solutions to the civil rights crisis," he argued. Contending that "people do not feel free . . . so long as they are denied jobs and their families are in want," Humphrey observed that it would be "hard for [African Americans] to retain their faith in the

American political system when the American economic system displays so little faith in them."[68]

But what could be done? Given Humphrey's New Deal roots, he might have proposed a WPA-style government jobs program, but he thought the best solution to economic problems in the ghetto was Kennedy's proposed tax cut. The administration had chosen a tax cut rather than massive new government spending as the way to address the problem of poverty generally. A tax cut presumably would be easier to get through a conservative Congress than new programs, but it also reflected liberalism's fascination with the "new economics" that confidently posited the ability of the government to promote employment and create prosperity through the right combination of fiscal and monetary policy. Humphrey expected that the tax cut would spur sufficient economic growth to avoid the nightmare scenario of whites and blacks competing for a dwindling supply of jobs. "We can never stem racial tension and discord in this land so long as a man or woman of one color can get a job only by taking it away from a man or woman of another color, he noted. "It is a happy circumstance that the extension of the right to vote . . . does not take the right away from anyone who has enjoyed it all along. . . . But when people in huge numbers are unemployed because there are not enough jobs to go around, they cannot . . . obtain jobs without taking them from others."[69]

Humphrey believed that government would have to do something more than ensure general prosperity to help blacks achieve economic equality, however. After all, the 1950s had been a period of economic boom, yet African Americans still lagged far behind whites in many respects. Accordingly, Humphrey introduced a fair employment bill in July that differed enormously from his previous FEPC proposals. Contending that blacks had been "the principal victim[s] of a vastly complex system of self-perpetuating practices, traditions, and process that [had] denied [them] true parity in the national job market," he called for a broadening of the definition of employment discrimination. Under the old FEPC model only overt, intentional discriminatory acts by individuals were considered illegal. But much discrimination, Humphrey now recognized, occurred also as a result of longstanding "impersonal institutional processes." Businesses discriminated without even knowing they did so. (For instance, recruiters often failed to visit black schools, or promotions were based on job assignments not open to African Americans.) Under Humphrey's plan all employers had to ensure "parity of access" in advertising, recruitment, training, and promotion and had "an affirmative obligation" to develop a broad policy of equality of opportunity. Humphrey also finally acknowledged that the model in effect in hundreds of cities and states for approximately twenty years, which involved the filing of complaints by individuals claiming they had been discriminated against, had yielded extremely limited results. Pointing out that many state FEPCs acted upon an average of less than one hundred complaints per month, Humphrey sought to shift the burden from individuals by investing authority in a single Labor Department official who would initiate investigations, make findings, and issue orders. The administrator's decisions would be enforced by an independent Equal Employment Opportunity Board, with the possibility for appeal by either party in the federal courts. He also hoped to strengthen job training programs for African Americans, many of whom he believed were ill-equipped for life in the urban North after leaving the rural South. "The emphasis . . . needs to be on training people to do work," he noted. "This is much better than keeping people on relief and permitting them to just erode and waste away." These proposals signaled a shift well beyond the traditional models of equal employment opportunity policy that Humphrey had espoused since the 1940s. A targeted effort was needed, he had concluded. Greater emphasis had to be placed on training blacks to compete, a far more active approach than simply enforcing nondiscrimination laws. Though he favored a more "affirmative" approach to the problem of black unemployment, he was by no means ready to join the small but growing chorus of civil rights activists who sought preferential treatment for minorities and wanted to hold equal group outcomes, not equal opportunity for individuals, as the measure of success. "No one seeks charity or special consideration for any group or segment in our society," Humphrey firmly declared. "We seek only to guarantee equal opportunity for every person."[70]

Humphrey's proposals drew little attention because government officials and civil rights leaders focused on the president's legislation and developments in the South. Having been disappointed by Congress's failures too often before, African Americans refused to retreat into their homes and trust legislators to act. Birmingham had shown that massive direct action would produce a response from the nation's officials, and thus King and other black leaders proceeded with plans to stage a rally in Washington, D.C. Like the Kennedy administration, Humphrey initially opposed a mass protest. Rumors of sit-ins at the Capitol and encampments on the White House lawn greatly worried him. He drafted a letter to King stressing that a march on Washington would "be the wrong kind of effort" and make at best only a "negligible" contribution toward enactment of the president's legislation. At worst, Humphrey noted, it could lead to violence that would stiffen the opposition to Kennedy's bill. Humphrey instead lamely suggested that King substitute a "Freedom Lobby" in which two civil rights activists from each state would come to Congress with petitions on behalf of the Kennedy package. It is unknown whether Humphrey sent the letter, but he clearly was hoping to harness the civil rights movement into more formal political channels.[71]

Determined to keep the pressure on Congress and the president, King and other black leaders refused to back down. Humphrey joined the two hundred thousand Americans who came to Washington on a steamy August day to attend the March for Jobs and Freedom. He met with a Congregational Church group and the Minnesota delegation that morning and then attended the afternoon ceremonies at the Lincoln Memorial, where he heard King movingly tell of his vision of an America characterized by racial harmony. On the Senate floor that night he praised the crowd for its "self-discipline, good manners, and . . . respect for law and order." African Americans had suffered "cruel injustices," yet they were filled with "a sense of understanding . . . and charity." Calling the march "a blessed event," Humphrey predicted that it had rallied countless Americans to the cause of racial justice and would help spur enactment of the president's civil rights bill.[72]

Tragedy in Birmingham three weeks later reminded Humphrey of how difficult progress would be. On September 15 a bomb exploded in the Sixteenth Street Baptist Church during services. Four young African American girls died; fourteen other people were injured. Angered by such a brutal deed, a handful of black youths set fires and hurled rocks at the police. King asked that federal troops be sent to the city. Two days after the bombing Humphrey joined three colleagues in asking Kennedy to proclaim September 22, the 101st anniversary of the Emancipation Proclamation, a day of national mourning. Humphrey delivered a stinging address on the floor of the Senate that was far more inflammatory than anything he had ever said about race relations in the South. Continuing to hold to his exaggerated faith in the basic goodness of most poor white southerners, whom he regarded as having been deliberately misled by elites regarding racial issues, Humphrey laid the blame for the church bombing squarely on the section's political leaders:

> I condemn that leadership . . . which has sought to keep wages down throughout the South by keeping Negroes uneducated and untrained. I condemn those leaders in the South who have sought to prevent the growth of labor unions by setting white worker against Negro worker. . . . What is so sickening about the whole matter is that these policies have been to a large degree followed because of money—to save money that might otherwise have been used to educate . . . to raise workers' salaries and to improve their working conditions. . . . And so, for profit, for money, the

whirlwind of racial hatred and violence has been encouraged—not per-mitted—but encouraged and invited by the stubborn and determined hard core of segregationists who are reactionary, politically and economically.

The next day he met with a group of church leaders who had traveled to Washington to express moral outrage over the bombing. The country was facing "a grave crisis," Humphrey told them, and action on civil rights was desperately needed.[73]

But when would progress occur? Kennedy's civil rights legislation had run into trouble on Capitol Hill, where lawmakers were wrestling over the details. By October Humphrey had received reports that House Republicans would only accept a civil rights bill if it did not include FEPC, did not ex-pand the attorney general's powers to bring civil rights suits in any way, had voting provisions that applied only to federal elections, and excluded all re-tail stores from its public accommodations section. Sensing that civil rights advocates had lost much of the momentum from the summer, Humphrey feared that Kennedy's package would have to be compromised severely to win Republican support for cloture. He pessimistically told his Senate col-leagues, "I would be less than honorable . . . if I did not say that when we get down the line we shall have to make a judgment as to what we can really pass in this body and how we can stand together to support it." These were hard-ly the words of a man looking forward to breaking the back of Jim Crow.[74]

VI

Humphrey's exhaustive efforts on behalf of compromise during the Eisen-hower and Kennedy administrations represented a continuation of trends ev-ident during the early 1950s. Humphrey further demonstrated that he was a loyal Democrat who was eager to work with more moderate party leaders on civil rights issues. Political concerns played an important role in this strat-egy, for Humphrey knew that to advance he needed to assuage fears that he would not compromise on the race issue. Unity was also good for the party, he thought. Humphrey believed that the Democrats could not "be a major-ity party if the southern boys were out." There were strong psychological motivations for such a course too. Humphrey clearly enjoyed the attention he received from powerful people. Johnson regularly dropped by his office to talk over important matters, and Kennedy had made Humphrey part of his weekly White House breakfast meetings with legislative leaders. By the early 1960s Humphrey had cemented his standing as a leader of growing

stature, and he would not jeopardize this by leading confrontational challenges such as his 1948 effort. Harsh criticism of Johnson and Kennedy's civil
rights policies would certainly weaken his relationship with these men. Finally, Humphrey continued to believe that, despite all the chaos and injustice
swirling through the South, there were moderate whites in Dixie with
whom he could cooperate to facilitate orderly progress.

Contemporary critics blasted Humphrey for unnecessarily acquiesing to
party leaders, and in doing so they implied that he had set the civil rights
struggle back. It is unclear, though, how a more confrontational approach
would have resulted in any improvement in the legislative situation. To enact
a civil rights bill required substantial Republican help, and assistance from the
GOP was probable on only the mildest of bills during the 1950s and early
1960s. Unfortunately, few Republicans were willing to support FEPC or
grant the attorney general broad powers to address voting rights or desegregation. Only when black voters in the North and African Americans across
the South had decided to stand up for their rights did the legislative wheels
begin to move.[75]

Substantively, the civil rights debate underwent two critical shifts during
the Eisenhower and Kennedy years. First, liberals like Humphrey were more
willing to greatly increase the powers of the federal government to deal with
racial matters. This was evident in Title III, the voter registrar plan, and Humphrey's bills to deal with job training and equal employment opportunity. As
massive resistance spread across the South and as economic conditions for
many blacks worsened in the North, Humphrey sought to remove much of
the burden for redress from the individual and place it on the shoulders of
the federal government. Relying only on the court system to protect voting
rights or rule on employment discrimination after an individual had brought
suit, Humphrey and others realized, offered those who discriminated a way
to delay racial justice because individual court cases took so long to resolve.
More important, economic issues receded to the background during these
years. Though Humphrey continued to submit FEPC legislation and highlight the economic troubles of many African Americans, equal economic opportunity no longer topped his legislative agenda. He now focused more
heavily on voting rights and desegregation. The determined opposition of
southern Democrats and the refusal of the Republicans to support FEPC
helped force Humphrey to set his sights on much more modest aims, such as
his civil rights commission bill. The debate about the economic position of
blacks that had dominated the civil rights struggle during the late 1940s had
been snuffed out in part by the politics of anticommunism as opponents of
FEPC had successfully branded it un-American. Developments outside of

Congress also played a role in this transformation. Many African Americans saw the struggle for equality as a multifront battle. They wanted improved economic opportunities, but they also stressed the right to vote and launched numerous campaigns across the South to eradicate segregation. Seeking to make the Fifteenth Amendment a reality for blacks in the South threatened those whites who used the political system to cement their power, while confronting segregation directly also presented a stern challenge to the social order. In retrospect it is clear that civil rights leaders overestimated the power of the ballot and desegregation to transform political and economic relations in the South, but they were nonetheless right to believe that the franchise and integration would improve the lot of African Americans. Fighting and winning on three fronts (voting, integration, economics) simultaneously, however, proved impossible. The issue of political and social rights for blacks had supplanted economics as the top racial concern of the leading advocates of racial justice. Finally, though *Brown* represented a monumental victory, it also unintentionally deflected attention away from economic issues as the South soon plunged into a crisis over desegregation. Liberals such as Humphrey now made voting rights their highest priority in part out of a sincere belief in the importance of the ballot but also because they saw voting as a more achievable aim given the trauma aroused by the desegregation issue and the lack of progress on FEPC.[76]

Soon after Kennedy was assassinated in Dallas in November, it became clear that his civil rights bill would remain the center of attention. Would Johnson fully embrace the Kennedy plan, or would he permit southerners to eviscerate the legislation, as he had in 1957 and 1960? Humphrey learned the answer to that question a few days after the assassination when he had dinner with the new president. Johnson was to speak before a joint session of Congress the next day, and Humphrey stayed late into the night and helped persuade the president to cast the civil rights measure as a tribute to Kennedy. "No memorial or eulogy," Johnson firmly told lawmakers and a national television audience, "could more eloquently honor President Kennedy's memory than the earliest possible passage of the civil rights bill for which he fought so long. We have talked long enough in this country about equal rights. . . . It is now time to write the next chapter—and to write it in the books of law." Humphrey, who had spent more than two years waiting for Kennedy to take such a forthright stand on civil rights, eagerly anticipated helping the new president do just that when Congress reconvened in January.[77]

5

A Moment of Triumph
The 1964 Civil Rights Act

I

As 1964 opened Humphrey had an even greater sense of urgency regarding racial matters. The Birmingham police attacks on civil rights marchers, the murder of Medgar Evers, riots at the University of Mississippi, the killing of a Freedom Walker, and the Birmingham church bombing, had "spawned a terrifying record of violence" during the previous year, he declared, and would produce "a generation of angry citizens." These tragic events were related to segregation and voting rights in the South, but at the same time Humphrey continued to insist that the more important problem was economic opportunity for all. "For the average Negro the issue of civil rights is tied most directly to the problem of jobs," he pointed out. "For the average Negro family this 'citizenship gap' means an income that is far less than the average white family." Sixty percent of African American families, he observed, made less than $4,000 a year, compared to only 28 percent for white families. The gap between white and nonwhite wages had increased too. In 1939 the difference was about $650 a year, but twenty-five years later it had grown to more than $2,000.[1]

Whether the federal government would move on this front was very much in doubt, for the president's civil rights bill chiefly concerned segregation. Johnson told Senate Majority Leader Mike Mansfield to designate Humphrey floor manager for the looming battle in the Senate. Both the president and the majority leader wanted to stay above the day-to-day wrangling, and Humphrey's identification with the issue, his ties to civil rights groups, and his communication skills made him a natural choice. Johnson called Humphrey to the Oval Office in February and challenged him directly. "You have got this opportunity now, Hubert, but you liberals will never deliver," the president bluntly stated. "You don't know the rules of the Senate, and your liberals will be off making speeches when they ought to be present in the Senate. I know you've got a great opportunity here, but I'm afraid it's going to fall between the boards." Richard Russell, Johnson predicted, would use his encyclopedic knowledge of Senate rules to defeat the bill. Humphrey canceled numerous engagements and eagerly prepared to prove Johnson wrong.[2]

The president placed a heavy burden on Humphrey's shoulders. Civil rights leaders, eager to take advantage of the public support generated by the violence in Birmingham, viewed this as a historic opportunity to enact a strong bill. Indeed, Martin Luther King and other civil rights leaders had sharply criticized the Kennedy administration during the fall for its efforts to persuade liberals in the House not to strengthen the measure out of fear that doing so would hurt the legislation in the Senate. If the southerners defeated the bill, or watered it down substantially, a new wave of civil rights demonstrations would erupt and likely result in additional violence. The outcome of the civil rights fight would also influence Humphrey's political future. Many liberals had already begun a movement to bring pressure on Johnson to select him as his running mate for the fall election, but failure to navigate the bill through the Senate would certainly doom those prospects. Humphrey desperately wanted the job. Whether he ended up on the Democratic ticket or not, Humphrey privately noted, losing the civil rights fight would be "a staggering blow" to himself personally and "could spell the defeat of Johnson in November."[3]

The House approved the civil rights legislation in early February, 290–130. In a good omen for the pro–civil rights forces in the Senate, House Republicans, who had usually voted against civil rights measures, supported the bill 138–34. Humphrey's analysis that the violence in Birmingham had created a new political climate appeared to be accurate. Owing in part to extensive efforts by Republicans, the measure that emerged from almost nine months of debate was substantially stronger than that which Kennedy had submitted. Most important, the House had added an employment provision (Title VII). To avoid the controversy stirred up by FEPC, it had included a five-member Equal Employment Opportunity Commission (EEOC) that would investigate charges of employment discrimination and have the authority to bring suits on behalf of individuals. The commission would not have the power to compel corrective action—only a federal court could do that. Other significant parts of the bill included strengthening voting rights in federal elections (Title I), eliminating segregation in most public accommodations (Title II), allowing the attorney general to initiate suits to end segregation in public facilities (Title III), providing assistance for school deseg-regation and authorizing the attorney general to initiate suits to desegregate public schools (Title IV), extending the Civil Rights Commission for four years (Title V), and requiring the cutoff of federal funds to programs that dis-criminated (Title VI).[4]

Humphrey was accustomed to being a spokesperson for civil rights, but now he had to master the intricacies of the parliamentary process. To halt the certain Senate filibuster, he could make concessions on the bill, persuade Mansfield to hold round-the-clock sessions to wear out the southerners, or seek cloture. Humphrey quickly rejected the first two options. He believed a strong bill was needed to address the burgeoning civil rights problems in the South and to satisfy civil rights groups. Round-the-clock sessions would pose a health risk to many of his colleagues and cause tempers to flare. Hum-phrey hoped to avoid "an acrimonious, bitter name-calling debate" and re-solved to "preserve a reasonable degree of good nature and fair play in the Senate." That left cloture, which had never been achieved on a civil rights measure. Because only about fifteen northern Democrats and Republicans who had long supported civil rights were firmly in his camp, Humphrey would need the votes of western Democrats, and, more important, approxi-mately twenty-five midwestern and western Republicans. Both groups of senators tended to be skeptical about federal power and had few African American constituents. Obtaining their votes meant winning the support of Minority Leader Everett Dirksen of Illinois. If Dirksen favored the civil rights legislation, then other Republicans could safely back it too. Getting Dirksen on board would not be easy, for though he had voted for civil rights measures in the past, the minority leader had publicly voiced his concern that Title II and Title VII, arguably the two most important sections of the bill, were too hostile to private property rights and businesses. Courting Dirksen, therefore, ran the risk of having to accept compromises that would weaken the measure. Humphrey nonetheless began to woo the minority leader early that spring. "It is not Hubert H. Humphrey that can pass this bill," he regularly told Dirksen. "Ultimately, it boils down to what you do."[5]

At the same time, Humphrey had to confront a potential rebellion among staunch civil rights advocates. Worried that Humphrey would grant too many concessions to the Republicans, representatives from civil rights groups and other liberal organizations insisted on the House bill as an absolute minimum and even talked of strengthening it. On February 28 Humphrey conferred with Clarence Mitchell, chief lobbyist for the Leadership Conference on Civil Rights, Joe Rauh, and several senators and their legislative aides. Stress-ing the need for civility during the long debate that lay ahead, Humphrey rejected Mitchell's suggestion that senators absent from quorum calls be arrested for failing to carry out their constitutional duties and brought to the Capitol. Calling the group's attention to the New York City police chief's fear of an outbreak of demonstrations if the bill went down to defeat, Humphrey advised them to keep their temper during the debate. "Dirksen doesn't want anybody picketing him," Humphrey informed Mitchell. (Civil rights groups in Illinois had recently demonstrated against the senator.) Bipartisanship, Humphrey maintained, was essential. He would meet regularly with Republican leaders of both houses as well as representatives of civil rights groups. Concluding that the House bill was strong enough to satisfy the civil rights lobbyists, Humphrey instructed his colleagues that any effort to strengthen it had to be cleared with him or Mansfield, lest the pro–civil rights team become disorganized, as it had so often in the past, and fail to win the support of Dirksen and other midwestern Republicans.[6]

Humphrey continued his pursuit of Dirksen a few days later during an appearance on "Meet the Press." He astutely tried to step out of the limelight by giving Dirksen the chance to be the hero. The minority leader would "not be found wanting" when the time came to support the civil rights bill, Humphrey predicted. The pro–civil rights forces would win, he confidently asserted, because public opinion was on their side and because Dirksen "thinks of his country before he thinks of his party." After the program ended, an elated Johnson called Humphrey at the television station. "Boy, that was right," the president stated. "You're doing just right now. You just keep at that. Don't let those bomb throwers, now, talk you out of seeing Dirksen. You get in there to see Dirksen. You drink with Dirksen! You talk with Dirksen! You listen to Dirksen!"[7]

The following day Mansfield moved that the Senate proceed to consider the House civil rights bill. The southerners, led as usual by Russell, promptly launched a filibuster. With nineteen firm votes against cloture, Russell only needed fifteen more to keep the filibuster going indefinitely. As usual, the crafty Georgian had organized his forces into three teams, with each speaking approximately eight hours while the other two rested. The southerners immediately attacked the bill, even though it was not technically up for debate, in hopes of swaying public opinion to their side and convincing colleagues to vote against it. Denouncing the legislation as "much more drastic" than measures proposed during Reconstruction, Russell accused the civil rights proponents of hiding their true objectives behind "the finest feat of propaganda that [had] immersed this nation in many years." The new authority granted to the federal government represented "the realization of a bureaucrat's prayers." Russell zeroed in on the employment section.

Claiming that civil rights advocates had misled the public about Title VII when they asserted that it would simply guarantee equal opportunity for all, he maintained that the bill would force hiring and promotion quotas based on race. "The idea of recompense and special favoritism in order to atone for either past history or for some present conditions has become widespread," he charged. "It is carried in every provision of this bill." Several days later, George Smathers of Florida revived the argument that an FEPC-type agency would force companies to base employment decisions on racial quotas and thus lead to less qualified African Americans obtaining jobs and promotions instead of whites. The state FEPC in Illinois he noted, had recently decided that Motorola's hiring test was unfair to "culturally deprived and disadvantaged" groups and ordered the hiring of an African American applicant who had filed a complaint.[8]

Though the southerners held the upper hand for the moment, Humphrey decided that attacks on the bill's substance could not go unanswered. The quota argument especially worried him. Humphrey opposed using race in hiring decisions on principle, but he understood that the quota issue, which had been used to defeat FEPC legislation during the 1950s, was potentially disastrous because a bipartisan coalition would never coalesce if working-class Democrats, who had long feared competition for jobs from African Americans, and Republicans, who championed individual responsibility and the free market, could be convinced that the bill allowed for any kind of special treatment for blacks. Greatly disturbed by the Illinois FEPC ruling, Humphrey contended that an employer should consider merit only. "I want to make it crystal clear that I do not believe that, because a man has had bad luck early in life, he should automatically be given a job if a company has certain standards for that job," he informed Senate colleagues. "People can go too far in these areas. If there are to be standards that are nondiscriminatory, that is exactly what they should be. There should not be swept into the question many outside issues, such as whether or not one has been 'culturally deprived.' "[9]

The anticipated filibuster was underway, but Humphrey had devised several means to combat it. A favorite (and frequent) southern parliamentary maneuver during a filibuster was the quorum call, which allowed Russell's forces to rest during the time needed to round up fifty-one senators to come to the floor. More dangerous for Humphrey was the chance that just enough senators would find the calls annoying and give in to southern demands to weaken the bill. Humphrey devised an elaborate system to prevent this. He arranged to have six Democrats on duty each day, each of whom was to produce four to six Democrats on the floor quickly after the call was made. Re-

publican Thomas Kuchel of California would be responsible for getting sixteen colleagues from across the aisle. A special telephone system was installed
in each office to speed the process, and senators were to notify the leaders
well in advance of when they would be out of town. Humphrey's scheme
would keep other Senate business from being done and prevent many legislators from tending to matters in their states, but that was his goal. By making them, and the public, angry over the slow pace of action in the Senate,
Humphrey hoped to build support for cloture. Humphrey also had two senators, one Democrat and one Republican, take primary responsibility for
each title. These individuals would become experts on their section of the
bill, explain it to the Senate and to the public, and counter southern arguments against it. This division of labor not only took a great deal of responsibility off Humphrey's shoulders, but, more important, promoted a bipartisan spirit. He later recalled that it kept colleagues "in sharp debate with the
opposition" and made them "ever more committed" to the task at hand.
Humphrey also scheduled at least four pro–civil rights senators to be on the
floor at all times to participate in debate and questioning and guard against
southern maneuvers. On March 11 Senator John Stennis of Mississippi discovered that the pro–civil rights team had yet another organizational tool.
When Stennis arrived at his desk that morning he found an unsigned newsletter that refuted some of the arguments he had made against the civil rights
bill the previous day. "Who is the constitutional lawyer who is sending
around these unsigned articles to senators?" a confused Stennis inquired.
Humphrey immediately claimed responsibility. The letter had been drafted
the previous night by his and Kuchel's staff to keep senators abreast of the debate. "For the first time," Humphrey boasted, "we are putting up a battle." The
letter would be published daily and contain schedules of that day's activities,
summaries of recent developments regarding the bill, and ammunition to
rebut southern criticisms. Finally, Humphrey held daily meetings to discuss
the progress of the legislation and plot strategy. Occurring just prior to the
start of each day's session, the meetings were to be attended by pro–civil
rights senators, members of their staffs, officials from the Justice Department,
and, following a request by Mitchell, a representative from the LCCR.[10]

Public pressure was especially important, Humphrey thought, to convince western and midwestern senators who had usually voted against civil
rights legislation to support cloture and the bill. Hoping to stir up grassroots
activity on behalf of the legislation, he urged pro–civil rights senators to appear on television and send out newsletters as often as possible. He conferred
with actor Marlon Brando, who used his contacts in Hollywood to persuade
television celebrities Johnny Carson, Steve Allen, Jack Paar, and Hugh

Humphrey's civil rights reforms in Minneapolis led many city leaders to look to him for guidance. Here Humphrey meets with civil rights activists in Los Angeles in 1947 to discuss creating a Fair Employment Practices Commission.

In 1948 Humphrey led the successful liberal battle for a strong civil rights plank in the Democratic Party's platform.

During the 1950s and early 1960s Humphrey worked closely with NAACP leader Roy Wilkins on behalf of civil rights legislation in the Senate.

Prior to the outbreak of widespread civil rights demonstrations in the South during the early 1960s, Humphrey was one of just a handful of senators to advocate civil rights legislation. Here northern civil rights proponents from both parties meet to plot strategy in 1957. Left to right seated: Clinton Anderson (D-N.Mex.), Irving Ives (R-N.Y.), Paul Douglas (D-Ill.), H. Alexander Smith (R-N.J.); left to right standing: Fred G. Payne (R-Maine), Prescott Bush (R-Conn.), Humphrey, Joseph Clark (D-Pa.), Richard Neuberger (D-Ore.)—hidden, Thomas Kuchel (R-Calif.).

Humphrey led the Senate fight for the landmark 1964 Civil Rights Act. Here President Lyndon Johnson greets Humphrey after signing the bill into law.

Humphrey dedicates a recreation area in 1967 in Washington, D.C., as part of the Johnson administration's Youth Opportunity Campaign.

Humphrey took a strong interest in economic and social problems confronting the nation's cities. Here he talks with Washington, D.C. civil rights leaders Marion Berry and Curtis Mayfield about their efforts to clean up blighted neighborhoods (ca. 1966).

Humphrey tried to make economic opportunity for African Americans a major theme of his 1968 presidential campaign. Here he and UAW leader Walter Reuther meet with Leon Woods, manager of the Watts Manufacturing Company, and Ted Watkins, project administrator of the Watts Labor Community Action Council.

During the 1970s Humphrey joined with Representative Augustus Hawkins (D–Calif.) in calling for full employment as a way to solve the social and economic problems that many African Americans faced. President Carter signed a drastically weakened version of Humphrey-Hawkins in 1978.

Downs to educate their audiences about the measure and give air time to pro–civil rights legislators. On March 7 Humphrey met with representatives from several religious groups, who were organizing lobbying efforts on behalf of the bill, to hatch plans for an interfaith rally in late April. "The secret of passing this bill is the church groups," he told his colleagues, because they would contribute a powerful moral tone to the debate that many senators would find impossible to resist.[11]

Initially, however, the pro–civil rights forces were losing the public relations battle because of a massive effort by the Coordinating Committee for Fundamental American Freedoms. Composed of far-right conservatives and financed in part by the state of Mississippi, the committee placed ads in dozens of newspapers maintaining that the civil rights bill was a "100 Billion Dollar Blackjack" that would rob Americans of numerous political freedoms, abolish the rule of law, lead to a "dictatorial" federal government, and prescribe "preferential treatment of minorities" in employment and other areas. The committee, which carried an air of respectability because one of its leaders had been president of the American Bar Association, supplemented the newspaper effort by mailing anti–civil rights newsletters to union members and suburban home owners. Committee officials spent two hundred thousand dollars by mid-March, more than any registered lobby had in 1962. Many northern and western senators reported that their mail was running four to one against the legislation and that much of their constituents' objections were based on the misinformation and distortions contained in the ad. Denouncing the ad as "an outrageous lie" that represented "muckraking at its worst," a worried Humphrey immediately countered with a spirited defense of the bill on the Senate floor. "Nothing in the bill would permit any official or court to require any employer or labor union to give preferential treatment to any minority group," he declared. A week later, he went to the White House and urged the administration to work with religious organizations and the Democratic National Committee to sway public opinion to the pro–civil rights side.[12]

The southerners' talkathon soon came to a halt, but only as a result of a tactical consideration by Russell. Concluding that continuing the filibuster on the motion to consider would only hurt his cause, the Georgia senator agreed to a roll call on whether to bring the legislation itself up for debate. Though Humphrey had talked of attempting a cloture vote, he refrained from doing so when he realized he still lacked the votes. On March 26 the Senate voted 67–17, with only the southern Democrats in opposition, to make the civil rights bill its pending business. "We shall now begin to fight the war," Russell ominously announced. The next filibuster, set to begin when Congress returned in a few days from the Easter recess, would be on the legislation itself.[13]

II

The Senate finally took up the civil rights bill on the snowy afternoon of March 30. Deciding that the debate would be one of the more important in American history, CBS placed reporter Roger Mudd outside the Capitol, where he would provide updates on the proceedings several times a day to national television and radio audiences. Shortly after noon Humphrey rose to open debate for the civil rights advocates by maintaining that the purpose of the legislation could be summarized in the Golden Rule. "The American Negro does not seek to be set apart from the community of American life," he explained. "He seeks to participate in it." Humphrey analyzed the measure title by title. He vividly outlined the travesty of segregated public accommodations in the South by noting that in Augusta, Georgia, there were five hotels that allowed dogs as guests but only one that permitted African Americans. In Columbus, Georgia, he continued, dogs could stay at six hotels but African Americans none, while in Charleston the ratio was ten to zero. Regarding school integration, Humphrey pointed out that because less than 1 percent of all African American students attended desegregated schools in seven southern states and because private citizens lacked resources to sue individual school districts, the attorney general had to become involved if compliance with *Brown* were ever to be achieved. Humphrey dealt at length with Title VII. The unemployment rate for nonwhites, he noted, was more than twice that for whites. Worse yet, this gap had widened since the late 1940s because of discrimination, a lack of educational opportunities among African Americans, and technological changes in the economy. The EEOC was thus urgently needed. Humphrey again unequivocally stated where the pro–civil rights forces stood regarding the sensitive issue of racial quotas. "Contrary to the allegations of some opponents of [Title VII], there is nothing in it that will give any power to the [EEOC] or to any court to require hiring, firing, or promotion of employees in order to meet a racial 'quota' or to achieve a certain racial balance," he asserted. "That bugaboo has been brought up a dozen times, but it is nonexistent. In fact, the very opposite is true. Title VII prohibits discrimination. In effect, it says that race, religion, and national origin are not to be used as the basis for hiring and firing. Title VII is designed to encourage hiring on the basis of ability and qualifications, not race or religion." Concluding that this "long overdue" legislation was not a solution to all of the ills plaguing African Americans, Humphrey nonetheless insisted that it would at least provide them with "the same rights and the same opportunities that white Americans take for granted." Having spoken for three and a half hours, Humphrey turned the floor over to his allies. During the next few weeks, each title was even more thoroughly explained by the two senators who were primarily responsible for it.[14]

Still lacking the votes for cloture, Humphrey had to let the southerners talk. Johnson told him in late March to go to round-the-clock sessions so that antipoverty legislation could be enacted by summer, but Humphrey replied that Mansfield opposed such a move out of concern that it would lose votes for cloture and endanger the health of older senators. That left only one course of action—continue to debate the southerners while trying to round up support for cloture. The nonsoutherners who were not firmly in the pro–civil rights camp, Humphrey hoped, would grow weary of the talkathon and demand that the bill be brought to a vote. "The whole thing is timing," he remarked. "We've got to hold on until the pain is miserable, till it's really agony."[15]

Meanwhile, Humphrey kept to his plan of working with Dirksen. The minority leader sounded as cagey as ever. On April 7 Dirksen met with his Republican colleagues and presented a package of forty amendments to Title VII that would weaken federal involvement in employment matters. Fearing that Dirksen was out to gut the bill, Joe Rauh and other civil rights lobbyists worried that Humphrey would sell out to get cloture. Humphrey counseled the pro–civil rights forces not to panic. "[Dirksen's] trying to be constructive," he reassured them. Mitchell and others were not convinced. They wanted to avoid negotiating with Dirksen and attempt to wear out the southerners by moving to round-the-clock sessions, but Humphrey insisted on holding to the original strategy.

"We will have to plan on cloture. Nobody won a war on starving the enemy. We must shoot them on the battlefield," Humphrey observed.

"You are shooting the friends if you trade with Dirksen," Mitchell contended.

"We don't have sixty-five votes for cloture."

The lack of enough cloture votes meant that Humphrey would have to wait for Dirksen, but the minority leader reported that he was not yet ready to deal.[16]

Privately, Humphrey had begun to worry that his strategy was failing. Democratic attendance at the frequent quorum calls by the southerners was abysmal—an average of only twenty-four out of a goal of thirty-six. Republicans and even a few southern Democrats had been ensuring a quorum.

Not only was Democratic attendance a serious problem, but the southerners were able to get a good rest because obtaining a quorum was taking nearly an hour. Fearing that Johnson's prediction of not being able to overcome
the filibuster might prove accurate, Humphrey wrote Democratic colleagues
about the importance of attending quorum calls and informing the leadership about all out-of-town engagements. Only thirty-nine senators answered
the quorum call on April 4, however. Having known several days in advance
that a quorum could not be met because many senators would be home
tending to political affairs, Humphrey decided to use the occasion to make
a point. At a meeting in his office that day he read the names of the missing
and wondered aloud why they were gone. He then sent telegrams to the absent Democrats. When they returned Humphrey met with them, gave them
a list of scheduled sessions through mid-May, and warned that he would
scold them publicly if they were absent again. Humphrey's feigned tirade
succeeded. A week later, the pro–civil rights forces met a quorum in just ten
minutes. Two days after the LCCR assisted in bringing senators from a baseball game by police escort to Capitol Hill in just twenty minutes.[17]

Political events in the heartland gave Humphrey additional reason for
concern. On April 7 Governor George Wallace of Alabama won 33.9 percent
of the vote in the Wisconsin Democratic primary, a far better showing than
most political observers had expected. Though he finished second, Wallace
rightly proclaimed that the surprising result showed that anti–civil rights
sentiment was strong outside the South too. Dirksen interpreted the Wisconsin vote as a sign of public backing of his efforts to limit federal enforcement of the civil rights legislation, but Humphrey gamely tried to downplay
Wallace's impact. "I can count. Governor Wallace's effort was a flop, f-l-o-p,"
he told the press. "His campaign was a fizzle, f-i-z-z-l-e. . . . [In] most midwest states if you put your name on the ballot you get 25 percent of the vote,
dead or alive." The vote was not as benign as Humphrey had indicated. In an
ominous development for the Democrats, Wallace ran especially well in the
Polish, Italian, and Serb working-class neighborhoods of Milwaukee. The
Democrats thus had to be careful about how far they pushed civil rights lest
they upset an integral part of the New Deal coalition.[18]

Trouble was also brewing on Humphrey's left. If the filibuster gravely
weakened or killed the legislation, King warned Humphrey, African Americans would "engage in some type of direct action" in Washington. Several
days later, the Brooklyn chapter of CORE proposed to express its frustration
over the lack of social and economic improvement for African Americans by
conducting a "stall-in" at the upcoming World's Fair in New York. The techniques rumored to be considered by CORE included causing massive traf-

fic jams by having members sit on highways leading to the fair and forcing delays at the gate by paying admission with pennies. Whereas the use of police dogs and fire hoses in Birmingham had generated tremendous goodwill for civil rights, Humphrey commented, a stall-in would "have the same reaction in reverse." He and Kuchel thought the issue to be so potentially damaging to their cause that they released a joint statement advising against any massive disruption of the fair. "Civil wrongs do not bring civil rights," they contended. "No one can condone violation of the law." Instead of a stall-in, the pair recommended that CORE use "the same good manners, forbearance, and devotion" that had been employed by participants in the March on Washington if it wanted to advance racial justice. Much to Humphrey's relief, the stall-in never occurred.[19]

Nevertheless, Humphrey still feared that southerners were winning the public relations battle. "We have to hammer away," he told a meeting of the civil rights advocates. "We have to get at the racial quota argument." To counter this and other southern propaganda, Humphrey supplied his allies with a fact sheet describing the offensive that had been mounted against the bill and a question-and-answer book dealing with the basic issues. He also urged colleagues to mention the civil rights debate whenever possible and distributed to all pro–civil rights senators information that one of them was using in his newsletters to constituents. The campaign succeeded brilliantly. As a result of this and similar efforts by civil rights, labor, and religious organizations, Humphrey reported in mid-April that his mail, which had been two or three to one against the bill, was running three to one in favor of it. Other senators also witnessed a marked turnaround. Though Humphrey welcomed this reversal of public opinion, he was still a long way from victory. Dirksen's amendments had divided the GOP; liberal Republicans worried that they would unduly weaken the bill while conservatives supported them. More important, Humphrey announced that he still needed several votes for cloture.[20]

By the end of April, however, Humphrey had grown more optimistic about the chances for breaking the filibuster. Public opinion was overwhelmingly behind the legislation, and with an election looming that fall it would be bad politics for the GOP to stand in its way. House Republicans, moreover, wanted a strong measure. As a result of pressure from them, as well as Humphrey, Dirksen reduced his forty-plus amendments to twelve. On April 21 he assured Humphrey that he would use his influence to round up Republican votes for cloture and for the bill itself. The outlook for civil rights, one of Humphrey's legislative aides cheerfully noted, appeared to be "quite good."[21]

The southerners abruptly changed their tactics in late April by submitting an amendment that would guarantee a jury trial to anyone accused of violating court orders in all civil rights cases. The amendment, and not the entire bill, thus became the subject of debate. The House measure had provided for jury trials in only certain instances, but the southerners insisted, as they had in 1957, that jury trials were an inalienable right in all cases. The civil rights proponents suddenly found themselves in the difficult position of having to explain the complex legal reasoning why they opposed this plan. Worried that success of the jury amendment would be a tremendous psychological blow to the pro–civil rights forces, Humphrey met with Dirksen, Mansfield, and Justice Department officials to craft a more acceptable alternative. Though they agreed on a new amendment to be sponsored by Dirksen and Mansfield, there was considerable disagreement over how to proceed. Dirksen wanted a cloture vote just on the amendment. On the other hand, Humphrey favored postponing any cloture attempt because he still did not have enough votes.[22]

While Humphrey wrangled with Dirksen about the jury issue, religious groups intensified their efforts on behalf of the legislation. The National Council of Churches and the U.S. Catholic Conference, as well as several Jewish organizations, met regularly with legislators. As part of an extensive grassroots educational campaign throughout the Midwest, clergy asked parishioners to contact their representatives. Trios of Catholic, Protestant, and Jewish seminarians initiated a round-the-clock vigil at the Lincoln Memorial until the measure was passed. More than four thousand church leaders packed the gymnasium at Georgetown University in late April for a civil rights rally. Another fifteen hundred sat in an adjacent hall. Wanting a peaceful and positive event, Humphrey, who was one of three legislators to attend the gathering, had asked that participants refrain from personal attacks on the bill's opponents, and he got his wish. The evening was filled with music and speeches on the need for racial equality. Over the next several days many who had attended the rally met with members of Congress. As Humphrey had hoped, they paid special attention to midwestern and western senators.[23]

Though lobbying efforts by religious groups turned up the pressure on many senators, Humphrey still had not yet reached a final agreement with Dirksen regarding the minority leader's amendments. Humphrey recognized that some concessions to the Illinois Republican had to be made if the bill were to be enacted, but he also knew he could not let Dirksen completely set the terms of debate. On April 28 he enlisted Johnson in his effort to hold back the minority leader. Telling the president that "victory was in sight," Humphrey urged him to "lay down the law" to those who wanted to weaken the legislation. When Dirksen went to the White House the next day expecting to convince Johnson to accept his amendments as the price for a civil rights bill, the president held firm.[24]

At the same time, Humphrey asserted his independence from the civil rights lobbyists. Clarence Mitchell reported that African Americans were growing restless and demanding no compromise whatsoever.

"Some of the Negro groups would tar and feather and hoot off the stage those who support the Dirksen amendments," he told Humphrey on April 30.

"What should we do, Clarence? Let's put it on the table," Humphrey demanded.

"The missing ingredient is to compel the attendance of the absent senators."

Because so few senators were present on the floor at any one time, Mitchell feared that the filibuster would soon wear out the pro–civil rights senators. By forcing truant senators to be present during the southerners' speeches, he thought, Senate leaders would increase support for cloture. Humphrey disagreed and resolved to continue to work with Dirksen to find an acceptable bill and then seek cloture.[25]

Like Mitchell, Humphrey was concerned over the lack of progress. "Let me assure you that when a hot summer comes and people grow more restless in tenements and on the highways seeking accommodations, and youngsters pour out of our universities, then the danger signals are up in America," he told a meeting of the civil rights proponents. "I don't want responsible Americans like Roy Wilkins being repudiated. Unless this Senate provides a framework of law, then wild men will take over." Humphrey's frustration over the slow pace of action in the Senate may have explained his comment the following day that the White House was willing to bargain. Humphrey's remark brought Johnson's wrath down upon him. Eager to maintain a public posture of no compromise, the president immediately telephoned Humphrey after his speech and, according to one source, gave him "unshirted hell." Humphrey quickly backtracked, saying that he was only stating his opinion of what the president would do. He refused to confirm directly his conversation with the president, but there was little doubt what had happened when he looked up at the press gallery during a quorum call, grinned broadly, and tugged upwardly on his ears, a clear reference to Johnson's regular treatment of his two beagles.[26]

Humphrey thought the breakthrough he had been waiting for finally occurred on May 5, when Dirksen agreed to open negotiations. That morning Humphrey, Mansfield, Attorney General Robert Kennedy, and several other senators and Justice Department officials met in the minority leader's office. To nearly everyone's surprise, however, Dirksen announced that he had dozens of new amendments, not just one, as he had previously indicated. Some were relatively simple matters dealing with language, but others were more substantive. Resolution of the civil rights bill would take even longer than Humphrey or anyone else who favored it had expected.[27]

Humphrey soon encountered additional difficulties, this time on the Senate floor. Russell had agreed to end the debate over the jury issue and bring it to a vote. Why he did this is unclear, though it is possible that he took seriously Humphrey's public statements that the civil rights proponents had the votes for cloture. The pro–civil rights camp proved to be in utter disarray, however. The matter up for consideration was not the Dirksen-Mansfield amendment, as Russell had promised, but rather a perfecting amendment to the original southern jury trial plan. The Senate defeated it, but only by a 45–45 vote. Humphrey's team suffered defeat on the next vote, a motion to table the perfecting amendment so it could not be brought up later. When the jury plan was taken up again, Humphrey's side won by just one vote because a senator switched positions. "Occasionally [the Senate] is a quorum of frustration," Humphrey commented angrily. The razor-thin victory raised doubts about whether some Republicans previously thought to be certain supporters of cloture would side with Humphrey. It also demonstrated that Humphrey did not have his team under control, and as a result he put off a vote on the Dirksen-Mansfield amendment. As had been true so often before, northern and western senators appeared to lack the cohesion of the southerners. "I will say that it will be somewhat of a major miracle if the pro civil rights forces can get themselves back in order and push ahead with some degree of resolution and determination," Humphrey's top civil rights aide wrote in his diary. "Of course, the southerners have their problems and . . . they are probably more profound than ours. But right now, ours look pretty profound.[28]

Tensions soon flared between Humphrey and several civil rights lobbyists, who, in hopes of protecting Title II and Title VII, still urged him to refrain from negotiating with Dirksen. Accepting the minority leader's plans to limit federal involvement, Roy Wilkins warned, would "arouse sharp and cynical resentment in the Negro community" and lead to "many years of tension and abrasive racial relations." Similarly, James Farmer of CORE and Martin Luther King intimated that mass protests would occur in the nation's capital if the Senate did not pass a strong measure by summer. The LCCR firmly opposed any talks with Dirksen, and UAW chief Walter Reuther expressed concern that minority leader would seriously weaken the bill. Humphrey reassured the lobbyists that though Dirksen was needed for cloture the pro–civil rights forces would make no damaging compromises.[29]

Negotiations between Dirksen, the Justice Department, and Senate Democrats continued each day in the minority leader's office. The chief sticking points continued to be cloture procedures, public accommodations, and employment. By now, however, Humphrey and other liberal Democrats had concluded that Dirksen needed their support as much as they needed his, for the GOP's political interest lay in a strong civil rights bill. Humphrey firmly opposed Dirksen's plan for cloture on each title (instead of one cloture vote on the entire bill), and he resisted attempts by the minority leader to create a new title that would delineate the attorney general's enforcement powers regarding every section of the bill. Such an addition could be knocked out of the measure, leaving only a handful of goals with no means of achieving them, Humphrey rightly pointed out. Nevertheless, he knew he had to give some ground because he had only fifty-four certain votes for cloture. He accepted two of Dirksen's more important amendments that clarified and somewhat limited federal involvement in civil rights enforcement. Regarding Title II, Humphrey agreed to let local agencies attempt to resolve public accommodations and employment issues before the federal government became involved. The Justice Department would be allowed to initiate lawsuits on behalf of individuals claiming discrimination, but it could become involved only where "a pattern or practice" of discrimination existed. Second, the EEOC's powers to bring individual employment discrimination suits were stricken from the bill. The attorney general would instead be given powers to initiate suits to deal with "a pattern or practice" and be allowed to intervene in individual suits, but only after someone had brought the case. These two changes ensured that the bill was aimed primarily at the South. But that would be all Humphrey would accept. To demonstrate his resolve to Dirksen, he arranged for liberal Joseph Clark of Pennsylvania to storm out of a negotiating session in mock furor over one of the minority leader's amendments to Title VII. "It's a goddamn sellout," shouted Clark as he slammed the door. "See what pressure I'm up against?" Humphrey asked Dirksen. "I can't concede any more on this point." Eager to have the civil rights issue disposed of quickly because party conventions were nearing, the minority leader backed down. By May 13 all remaining differences had been ironed out. Knowing that he would still have to sell the compromise legislation to his colleagues and the civil rights lobbyists, Humphrey nervously remarked, "I feel like someone who's going down a ski jump for the first time. After you're five feet down, all you can do is hope that you don't land on your head."[30]

The filibuster had taken its toll on Humphrey, however. He could count only fifty-five votes to halt what had become the longest talkathon in Senate history. Seeking to mollify the civil rights lobbyists, Humphrey suggested that cloture would be attempted in late May. When Kuchel approached him about this, a discouraged Humphrey confessed, "Tommy, I'm talking out of both sides of my mouth." There would not be a cloture vote before early June, he told the California senator. Because even this deadline would be difficult to meet, Humphrey decided to turn up the heat on his nonsouthern colleagues by taking his case directly to the voters of the Midwest. Speaking at a Jefferson-Jackson Day fund-raiser in Des Moines on May 9, he urged citizens to lobby their senators to at least support cloture. "Eighty-one North, East, and Western senators have the civil rights bill in their hands," Humphrey told the gathering of Democrats. "Just give me two votes from Iowa, two from Nebraska, and two from Kansas." He instructed Mitchell three days later, "Clarence, it is time for the NAACP and the AFL-CIO to put their fingers on the eighty-one other senators around here. . . . Every day we wait for cloture is nibbling away at the bill." Humphrey was not the only one eager for a vote. At a breakfast meeting with congressional leaders the next morning, Johnson berated Humphrey for the lack of progress in the Senate. The president demanded round-the-clock sessions, but Humphrey, thinking it was better to win senators to his side through personal persuasion and public pressure, told Johnson that he would take no such action. By late May Humphrey's strategy appeared to be working. Dirksen's amendments, Humphrey revealed, had won some votes for cloture. Mansfield announced on June 1 that the Senate would attempt to shut off the filibuster eight days later. Fearful that the pro–civil rights force might win, the southerners questioned the delay and demanded the vote be taken immediately. Owing largely to extensive lobbying by religious groups, Humphrey was closing in on his target of sixty-seven, but he still needed the support of several midwestern and western colleagues. The civil rights proponents, therefore, held the Senate floor to explain the revised bill as the religious lobbyists continued their efforts. Ironically, Humphrey's team was now engaged in a delaying tactic.[31]

As the pro–civil rights forces attempted to round up votes for cloture they again found themselves on the defensive, especially regarding employment, the withholding of federal funds to programs that discriminated, and school desegregation. "Title VII," Humphrey countered, "does not require an employer to achieve any sort of racial balance in his workforce by giving preferential treatment to any individual or group." Asserting that "inadvertent or accidental discriminations will not violate the title or result in entry of court orders," Humphrey insisted that Title VII simply meant "that the respondent must have intended to discriminate." Title VI, he assured the southerners, would cut off federal money only to the program under question, not the recipient general-ly. A company or institution, therefore, could still obtain federal funding as long as it did not discriminate in all of its activities. As for school desegregation, Humphrey confirmed southern claims that the legislation ignored de facto segregation in the North when he stated that the bill would not permit the busing of children to achieve racial balance. "In fact, if the bill were to compel [busing], it would be a violation, because it would be handling the matter on the basis of race and we would be transporting children on the basis of race," Humphrey commented. Racial gerrymandering of school districts would be illegal, therefore, but segregation arising from housing patterns would not. All three of these areas would become bitterly contested issues in subsequent years, when civil rights proponents would take positions directly opposite Humphrey's. The senator, though, had laid down a clear record of legislative intent based on principles of discrimination being rooted in conscious deci-sions and not using race as a criteria for social or economic policy.[32]

A sudden and unexpected revolt among midwestern Republicans, led by Iowan Bourke Hickenlooper, added to Humphrey's problems. The rebellion occurred as a result of opposition to portions of the bill and Hickenlooper's resentment over the attention that had been lavished on Dirksen. On June 5 a dejected Dirksen told Humphrey that the outlook for cloture was grim be-cause several senators previously thought to be firmly in the pro–cloture camp seemed to be slipping away. Hickenlooper and his allies demanded that the cloture vote be moved to June 10 and that the Senate consider three new amendments. Humphrey had to make a decision quickly. He knew that if Hickenlooper were not given a hearing the Iowan and his allies might not vote for cloture and the civil rights bill would succumb to the southern fil-ibuster. On the other hand, approving the amendments would weaken the legislation and stir the wrath of civil rights groups. While Humphrey debat-ed what to do, he lobbied three midwestern senators and obtained their votes for cloture. More confident that cloture could be achieved, Humphrey worked out a deal with Hickenlooper whereby the Senate would vote on the three amendments on June 9. The Senate approved only one of them. The stage was set for the long-anticipated showdown over cloture.[33]

III

The night before the roll call Humphrey stayed in his office well past midnight going over procedural details and double counting votes. He phoned the president at 7:30 to inform him that he had the necessary support. Johnson remained skeptical, but Humphrey indicated that he was certain he would win. Humphrey then called three more senators in hopes of increasing his total.[34]

The Senate galleries filled early on the morning of June 10 with onlookers who wanted to be present for what they anticipated would be a historic moment. Many House members stood against the Senate walls. CBS newsman Roger Mudd, who had diligently covered daily developments since February, prepared to broadcast the vote on live television and keep a running total for viewers on a large scoreboard. Reporters jammed into Humphrey's office before the session. His longtime ally and friend Cecil Newman, editor of the *Minneapolis Spokesman*, joined him for a toast of orange juice. Humphrey then made several phone calls trying to clinch some more votes. An hour before the session opened he gave a Democratic colleague a note that said he had sixty-nine votes for cloture, two more than needed. Thinking that there was a possibility of picking up additional support, he confidently strode to the Senate chamber when the bell rang at ten o'clock. Russell gave one last speech against the bill. Humphrey spoke to his colleagues for just two and a half minutes. Following a thirty-minute address by Dirksen, it was time to vote.[35]

The galleries grew quiet for the tense drama of the roll call. Like many of his colleagues, Humphrey kept a tally as each senator rose to announce his vote. A poignant moment occurred when Senator Clair Engle of California, who was battling cancer, was wheeled into the chamber. Unable to speak, he signaled his approval for cloture by pointing at his eye three times. Several minutes later, Senator John Williams of Delaware provided the sixty-seventh vote. Humphrey triumphantly raised his hands over his head and looked up into the gallery as reporters scrambled to file their stories. The final vote was 71–29. Forty-four Democrats and twenty-seven Republicans backed cloture, while twenty-three Democrats and six Republicans comprised the losing side. Nineteen of twenty-one western Democrats sided with Humphrey. Thanks in large part to the religious groups and the leadership of Dirksen, all but one midwestern and four western Republicans supported cloture. This was only the twelfth time cloture had been invoked on any issue, the first for a civil rights bill. The seventy-five-day filibuster was over at last.[36]

Refusing to concede defeat, Sam Ervin, Strom Thurmond, and a few other southerners offered hundreds of amendments over the next several days. Though Humphrey and the pro–civil rights forces were somewhat disorganized at first, they gradually decided that the best approach was to vote down the amendments as soon as they came up. The Senate quickly did just that. There were a few close votes, but most were rejected by lopsided margins of three to one or four to one. Humphrey did accept several amendments that he regarded as harmless to the bill in hopes of promoting goodwill among his colleagues and hastening the final vote on the legislation itself. The Senate approved a Justice Department revision of Ervin's amendment regarding double jeopardy, and on June 13 Humphrey agreed to a proposal that would not prevent an employer from making hiring decisions based upon an abilities test given to all job applicants. Recalling that the Motorola case had been "discussed, discussed, and cussed" by civil rights proponents, he declared that the amendment was acceptable because it did nothing to undermine the standard of intentional discrimination in employment cases.[37]

Four days later, Humphrey experienced professional triumph and a personal setback. Following several days of negotiations, Humphrey, Ervin, and Thurmond worked out an agreement that would enable the final vote on the measure to occur within two days. That afternoon, however, Humphrey was called off the Senate floor to take a phone call from his wife, who informed him that a biopsy was to be performed on their son, Robert, for a malignant tumor in his neck. Humphrey sat in his office crying as Rauh and Mitchell attempted to console him. Though he wanted desperately to be with his family, Humphrey decided to remain in Washington until the civil rights measure passed the Senate.[38]

The Senate galleries filled early on June 19 with those eager to witness the long anticipated vote on the legislation itself. Following defeat of a motion to send it to the Judiciary Committee, Humphrey rose to present his last address regarding the bill. Noting that the eighty-three days of debate, the longest in Senate history, had been "difficult and demanding," he acknowledged that the measure did not satisfy everyone. Nevertheless, he insisted the Senate had done its job well and pointed out that compromise had been the essence of the legislative process since the debates on the drafting of the Constitution itself. The process of give and take had resulted in "the greatest piece of social legislation of our generation." But, Humphrey cautioned, this was no time for gloating, for there was much more work to be done regarding education, jobs, and other areas of racial justice. "As we enact the Civil Rights Act of 1964, then, let us be exalted but not exultant," he concluded. "Let us mark the occasion with sober rejoicing, and not with shouts of victory."[39]

The Senate proceeded to vote that evening. The galleries erupted in loud and lengthy applause shortly before eight, when the clerk announced that the bill had passed, 73–27. Forty-six Democrats and twenty-seven Republicans supported the measure, while twenty-one Democrats and six Republicans opposed it. As on the cloture vote, nearly all the midwestern Republicans and western Democrats that Humphrey had targeted sided with him. After the roll call Humphrey, Dirksen, and other civil rights advocates gathered in Mansfield's office to celebrate their triumph. As Humphrey left the Capitol later that night, a crowd of several hundred citizens who had not been able to obtain seats in the galleries greeted him. Many who had gathered were African American. Some people shouted "Freedom." Others praised Humphrey for doing "a good job." "You gave us justice, senator," a student told him. "Thank you." Humphrey was buoyed by the crowd, but the long ordeal had clearly taken its toll. "I feel like a heavy load has been lifted from my shoulders—a wonderful sense of relief and quiet joy," he wrote columnist James Reston of the *New York Times*.[40]

Humphrey met another hero's welcome when he arrived in Minneapolis the next day to be with his son. A jubilant crowd of one hundred people greeted him with cheers and applause when he stepped off the airplane. Some carried banners proclaiming "Minnesota Is Proud of Humphrey," and "Well Done." One person showed Humphrey a browned and tattered sixteen-year-old picture of him being carried through the Great Northern railroad station following his return from the Democratic convention in Philadelphia. Though there was no parade through downtown Minneapolis this time, the parallels to 1948 were obvious. The bill, Humphrey told the crowd, constituted "an expression of the beauty of our country." He also warned against thinking that the fight for racial justice was over. "It doesn't mean much if you have the right to sit at the lunch counter if you don't have the dime to buy the cup of coffee," he reminded them.[41]

Two week later, Humphrey returned to Washington knowing that his son would recover. The House approved the measure on July 2, and the president signed it at a nationally televised ceremony from the White House that evening. Humphrey attended the momentous occasion along with several civil rights leaders and numerous members of Congress. The 1964 Civil Rights Act, Martin Luther King had declared, was "a good and meaningful bill," while Urban League president Whitney Young called it "the greatest single triumph for human rights . . . since the Emancipation Proclamation." Knowing that this was a historic occasion, Humphrey asked the president for the manuscript of his remarks, but he was disappointed to discover that someone had already snatched it.[42]

IV

The 1964 Civil Rights Act was an enormous victory for racial justice. The pro–civil rights camp had slain Jim Crow by enacting a tough public accommodations law. They had given the federal government considerable power to compel equality by outlawing the use of federal funds in programs that discriminated. They had taken an unequivocal position against discrimination in employment and established a federal apparatus to combat it. For Humphrey the statute represented the culmination of more than a decade of work. Ideas that only a few years earlier had commanded the support of only a handful of members of Congress now enjoyed overwhelming support.[43]

An extraordinary confluence of events had led to this remarkable development. Most important, countless African Americans throughout the South had set the stage by heroically standing up for their rights. The reaction of southern whites to the African American protests, especially in Birmingham, had created a sense of national outrage. The assassination of Kennedy, firm leadership by Johnson, Russell's mistaken belief that a filibuster could not be broken, the lobbying of religious and other pro–civil rights groups, and Dirksen's support for the legislation were also essential. Humphrey, though, could justly take pride in his considerable efforts. Several times during the debate the bill could have been lost or weakened severely, but Humphrey's organization, perseverance, and determination to keep the debate from becoming bitter were critical to the civil rights advocates' success. Political observers were quick to praise Humphrey. The civil rights struggle, columnist Walter Lippmann noted, had demonstrated that Humphrey was "the kind of statesmanlike politician without which our system of government does not work." Humphrey and Dirksen, he continued, had "worked in the best traditions of the Senate." Likewise, the *Washington Post* editorialized that America would "long and gratefully remember" Humphrey's role in guiding the bill through the Senate. Even the southerners acknowledged that Humphrey's leadership played a decisive role in achieving cloture and passing the bill. Indeed, Russell told Mitchell that Humphrey's patience and refusal to attack the southerners directly would help the South see its defeat as the result of a fair and honorable battle and thus help acceptance of the new law.[44]

The 1964 Civil Rights Act was a rare instance when politics and principle merged perfectly. Knowing that his side would lose if the southerners successfully labeled the legislation a "quota bill," Humphrey recognized that civil rights advocates had to mount an aggressive public relations campaign to define the debate as a moral issue over equal opportunity for all citizens, regardless of race. This was a winning political strategy, but it also represented liberalism's approach to racial matters. The issue of quotas and race consciousness had been debated frequently throughout the early 1950s regarding FEPC, and so too was it a critical part of the debate in 1964. Humphrey left a very clear record of how he felt about this matter. Like most Americans, he was unwilling to accept the ideas of compensatory justice or group rights. He had expressed opposition to making decisions based on race on numerous occasions during the debate, even when those decisions would ostensibly benefit African Americans. Whether one was considering employment, education, or public accommodations, race, in his view, should not be taken into account at all. In cases of discrimination the crucial issue was intent. Statistical disparities in the composition of a workforce or a student population in and of themselves would not prove discrimination, he believed. Humphrey felt so strongly about these matters that he inserted provisions into the law specifying that the aim of Congress was not to provide for busing or to grant "preferential treatment" to minorities regarding employment matters. These would become hotly contested issues in a few years, but in 1964 Humphrey and his allies, including leading civil rights organizations, sought a color-blind society. Racial progress, in his eyes, would come when race was eliminated from policy decisions and as a result of blacks continuing to advance in education. Humphrey's goal was to ensure equal opportunity, not equal results. He wanted blacks to advance socially and economically, to be sure, but he was staunchly opposed to the state trying to guarantee outcomes.[45]

Humphrey fully realized that Republican help was essential in getting the legislation through Congress, but he also expected that the Democrats would reap most of the political benefits. After all, the bill had become law while the Democrats were in control of the executive and legislative branches. Most whites supported it, and African Americans would continue to identify the Democrats as the party that protected their rights. George Wallace had appeared as a dark cloud on the horizon in the spring, but by summer he had largely faded from the national spotlight. The likely Republican presidential nominee, Senator Barry Goldwater of Arizona, was one of the few nonsoutherners to vote against the bill. The only potential problem lay in Dixie. Indeed, Johnson had commented to an aide that by signing the civil rights bill, he had "delivered the South to the Republican Party for a long time to come." The upcoming Democratic convention and fall campaign would test whether Humphrey's political optimism was warranted.[46]

6

Preserving the New Deal Coalition
The Politics of Race in 1964

I

The Civil Rights Act was aimed primarily at the South, but just two weeks after Johnson signed the bill racial issues in the urban North became the focus of national attention when an off-duty New York City police officer killed a sixteen-year-old African American boy who had allegedly threatened him with a knife. For five consecutive nights hundreds of African Americans, who believed that the officer had used excessive force, set fires, looted stores, and hurled assorted objects at police. The riot resulted in 150 injuries, 500 arrests, and damage to more than 600 businesses. Several days later, racial violence broke out in Rochester after police arrested a drunken individual. Officers used tear gas, dogs, and fire hoses to quell the disturbance, which led to 4 deaths, 350 injuries, 800 arrests, and more than one million dollars in property damage. Smaller incidents took place in three other cities a week later, and in early August racial violence engulfed several cities in northern New Jersey. The days of peaceful protests by African Americans had suddenly and dramatically ended.[1]

For Humphrey the riots signaled that the nation found itself in a "terrible dilemma." African Americans were rightfully demanding to be full participants in society and understandably weary of being told to be patient, but achieving economic equality would be lengthy and difficult. Humphrey echoed conservatives' denunciation of violence, but he went on to accuse those who talked only about law and order of demonstrating "the profoundest misunderstanding of the social and economic forces at work in this country." Insisting that there were "not enough policemen in the world to hold down a section of a city or of a nation that lives in misery and poverty, frustration, hopelessness, sickness, and illiteracy," Humphrey argued that the riots resulted from material, not moral, deprivation. "Riots seldom take place in communities where unemployment is virtually non-existent, where families live in clean and spacious homes, where the level of education among adults and children is high, and where persons enjoy the opportunity to succeed or fail on the basis of their capabilities and initiative," he maintained. "We do not find many participants in the good life of mid-century America taking to the street in a spirit of hate, frustration, and vengeance. This is one of life's simple truths which some persons choose conveniently to ignore." Suggesting that new federal action was urgently needed because discrimination and structural changes in the economy had created an especially combustible situation that would only worsen, Humphrey believed that no one should have been surprised that bleak conditions had produced violence.[2]

But many whites were surprised, angry, and fearful. In San Francisco thousands of residents eager to discuss racial issues jammed the phone lines at a television station. Sheriff's deputies in Columbus practiced riot control by hurling plastic "bricks" at each other, while in Chicago housewives canceled trips to the Lincoln Park Zoo out of fear of being attacked by African Americans. One poll found that 87 percent of the public thought the riots had hurt the cause of civil rights. As far as many northern whites were concerned, African Americans in the North had nothing to be upset about because racism was a southern problem.[3]

Political commentators saw such developments as evidence of a small but growing "backlash" against the civil rights movement and forecast political trouble for the Democrats. The backlash would be "the overriding domestic issue of the election year," one popular magazine contended. Another called race "the most emotionally explosive domestic issue" of the fall campaign. "If violence continues," still another publication predicted, "anything can happen in the election." Johnson's lead over Republican presidential nominee Barry Goldwater had shrunk from fifty-nine percentage points in June to twenty-eight percentage points by August. That still left the president with a commanding edge, but the size of the drop in so short a time must have concerned him. Part of Goldwater's tremendous jump was no doubt due to the traditional boost that presidential challengers receive following their convention, yet it stemmed also from his strong denunciations of crime. Further rioting, therefore, portended trouble for the Democrats.[4]

In June the nation had seemed to be on the verge of forging a consensus behind civil rights, but now racial politics had grown considerably more complicated. Goldwater's triumph represented a shocking defeat for the liberal wing of the GOP, which played an important role in the enactment of the 1964 Civil Rights Act. Though Goldwater and Johnson met in July and pledged to refrain from using racial appeals to win votes, Humphrey worried that the Republican nominee might receive the backing of blue-collar whites in the urban North who felt encroached upon by a surging African American population and mistakenly believed that the Civil Rights Act would force businesses to replace whites with blacks. Humphrey admitted that this opposition to civil rights constituted "one of the really difficult problems" for his party, but, ever the optimist, he predicted that union members' concern over the economy and national security would keep them in the Democratic column that November.[5]

The riots also raised questions about Humphrey's political future. With an eye on occupying the Oval Office someday, he had been consulting with aides since January about how to become Johnson's running mate. Before the riots Humphrey had reason to be optimistic that Johnson would select him. He had demonstrated his leadership abilities in getting the Civil Rights Act through Congress, and several polls indicated that he was the first choice of numerous Democratic officials and delegates. Johnson, moreover, had sent signals that Humphrey was a strong contender. But racial violence led Humphrey to worry that the president might opt for someone less closely identified with civil rights. Several days after the New York riot he instructed his staff to lobby administration officials on his behalf and compile evidence on the advisability of choosing a pro–civil rights running mate. Meanwhile, anxious southern Democrats were launching a vigorous stop-Humphrey drive. White resentment against the Civil Rights Act gave the Republican nominee a 51–40 edge in the South according to one August poll. Having written off the East as too liberal, Goldwater needed to build on recent Republican gains in Dixie if he were to have any chance of victory. "We're in trouble, and Humphrey would make it worse," one southern official complained. "I just don't know what the president is thinking about. Man, we've had enough of these liberals to last a spell." To counter this campaign, Humphrey urged southern allies such as *Atlanta Constitution* editor Ralph McGill to spread the word about Goldwater's opposition to dozens of federal programs that had helped modernize the region. These efforts bore little fruit. A week before the Democratic convention, Humphrey had no support in the Deep South and only a trace in other southern states.[6]

The politics of race threatened Humphrey's chances in still another way. In April African Americans and liberal whites in Mississippi had formed the Mississippi Freedom Democratic Party (MFDP) and announced they would challenge the seating of the state's regular delegation at the convention on grounds that it was not loyal to the Democratic ticket and systematically excluded African Americans from participating in the political process. The MFDP thought it had an airtight case. When African Americans had tried to attend precinct meetings in June, they often found them canceled or were denied entry outright. The regular party passed resolutions that denounced the Civil Rights Act and urged the separation of the races when it held its annual convention a month later. Nearly all regular delegates, including the governor, would almost certainly back Goldwater. The MFDP, which firmly supported Johnson, met in early August and elected sixty-eight delegates, four of whom were white, to represent the Magnolia State in Atlantic City. Many white southerners, meanwhile, renewed the old threat of bolting the convention if the party backed the MFDP. With many leading southern politicians already intending to skip the convention out of anger over the Civil Rights Act, a walkout of southern delegates would likely mean a complete surrender of Dixie to Goldwater. The MFDP, therefore, threatened to undermine two things that Johnson badly wanted—a harmonious convention and a landslide victory in the fall.[7]

Humphrey slowly became embroiled in the MFDP controversy. His close friend and ally in 1948, liberal attorney Joseph Rauh, was the party's chief counsel. Rauh needed just 11 votes from the 110-member Credentials Committee and the support of 8 states to force a roll call on the issue. He expected to win once the matter went to the convention floor. By early August Rauh had persuaded 9 northern states, including New York, Michigan, and California, that the frequent violence in Mississippi warranted their support of the MFDP. The attorney's initial success worried the White House. An administration official who also was a friend of Humphrey's called the senator on August 12 and informed him he would not be vice president unless Rauh were stopped. Humphrey's aides immediately relayed the message to the attorney, who resolved to press ahead even though he too wanted Humphrey on the ticket. Likewise, UAW chief Walter Reuther was warning Rauh, who also was the union's chief counsel, that he would have Humphrey's "blood on his conscience" if he did not accede to Johnson's wishes.[8]

Humphrey telephoned Rauh the next afternoon after making an appeal to the Credentials Committee to seat both delegations. Rauh advised his friend that getting involved in the MFDP fight would be "stupid," and Humphrey agreed to stay out of it. He did not remain on the sidelines for long. On August 14 Humphrey concluded that seating both delegations would be a good compromise. (This had been done with two rival Texas delegations, one of which included a young Lyndon Johnson, in 1944.) Humphrey then called the chair of the Credentials Committee, who supported the plan. The administration promptly rejected it. The president summoned Humphrey to the White House on August 18 and instructed him to convince the MFDP to back down. From Johnson's perspective, Humphrey's liberal credentials and personal ties to Rauh and others involved in the fight made him the perfect choice to quell the rebellion. Humphrey, meanwhile, still did not know whether he would be Johnson's running mate, and thus he had every reason to suspect that the outcome of the MFDP issue would go a long way toward determining his fate. With the convention only a few days away, Humphrey had little time to act. He conferred with Rauh regularly in hopes of persuading his friend to drop out of the battle. If he resigned as chief counsel, Rauh told Humphrey, Communists would step in and only make things worse for the president. Clearly, the tense situation made both men uncomfortable, for the former allies were now working for very different purposes. Despite numerous conversations between the pair over several days, the stalemate continued.[9]

On Saturday, August 22, two days before the convention officially opened, the MFDP controversy intensified when each side argued its case before the Credentials Committee and a national television audience. The regular Democratic Party in Mississippi insisted that it was the only legitimate party because the national party recognized federal and state officials elected on its ticket. The MFDP, the spokesman for the regulars claimed, was not a legal political party because it had not met all the requirements under Mississippi law, such as holding conventions in every county. The regulars also charged that the MFDP enjoyed support among Communists and denied that blacks were forbidden from participating in Democratic activities. The pro-MFDP forces offered a powerful rebuttal. "Are we for the oppressor or the oppressed?" Rauh bluntly asked the committee after chronicling the blatant discrimination suffered by African Americans in the Magnolia Sate. A former sharecropper then provided the afternoon's most dramatic moment. After telling how she had been fired from her job for trying to register to vote and brutally beaten in jail by African American prisoners on orders from their white captors, Fannie Lou Hamer poignantly wondered, "Is this America, the land of the free and the home of the brave, where we are threatened daily because we want to live as decent human beings?" The president, who had ordered FBI surveillance of MFDP activities in Atlantic City, was outraged that the MFDP was disrupting one of the most important events of his career. He hastily called a press conference to divert attention from Hamer's moving testimony, but the networks rebroadcast it that night. Afterward the Western Union office in Atlantic City reported that an "avalanche" of pro-MFDP had poured in from around the country.[10]

Humphrey, meanwhile, dictated a revealing letter that evening to his close friend Eugenie Anderson, a Minnesota native who had been a part of the 1948 convention challenge and was now in Europe. The political situation, he stressed, was especially volatile. Humphrey expected a Democratic victory in the fall, but he warned Anderson that the campaign would be a "hard fought" effort that would "literally . . . shake the foundations of the Republic" as a result of "the noises that will be made from some very irresponsible forces" on the right. To Humphrey the Goldwaterites were "almost fanatical." Like many other Democrats, Humphrey sincerely believed that Goldwater represented a new and dangerous force in American politics. Though the Arizona senator was no bigot, his vote against the Civil Rights Act struck Humphrey as a dangerous omen if the Republican were elected. The Democrats had to be very careful how they approached racial issues, Humphrey asserted, and thus it was time to consolidate recent gains regarding racial justice rather than press ahead with new initiatives. "We always have people who want to go a little bit further than it seems possible to go at the moment." he observed. "I suppose one shouldn't be critical because I too have done the same. But in this instance when we have done so much in the field of Civil Rights, and we have so many problems in our great cities due to racial tensions, it seems to me that we ought to let well enough alone and let what we have done sink in and to be digested."[11]

As the convention opened, the administration offered to settle the Mississippi controversy by requiring the regulars to pledge their loyalty to the ticket, giving the MFDP seating but no voting privileges, and promising to investigate the problem of segregated delegations. In the Credentials Committee meeting on Sunday a representative from Oregon modified this slightly by suggesting that the MFDP be granted two votes. When the Credentials Committee could not reach a solution, one of its members, Walter Mondale, the attorney general from Minnesota and a Humphrey protégé, suggested that a five-member subcommittee be formed to study the problem. The committee agreed. Rauh pleaded with Humphrey that night for the administration to give his clients more than just guest tickets, a solution the MFDP rightly viewed as a "back of the bus" slap in the face. Though they talked well into the early morning hours, the pair failed to break the impasse because Humphrey had no authority to negotiate for the administration. He was nothing more than an intermediary whose job was to persuade the MFDP to accept the administration's plan.[12]

The search for an answer continued on Monday, August 24, the opening day of the convention. Meeting in his hotel room that afternoon with Rauh, Mondale, Martin Luther King, several members of the Credentials Committee, and a handful of representatives from the MFDP, Humphrey pushed the administration plan of seating the regular Mississippi delegation and making the MFDP guests of the convention. Edith Green, a pro-MFDP member of the Credentials Committee, again raised her idea of seating those members of either delegation who were willing to take a loyalty oath to the Democratic Party. Knowing that Johnson would never approve such a proposal because it gave legal recognition to the MFDP, Humphrey opposed it. The compromise, Humphrey told the MFDP, would enable him to become vice president. He then outlined all the things he would do to benefit African Americans when in power. Fannie Lou Hamer was not persuaded. "Well, Mr. Humphrey, do you mean to tell me that your position is more important to you than four hundred thousand black people's lives?" she pointedly asked. Humphrey gave an evasive answer. "Senator Humphrey," she continued, "I lost my job on a plantation in Sunflower County, but I think I did what was right, and God's taking care of me. And Senator Humphrey, if you do these things you will become vice president, but you will never be free to do the good things you're telling us about." Humphrey shook his head. Hamer went on, "Senator Humphrey, I'm going to pray to Jesus for you." The meeting ended later that day without any progress. Hamer's powerful testimony had so unnerved Humphrey that he resolved to exclude her from all future discussions. He had a tremendous amount of sympathy for the suffering the MFDP had endured, but now his chief goals remained the vice presidential nomination and party harmony.[13]

The convention began Monday night without a delegation from Mississippi on the floor. Humphrey arranged for the MFDP to have tickets in the public gallery for the opening session after the Credentials Committee had decided that afternoon to postpone a decision on the MFDP matter until Tuesday. The regular delegates were offered the same seating, but they refused. Rauh went to Humphrey's room that night to discuss the MFDP issue. The attorney wondered if Humphrey had heard anything about the vice presidency, but he reported that he had not. The MFDP affair and the uncertainty over his political future were taking a heavy emotional toll on Humphrey. "At this stage, honestly, I'm so tired of it, I honestly don't care anymore," he confessed. "I'm so tired of it all and I'm never at ease." Though the two talked well into the night, Humphrey reported that the administration would not budge.[14]

The search for an answer continued on Tuesday. Humphrey had breakfast that morning with Mondale, DNC leader David Lawrence, Walter Reuther, whom Johnson had summoned to Atlantic City in the middle of the night, and representatives of the MFDP. The MFDP's refusal to accept the earlier plan led the administration to slightly sweeten its offer: two members of the MFDP (who would be selected by the administration) would be seated and given voting privileges as at-large delegates; the other MFDP delegates would be classified as guests of the convention and not be allowed to vote; only the regulars who promised to support the Democratic ticket would be seated; a committee would be named to ensure that all future delegations were chosen without respect to race. This struck the administration as a way of acknowledging the moral power of the MFDP's case without producing a southern walkout. Like many at the convention, Humphrey viewed the MFDP as a protest organization, not a full-fledged political party. The MFDP would presumably be happy to receive the two seats and the pledge to prevent segregated delegations in the future. Humphrey asked Mondale if his subcommittee would agree to it. Mondale thought his group would.[15]

Martin Luther King, Bayard Rustin, and several other civil rights leaders urged the MFDP to take the offer, but the group flatly rejected it. The seating of both delegations or the Green proposal were the only compromises acceptable to the MFDP. The new plan's preselection of the two delegates (Aaron Henry, the African American head of the MFDP, and Ed King, a white clergyman) infuriated the MFDP as too domineering. Civil rights activist Bob Moses demanded that more than one black from the Magnolia State be seated. Humphrey replied that he thought the aim was not representation based on race but rather the end of discrimination. The choice of Henry and King, he argued, symbolized the goal of an interracial Democratic Party in Mississippi. Moses responded that he did not think that any of the regulars, whom he regarded as little more than a band of racists, should be allowed to be seated and thus represent him. Reuther then berated Moses for his obstinacy and reminded him of the UAW's considerable financial backing of civil rights organizations, but yet another meeting ended without a solution.[16]

Rauh, meanwhile, was pleading Humphrey's case to the MFDP delegates who had gathered at a nearby church. At the two o'clock meeting of the Credentials Committee, the attorney told them, he expected to be made an offer. He claimed to know only that something was in the works, not the specifics of any proposal. Rauh then appealed for racial tolerance in general and sympathy for Humphrey. If the MFDP refused to accept the compromise, he asserted, Johnson would choose someone less sympathetic to racial justice as his running mate. After Rauh had finished, Ella Baker offered a stinging rebuttal that summed up the feelings of many in the MFDP. "I don't care about traitors like Humphrey deserting their liberal [friends]," she thundered.[17]

Everything came to a head that afternoon. While the Mondale subcommittee presented the final compromise to the Credentials Committee, Humphrey conferred in his hotel suite with Reuther, Martin Luther King, and several members of the MFDP. Ed King wondered if the MFDP could fill in seats under the Mississippi standard if the regulars went home. Humphrey replied that they could not, for under the unit rule a single regular delegate could cast all of Mississippi's votes. Pointing out that the MFDP was livid at being told who its delegates would be, Ed King then suggested that the two seats be split into four half-seats, with the MFDP choosing whomever it wished to fill them. Because this likely meant that Fannie Lou Hamer would be a delegate, Humphrey immediately squelched the proposal. "We will tell you who your spokespersons are," he imperiously informed King. "You cannot change this compromise because Lyndon Johnson has said Fannie Lou Hamer will never speak at a Democratic Party convention." The president, Humphrey added, considered Hamer to be "illiterate." Infuriated at this cruel characterization of Hamer, Moses called Humphrey a racist. Humphrey beat a hasty retreat, saying that Johnson felt this way, not him. Nevertheless, Humphrey's unease with Hamer quickly became apparent. Surely, he argued, the MFDP had someone who would conduct him/herself better than Hamer supposedly would. The MFDP still refused to go along with the administration. Group leaders asked Humphrey if they could talk over matters with their delegates for an hour or so. Thinking that was a reasonable idea, Humphrey agreed. He then lobbied Moses to urge the MFDP to accept the proposal. Moses promised only that the party would discuss the situation. The door seemed open, albeit just a crack, for a resolution of the crisis.[18]

That door slammed shut a few minutes later. Just as Humphrey was about to agree to an hour-long break so that the MFDP could debate matters further, an aide rushed into the room and told Humphrey to turn on the television. Humphrey quickly rolled the set in. Everyone in the room sat motionless as a newscaster announced that the Credentials Committee had unanimously adopted the two-seat compromise. Humphrey could not believe what he was seeing. He thought there was still time to talk, but now he realized he had been used by the administration to stall the MFDP that afternoon while it ensured that the Credentials Committee accepted the compromise. Moses suspected that Humphrey had known all along what was going on. "You cheated!" Moses screamed at Humphrey as he stormed out of the room. The meeting abruptly adjourned.[19]

Though the convention roared its approval of the two-seat compromise Tuesday night, neither of the chief participants in the fight was satisfied. The MFDP had rejected the proposal that afternoon, and the regular delegation, which considered the loyalty oath an insult, left the convention that night. Another attempt was made to persuade the MFDP the following morning. Martin Luther King informed the delegates that Humphrey had promised him "a new day in Mississippi" if the MFDP accepted the compromise. Humphrey, King noted, had pledged that there would be, among other things, Civil Rights Commission hearings in the Magnolia State and an end to segregation in the Democratic Party. Following several hours of discussion, the MFDP rejected the compromise again. The two seats amounted to little more than tokenism. Hamer expressed the feelings of many MFDP members when she observed, "We didn't come all this way for no two seats."[20]

Ultimately, the MFDP fight boiled down to two conflicting and irreconcilable visions of racial progress. Humphrey saw politics as fundamentally about making deals that resulted in incremental change. He considered the offer of two at-large votes, which was unprecedented for the Democrats, as another step, albeit a small one, in the long march toward racial justice. More important, the Democratic Party had given its word to make things even better in 1968. Humphrey saw no reason why the MFDP should doubt the party's commitment. But the MFDP's experiences with politicians in Mississippi had been marked by lies, deception, and lawbreaking. MFDP members rightly considered the selection by the Johnson administration of their two representatives as yet another unjust denial of their political self-determination. Moreover, the promise of integrated delegations at future conventions rang hollow. Eager to preserve the New Deal coalition, the Democratic Party had refused to bar the seating of racist and disloyal southern whites since the 1950s. Because the Democrats were unwilling to provoke a full-scale rebellion among white southerners in 1964, the MFDP had no reason to think that the party would do so four years down the road. Furthermore, a change in the rules, even if it did occur, would likely mean few black delegates from the Magnolia State because there were few African Americans registered to vote in the South. Humphrey woefully underestimated how the enormous suffering endured by the MFDP delegates had created an intense desire that long overdue rights be granted immediately, not in 1968. The Green compromise represented a fair solution that had precedent in party history, but once Johnson had rejected it Humphrey, who had been bitten by the vice presidential bug, chose to follow the president rather than join the insurgents. The ultimate responsibility for the MFDP debacle belongs on Johnson's shoulders, but it is clear that Humphrey was an accomplice, albeit a sometimes unwitting one, in one of post–World War II liberalism's greatest moral failures. The convention, many MFDP members concluded, proved that white liberals such as Humphrey valued personal political gain more than racial justice. MFDP delegates, including Hamer and Ed King, had come to the convention thinking of him as an ally. They left wondering if the political system was so mired in compromise and backroom deals with racists that even someone like him could not be trusted. To be sure, Humphrey had severely damaged his credibility among many African Americans, but it would be a mistake to see the MFDP settlement as only a grave setback for racial justice. The promised commission to investigate racism in state parties did materialize in 1967. More important, it initiated significant reforms that helped open up the Democratic Party across the South to African Americans in the late 1960s and early 1970s.[21]

Many in the MFDP (as well as many scholars who have looked at this controversy) believed that Humphrey's position in Atlantic City stemmed solely from his political self-interest. There is no denying that Humphrey badly wanted to be vice president and that this desire influenced his thinking at the convention. But to suggest that personal gain fully explains Humphrey's approach to the MFDP affair grossly oversimplifies matters. As the letter to Anderson suggests, Humphrey was genuinely concerned over what conservative control of the Republican Party might mean for civil rights. His worry was not simply a rationalization for opposing the MFDP. He thought that Goldwater and the riots posed a political hazard for his party and the cause of racial justice. It is thus not surprising that Humphrey wanted unity. In retrospect it is clear that Humphrey greatly overestimated the threat Goldwater posed, but there was more on his mind than his political future.[22]

Not only had the MFDP affair been settled by the Credentials Committee on Tuesday, but so too was the matter of Johnson's running mate. Sometime during Humphrey's discussions with MFDP leaders, James Rowe, after spending forty-five minutes trying to get past the guards outside Humphrey's suite, was finally able to speak with the senator. "You're it," Rowe said simply. He then swore Humphrey to secrecy, even from Muriel. Humphrey, who had been anxious throughout the convention over rumors that the president was considering other candidates, was greatly relieved. He flew to Washington on Wednesday afternoon with Senator Thomas Dodd, whose presence left Humphrey wondering if the president were about to change his mind at the last minute. Johnson called Humphrey into the Oval Office shortly after five o'clock and told him that Dodd was just a diversion for the press. The vice president, Johnson warned, would have to be completely loyal. "You can trust me," Humphrey dutifully replied.[23]

The pair traveled to the convention hall late that evening, and delegates cheered wildly when the president announced his selection. Alabama tried to lead a southern rebellion, but the effort never got off the ground. The Minnesota delegation proudly placed Humphrey's name in nomination.

Hoping to demonstrate sectional unity, the president had arranged to have Senators George Smathers of Florida and Olin Johnston of South Carolina second Humphrey's nomination. Once the delegates had roared their approval in a voice vote at 12:30 Thursday morning, the world's largest pipe organ promptly filled the cavernous hall with the University of Minnesota fight song and "Happy Days Are Here Again." Standing on the rostrum with the president, Muriel, and his children, Humphrey savored the exhilaration of the moment.[24]

Though numerous southern Democrats had grown to like and respect Humphrey, many had trouble with the idea of him as their party's vice presidential candidate. "We realize Humphrey is a brilliant man, but he has a long civil rights identification that won't help us here," a South Carolina official observed before Johnson had revealed his choice. Most southern Democratic leaders grudgingly accepted Humphrey once he was selected, but, fearing that the senator's identification with racial equality would not go over well in Dixie, they immediately sought to downplay the race issue. Economic matters, one Tennessee official forecast, would dominate the campaign, and Humphrey presented no problem because he had "voted in the FDR tradition that was good for the South." Likewise, another southern leader predicted that Humphrey's "record of being interested in education, farms, and other things that benefited the South will help." A drive to sell Humphrey to the South began Thursday afternoon, when he received a standing ovation from the Georgia delegation, after Governor Carl Sanders had cited his support for farmers and blue-collar workers. Humphrey told the delegates that he would campaign in the South, but he clearly indicated that he wanted to shift the debate away from civil rights. "I want to . . . talk to your farmers and show them the blank pages of the opposition," he told the cheering delegates.[25]

Humphrey offered another signal that race would take a secondary role during the fall campaign when he gave his acceptance speech. Goldwater, Humphrey asserted, was one of the "shrill voices" who had "kidnapped" the GOP and turned it into "the party of stridency, of unrestrained passion . . . of bitter and partisan philosophy." Humphrey chiefly used civil rights to paint Goldwater as being out of step with his party and the vast majority of Americans. "Most Democrats and most Republicans in the United States Senate, in fact, over four-fifths of the members of his own party—voted for the Civil Rights Act of 1964," Humphrey pointed out. "But not Senator Goldwater!" Though he called upon the nation to join the president's quest to "end the shame of poverty, to end the injustice of prejudice and the denial of opportunity," Humphrey offered little regarding the festering problem of race relations in the urban North or the continuing difficulties in the South.[26]

II

The Democrats' Solid South, which had shown signs of cracking since 1948, appeared to be on the verge of crumbling altogether that fall. Polls showed that Goldwater would probably win Mississippi and Alabama, and reports from Georgia indicated that he might triumph there too. Secretary of Commerce Luther Hodges speculated that "civil rights trouble" would cost the Democrats his home state of North Carolina. Florida and Virginia were widely regarded as likely to go Republican, while Tennessee, South Carolina, and Louisiana were up for grabs. The president's home state of Texas was the only member of the former Confederacy safely in the Democratic column.[27]

Several days after the convention, Humphrey traveled to Johnson's ranch to plot strategy. His task would be to convince southern whites to vote their wallets rather than their racial animosities. "Now, I want you to head right for the South," the president instructed. "Talk about farms and farming. Don't preach. Just let them see you and make up their own minds that you don't have any horns. We'll win the South." A few days later, Humphrey revealed that five southern Democratic leaders had urged him to come to their states and that a "significant" part of his campaign would be spent in Dixie. Declaring that he might even visit Alabama and Mississippi, Humphrey insisted that the press had "overstated" the "problem" of his relationship to the South. "The civil rights law is an accomplished fact," he commented. "My record in the fields of farm price supports, rural electrification, TVA, farm credit, rivers and harbors appropriations—things that have meant so much to the South—will stand the closest scrutiny. It is a record of friendliness." Noting that he was "anxious to get to know the people of the South much better," Humphrey privately forecast that "when we get acquainted... the number one news story of this campaign will be my new relationship and affection with the South."[28]

The vice presidential nominee implemented Johnson's strategy on his initial foray into Dixie a few weeks later. His first stop was Wichita Falls, Texas. Given Johnson's extensive ties in the Lone Star State, it was a safe place to begin. After a nervous opening, Humphrey stressed to the small crowd that the nation had common problems and goals even though the press emphasized racial and sectional divisions. He then traveled to Arkansas, where he initially received a cool welcome at a Rural Electrification Administration office. When he suggested that Goldwater would end farm programs that had greatly helped cotton growers, however, the crowd gave him a standing ovation. The closest Humphrey came to discussing civil rights was to say simply that there should be "opportunity for all." Preferring to talk of how Democratic programs had contributed to the state's economic development, he quickly brushed aside reporters' questions about his opinion of Governor Orval Faubus's conservative stand on segregation by noting, "I didn't come down here to get into a squabble with the governor." The next stop was Houston, where Humphrey again asserted that the Democrats were the true friends of the farmer. Southerners, he indicated, would recognize what Democratic programs had meant to them and resist Goldwater's invitation to join the GOP.[29]

Humphrey continued these themes during another brief swing through the South ten days later. He praised Memphis for its peaceful and quick compliance with the 1964 Civil Rights Act, but he saved his strongest rhetoric for Goldwater's agricultural policies. A Republican victory, Humphrey warned, would cost the South three billion dollars a year and leave one in five farmers with "no income at all." The audience showered Humphrey with enthusiastic applause. The vice presidential nominee then traveled to Georgia, which was another relatively safe state for him to visit because Governor Sanders firmly supported Johnson. Nevertheless, the reception Humphrey received in the tiny cotton town of Moultrie hardly lived up to the South's reputation for hospitality. Many in the crowd carried Goldwater signs, booed lustily, and called Humphrey a "communist." Visibly upset, Humphrey told Sanders that he had "better do something about this." After a delay of several minutes, he gave a short speech and left. Humphrey mentioned the race issue at his second stop in Tifton, but only to accuse Goldwater of hypocrisy. The Republican nominee was using race to win the votes of southern whites, Humphrey informed the audience, but in the North the Republican Party had prepared a pamphlet touting Goldwater as pro–civil rights. "You know about us [Democrats], even if some of you don't like what you know," Humphrey said. Once again, farm issues occupied center stage as Humphrey blasted Goldwater's opposition to food for peace, farm price supports, and the Rural Electrification Administration. Humphrey carried these themes to excess at a Jefferson-Jackson Day dinner in Atlanta when he claimed that Goldwater would "turn out the lights in the countryside" and force farmers off their land "to root hog or die in the cities."[30]

Despite the warm reception Humphrey had received in several places, many southern politicians still viewed him as a political liability. Faubus, who was up for reelection, claimed he could not appear with Humphrey because he was "sick." Richard Russell was so unhappy with the selection of Humphrey and the Democrats' stand on civil rights that he did little to help the ticket in his home state and even refused Lady Bird Johnson's invitations to join her train tour of the South. Louisiana Democrats avoided mentioning Humphrey in campaign literature so as not to hurt Johnson and local candidates, while Democrats in North Carolina waved off visits from the vice presidential nominee. Likewise, the Democratic gubernatorial candidate in Florida did not want Humphrey to come to the Sunshine State.[31]

Humphrey's problems stemmed primarily from long held animosities, but they also arose because of Republicans' use of the civil rights issue to score points among southern whites. Senator Strom Thurmond of South Carolina, who had recently converted to the GOP, proclaimed himself part of a "truth squad" and followed Humphrey across the South. Humphrey, Thurmond later remarked, was the "ultimate" choice in extremism. The racial implications were clear. Republican organizers made headway among rural and small-town whites by spreading false rumors that the Civil Rights Act would lead to the loss of their jobs in textile plants and telling small business owners that the law would flood their establishments with African American customers. "There is a general feeling," an administration official noted after watching Humphrey in Georgia, "that [he] stimulates far more bad memories than good ones among Southerners and that he perhaps ought to work elsewhere in the future." The White House apparently agreed. Aside from a brief return later that month to two relatively safe border states, Tennessee and Kentucky, Humphrey stayed out of the South for the rest of the campaign. Humphrey's effort to shift the spotlight from race to economics had largely failed. The new relationship that Humphrey had hoped to forge with white southerners would not materialize that fall. Indeed, it would never develop.[32]

Numerous signs pointed to potential trouble for the Democrats in the North too. George Wallace's surprise showing in three primaries during the spring had revealed strong anti–civil rights beliefs among many whites that had only intensified during the year. Fair housing measures went down to defeat in Berkeley, Seattle, Detroit, and the Illinois state legislature. Four out of five members of the School Committee in Boston easily won reelection after basing their campaigns on opposition to integrated schools. Several union leaders feared defections of the rank-and-file to the GOP. One nervously remarked that the political situation reminded him of 1946 and 1948, when voters had proved nearly all the pundits wrong. In August Secretary of Commerce Luther Hodges had reported to Johnson that union members were "turning in disturbingly great numbers to Goldwater" out of fear that the Civil Rights Act would take their jobs and give them to African Americans. Twenty-six Democratic governors, Hodges continued, had indicated that the backlash existed in their states. Similarly, one governor wrote the president that the backlash stemmed from whites' concern that they would be discriminated against in future employment decisions and their perception that those who rioted or broke other laws were not being punished.[33]

Well aware that Humphrey had long enjoyed strong support from union members, Johnson sent him to the industrial North during the early campaign. In Youngstown, an area reputed to be a stronghold of white backlash, Humphrey reassured voters that the Civil Rights Act would not cause white workers to lose their jobs. The new law, he told a crowd at another Ohio stop, "was morally right, spiritually right, politically right, and economically right." Rather than discuss civil rights at length, however, Humphrey stressed the issue of war and peace. Goldwater could not be trusted with nuclear weapons, he repeatedly charged. Humphrey believed this, but his emphasis on foreign policy matters was no doubt meant in part to keep voters' minds off of racial matters.[34]

Goldwater, though, continued to seek support among blue-collar whites by demanding law and order, linking liberal welfare policies with crime and other urban violence, and lambasting the Civil Rights Act as a misguided attempt to legislate morality. "Choose the way of this present administration," the Republican nominee charged, "and you have the way of the mobs in the streets, restrained only by the plea that they wait until after the election to ignite the violence again." Though he had not mentioned civil rights groups or leaders by name, this was an unmistakable reference to an agreement by the NAACP, the Urban League, SCLC, and other organizations to refrain from demonstrations until after the election. Similarly, Goldwater insisted that those "who broke the law have found loud champions, eager investigators, and nearly fanatic apologists" in the Johnson administration.[35]

Humphrey initially tried to avoid the question of connections between race and crime altogether, but he could not do so for long. "The best thing that could be done would be to quit playing politics with the issue of human rights and the whole issue of civil disobedience," he stated. Goldwater, Humphrey declared before a Denver audience, was doing "a disservice to national unity and national understanding" by highlighting increases in crime. Pointing out that most white and black Americans were law-abiding people, Humphrey contended that violence was caused by "hoodlums, dope addicts, Communists, Klu Kluxers, and their ilk." Whites' concern over dramatic increases in lawlessness during the mid-1960s involved far more than racism, but race was nonetheless a significant part of their worry because crime had gone up in many African American neighborhoods. Though Goldwater's persistent criticism of the administration never put Johnson in danger of losing the election, it did threaten to undermine the broad support the president desperately wanted for his Great Society programs. Humphrey reassured voters that the Democrats would not tolerate violence, but he also tried to convince them that the answer to crime also involved a commitment to eradicating poverty. He spoke at length to a crowd in New Mexico about the growing unemployment rate among African American youth as potentially causing "great trouble" and pledged that the Johnson administration would assist state and local governments in keeping the peace. The Democrats would insist on adequate police protection for all citizens yet fight for social justice too, he told a television audience. Nevertheless, Goldwater's attacks had gotten under Humphrey's skin. At a stop in Evansville, which had given strong support to Wallace in the spring, he charged that Goldwater's opposition to the Civil Rights Act, not liberal permissiveness, constituted an "invitation to disorder and lawlessness."[36]

Humphrey also had to navigate the increasingly perilous waters of school integration in the North, where the issue was not de jure segregation but rather segregation rooted in housing patterns. Emboldened by the civil rights struggle in the South, African Americans in many northern cities were demanding integrated schools. Whites' fierce determination to maintain the status quo manifested itself most dramatically in New York City, where a two-day boycott, which had been called to protest an integration plan that involved busing students to achieve racial balance, resulted in a seventeen percentage point increase in absent students when schools opened in mid-September. Goldwater had strongly denounced busing. On the other hand, busing presented Humphrey and the Democrats with a thorny dilemma. To favor it meant risking the loss of political support among northern whites, who valued their neighborhood schools. (Many blacks were against busing for the same reason.) Conversely, to oppose busing would validate the long-standing claim of southern Democrats that northern liberals were hypocrites and, more important, perpetuate the de facto segregation of the North that had left tens of thousands of African Americans in clearly inferior schools. A few days after the New York boycott, reporters asked Humphrey where he stood regarding busing. The vice presidential nominee voiced his opposition and pointed out that the Civil Rights Act contained a specific antibusing provision. "I think the best thing to do is to build good neighborhoods," he observed. Humphrey then added, without any apparent sense of irony, "I don't want the federal government to be messing into this thing. . . . I think it ought to be handled locally."[37]

The question of liberal hypocrisy arose again several days later, when Republican vice presidential nominee William Miller, a conservative congressman from upstate New York, charged that Humphrey's Maryland home had a restrictive covenant in the deed. When reporters asked about the racial exclusion, Humphrey remarked that he had only learned of it when auditors had recently prepared a financial statement. The covenant, he pointed out, was not legally binding because of the 1948 Supreme Court decision outlawing such provisions. Humphrey indicated that he found the clause "distasteful" and "onerous" and thus felt no moral obligation to honor it. Republican attempts to embarrass Humphrey came to naught as the issue quickly disappeared.[38]

The failure of the covenant matter to catch fire with voters symbolized what was happening to the race issue in general by early October. The white backlash, which had dominated headlines during the summer, had subsided. There had been no instances of large-scale racial violence in either the North or the South since August. More important, the Democrats' strategy of painting Goldwater as a radical, especially regarding questions of war and peace, was working beautifully. White voters had not forgotten their racial animosities, of course, but, as Johnson and Humphrey had hoped, they were focusing on international issues more than racial tensions. A Gallup Poll found the Democratic ticket running well ahead of the Republicans in all regions but the South. Nationally, the Democrats were ahead 62–32, and they had even made up ground in Dixie, where the race was virtually a dead heat.[39]

Goldwater attempted to bring the race issue back into view during the final two weeks of the campaign. Declaring that "forced integration is just as wrong as forced segregation," he denounced busing as a "morally wrong" example of "doctrinaire and misguided equalitarianism" and demanded that the law protect "free association." The proper role of government was "to preserve a free society," not "to establish a segregated society nor to establish an integrated society." He continued these themes a week later at Madison Square Garden, where he lambasted busing as "a futile exercise in sociology that will accomplish nothing—but lose much." With Strom Thurmond at his side, the Republican nominee delivered his most stinging anti–civil rights rhetoric of the campaign during a speech at Columbia, South Carolina, that was televised by eighty-seven stations in fourteen southern states. "One thing that will surely poison and embitter our relations with each other," he asserted, "is the idea that some sort of pre-determined bureaucratic schedule of equality, and worst of all, a schedule based on racial quotas, must be imposed as the goal of the misnamed 'great society.' "[40]

As the contest neared its conclusion, Humphrey chose not to rebut Goldwater directly on the finer points of quotas, busing, or anything else related to civil rights even though the Republican had greatly distorted the Democrats' views. With the Johnson-Humphrey ticket well in front, there was no compelling political reason to change course. Holding to his strategy of trying to paint the Republican nominee as an extremist, Humphrey described Goldwater as "America's number one radical" and "the temporary spokesman of a faction of reaction." When Humphrey did touch on civil rights, he did so only vaguely in hopes of further marginalizing the Republican nominee. Goldwater was "unworthy" of being president because he had "repudiated the principles of Abraham Lincoln and his party." Similarly, Humphrey told a Kentucky crowd that political candidates should not make racial distinctions because America was "one nation, indivisible," while in Virginia he condemned the Republicans for defeating an antiextremist plank at their convention and refusing to condemn the John Birch Society. "The Goldwater party," Humphrey charged, had "permitted into its ranks those individuals and organizations whose stock in trade is the politics of hate."[41]

III

On the evening of November 3 Humphrey gathered with family and friends at a downtown Minneapolis hotel to await the election returns. There was little suspense that night, for the three major television networks predicted a Johnson triumph before eight P.M. Johnson and Humphrey enjoyed one of the more lopsided victories in American electoral history. Winning 44 states and 486 electoral votes, they received 61 percent of the popular vote. Late that night Humphrey attended a victory party at a nearby hotel. The nation seemed eager to build the Great Society.[42]

Johnson and Humphrey had good reason not only to celebrate but also to breathe a big sigh of relief. The white backlash in the North did not hurt the Democrats. Indeed, the vote totals for the Johnson-Humphrey ticket in numerous potential backlash areas was striking. Johnson trounced Goldwater by thirty percentage points in Gary, twenty in Baltimore, forty-four in Cleveland, and twenty-six in Chicago. The Democrats even enjoyed lopsided margins in areas that had experienced riots that summer: twenty-nine percentage points in Paterson, thirty-three in Elizabeth, and forty-four in Rochester. In two Polish wards in Milwaukee, where Wallace had done very well in April, Johnson won an astounding 82 percent of the vote. Northern

African Americans, moreover, overwhelmingly voted Democratic—95 percent in the East, 96 percent in the Midwest, and 97 percent in the West. In some African American districts the president won 99 percent of the vote. The New Deal coalition had held together in the North.[43]

The Democrats were not so fortunate in the South. Goldwater won five states in the Deep South—Mississippi, Alabama (where Johnson and Humphrey were not even on the ballot), Louisiana, South Carolina, and Georgia. He carried the Magnolia State with a whopping 87 percent of the vote. Johnson and Humphrey triumphed in Arkansas, Florida, Tennessee, North Carolina, and Virginia, but only because of African American votes. Indeed, they received 95 percent of African American ballots in Dixie. The MFDP controversy had not caused most southern blacks to desert the Democratic Party or to stay at home. Rather, they were ready to back the men who had led the battle for the 1964 Civil Rights Act. In an ominous development for the Democrats, however, only 45 percent of southern white voters supported Johnson and Humphrey. Overall, the Democrats lost the white vote in every former Confederate state except Texas.[44]

The controversies over the Civil Rights Act and the summer riots had led Humphrey to worry, not unreasonably, that the Democrats would be vulnerable on the race issue. That the New Deal coalition had not been fatally split over this matter resulted from Johnson and Humphrey's ability to make foreign policy and economic issues the focus of the fall campaign. They chose to downplay civil rights altogether. When Humphrey did mention race, he rarely went beyond using Goldwater's opposition to the Civil Rights Act as part of his larger attempt to cast the GOP nominee as an extremist. Racial equality and urban life were only the eighth most frequent topic in his speeches, well behind foreign affairs, extremism, nuclear weapons, and agriculture. Such a strategy proved successful in the short term, but the Democrats had ultimately done the nation a disservice by failing to directly confront a number of enormous racial problems—poverty, jobs, crime, voting rights, and school desegregation. Humphrey saw politics as educative, but the Democrats had squandered a valuable opportunity to inform the public about these simmering issues. Humphrey would have to deal with them once in office, however, and whether the New Deal coalition could survive the strains that they would surely impose remained to be seen.[45]

7

Civil Rights Enforcement and the
Assaults on Liberalism

I

Inauguration Day dawned cool but sunny in the nation's capital. Humphrey arose shortly after seven and, after having breakfast with Muriel, went down to the lobby to meet with reporters, who jokingly asked about his plans for the day. He simply noted that he would "try to be on time" for the festivities. Humphrey joined the president for a midmorning church service and later went to the White House. Upon completing the oath of office shortly before noon, he smiled, shook hands with Johnson, and kissed Muriel. More than a million people, the largest crowd ever, lined Pennsylvania Avenue for the afternoon parade. So tight was security that Native Americans participating in the event were instructed to remove the heads from their arrows. The festivities included the Doland High School band, which had traveled by bus from South Dakota to honor the school's most famous graduate. Humphrey, who had played the bass horn while a student there, was delighted. He capped off this exhilarating day by attending the five inaugural balls at various downtown hotels that evening.[1]

II

The vice president believed that the struggle for racial justice was entering a new era. The door to racial equality, Humphrey noted, was "only just ajar." With the important exception of voting rights, the old battles to remove legal segregation were largely over. The new agenda would include ensuring that segregation was eliminated in practice, and, more important, a commitment to improving economic opportunities for African Americans. Unemployment among blacks in 1964 stood at 9.6 percent, compared to 4.6 percent for whites. Similarly, 37.3 percent of black families earned less than three thousand dollars in 1964, while only 15.4 percent of white families did. Fifty percent of blacks were poor. Blacks had a life expectancy of seven fewer years than whites, and they completed on average approximately four fewer years of school. Blacks' infant mortality rate was twice as high as that for whites. Humphrey accepted much of the "culture of poverty" thesis that was fashionable among social scientists at the time. The poor were "different in respect to attitude and outlook" than the rest of society, he wrote. They were "fatalistic, suspicious, and alienated individuals who did not plan ahead." They were also "technological illiterates" unprepared for life in a service-oriented, high-technology economy. According to Humphrey, discrimination, a lack of good educational opportunities, and structural changes in the economy, not personal moral shortcomings, were the sources of their plight.[2]

But what could Humphrey do to address these issues? His new job was legendary for its obscurity and impotence. The president had declared a War on Poverty but had not yet indicated whether Humphrey would have a role in it. As vice president he was the head of the PCEEO. More accustomed to rallying public and legislative support for civil rights legislation than enforcing laws, Humphrey seemed ill-prepared for this position. His relationship with Johnson further complicated matters. Several of Humphrey's aides feared that Johnson would be a tough and demanding boss whose need for control and loyalty would cause the new vice president to lose power and influence in Washington. Humphrey, however, accepted this risk as the price of being a heartbeat away from the Oval Office and remained confident that his fifteen-year relationship with Johnson would enable his vice presidency to be more productive than most others.[3]

Humphrey did not have to wait long to learn where he fit into the administration's civil rights plans, for shortly after the election Attorney General Nicholas Katzenbach informed him that Johnson wanted his views on how better to coordinate the executive branch's civil rights enforcement efforts. A myriad of agencies had at least some civil rights responsibilities. These included, among others, the Civil Rights Division in the Justice Department, the Civil Rights Commission, the PCEEO, the President's Committee on Equal Opportunity in Housing, the National Labor Relations Board (NLRB), the Community Relations Service, the yet-to-be created EEOC, and the Sub-Cabinet Committee on Civil Rights. Title VI, with its requirement of nondiscrimination in programs that received federal money, meant that almost every federal agency would soon be involved with racial affairs. For Katzenbach the potential for confusion and duplication constituted "the overriding problem" facing the administration in this area. Yet rather than nominate himself for the difficult and politically sensitive job of coordinating civil rights enforcement, Katzenbach suggested that the administration place Humphrey in charge of a new interdepartmental committee. Katzenbach's plan appealed to Humphrey, who thought that an interagency committee would enable him to have a role in implementing the 1964 Civil Rights Act and bring some prestige to his office. Johnson followed up nine days later by asking Humphrey to provide by January specific recommendations regarding the coordination of the federal government's civil rights activities.[4]

Several proposals emerged as a result of Humphrey's numerous meetings with government officials and civil rights leaders during December. The NAACP's Clarence Mitchell wanted to designate the Civil Rights Commission as a central clearinghouse and involve Humphrey only when lower level staff members proved unable to resolve a problem. Carl Auerbach, who had worked with Humphrey on the 1957 Civil Rights Act, recommended that Johnson delegate to the vice president some of his authority to enforce civil rights laws. Humphrey would assist various agencies as the need arose and as the president wished, thus freeing him from daily administrative duties, which Auerbach doubted that he could perform well. LeRoy Collins, head of the Community Relations Service, favored a far more centralized approach in which the vice president, as head of a new committee with broad enforcement powers, would become a civil rights "czar" while agencies such as the PCEEO and the Civil Rights Commission would be abolished. Katzenbach, meanwhile, stuck to his proposal to establish an interdepartmental coordinating body.[5]

Despite the misgivings of several of his aides, Humphrey accepted the essentials of Katzenbach's plan when he submitted a thirty-six page report to the president in January. Because the battles for racial justice demanded "more than the lowering of bars to equal opportunity" and centered on economic matters, Humphrey pointed out, civil rights issues would "defy quick or easy solution." The existence of numerous federal civil rights programs had "created special problems of interagency coordination," Humphrey continued. More troublesome was the fact that civil rights issues could not be neatly compartmentalized. Unemployment among African Americans might stem from employer bias, but it could also be related to an individual's lack of education or job training. To remedy these shortcomings, Humphrey proposed the creation, by executive order, of a President's Council on Equal Opportunity (PCEO) that would be led by the vice president. Humphrey suggested that it be comprised of sixteen people, including Cabinet members and the leaders of federal agencies such as the Civil Rights Commission, the Office of Economic Opportunity (OEO), and the EEOC. Its functions would include helping agencies work together, ensuring consistency across federal programs, planning in advance to avoid future racial unrest, meeting with state and local leaders, serving as a liaison with private groups, and developing and evaluating public policy. As a Humphrey aide recalled later, it was supposed to be a combination "watchdog, cajoler, coordinator, and adviser." Ultimate responsibility for civil rights enforcement would remain with individual agencies. Though Humphrey admitted that the PCEO would be "no panacea" and even hinted that it was not necessarily a permanent structure, he confidently assured Johnson that it would "meet present needs and [foster] bold and creative action." Humphrey's report precipitated a monthlong debate among the president and his aides. Despite misgivings that another agency would exacerbate the confusion and duplication that already existed, Johnson signed an executive order in February creating a PCEO.[6]

The new group met for the first time on March 3. Humphrey pointed out that it would have a yearly budget of just $289,000, which would be supplied by the agencies comprising it, and a small, flexible staff whom he promised to "work the hell out of." Humphrey instructed the council to be "as ingenious in eliminating discrimination . . . as segregationists are in finding ways to maintain the status quo." The PCEO would not simply help eradicate discrimination but also assist in promoting federal outreach programs aimed at blacks. Its functions were thus partly affirmative in nature. Along these lines, Humphrey designated Secretary of Labor Willard Wirtz to head a Task Force on Employment, which would study overlapping jurisdiction among federal authorities in this area and propose ways to increase job opportunities for African Americans. To deal with the implementation of Title VI, Humphrey asked Education Commissioner Francis Keppel to lead a Task Force on Education. Informed that riots could occur in as many as twelve cities that summer, Humphrey also established a Community Relations Task Force to develop ways to mitigate both the short-term and underlying causes of urban unrest. Avoiding urban unrest, the vice president told the group, was of utmost importance.[7]

The main issue concerning the PCEO in the South was Title VI enforcement. Covering almost two hundred federal programs worth nearly fourteen billion dollars, Title VI offered a powerful weapon to combat discrimination, but this enormous scope also presented a potential bureaucratic nightmare. Moreover, it said nothing about the rate or methods by which discrimination was to be eliminated. It did not even define discrimination.

Federal departments, therefore, had the difficult task of determining what was acceptable compliance. The most pressing need for Title VI was in fighting school segregation because, ten years after *Brown*, only 2 percent of southern African American students attended desegregated schools. White southerners predictably wanted to give local districts wide leeway in developing compliance plans. On the other hand, some liberals favored eliminating funding for any district that did not integrate immediately. Fearing that a complete cutoff of funding would go against the long established practice of local control of schools and give arch segregationists a point around which to rally public support, Humphrey rejected such an approach. He also worried that it would result in the elimination of programs benefiting African American students. Voluntary compliance through careful negotiation between federal and local officials, he expected, represented a far better approach than using Title VI as a club to demand immediate change.[8]

The PCEO soon began assisting HEW to prod recalcitrant districts. By failing to issue instructions for school districts' compliance with Title VI, Humphrey noted, the federal government was vulnerable to a legal challenge if it ever attempted to cut off funds. The need for guidelines became even more urgent after Johnson signed the Elementary and Secondary Education Act in April. Because the new law provided millions of dollars to districts with poor children, federal aid to southern education was about to increase dramatically. Accordingly, the PCEO encouraged HEW to develop clear and specific instructions, which it did later that month. Here, though, the PCEO was simply repeating what local leaders and some HEW officials had been suggesting for months. The PCEO was more instrumental in two other areas. It persuaded HEW to insist on integrated teaching staffs in desegregating districts and helped arrange for thirty people from the Justice Department to provide assistance in reviewing the backlog of integration plans that had piled up during the summer. Yet even with this extra help HEW still lacked enough staff to process all the plans by the time school opened. The shortage of personnel, along with the often protracted negotiations involved in school cases, meant that HEW would not meet the fall deadline. This was far from ideal, Humphrey observed, but it was better than quick approval of unsatisfactory plans.[9]

But what was Humphrey considering adequate? On one level the guidelines presented a strong challenge to totally segregated districts. They required the opening of all grades by fall of 1967, forbade segregation on school buses and in school activities, and indicated that actual desegregation, rather than the theoretical opportunity for desegregation, would be the test of compliance. But the guidelines nonetheless left the South with several large loopholes. They permitted freedom of choice plans, which placed the burden of desegregation entirely on African Americans willing to volunteer to attend white schools. The guidelines stipulated that a school district operating under a federal court order to desegregate would be in compliance. From a purely legal angle this approach represented an entirely reasonable way to avoid conflict between the executive and judicial branches—the former would accept whatever the latter held to be the standard. In practice, however, this meant that desegregation would be a very lengthy affair because many court orders allowed several years to achieve full integration.[10]

The PCEO also tackled the issue of discrimination by state branches of federal agencies. Problems in Alabama were the most egregious. The dozens of violations by state and federal government officials there included the open defiance of Title VI by welfare agencies, employment discrimination, refusal to distribute surplus food to blacks in retaliation for voter registration and other civil rights activities, and the operation of public housing on a completely segregated basis. Because these and other unlawful practices fell under the jurisdiction of several federal agencies, the situation appeared tailor-made for the PCEO. Federal agencies simply wanted written statements promising not to discriminate, but state officials would not even agree to this. Humphrey and the council held several meetings with the federal agencies involved to develop a uniform strategy. When Alabama showed no sign of ending its defiance, the PCEO scheduled fund cutoff hearings for late August. Subsequent negotiations with state officials led to a postponement, but when the PCEO realized that Alabama was merely trying to stall for time it rescheduled them for October. The state eventually agreed to submit the required forms. Even getting a promise to comply with antidiscrimination laws, much less actual compliance, was proving to be time-consuming and difficult.[11]

Humphrey and the PCEO were able occasionally to go beyond crisis management efforts regarding Title VI, but here, too, results were limited. The PCEO recruited and trained a pool of hearing examiners who were to process fund cutoff cases. It held numerous meetings with federal agencies to ensure uniformity in implementation and developed a program whereby the twelve agencies providing federal assistance for hospitals and other health care facilities would use a standardized form and have compliance reviews conducted by one agency (HEW). It worked out a similar arrangement for institutions of higher learning.[12]

Employment policies also desperately needed coordination, because several agencies, including the PCEEO, the EEOC, and the NLRB, had responsibilities in this area. Humphrey advised the president that the EEOC, which would be established that summer, provided a good opportunity to "clean up the equal employment area." This included doing something about the PCEEO, which needed money (it was nearly broke in February) and had substantial performance shortcomings. Humphrey hatched plans to temporarily house contract compliance duties in the PCEO until the EEOC could get off the ground and transfer responsibility for equal opportunity in federal employment to the Civil Service Commission. This proposal soon ran into trouble on Capitol Hill, where conservative senators in both parties eager to thwart antidiscrimination enforcement altogether were attempting to delete from the budgets of federal agencies money equal to their expected contribution for contract compliance and to prohibit the use of other money for this purpose. By the end of the summer opposition in Congress was so strong that Humphrey considered sending the compliance program immediately to the EEOC, which had begun operations in July. He worried, though, that adding to the responsibilities of the fledgling EEOC would circumvent congressional intent (the 1964 Civil Rights Act gave the EEOC powers only to mediate and conciliate employment conflicts, not cancel contracts or issue orders affecting firms and unions doing business with the government) and anger civil rights groups. He avoided these operational and political difficulties by reaching an agreement with Congress whereby contract compliance would be funded by agency contributions through the first quarter of 1966 and by congressional appropriations thereafter. Having cleared this hurdle, Humphrey continued his efforts to prepare an executive order eliminating the PCEEO.[13]

The PCEO also had to deal with crisis situations regarding employment. The Cleveland branch of the NAACP had brought pressure on the federal government that spring by organizing marches to protest discrimination in unions that were working on a federal construction site. The NAACP demanded that the federal government cancel contracts. This confrontation pitted two important Democratic constituencies against one another, but the PCEO reassured union leaders that the government "would not take precipitous action" in response to the marches. Instead, it hoped to work out a long-term affirmative recruitment plan. When union leaders stalled regarding its implementation, Humphrey helped ease tensions by meeting with them and encouraging the adoption of standardized admission procedures. The PCEO followed this up by working with the Urban League and the NAACP to prepare applicants for the union's exams. Affirmative recruitment and job training offered more promising approaches, Humphrey believed, because "elimination of all discrimination in the building trades would probably not really open up many new jobs to Negroes." Most African Americans lacked the skills necessary for immediate admission to the unions. Here again, however, compliance proved to be a lengthy and uncertain process, for by late fall few African Americans had found jobs with the unions. The approach taken by the PCEO in the Cleveland case reflected Humphrey's acceptance of a relatively new model of employment equality. Affirmative action during the early 1960s was an ambiguous concept, but it clearly meant doing more than simply requiring employers or unions not to discriminate in employment decisions. To Humphrey and others within the Johnson administration it suggested that more aggressive efforts be taken by unions, employers, and government to reach out to minorities to ensure special training and educational programs and fair recruitment. Such efforts would presumably expand the pool of minorities able to compete with whites. Affirmative action, though, still demanded that individuals be treated without regard to race regarding employment decisions. This type of "soft" affirmative action contrasted sharply with the "hard" affirmative action of later years, which allowed for consideration of race in matters such as hiring.[14]

Worried that situations such as Cleveland could provide the spark to set off another summer of urban unrest, Humphrey and the PCEO's Community Relations Task Force soon agreed on two principles of operation. First, mayors would be reminded that riot prevention was chiefly a local concern. The federal government would not, and could not, assume primary responsibility in this area. Second, the PCEO would be as responsive as possible in providing federal resources wherever they were needed most. The task force targeted eleven northern cities for special attention. Conferring with nine of the eleven mayors that spring, LeRoy Collins learned that friction between African Americans and the police, high unemployment, inadequate housing and education, and poor communications with civil rights groups had led to dangerous situations. He promptly assigned a consultant, who was to help minority groups take advantage of the federal programs and facilitate communication between minorities and federal and local officials, to each of the cities (Chicago and Los Angeles declined) and made preparations to increase federal antipoverty efforts in them. By June an extra fifteen million dollars in special summer program projects was set to be approved under the Community Action Program of the Office of Economic Opportunity (OEO). Similarly, thirty-one thousand jobs costing twenty million dollars were to be funded by the Neighborhood Youth Corps. "Although these and other activities by Federal agencies have generated significant and constructive summer activities, no optimistic predictions can be made about this summer," Humphrey gloomily wrote Johnson. "The problems of the urban slums are so large and so profound, and the anger, alienation, frustration, and despair of the Negroes who live in them are so great, that crash programs cannot be viewed as any dependable insurance against disorder."[15]

Fears of urban unrest also helped cause Humphrey to direct the PCEO Task Force on Employment to study teen unemployment. He was no stranger to this issue, for since the 1950s he had routinely introduced legislation dealing with teen delinquency, recreation, and unemployment. Teenage unemployment was roughly 15 percent in the first quarter of 1965, four times that of adult workers and one-third higher than the teen rate in 1957, the task force reported. As a result of the maturation of the postwar baby boom, the teen labor force, which had grown only by 78,000 per year between 1947 and 1964, would balloon by an average of 255,000 per year until 1970. The problem would be exacerbated during the summer, when more than a million teenagers would enter the labor force until school resumed. Predictably, the employment outlook for nonwhites was far worse than that for whites. Unemployment among teenage nonwhite males stood at 22.4 percent in the first quarter of 1965, almost 100 percent higher than that of their white counterparts. This represented a substantial deterioration since 1957, when the gap was 50 percent, and 1948, when the black rate was lower than the white rate. Technological changes, a lack of adequate educational opportunities, and discrimination had resulted in limited employment prospects for African American youth, the task force observed.[16]

Teen unemployment greatly concerned Johnson too, and in April he asked Humphrey to form a Cabinet Committee on Employment to look for ways to increase employment opportunities for disadvantaged youth, especially those in northern cities where the likelihood of violence was great. Invoking memories of the National Youth Administration of the 1930s, Johnson announced six weeks later that he was placing Humphrey in charge of a Youth Opportunity Campaign. The president set a target of finding five hundred thousand jobs over and above the normal summer hiring done by the government and private companies. Government agencies would be directed to hire one extra person for every one hundred people already employed, and private employers would be asked to make a similar effort. Special attention would be given to disadvantaged youth. Administration officials privately conceded that there would still be thousands of jobless youth if these goals were reached, but they thought the problem so serious that an effort had to be made.[17]

The Youth Opportunity Campaign embodied the same assumptions as the broader War on Poverty. Rather than provide direct cash assistance to the poor, the Johnson administration sought to aid the disadvantaged in acquiring skills that would allow them to compete in the booming economy. Work experience obtained during the summer months would presumably enable disadvantaged youth, especially black teens, to move on to more stable and better-paying jobs, become more fully integrated into the mainstream economy, and achieve long-term independence. It was the type of government program that a New Deal Democrat like Humphrey loved. Here seemed to be the perfect opportunity for government to do good.[18]

Though he clearly had his work cut out for him because school ended in less than a month, Humphrey enthusiastically plunged into the Youth Opportunity Campaign. The federal government soon sent out more than a million letters urging businesses, civic and private organizations, educators, state officials, and unions to provide jobs for the nation's youth. "Get on that telephone," Humphrey exhorted a group of federal employees. "Just get on there . . . and say, 'John, how are you doing on that Youth Opportunities Campaign?' Then call him the next morning and then call him at night, and call him the next morning." The situation, Humphrey stressed, was so urgent that "either we're going to do something about this in a constructive way or we'll have to pay serious costs in other ways." Humphrey mailed letters to every mayor of a city with more than ten thousand people and the heads of the one thousand largest companies. He followed this up by meeting with representatives of the National League of Cities, the National Association of Counties, and the International City Managers Association. Local action, Humphrey repeatedly emphasized, would make or break the campaign. The massive publicity blitz continued into early June. Five thousand radio stations, seven hundred television stations, and fourteen hundred newspapers received press kits. Several major league baseball teams flashed news of the program on their scoreboards. Word of the campaign appeared in countless places, including stock car races in Atlanta, a rodeo in Idaho, department stores in Philadelphia, and the Shrine Circus. Ozark Airlines put flyers in the seats on its planes. Ed Sullivan endorsed the campaign on one of his television shows. By the end of the month 550,000 jobs had been pledged. No one knew how many would go to African Americans, however. There was another problem—more than a million teenagers had applied for work. Concerned about the government's inability to meet rising expectations, Humphrey increased the goal to 750,000 and prepared letters for five hundred additional companies.[19]

Even as Humphrey attempted to arouse support for youth employment, he kept close watch on the administration's voting rights bill, which Johnson had submitted that spring following violence in Selma, Alabama. The president signed the landmark legislation on August 6. For Humphrey the ceremony marked "one of the truly great days in the life of the nation." The federal government had delivered another decisive blow against legal discrimination in the South. The new law's chief provisions were an automatic trigger mechanism that gave the attorney general power to suspend literacy tests where black voter turnout in 1964 had been less than 50 percent of the eligible population, authorization for the attorney general to dispatch federal registrars upon receipt of twenty complaints of the denial of voting rights, and a requirement that states submit proposed changes in voting laws to the Justice Department for approval. The Voting Rights Act and the numerous antipoverty programs recently approved by Congress gave Humphrey good reason to think that progress in redressing America's racial ills, though not always as swift as he or others would like, would at least be orderly.[20]

Events in Los Angeles several days later severely tested that faith. When police officers in the predominantly African American neighborhood of Watts arrested a black man for drunken driving, an angry crowd gathered and began to overturn cars and break store windows. For the next six days television captured the vivid images of thousands of African Americans rioting, looting, and setting fire to hundreds of shops. The National Guard restored calm, but only after the violence had exacted a horrible toll—thirty-four dead, more than a thousand injured, and four thousand arrested. Nearly a thousand buildings had been damaged or destroyed at an estimated cost of thirty million dollars in the worst episode of racial violence in the nation's history.[21]

Though Republicans pointed to the riot as proof that the War on Poverty was a grand failure, Humphrey continued to link violence with the lack of economic opportunity. Speaking to a group of veterans, he insisted that respect for law and order had to be upheld, but he added that all Americans should "deplore injustice as well as violence." At a conference on equal opportunity a few days later, Humphrey wondered, "What can we expect when hope is resolutely crushed from the young, when there are no jobs even for the educated, and no homes in good neighborhoods even for the hardworking?" Declaring that "nothing is more important to the Negro in his struggle to free himself from his circle of frustration than the ability to have and to hold a good job," Humphrey observed that most African Americans were "on the verge of a major economic crisis." Automation was reducing the demand for unskilled labor, but, because more than half of black men over age twenty-five had little more than an elementary education, many African Americans could look forward only to greater economic misery. Pointing out that the black unemployment rate was twice that for whites, Humphrey called upon business, labor, and government to "go out and affirmatively seek those persons who are qualified and begin to train those who are not," for "the problems of spirit [in the black community]" were "intimately tied to more and better job opportunities." African Americans who demanded more jobs and better training programs were not seeking preferential treatment but rather were recognizing "a fundamental fact of life." Only when the privileged helped make equality a reality for all, Humphrey contended, would "the other America become an America that cherishes respect for law and order."[22]

The administration also faced attacks from its left. Many civil rights leaders were outraged over the Moynihan Report, a study of African American urban life that pointed to rising crime, illegitimacy, drug use, and unemployment among blacks. They charged Assistant Secretary of Labor Daniel Patrick Moynihan, the report's author, with "blaming the victim" when he should have been emphasizing structural factors in the economy and discrimination as the sources of these problems. Though many critics had misread the report (Moynihan had stressed macroeconomic forces), these protests were forceful enough to cause the administration to rethink the arrangements for its upcoming White House Conference on Civil Rights, which Johnson had scheduled for that fall. The agenda was to include housing, employment, voting rights, Title VI, education, crime, and African American family life, but civil rights leaders wanted the conference to avoid discussion of this last issue. Many administration officials concurred. Humphrey, who later commended Moynihan for an analysis of black life that was "compassionate, sensitive, and correct," argued that the administration needed to deal "candidly, carefully, and in depth" with issues such as the African American family if it expected the conference to have any value. The president had originally conceived of a gathering to highlight new directions in civil rights policy, but the imbroglio over the Moynihan Report convinced Humphrey and several White House staff members to break the conference into two parts—a small working session during November to debate ideas and offer solutions, and a larger follow-up conference the following spring to approve the recommendations.[23]

Amidst the controversy over the riots and the Moynihan Report Humphrey took stock of the PCEO's activities and concluded that there was a great deal of room for improvement. LeRoy Collins had reported that the War on Poverty's employment programs failed to meet the needs of low-skilled African American males and that city leaders were either unable or unwilling to acknowledge or grapple with the underlying economic and social problems plaguing many blacks. Improved job training programs, increased participation of African Americans, and better coordination of existing federal antidiscrimination efforts were sorely needed for the Task Force on Employment to go beyond marginal efforts. Job training and education,

Humphrey acknowledged, were "meaningless" if they did not result in employment. Education constituted another area fraught with difficulty. Noting that civil rights groups in the North were paying more attention to de facto segregation, Humphrey predicted that the issue would "become even more emotion-laden as time goes on," yet the government had "not charted a clear course" in this area. There was considerable doubt whether Title VI could even be used in the North because no district there had a de jure policy of segregation. Title VI did apply to the South, of course, but Humphrey, who continued to think that simply cutting off funds would only stir white resentment, was still searching for a way to speed desegregation. As for discrimination in other federally assisted programs, Humphrey knew that the government had only begun to enforce Title VI. Though a PCEO survey indicated that the vast majority of recipients of federal money had committed themselves to a policy of nondiscrimination, verbal promises often meant nothing in the absence of continued federal pressure.[24]

Humphrey thus concluded that the PCEO had a good deal of work to do, but recent administration actions left him uncertain about the council's role. Joseph Califano, who had taken command of the administration's domestic programs in July, regularly kept Humphrey waiting outside his office whenever the vice president wanted information regarding civil rights. More important, Humphrey had fallen out of Johnson's favor after privately expressing doubts in February about the president's Vietnam policies. Johnson would not see him about *any* matter. Humphrey finally became so exasperated that he wrote Appointments Secretary Marvin Watson in August asking how he could best serve the president. In dealing with Watts, school desegregation, enforcement of the 1964 Civil Rights Act, and planning for the White House Conference on Civil Rights, Humphrey pointed out, Johnson and his aides had neglected to inform the PCEO of their activities, failed to seek its advice, or undertaken projects on which the council was already working. This duplication and lack of communication not only puzzled Humphrey but federal agencies, state and local officials, and civil rights organizations as well.[25]

While Humphrey was looking forward to increasing the PCEO's role in civil rights matters, the president was secretly planning to shut it down altogether. Johnson, who had misgivings about creating the body in the first place, viewed it as another layer of bureaucracy that impeded civil rights enforcement. Watts, moreover, had caused the president to want total control over the administration's civil rights activities. Califano, who was looking to increase his own power within the White House, helped sway the president's thinking by offering regular criticism of Humphrey. "I want you and Nick

[Katzenbach] to put together a plan and get the civil rights programs out from under the vice president," Johnson told Califano in September. The attorney general produced a detailed proposal two days later that extensively reshuffled the administration's civil rights effort. Katzenbach recommended termination of the PCEO and the PCEEO. Title VI coordination would fall to the Justice Department. The Community Relations Service, which had been lodged in the Commerce Department, would also be transferred to Justice. The Civil Service Commission would assume responsibility for policing the federal government's employment policies, while federal contractors would be monitored by the Labor Department. These changes would move civil rights closer to Johnson's control and leave Humphrey with no formal responsibilities in this area. The attorney general did suggest, however, that Humphrey be used "as a trouble shooter or evaluator on specific programs or problems which the President assigns him." White House aide Lee White then concocted a script in which Humphrey would "show his 'bigness' " by announcing that he had made the suggestions. The president would follow with "a very warm letter" thanking him for his hard work.[26]

Unaware that its fate was sealed, Humphrey's group continued to function as normal. Ironically, the PCEO was furnishing its new offices as the president put the finishing touches on its demise. On September 21 Humphrey invited Martin Luther King, Whitney Young, Clarence Mitchell, and other civil rights leaders for a cruise down the Potomac on the presidential yacht. Pointing to the violence that many civil rights workers encountered when they tried to get more African Americans on the voting rolls, Mitchell strongly urged the vice president to have Johnson send more registrars to the South. After listening to this and other vehement complaints about administration civil rights policies, Humphrey promised more vigorous action. The following day he was to hold the third meeting of the PCEO and then discuss with several administration officials ways to address the problem of de facto school segregation in the North.[27]

Johnson summoned the vice president to the White House shortly after noon on the day after the cruise. Humphrey had no idea what the president wanted. Without identifying the source of his information, Johnson told him about recommendations he had received that would improve civil rights enforcement by eliminating the PCEO and shifting its functions to the Justice Department. Sensing the impending doom of his group, Humphrey turned pale. Johnson then proceeded to walk through a charade of seeking the vice president's opinion.

"Do you think it's a good idea to strengthen our civil rights efforts this way?" Johnson asked.

"I told you I would do whatever you wanted me to do. If you believe that's where these programs should go, then that's the way we'll do it."

"I thought you'd agree, Hubert," the president returned.[28]

Johnson moved swiftly once he had humiliated Humphrey. The president immediately instructed Califano to draft a memo in the vice president's name outlining the changes. Califano took a copy to Humphrey's office the following night. Still shaken by the news, Humphrey told Califano he would get back to him after he had talked with the PCEO. Califano then indicated that Johnson expected him to sign the memo immediately. Humphrey reluctantly did so. Joining Press Secretary Bill Moyers at the White House for the announcement several hours later, Humphrey dutifully followed Lee White's script. A skeptical press corps wondered whether this represented a slowdown in civil rights enforcement, but Humphrey insisted that just the opposite was true. He revealed a glimpse of his true feelings only once, when a reporter mused that Humphrey no longer had an official title. "That is correct, except vice president," he quipped. As for the "very warm letter" that Humphrey was supposed to receive from Johnson, the president simply gave him a brief formal note thanking him for the recommendations. As Humphrey's top civil rights aide later recalled, the vice president had once again "played the good soldier" in the face of Johnson's demands.[29]

News of the shake-up greatly disturbed liberals, who feared that the administration was assigning civil rights a lower priority. To Whitney Young the elimination of the PCEO gave "reason for some misgiving" and prompted "some disturbing questions." One dejected civil rights leader commented, "We are back where we were five years ago." Many had more faith in Humphrey than in Katzenbach, whom they criticized for being too slow in enforcing the Voting Rights Act and refusing to protect civil rights workers in the South. Amidst the outcry from many of his longtime allies, Humphrey gamely held to the administration line that the shake-up would improve civil rights enforcement.[30]

Given the performance of the PCEO, liberal reaction to its demise stemmed more from hopes for what it might do rather than pride in what it had done. The council had achieved some positive results in coordinating civil rights policy, especially related to Title VI, but its accomplishments were minimal overall. It never lived up to Humphrey's promise for "bold and creative action." Some of the PCEO's shortcomings, such as its tiny budget, poor relations with agencies and the White House, and lack of support from the president, were beyond his control. The problems ran deeper than this, however. The very conception of the PCEO greatly hampered its effectiveness. In this case Humphrey's instinct for compromise served him badly. He tried to walk a middle ground between centralization of civil rights activities and keeping them completely with the agencies. Because the PCEO lacked responsibility for enforcement of most affirmative programs, it wielded little influence with federal agencies. Most agency heads did not look to Humphrey or the PCEO for guidance, and he largely failed to convince them to make civil rights a higher priority. The work of the PCEO was thus primarily redundant or peripheral. Johnson's initial fears had been borne out.[31]

Humphrey also experienced another civil rights setback that September. The Youth Opportunity Campaign had yielded rather modest results for African Americans. Humphrey claimed that the program generated nearly nine hundred thousand jobs, which he called "a stunning success," yet he had no way of knowing how many of those pledges represented additional hires, as was originally hoped, or if the companies promising jobs would have employed the youths anyway. Whatever the case, few businesses or government agencies took any special interest in black teens. Nonwhite youth unemployment for the summer months was 22.2 percent, still nearly twice as high as the white rate. This was hardly surprising. The Youth Opportunity Campaign had noble intentions, and Humphrey had identified a grave problem, but the effort suffered from serious handicaps from the start. Because it was launched just a few weeks before school ended, businesses had little time to make plans. Moreover, the government offered them no financial incentive to hire additional workers, especially those who lacked skills. The result was a crash program that made little difference in the lives of black youth.[32]

Altogether, the first year of Humphrey's vice presidency had failed to live up to his high expectations. Early in the year Johnson had used him primarily to forestall criticism from civil rights groups who wanted the administration to move more quickly in a number of areas. By summer Humphrey found himself frozen out of critical administration decisions. The PCEO and the Youth Opportunity Campaign had accomplished little. Finally, the uprising in Watts signaled that the federal government had failed to meaningfully address the issue of equal economic opportunity for African Americans, the matter Humphrey had deemed most important.

III

Humphrey now became the principal spokesman for the administration's racial policies. This would be a difficult task, because the consensus that had led to the 1964 Civil Rights Act and the Voting Rights Act was fraying. Never strong anyway, white support for providing economic aid to the ghetto soured after Watts. At the same time, questions regarding voting rights enforcement, protection for civil rights workers in the South, and the War on Poverty had led many African American leaders to criticize the administration for not doing enough for blacks. Seeing the November planning session for the White House Conference on Civil Rights as an opportune moment to reassert the need for unity and continued federal action, Humphrey told the fifty people who had come to the Washington Hilton Hotel that most Americans had "[failed] to realize that the most difficult and challenging task still has not been faced squarely, that we are now in a period where . . . greater, not less, courage, greater and not less sacrifice and wisdom and understanding will be required of the American people of all races, colors, and creeds." The 1964 and 1965 laws had simply "established the ground rules by which we can wage the struggle." Few quarreled with these aims, but there was much disagreement over how to achieve them. The two-day event, which included a session on the African American family, produced a wide range of proposals and generated a good deal of criticism over the administration's failure to initiate voter registration drives in the South and its decision to restore thirty-two million dollars in federal funds for Chicago schools after the money had been denied because of a finding of segregation by HEW. Humphrey grew evasive and defensive when pressed about these and other issues the administration wanted to avoid.[33]

Humphrey again played a central role in administration plans to help the nation's youth and keep peace in the cities. Unless the problems of urban youth were addressed, he warned, "city after city will explode and Watts will look like an afternoon picnic." In March 1966 Johnson named him chair of a Special Task Force on Summer Domestic Programs. Submitting its report at the end of the month, the group predicted that 1.8 million youth between the ages of sixteen and twenty-one would be unable to find work unless the federal government offered assistance and that 2.7 million children under age fourteen lacked supervised care. To meet those pressing needs the task force proposed an expanded Youth Opportunity Campaign that included jobs, recreation, education, and health care. Children of all races would participate, but the task force called upon the federal government to pay special attention to African American youth because there was an "urgent need for hard, visible evidence that things are really changing for the better."[34]

Johnson formally launched the Youth Opportunity Campaign in April by urging businesses to hire an extra one million teens. Humphrey would once again head the effort. Within ten days of the president's announcement he sent letters and promotional kits to the mayors of every city with a population of more than ten thousand people, radio and television stations, governors, trade and professional associations, city managers and county officials, state employment service offices, newspapers, and mass circulation magazines. Promotional efforts were also undertaken by baseball teams, the entertainment industry, and numerous businesses. In all the material sent out from his office, Humphrey stressed the need to hire disadvantaged youth. He received more than thirty thousand replies within the first seven days of the campaign (as opposed to seven thousand letters in all 1965). It was again impossible to know how many of the 150,000 jobs pledged would go to African Americans, but Humphrey found the initial response encouraging.[35]

Meanwhile, disenchantment with white liberals had reached new levels among some blacks. Believing that the administration needed to do more to protect civil rights workers in the South, SNCC denounced the White House Conference on Civil Rights as a sham and boycotted the June event. CORE participated only because its leader hoped to add his criticism of the Vietnam War and the War on Poverty to the predetermined agenda. Several weeks later, the group renounced nonviolence, rejected integration, and embraced the nascent concept of Black Power, which saw no need for white liberal allies, no value in integration, no need to be color-blind, and no use for working within the existing political system. In its most extreme form it asserted the superiority of African Americans to whites. Black Power thus directly contradicted nearly all of Humphrey's beliefs about race relations.[36]

Deeply troubled by these developments, Humphrey reasserted his liberal faith in two important speeches that summer. He took a thinly veiled swipe at Stokely Carmichael and other radical civil rights leaders by denouncing those "who appear more concerned about their own positions than about the plight of those less fortunate, less articulate members of their race." All of American history, he told the crowd gathered for the White House Conference on Civil Rights, pointed to the failure of separatist movements. Even more significant was the speech Humphrey gave a month later at the NAACP's convention. Violence would only hurt African Americans in the long run, he contended. Whereas CORE and SNCC were turning inward, Humphrey called upon the NAACP "to reach out into the total American community and enlist vital new sources of energy and strength." Economic justice required more than "crying 'freedom now' on a picket line." It demanded a balance between "dedication to *action*" and "commitment to *achievement*" by both whites and African Americans. Groups such as SNCC and CORE had too much of the former and not enough of the latter, Humphrey implied. He saw an enormous difference between "legitimate pride in the achievements and contributions of one's forebears" and Black Power:

> It seems to me fundamental . . . that we cannot embrace the dogma of the oppressors—the notion that somehow a person's skin color deter-mines his worthiness or his unworthiness. Yes, I say to you, frankly and honestly, racism is racism. . . . We must reject all calls to racism, whether they come from a throat that is white, or a throat that is black. It's all the same. . . . We must strive to perfect *one* citizenship, *one* destiny for all Americans. That's our goal. Integration must be recognized as an essen-tial *means* to the *ends* that we are seeking—the ends of freedom and jus-tice and equal opportunity.

Reaction to Humphrey's speech reflected the deepening fissures among African Americans. The audience, which viewed Humphrey as a longtime ally, gave him a rousing standing ovation. Conversely, one radical leader ac-cused him of having a "purely racist reaction" to Black Power.[37]

Humphrey again affirmed his liberal beliefs twelve days later, this time by attacking conservatives who called for "law and order" and cuts in anti-poverty programs. Insisting that "the National Guard is no answer to the problems of this country," he vigorously asserted before a gathering of coun-ty officials in New Orleans that violence would not stop until the poverty of the inner city had been eliminated. "I'd hate to be stuck . . . in a tenement with the rats nibbling on the kids' toes. . . with the garbage uncollected . . . with the streets filthy . . . with little or no recreation . . . because I've got enough spark left in me to lead a mighty good revolt under those condi-tions," Humphrey declared. Occurring at the same time as a riot in Chica-go, the speech brought a hailstorm of criticism upon him. House Minority Leader Gerald Ford of Michigan described it as "incredibly irresponsible" and demanded that Johnson repudiate the vice president. One newspaper noted that the speech "will not fail to inspire further violence and disrespect for the law," while another called Humphrey's timing "tragic." Johnson was furious. Concerned that the Republicans would exploit the address for po-litical gain, Humphrey mounted an aggressive counteroffensive by sending letters to numerous editors quoting a recent law and order speech he had given to the FBI. But it was too late. His poor choice of words had provid-ed strong ammunition for critics who had begun to link liberalism with urban unrest.[38]

Humphrey continued his elusive search for consensus in August, when growing white hostility toward African Americans caused him to question the tactics of Martin Luther King. The SCLC leader had decided to shift his attention to northern ghettos and fight for jobs, housing, and education for blacks. Chicago would be the site of his first mass effort in the North. Italians, Poles, and Irish residents of the Windy City, however, showed their fierce opposition to integrated neighborhoods by overturning cars, throwing rocks, waving Confederate flags, and shouting at King and his followers, "Go back to Africa. We don't want you here." King resolved to press ahead. Humphrey, though, called for a temporary halt to the marches. Such an appeal was no doubt partly intended to boost his political standing among whites following the New Orleans debacle, but it also reflected his belief that African Americans would not advance without the support of most whites. Asserting that the demonstrations had "gotten out of hand," Humphrey remarked that "the cause is suffering—the cause of social justice." Rioting, white backlash, and fighting among civil rights groups, he mournfully observed, had made the summer of 1966 a time of "trying days."[39]

Mounting political problems were only the beginning of the bad news for Humphrey. The administration's 1966 civil rights bill, which dealt chiefly with housing discrimination, was in trouble on Capitol Hill. Humphrey offered Johnson a list of suggestions to achieve the desired goals through means other than legislation, but the president ignored them. Furthermore, Humphrey's efforts to bring jobs to the African American sections of Los Angeles were yielding few dividends. He had paid close attention to developments there following the Watts riot in hopes of preventing another outbreak of violence. Told in July that antipoverty efforts were making little difference in the lives of many African Americans, he met several times with federal officials and corporate leaders in the area to improve the administration of programs and secure employment for those who needed it most. Humphrey hoped to convince defense and aerospace contractors to hire low-skilled African Americans by offering to have their wages paid by the Department and Labor and the Office of Economic Opportunity. Despite much exhortation from the vice president and a professed willingness by defense contractors and other companies to cooperate, the results, as one OEO official confessed, were "minimal" because too few employers were willing to hire unskilled employees.[40]

A similar fate had befallen the 1966 Youth Opportunity Campaign. Humphrey claimed that it had generated 1.1 million jobs overall and led to a drop in teen unemployment, but he again had little firm evidence that the campaign had been directly responsible for opening up additional jobs above and beyond normal summer hiring. More important, he privately admitted that the effort "made no appreciable gains" in reducing the unemployment rate for black youth. It remained approximately 23 percent, more than twice the white rate. Employers, his top civil rights aide lamented, had shown little interest in helping the less fortunate. African Americans who did locate summer work through the program often found that the jobs usually offered no skills to help them out of poverty. One noted, "Every time I go to the [United States Employment Service] they want to know if I got a record, and they tell me all they got is one of those dishwashing, or jump off the paper truck kind of jobs. Man, that's jive talk. I can do more than just wash dishes, or jump off the paper truck." Blacks understandably wanted permanent jobs, not low-paying temporary work. Similar difficulties plagued the recreational programs. Humphrey proudly announced that more than 200,000 youth participated in Neighborhood Youth Corps programs, 570,000 enrolled in Headstart, and more than 900,000 took part in camping and other activities. He personally raised seventy thousand dollars to provide lighting for thirty playgrounds in the nation's capital. The federal government spent four hundred million dollars on special summer programs in 1966, yet many were hastily drawn and poorly implemented, reached only a small portion of those in need, and had little or no long-term benefit for participants. By fall the government had done no analysis of which programs worked best, had no cost/benefit data, and had no solid information on how many poor youth were helped. There was plenty of blame to go around. Local officials, business leaders, and federal agencies all contributed to the campaign's shortcomings. The administration had again offered no financial incentive for business to hire additional workers. Humphrey, meanwhile, was better at publicizing the campaign than at daily oversight or following it up with badly needed studies about its effectiveness.[41]

These enormous problems, the Task Force on Summer Programs concluded, could be fixed through several reforms, including the creation of a full-time staff that would work with Humphrey throughout the year on planning and coordinating youth activities. This would presumably reduce the frenetic pace that had led to many of the implementation difficulties. Johnson signed an executive order in March placing Humphrey in charge of the President's Council on Youth Opportunity (PCOYO). The vice president launched the 1967 Youth Opportunity Campaign two weeks later. This time, he assured reporters, the federal government would do a better job of reaching African Americans. Privately, Humphrey worried that it would not. Due to congressional budget cuts, reduced budget requests by federal agencies, and a shortage of funds for reallocation to summer programs, the summer campaign for 1967 would have ninety million dollars less than the previous year and reach 2.6 million fewer youths. Humphrey diligently searched for ways to raise more money, but legal and time constraints made success unlikely.[42]

Humphrey also worried about how the politics of race was hurting the administration. Anti–civil rights sentiment played a prominent role in several Republican victories in the 1966 elections, and George Wallace was preparing to run for president again. Wallace would probably campaign as a third party candidate, and Johnson feared that the former Alabama governor would capitalize on racial animosities to draw the votes of white southerners away from the Democrats. Hoping to shore up his party's standing in Dixie, Humphrey accepted the invitation of Georgia Governor Lester Maddox for a meeting in Atlanta. The trip would plague Humphrey for years. During a forty-five minute conversation Humphrey lobbied Maddox to back Johnson in 1968. "The governor of Georgia is a good Democrat," a smiling Humphrey told reporters afterwards. "The Democratic Party is a big house. It has room for all of us." Maddox voiced his agreement. The following morning many news accounts included a picture of Humphrey walking arm in arm with Maddox. The sight of the man who had spearheaded the 1964 Civil Rights Act through the Senate so closely allied with someone who had become a public figure by brandishing guns and ax handles to keep African Americans out of his restaurant prompted some to wonder if Humphrey had softened his stance on racial justice. He tried blithely to dismiss all the attention, but the meeting offered ammunition to critics who contended that liberals were too mired in compromise with racists such as Maddox.[43]

Thinking that Georgia would vote Democratic in 1968, Humphrey returned to Washington and resumed work on the Youth Opportunity Campaign. He set a goal of 1.2 million summer jobs as an "absolute minimum" and hoped to approach 2 million. To reach those lofty targets Humphrey oversaw a whirlwind publicity campaign far greater than those in each of the two previous years. He met with many leaders from state and local governments, businesses and unions, and federal agencies. "I'll lay it on the line— we need preventive medicine before we're struck down by the disease of violence," he bluntly informed prominent members of the Washington business community. "I'm not telling you what to do, but you go up to the Metropolitan Club and spend more on drinks in an hour than it takes to send a kid to camp for two weeks." Word of the campaign reached the public in dozens of other ways, including free want ads donated by many newspapers, advertisements in popular magazines such as *Look* and *Life*, radio spots narrated by actor Charlton Heston, and displays on the marquees of Holiday Inn motels. A giant electronic sign in Times Square flashed word of the Youth Opportunity Campaign 240 times each day. The enormous publicity effort, a supplemental congressional appropriation of seventy-five million dollars, and initial indications that mayors and businesses were better organized than before led Humphrey to think that this would be the largest and most successful summer undertaking yet.[44]

This optimism proved to be premature. In Cincinnati programs were poorly administered, and, more important, many businesses had given only lip service to employing teenagers. City leaders in Los Angeles had followed Humphrey's advice to set up a Youth Opportunity Council, but they lacked commitment to and communication with disadvantaged youth. There, too, many businesses and federal agencies were reluctant to hire them. Birmingham's program was "woefully inadequate," a PCOYO staff member wrote. Not only had the mayor refused to create a youth council, but nearly 4,000 teenagers had applied for only 314 nonagricultural jobs. A similar situation existed in Louisville, where the State Employment Service was flooded with phone calls but had few jobs to offer. The business community in Jersey City, Humphrey angrily noted, displayed a "near total indifference" to problems there. In Washington just 124 of the 1,084 jobs pledged by private business through mid-June were located in the District of Columbia; the rest were in suburban Maryland or Virginia, and few teens had adequate transportation to these locations. Businesses in the nation's capital had contributed "not much of anything," a PCOYO official lamented. More disadvantaged youths filled government jobs by early July than in all the previous summer, but demand was so high and positions so scarce that in late June hundreds of irate African American teens stormed a Washington employment office to protest. When no one in the group received a job, many staged a sit-in at the PCOYO office five days later to call the attention of businesses to their needs. Failure to meet rising expectations, Humphrey readily acknowledged, posed a serious problem. "In all too many of our cities," he privately lamented, "the summer youth campaign is receiving inadequate attention from City Hall and the so-called establishment." Humphrey approached numerous mayors and again urged them to lobby the business community. He also contacted newspaper editors and requested that they bring pressure on reluctant city leaders by running stories on the lack of jobs or recreation. In some cases the vice president went beyond his customary role as advocate and became directly involved in negotiations to make jobs or recreation more available to poor children. Despite a Herculean effort by Humphrey and the PCOYO staff, the vice president regrettably informed Johnson in midsummer that African American teen unemployment remained "a problem."[45]

More dramatic evidence of the failure of War on Poverty programs occurred on July 12, when thousands of African Americans of all ages began to loot stores and set fires in Newark upon hearing a rumor that the police had beaten to death a black cab driver. Plagued by the highest African American unemployment rate in the nation, rampant crime and drugs, and dilapidated housing, the city was a tinderbox that only needed a small spark to set it ablaze. Flying above Indiana as the violence progressed, Humphrey telephoned New Jersey governor Richard Hughes to express his sympathy. He told the governor to call if he could be of any assistance. The press, however, reported that Humphrey had offered federal aid. Johnson was livid. "[Humphrey] has no authority, spell it out, N-O-N-E, to provide any federal aid to Newark or any other city . . . in America," the president barked to Califano. When another account suggested that Humphrey had promised to send U.S. marshals, Johnson told Califano he wanted the vice president gagged before he "brings down the administration." Califano called Humphrey the next day and relayed the president's concern. The vice president thought Califano was kidding and indicated that he had made no such promises. He soon humbly expressed his regret over the whole affair to the president. Johnson accepted Humphrey's account of his conversation with Hughes and placed him in charge of a special Cabinet working group on the crisis in the nation's cities. Hughes eventually called in the National Guard, but the riot led to more than 25 African American deaths, 1,200 people wounded, and ten million dollars in property damage. Humphrey blamed the riot on "three hundred years of neglect that is now trying to be corrected in ten years." Though he insisted that violence would "not be tolerated," he also told a largely white audience that "opportunity can't be something just for you and me."[46]

Violence broke out in Detroit a few days later. Unlike Newark, the Motor City had a good economy and a highly touted antipoverty program, but the mass arrest of African Americans at a nightclub that was selling alcohol past closing time led to a rampage of burning and pillaging. Mayor Jerome Cavanaugh phoned Humphrey to report that the situation was "getting out of hand" and to inquire about federal troops. "If it can happen in your town, it can happen anywhere," a disturbed Humphrey told him. Requests for troops, the vice president carefully indicated, would have to be made to the attorney general. Humphrey did go to Johnson with requests from the office of Senator Philip Hart of Michigan that the federal government deploy the Army, but Johnson flatly refused. Badly shaken by the violence, Humphrey disappeared for several hours. Governor George Romney soon called out the National Guard, which reestablished peace but was also largely responsible for most of the forty-three deaths and the wounds suffered by a thousand people. The six-day melee, the worst race riot in modern American history, led to four thousand fires, which destroyed more than 1,300 buildings.[47]

Humphrey's belief that the riots were fundamentally rooted in economic deprivation reflected conventional liberal thinking of the day, but subsequent analysis of the wave of rioting that swept through American cities during the second half of the 1960s reveals that such a view was too one-dimensional. To be sure, Newark was a desperately poor city, but African Americans in Detroit and Los Angeles fared relatively well on measures of economic standing. Black unemployment in the Motor City during 1967 stood at just 3.4 percent, while the poverty rate for African Americans there was just half the national average. The home ownership rate for blacks in Detroit was the highest in the nation. Moreover, the gap in income among typical white and black families was only 6 percent. According to a 1964 study by the National Urban League of social and economic conditions in the nation's sixty-eight largest cities, Los Angeles was the best place in the United States for African Americans to live. Clearly, the causes of the violence were more complex than Humphrey had acknowledged.[48]

Two massive riots within a week created a crisis atmosphere at the White House. Republicans blasted the War on Poverty as a colossal failure while critics on the left demanded that the president provide more money for the poor. Humphrey held three lengthy meetings with the Cabinet working group on the cities within three days. Over the next two weeks they met five additional times. The members, he informed the president, "were more deeply concerned than ever before" because the riots indicated "widespread rejection of our social system and not simply dissatisfaction with conditions." Furthermore, they were worried that "shockingly large numbers of Americans, including many liberals, [were] displaying extremely hostile racial attitudes." The group initially explored the possibility of creating a massive jobs program involving significant new spending. Such an approach went against the intellectual foundations of the War on Poverty, but it struck many as the only solution. When Califano received word of such plans, he quickly informed Humphrey that the administration was already having enough trouble getting Congress to approve its budgetary requests for existing programs. Humphrey got the message. His group dutifully retreated by simply recommending that existing programs be fully funded and repackaged in hopes of increasing public support. Califano, meanwhile, advised Johnson that Humphrey's group should be "tactfully disbanded."[49]

The riots left Humphrey extremely depressed, but he held to his faith in the War on Poverty. The government needed to encourage the unemployed to seek jobs because individuals denied opportunities for centuries would not suddenly believe that things had changed simply because a law had been passed. Rather, the trick was "to reach out and find [the unemployed]" and to help ensure that there were jobs for them. Along these lines, he urged Johnson to lobby one hundred large corporations to provide five hundred jobs each for the "hard core" unemployed who would be recruited by black ghetto leaders. Thinking that the public was "getting a little weary of straight welfare programs," Humphrey encouraged Johnson to focus on employment matters by expanding job training programs, offering tax incentives for employers to hire low-skill workers, and even creating a government jobs program to employ those unable to find work in the private sector. The president, who was preparing to cut spending and raise taxes to pay for the war in Vietnam, did announce in the spring of 1968 a program intended to provide five hundred thousand jobs for the hard-core unemployed, but he did not give it a high priority.[50]

Humphrey's despair over the urban crisis landed him in more political trouble that fall. During an emotional address in which his voice was sometimes near breaking, he appealed to delegates at the National League of Cities convention for domestic peace and social justice. This was standard liberal rhetoric, but Humphrey also offered a stinging attack on Congress. Pointing to recent cuts in or failure to approve altogether several antipoverty programs, he charged that legislators abetted "frustration" and displayed a lack of urgency regarding urban problems. One Republican accused him of "political demagogy of the worst kind." Even Senate Democratic leader Mike Mansfield commented that he was "somewhat disturbed" that Humphrey would implicate Congress for the riots. An angry Johnson ordered Humphrey not to repeat it. Humphrey also upset the president during a trip to Detroit during the week following the riot. Speaking to the National Association of County Officials after a tour of several riot-torn neighborhoods, Humphrey suggested that America be willing to pay "whatever it will take" to rebuild its cities and compared the Model Cities program to the Marshall Plan. Reporters interpreted his remarks as a call for a new and expanded urban effort similar to what Urban League head Whitney Young had advocated since the early 1960s. When Humphrey returned to Washington the president demanded to see him immediately. "Hubert, what makes you think that you can go around announcing programs like that?" Johnson pointedly asked. "I've got all the problems I can handle." Humphrey quickly sought to get back in Johnson's good graces by telling reporters that he had no major differences with the president on urban policy and warning against "checkbook solutions" to domestic problems.[51]

The riots presented a discouraging picture, but so too did the results of the Youth Opportunity Campaign. Many governors and mayors did little or nothing. According to government reports, none of the thirty-three large cities to which the PCOYO had given special attention had adequately prepared for the summer. Only fourteen had created a Mayor's Council on Youth Opportunity, and just six of those had even a single staff employee. Communication between city and community leaders was often poor or nonexistent. Businesses fell far short of meeting the demand for jobs. Nonwhite teen unemployment rose slightly from the previous summer to 23.5 percent, still more than twice as high as the white rate. Humphrey privately admitted to being "relatively disappointed" in the lack of support from city and business leaders. "It is incredible that they would ignore as many communications as went out to them," he complained. But not all the problems could be attributed to city officials and business leaders; the federal government deserved a good share of the blame too. Though the PCOYO began work on the summer programs earlier than ever, there was still too little time for many businesses and city governments to prepare adequately. Federal money frequently arrived late in the spring or early in the summer. The results of such bureaucratic snafus included uncoordinated and superficial programs, lost job opportunities, and administrative chaos. Programs were often isolated experiences with little or no meaning after they ended abruptly in September. Administrators of recreation programs measured success almost exclusively by the number of participants, and even this crude yardstick was inaccurate because attendance totals were inflated by counting casual, late, or one-time participants. Because thousands of youth took part in more than one program, there was double and triple counting. The PCOYO, moreover, had only a cursory understanding of local conditions. Its field representatives spent just six days in each of the thirty-three largest cities. When businesses pledged jobs, the PCOYO again had no valid data on how many of them went to disadvantaged youth or if those jobs were over and above normal summer hiring.[52]

All too aware of these serious flaws, that fall Humphrey established six working groups to develop plans for 1968 and revised the PCOYO staff structure to implement proposed programs more rapidly. By December he had contacted mayors of the fifty largest cities and recruited Henry Ford II to chair a spring national Jobs Fair for disadvantaged youth. Humphrey followed these activities up in January with a three-day conference for six hundred civic, business, labor, religious, and social leaders that he hoped would produce a groundswell of energy and ideas for earlier and better planning of summer programs. The conference, however, quickly degenerated into a sometimes hostile series of exchanges between the audience and federal officials when the administration revealed that it would not seek another $75 million supplemental appropriation for summer programs in 1968. Humphrey defended the administration's decision by saying that funds could be used more effectively, but unconvinced delegates overwhelmingly approved a resolution condemning the cutback and calling upon the administration to provide an additional $275 million. Humphrey quelled the rebellion by promising to lobby Congress for the money. Chances for success were slim, though, because the administration had committed to reducing spending to win congressional support for a tax increase.[53]

As usual, Humphrey poured a tremendous amount of energy into the youth campaign. He met with leaders of the sports and entertainment industries about participating in recreation efforts. In addition to its usual public relations efforts, the PCOYO launched an expanded communications program that included a weekly newsletter, special films, advertisements, and a closed-circuit television session involving Humphrey and local leaders in fifty cities. Wary of arousing expectations in the nation's youth, the PCOYO no longer asked them to contact a local employment office if they wanted a job. Instead, it focused more heavily on urging employers to hire disadvantaged teens. Financial difficulties presented the PCOYO with its most significant problem that spring, however. As a result of congressional budget cuts, the Neighborhood Youth Corps was preparing to eliminate funding for tens of thousands of summer jobs for needy youth around the country. The administration was shifting money away from summer programs to manpower training efforts in hopes of better addressing the problems of long-term unemployed adults. "Unless additional monies are in hand," Humphrey's top civil rights aide reported, "the situation will be most critical." Humphrey urged Cabinet members to squeeze their budgets for an extra seventy-five million dollars for summer programs so that funding would at least equal the previous year's level. He also approached Senate leaders about a supplemental appropriation and made arrangements with the Labor Department to secure added funding for the Neighborhood Youth Corps. These efforts met with some success, and by the end of the month the budgetary outlook for the 1968 summer youth campaign appeared to be improving.[54]

Urban America needed all the help it could get, according to the Kerner Commission. Appointed by Johnson in the summer of 1967 to study the sources of and remedies for urban violence, the group, which was headed by Governor Otto Kerner of Illinois, issued its report in March. It criticized many of the administration's antipoverty programs and concluded that the nation was moving toward "two societies, one black, one white—separate and unequal." Its recommendations included vastly increased federal spending in several areas, among them the possibility of creating public service jobs to aid the poor. The first high administration official to comment publicly on the report, Humphrey appeared to sympathize with it initially. Indeed, in 1965 he had publicly expressed similar worries about a two-tiered society. "If this nation can afford to spend $30 billion to put a man on the moon, it can afford to spend what it takes to put a man on his feet right here on earth," he now asserted. Three days later, however, he observed that the group's findings were "open to some challenge" and argued that progress against poverty under Johnson had been "dramatic" because the nation had increased its spending on job training, education, and other antipoverty efforts to unprecedented levels. If the report's prediction of a racially divided America came true, Humphrey maintained, "it will be not so much because any specific government failed. It will be because our free society failed." None of this was wrong, but in the spring of 1968 such statements sounded defensive and only deepened the belief among many that the Johnson administration would not meet the needs of the nation's cities. Humphrey broadened his attack on the commission three weeks later by declaring that its conclusion that white society condoned slums "[came] dangerously close to a doctrine of group guilt." The reasons behind Humphrey's increasingly critical stance are unclear, though it is likely that here again he had angered Johnson by initially seeming to endorse massive new social spending. After his criticisms of the report raised charges that he was out of touch with developments in urban America, Humphrey tried to find a middle ground. By the end of the month he had declared his support for its "principal conclusions."[55]

Understandable confusion over where Humphrey stood regarding the Kerner Commission report constituted just a tiny part of his political misfortunes that spring. Just four years earlier, there had been widespread support for civil rights and the War on Poverty. Liberalism seemed invincible. Now, however, it appeared powerless to enforce civil rights laws, halt the surging crime wave, or lift people out of poverty, and as a result critics on the left and the right commanded growing attention. Disaffection with the war in Vietnam and violence in the nation's cities caused Johnson's approval rating to plummet to 41 percent. To make matters worse, Senator Eugene McCarthy of Minnesota had declared that he would challenge Johnson for the Democratic presidential nomination. McCarthy stunned the nation on March 12 when he won 42 percent of the vote and finished second in the

New Hampshire primary. His impressive showing dramatically revealed the president's vulnerability. Several days later, Johnson's longtime nemesis, Senator Robert F. Kennedy of New York, launched his bid for the nomination. These were shocking developments, but an even bigger surprise occurred when Johnson announced on March 31 that he would not seek another term as president. The Democratic race was blown wide open, and Humphrey now had to decide if he wanted to join it. To be sure, he was part of an unpopular administration, but as vice president Humphrey would still be the leading contender for the chance to run in the fall election, a contest in which racial issues would inevitably loom large.[56]

8

Order and Justice
The Politics of Race in 1968

I

Four days after Johnson's withdrawal, Humphrey joined three thousand Democrats at the Washington Hilton Hotel for a party fund-raiser. Many eagerly hoped that he would announce his candidacy for the party's presidential nomination, but Humphrey was still weighing his options. He did, however, make a dramatic announcement. Shortly after dinner the vice president rose and solemnly said, "One of our nation's renowned leaders, the Reverend Martin Luther King, has been shot, and he is dead." Though word of the assassination had spread earlier that evening, many in the audience gasped nevertheless. Describing King's death as a "great tragedy" that brought "shame to our country," Humphrey called upon the nation to renew its commitment to equal opportunity for all. After the House chaplain had said a prayer at Humphrey's request, the vice president conferred with Senator Edmund Muskie of Maine, who agreed to cancel the rest of the program. That night, as a stunned Humphrey traveled home, riots broke out in Washington, Baltimore, Detroit, Boston, Chicago, Philadelphia, and dozens of other cities.[1]

After attending a memorial service for King at the National Cathedral the following day, Humphrey traveled to Long Island. Visibly shaken, he told one thousand businessmen:

> If [King's death] becomes a signal for black Americans to strike out in rage and retaliation, then we will have made a mockery of all for which he lived and died. If it leads white Americans . . . to turn from the tortuous road which leads to progress and equality, then we will have strength-

ened that very doctrine which he defied—the sense that the world has gone mad and that mortal man cannot set it right. . . . If we *do* rededicate ourselves to the mission of healing the torment of our poor and our hungry, our deprived, and our illiterate—then truly this tragedy will be remembered, not as the moment when America lost her faith, but as the moment when America found her conscience.

The positive reaction of the crowd left Humphrey hopeful that something good might come of the tragedy. Such a feeling did not last long, however, for as his plane landed at National Airport that night a stunned Humphrey sat in silence as he looked out at nearly a dozen fires raging below. As one of Humphrey's aides later recalled, the vice president was "sickened" by the terrible sight. Violence had been so rampant in Washington that Humphrey's plane was delayed in New York because the Secret Service could not guarantee safe passage to his office. As Humphrey traveled to the White House, he saw the streets lined by troops with bayonets. For the first time since the Civil War, Washington was under military protection. Humphrey attended King's funeral in Atlanta as rioting continued to spread. More than fifty thousand federal and National Guard troops were deployed in more than one hundred cities within a week after the assassination. Twenty thousand people were arrested and thirty-nine died as a result of the violence.[2]

The turmoil that followed King's death spelled deep trouble for the Democrats. By the spring of 1968 39 percent of the public thought that Johnson was pushing integration too fast. Many whites, moreover, saw law and order as the most important domestic issue. Sixty-three percent of the public thought that the courts were not dealing harshly enough with criminals. Though the Kerner Commission reported an unofficial total of 164 riots in 1967 alone, mass urban unrest was one part of a much larger problem. Between 1957 and 1967 the crime rate for robbery and burglary had more than doubled, the rate for aggravated assault had nearly doubled, and that for murder had increased 20 percent. Such alarming statistics provided plenty of fodder for American Independent Party candidate George Wallace. "Law and order" was not simply a code phrase for racism, for many African Americans were also deeply troubled by violence, but there clearly was a racial dimension to the issue since much of the surge in crime had occurred in cities with large numbers of blacks. Liberals, many Americans had come to believe, were too preoccupied with solving the "root causes" of crime and too little concerned with the victims of crime. That the public's dissatisfaction with the status quo would mean an uphill fight for Humphrey was evident in an April poll showing him trailing likely Republican nominee Richard Nixon 43–34 percent. Wallace brought up the rear with 9 percent.[3]

Despite appeals from labor leaders and Democratic officials to announce his candidacy in early April, Humphrey initially wavered. With memories of 1960 lingering his mind, he feared another defeat after being used as a punching bag for Kennedy, whom he believed would not hesitate to employ "ruthless methods" against him. But Humphrey desperately wanted to be president, and he soon began to plot his strategy to capture the Democratic nomination. Whereas Kennedy and McCarthy had chosen to practice the "new politics" of demonstrating broad public support by entering the handful of primaries that were held that spring, Humphrey elected to take the more traditional route of lining up the backing of state and local party leaders because they still chose the vast majority of convention delegates. This approach played to Humphrey's strength, for during his twenty years in Washington he had built up ties with many Democrats across the country. Such a strategy would avoid a direct confrontation with Kennedy, who had been drawing large and enthusiastic crowds since he had entered the race in March, but it also meant that Humphrey would have to look for support in the South, where there were no primaries but hundreds of delegates to be won. Thinking that Humphrey was the best of a bad lot, southern Democratic leaders quickly lined up behind the vice president despite differences over racial issues. "I'm not happy about Hubert," one governor remarked, "but I'd certainly go along with him before I'd come within a mile of Bobby." A Texas official privately told his party, "Well, I never thought I would see the day I was pushing for Humphrey . . . but if this is what it takes to kill off Kennedy and McCarthy, why don't we come out and say we are for Humphrey?" Southern Democrats hated Kennedy for his liberal views on race, smoking, and law and order, and they opposed McCarthy's stance on Vietnam. They also feared that either candidate would be more of a drag on state races in the fall than the vice president. Humphrey welcomed the support of state leaders, but he did not back off of sensitive subjects during two visits to the South in April. During a trip to Mississippi, his first as vice president, Humphrey appealed for a "new commitment" to end poverty and prejudice. More important, he expressed his support for an integrated convention delegation from the Magnolia State. The Democrats had made a pledge in 1964 to end lily-white delegations, he reminded state party leaders, and he intended to see that it was honored.[4]

Humphrey finally announced his candidacy on April 27. Critics quickly seized upon his inane remark about "the politics of joy" as evidence that

Humphrey's liberalism had outworn its usefulness, but in their eagerness to dismiss him they overlooked other parts of his statement that showed he was well aware of the seriousness of the nation's racial problems. Nixon and Wallace had cast law and order as separate from racial justice and stressed the former over the latter, but Humphrey would try to unite them as two sides of the same coin. "I believe we can make law and order not only compatible with justice and human progress, but their unflinching guardians," he declared. "I believe we can build cities and neighborhoods where all our citizens may walk together in safety and in pride and the spirit of true community." By pairing order and justice Humphrey was taking a substantial political risk that he could convince voters to see the two as connected. As he had throughout his political career, Humphrey assumed that there was a reservoir of goodwill among the public that could be tapped. Most voters, however, seemed to want tougher anticrime policies, not greater funding for antipoverty programs.[5]

Humphrey spoke regularly during the early part of the campaign about the importance of confronting directly the economic problems facing African Americans and the need for harmony between the races. Addressing the U.S. Chamber of Commerce, he appealed for businesses to train the "hard-core unemployed." There was "no satisfaction in the superficialities of opportunity that is equal in form but not in fact," he told a group of African Americans. "The enduring morality of brotherhood and love and justice, not violence" he declared before a convention of African American ministers, "must be the accepted standard if we are going to accomplish what each one of us wants." Few liberals would have quarreled with such rhetoric, but Humphrey refused to put forth any specific proposals to achieve his goals. He did, however, reject the idea of a guaranteed income for the poor because he believed that simply sending them a check each month would not lead to a sense of self-worth or give the poor a stake in society. Jobs, the vice president insisted, were a more difficult but far better solution. Humphrey's vague positions led Kennedy to blast him as a "status quo" candidate who gave people "pabulum and tranquilizers," while McCarthy, in an unmistakable reference to the Youth Opportunity Campaign, attacked him for expecting that "the young men of the ghettos should rejoice that the government has given them a few summer jobs to keep them off the street." Humphrey, who was amassing hundreds of delegates and had even drawn within three percentage points of Nixon by mid-May, saw no compelling political reason to get into a debate with his two Democratic opponents regarding the details of urban policies.[6]

While McCarthy and Kennedy concentrated on winning primaries, Humphrey continued to search for delegates in the South. Concluding that he needed to win at least a few southern states if he were to triumph in November, the vice president attempted to reach southern whites by noting that "there are a lot of people who would rather point at you than look in the mirror" regarding racial matters. Upon the death of Alabama Governor Lurleen Wallace, wife of George Wallace, Humphrey conveyed his sympathy to his rival and sent one of his chief assistants to the funeral. Similarly, on "Meet the Press," Humphrey commented that both he and the South were "growing up." These actions, campaign aides cheerfully reported, had gone over especially well with many southern whites. Humphrey's pursuit of white votes in Dixie represented a combination of cold political calculations and his longstanding idealism about the region's future. In some cases the vice president welcomed the support of state officials (such as Governors John J. McKeithan of Louisiana and Bob McNair of South Carolina) with poor civil rights records. But to suggest, as some critics did, that he was selling out his views on racial equality simply to win the nomination greatly oversimplified Humphrey's position. He had thought since the 1940s that there were nascent progressive forces in the South, and there was evidence to support his belief that the white South had changed for the better regarding racial matters. Segregation in public accommodations had crumbled rapidly, and as a result of the Voting Rights Act nearly a million African Americans had registered to vote. Though there remained much to be done, Humphrey expected progress to continue. He interpreted the rise of governors such as Terry Sanford in North Carolina and Buford Ellington in Tennessee during the 1960s as signs that progressive leadership was strengthening. Southern liberals would not always go as far as he wanted, but, unlike the staunch segregationists who had come to power in the wake of *Brown*, they understood that the South had to solve its race problem if it were to be brought into the mainstream of the nation's social and economic development. Nixon and Wallace could fight for the votes of die-hard southern conservatives, then, while Humphrey won this new South.[7]

The battle between Humphrey and Kennedy never reached a culmination, for on June 4 the New York senator was tragically murdered in Los Angeles at a party celebrating his victory in the California primary. Occurring just two months after Martin Luther King was gunned down, Kennedy's death shocked Humphrey. He stopped campaigning for several days and attended the senator's funeral in New York. Like many other Americans, Humphrey wondered when the violence would end. He soon offered an impassioned plea for the "relentless" pursuit of law and order. Declaring that "violence, crime, looting, burning, cannot be condoned and must be stopped," Humphrey called for strengthening state laws against rioting, increased federal aid for local police forces, registration of *all* firearms, expanded antidrug enforcement policies, and the establishment of councils for civil peace in every state and many cities. Violence was morally wrong, Humphrey maintained, but he also suggested that it would hurt the struggle for racial equality because it was the unwitting "ally of reaction [and] could be used as an excuse for not doing the things that need to be done in this country." Humphrey continued to insist that the future of the nation depended upon recognizing that "civil order and civil justice are twin imperatives." If the public expected a reduction in violence, he asserted, it had to make sure that the poor had food, education, and jobs.[8]

Two camps were waging a tug-of-war for Humphrey's mind on how to handle law and order and racial issues. One saw most whites as against increased social spending for the poor, fearful of crime and urban unrest, and generally hostile to civil rights. These advisers urged Humphrey to downplay racial matters because most voters were "unpoor, unyoung, and unblack." Writing in the *New Republic*, Irving Kristol astutely observed that even if Humphrey won the election he would have to secure the backing of middle-class whites to pass any proposals to aid blacks in the nation's cities. Conversely, others recommended that "every effort" be made to highlight Humphrey's civil rights record because African Americans constituted the deciding factor in sixteen states worth 317 electoral votes. The danger regarding the African American vote was not that it would be lost to Nixon or, of course, Wallace, but rather that blacks would sit the election out if they did not find a candidate who addressed their needs.[9]

As the Democratic convention neared, Humphrey followed the advice of the latter group. He was the only presidential candidate to identify himself with Poor People's Campaign. Ralph Abernathy, a longtime aide to Martin Luther King, had organized a mass protest in Washington that spring to dramatize the plight of the downtrodden and prod Congress to provided additional funding for jobs, a negative income tax, and low-cost housing, among other things. Humphrey sent a letter to Abernathy outlining his support for programs to alleviate hunger, revamp the "destructive and demeaning" welfare system, and provide greater health care for the poor. He also attended Abernathy's June rally in Washington. Humphrey, moreover, endorsed legislation that would create 2.4 million jobs for the "hard-core" unemployed through aid to private businesses and the establishment of public service employment.[10]

The vice president offered two more detailed plans in July. Declaring that America had fallen "far short of the mark" in mobilizing sufficient will and resources to solve urban problems, Humphrey first proposed a Marshall Plan for the cities. The centerpiece of this effort was a national urban development bank. The federal government would appropriate a relatively small amount of funds to get several regional banks started. The institutions, which would be financed largely through the sale of bonds that would be guaranteed by the federal government, would make loans to public and private borrowers for inner-city investment in housing, business, and other development. The federal government would underwrite especially risky ventures. The banks, moreover, would offer technical management and aid in urban planning. Humphrey did not put a price tag on the level of investment, but he did say that he envisioned "billions" of dollars in loans being made by the banks. Local bank boards would be comprised of politicians, business leaders, and representatives of the poor. The great virtue of the banks, Humphrey believed, was that they would promote better coordination and long-range urban development because city leaders would not have to deal with the "scattered efforts" that the federal government had undertaken in recent years. The banks would also meet urban economic needs directly, for they would channel money into the cities without having to go through Congress, which had refused to fully fund many Great Society programs in recent years. Other elements of Humphrey 's Marshall Plan were less well-defined. They included placing a lien on increasing tax revenues and using a large portion of an expected "peace dividend," which would come as a result of winding down the war in Vietnam and negotiating strategic arms reductions with the Soviet Union, on urban programs. Humphrey also suggested a system of tax and other financial incentives for private enterprise to invest in urban areas. Indeed, free enterprise "would do most of the job" in solving the urban crisis. The Marshall Plan for the cities, Humphrey hoped, would receive broad public support because it conjured up memories of an overwhelmingly successful program in the aftermath of World War II.[11]

Nearly three weeks later, Humphrey unveiled a program to promote minority entrepreneurship. Only one in a thousand African Americans owned a business, compared to one in forty whites. Urging whites to give blacks "a chance to succeed within the system," Humphrey contended that minority ownership of businesses would enable inner-city residents to become "productive, self-sustaining, and involved members of society." He proposed to funnel capital to the inner city through a liberalization of Small Business Administration policies regarding loans for inner-city projects and to increase efforts by the Department of Commerce and other federal agencies to assist private companies in creating inner-city branches that would be managed by local residents. As with the Marshall Plan for the cities, Humphrey stressed that the private sector had to generate the majority of the necessary resources. Capital was essential for getting businesses started, but Humphrey also thought that African Americans needed training, technical expertise, and access to markets. He favored expanding several federal job training programs to include instruction in management skills, enlarging the federal program to ensure that minority businesses received full and equal consideration in the awarding of federal contracts and subcontracts, amending the G.I. Bill to allow for payment for entrepreneurial training, and creating a National Committee on Minority Business that would bring to the federal government's attention the needs and ideas of inner-city businesses. Humphrey's Marshall Plan for the cities and efforts to promote entrepreneurship were consistent with the Great Society's goal of assisting the poor to help themselves rather than providing a direct income supplement. Indeed, Humphrey continued to oppose a guaranteed annual income or a negative income tax. Politically, Humphrey needed to match Nixon, who had endorsed "black capitalism" the previous fall. Though there were many similarities between Humphrey and Nixon's plans, the vice president rightly charged his opponent with offering more rhetoric than substance. "Talking about black capitalism without capital is just kiting political checks," Humphrey asserted. "Of course it will take money."[12]

The proposals for a jobs bill, a Marshall Plan for the cities, and minority entrepreneurship represented part of an effort by Humphrey to separate himself from Johnson. Having loyally defended the president's foreign and domestic policies for three years, Humphrey knew that voters' perceptions of him as Johnson's lackey constituted an enormous obstacle on his road to the White House. A Humphrey administration, the vice president now insisted, would mark "the beginning of a new liberal struggle." Whereas Humphrey had once held to the administration's line that attempts to increase spending on antipoverty programs would be futile because of a conservative Congress, he began to argue that funding for such efforts needed to be boosted lest the nation pay a greater price in terms of crime, delinquency, and lost productivity. Cost was now "something that [had] to be met rather than a pretext for inaction."[13]

Humphrey hoped that these issues would cause his candidacy to catch fire with African Americans, many of whom opposed his position on the war in Vietnam and had rallied to Kennedy that spring. Like many areas of his campaign, Humphrey's effort among blacks was poorly organized. His staff had arranged a meeting with African American Democratic leaders in April, but a month later Humphrey had to instruct his advisers to "put extra effort" into building support among this important constituency. There was little follow-up by midsummer. Just a month before the Democratic convention the Humphrey campaign lacked clearly defined areas of responsibility regarding racial issues and, due to a shortage of money, had undertaken little voter registration in African American neighborhoods. Humphrey's difficulties among blacks were evident during a campaign visit to Los Angeles in July. Kennedy had drawn sizable and enthusiastic crowds in May, but Humphrey attracted just six hundred people to a voter registration rally near Watts. Less than five minutes after the vice president began to speak several dozen young African Americans forced him off the stage through a chorus of booing. Several shouted, "Honkie, go home." There even was a brief threat of a brawl among members of the audience. Greatly upset at these developments, Humphrey nonetheless vowed that he would "not be driven away" from black neighborhoods. The following day's event in Watts was little better. Though he gained the endorsement of popular singer James Brown, Humphrey received only a lukewarm reception from the tiny crowd. His clumsy attempt to dance "the bougaloo" with Brown flopped badly. One African American assemblyman astutely summed up the situation when he glumly observed that his constituents would "go Democratic if we can get them out, but right now that's a big if."[14]

II

Developments at the Republican convention in Miami several weeks later confirmed that Humphrey would have a hard time in the South. Richard Nixon won the GOP presidential nomination by allying himself with Strom Thurmond. The arch-conservative South Carolina senator helped the former vice president thwart a last-minute challenge from Governor Ronald Reagan of California by swaying southern support to Nixon, who had assured southern delegates that he was against busing to achieve school integration and that he would softly enforce the recently strengthened school integration guidelines issued by HEW. Nixon also helped himself among southerners by selecting Governor Spiro Agnew of Maryland, who had recently blasted moderate black leaders in Baltimore for their failure to condemn radicals involved in the April riot there, as his running mate. The infamous "southern strategy" had been born. Nixon could not expect to outbid Wallace for white votes in the Deep South, but the Republican nominee realized that playing upon white hostility toward civil rights would win him wide support in other southern states. Dubbing the Republicans the "Nixiecrats," Humphrey gamely insisted that Nixon's alliance with Thurmond created an opening for him in the South.[15]

But Humphrey faced some choices of his own regarding the South. Billing itself as the "loyal Democrats of Mississippi," an interracial coalition that included the MFDP, the state NAACP, labor groups, and other organizations prepared to challenge the seating of the regular Mississippi delegation at the upcoming Democratic convention. Humphrey, who had been closely monitoring developments in Mississippi, knew that his integrity was on the line. He had promised an integrated delegation as part of the deal offered the MFDP four years earlier, and he had called for one that spring. He dispatched Senator Walter Mondale to Jackson in early August to assure the insurgents that he would support their case before the Credentials Committee. Humphrey also made public a letter he had written to the head of the Special Equal Rights Committee, which had been set up in 1967 to make certain that state parties were open to all, urging an investigation of alleged discrimination in Mississippi.[16]

Hostility among the regular Mississippi delegation and other conservative southern Democrats who were likely to back Nixon or Wallace in the fall was to be expected, but Humphrey's endorsement of the challengers also brought howls of protest from many of his southern allies, who had advised him to postpone making a decision until the matter had come before the Credentials Committee. They, too, wanted the regular Mississippi delegation thrown out, but they feared that Humphrey had unwisely prejudged the issue and thus allowed conservative southerners to claim that Democrats were pandering to the African American vote. Humphrey's decision in the Mississippi matter led many southern states to contemplate giving their support to one or more of the five southern favorite-son candidates, the segregationist Lester Maddox, or even Lyndon Johnson. Though Humphrey's victory seemed certain by early August, a lengthy fight during the first ballot or a second-ballot nomination would indicate that he was a weak candidate. Furthermore, the Humphrey camp worried that a walkout by several southern delegations would doom the vice president's already slim chances in Dixie that fall. As one of his chief aides noted, the campaign had "some serious trouble brewing" in the South.[17]

While Humphrey contemplated how to keep the New Deal coalition together, the Credentials Committee, which was comprised chiefly of Humphrey supporters, began a series of meetings in Chicago several days before the convention to settle the Mississippi affair. It followed Humphrey's lead by voting 84–10 to oust the regular delegation and seat the interracial challengers, most of whom backed the vice president. Humphrey, a campaign aide reported, was "very gratified" by the decision. Longtime civil rights activist Bayard Rustin called it "a great moment for the Democratic Party, one that I'll remember to the day I die." For the first time ever, a delegation had been excluded from the convention on grounds of racial discrimination. This repudiation of the staunch segregationists represented a victory for the ideal of an interracial Democratic Party in Mississippi and other parts of the South and helped pave the way for the dramatic increase in black Democratic leaders across the South in the 1970s.[18]

A wary Humphrey flew to Chicago on August 25. Though he appeared to have more delegates than necessary to secure the nomination, he still could not be certain of victory. The Mississippi fight, as well as divisions within the Georgia delegation, where a group of whites and African Americans was challenging the seating of the regulars on grounds of discrimination, led some southerners to talk of favoring another candidate. Rumors that Johnson would enter the race at the last minute swirled about the convention hall. The leader of the powerful California delegation, who had backed Kennedy, said that he found the idea of supporting Humphrey "very difficult." Mayor Richard Daley of Chicago intensified Humphrey's anxiety when he did not pledge Illinois's delegates to him that evening as the vice president had expected. Word that Senator Edward Kennedy of Massachusetts might become a candidate only heightened Humphrey's worry that the prize he had sought for so long would somehow be snatched away at the last minute.[19]

As the convention opened, the Democrats still had to decide several matters related to race and section. First up was the unit rule, which required that all of a state's delegates vote for one candidate. Liberals considered the rule an antiquated means of promoting "bossism." Southerners, on the other hand, used it to maintain control of their delegations and increase their bargaining power. Humphrey's instinct to please brought him a storm of trouble on this contentious issue. A few weeks before the convention he had attempted to shore up his standing among liberals by calling for the abolition of the unit rule. His private delegate tabulations had convinced him that he could afford to lose a few southern votes. When angry southerners confronted him about the issue, however, Humphrey immediately tried to backpedal by privately reassuring Governor John Connally of Texas that he would stand by the unit rule in Chicago. Further complicating matters was the fact that Humphrey's staff had released a letter a few days before the convention in which the vice president had written to the Credentials Committee endorsing elimination of the unit rule "at this convention." Southerners were outraged. Humphrey, who was telling Connally one thing and the committee another, had bungled the affair badly. "Hell, I wish I hadn't written that sentence," the vice president lamented. Connally, meanwhile, was frantically calling other southern governors urging them to refrain from endorsing Humphrey. He also asked Johnson, who was at his ranch in Texas, to persuade Daley to continue to withhold his support from the vice president. If these delegations, which counted for more than six hundred votes, could unite, they could force Humphrey to side with them on the rule. Fearing just such a coalition, Humphrey pledged to Connally that he would do whatever he could to preserve the rule for the Chicago convention. The southern rebellion had been quelled, at least temporarily, yet despite the opposition of Humphrey and the South the delegates struck the unit rule down in a narrow roll call vote.[20]

Humphrey also worked to cement his standing among white southerners by siding with the regular delegations during several other credentials challenges. Buoyed by the Mississippi decision, insurgents in several southern states, joined by the McCarthy forces, prepared for a floor fight. Humphrey stuck to a plan to split the Georgia delegation that he had developed earlier, but he decided to oppose the other challengers outright. The vice president was not siding with lily-white delegations, yet the insurgents were far more racially balanced than the regulars. Most delegates in Chicago followed Humphrey's lead. They decided to split the Georgia vote and then handily defeated challenges in Texas, Alabama, and other southern states during a series of roll call votes. Humphrey's stance was especially critical in preventing Connally's Texas delegation from deserting him. Once the Lone Star State decided not to rebel, other southerners quickly fell into line behind the vice president. Edward Kennedy, meanwhile, had foreclosed the possibility of a draft. Humphrey's triumph was now a mere formality.[21]

With the unit rule and the delegate challenges settled, Humphrey focused on shoring up support among blacks and nailing down the nomination. As aides put the finishing touches on his acceptance speech, the vice president invited reporters to photograph him having lunch with African American sports legends Jackie Robinson and Elgin Baylor. Nixon, he told the athletes, had made a "calculated decision" to court racists. Calling Nixon's appeals for law and order "subdued racism," Humphrey vowed not to compromise his lifelong commitment to equality. Carl Stokes, the African American mayor of Cleveland, seconded Humphrey's nomination that night. The nation, however, would not see the mayor because the networks had decided to show instead what was happening in the streets of Chicago, where the police had for several hours been engaging in a brutal crackdown on the antiwar demonstrators. The networks returned for live coverage of the roll call, which began shortly after eleven. Humphrey, who had been greatly shaken by the events in the streets below, kept a running count of the totals as he watched television in his twenty-fifth floor suite at the Conrad Hilton Hotel. His victory became official when Pennsylvania announced its vote. A jubilant Humphrey leaped to his feet and shouted, "That's it. That's it. That's it."[22]

Humphrey then turned his attention to the selection of a running mate. Fearful that a ticket of Humphrey and another northern liberal would be a drag on local races across Dixie, Connally led a delegation of southern governors to Humphrey's suite two hours after the balloting to bring pressure on the nominee to take a southerner. The following day Johnson urged him to select former North Carolina governor Terry Sanford. In a rare display of independence from Johnson, Humphrey chose Senator Edmund Muskie of Maine. Muskie was an intelligent, dignified, and competent man, well qualified to become president if anything ever happened to Humphrey. Politically, however, the choice made little sense because the Maine senator could offer no help for the Democrats among white southerners, blue-collar whites in the North, or African Americans.[23]

Humphrey delivered his acceptance speech that night to a crowd of thirteen thousand delegates and thousands more across the nation who were viewing the dramatic developments in the Windy City on television. "Rioting, sniping, mugging, traffic in narcotics and disregard for law are the advance guard of anarchy and they must and they will be stopped," he firmly declared. He promised to "use every resource that is available . . . to end for once and for all the fear that is in [the] cities." As he had throughout the spring, the vice president coupled his demands for law and order with an urgent appeal for racial justice. Declaring that "winning the presidency is not worth the price of silence or evasion on the issue of human rights," Humphrey insisted that the country had to choose whether it would be "one nation . . . or a nation divided between black and white, between rich and poor, between North and South, between young and old." Asserting that there was a "basic goodness" within the electorate, Humphrey believed that the public would reject the divisive appeals of Nixon and Wallace and instead "stand up for justice and fair play."[24]

III

Following the tumultuous week in the Windy City, Humphrey went to his vacation home in Minnesota to plot strategy for the fall campaign. Much of the public disapproved of the administration's policies in Vietnam and in the nation's cities. Prior to the convention Nixon led Humphrey by sixteen percentage points, and surely that gap had not been closed by the violence in the streets of Chicago. Despite these disturbing signs, Humphrey had some cause for hope. He never thought Wallace had a chance to win, but summer polling data indicated that the former Alabama governor's candidacy helped Humphrey in two ways. As long as Wallace received 15 to 20 percent of the popular vote, he would pull conservative voters away from Nixon. Furthermore, Humphrey expected that Wallace's presence would force Nixon to move to the right in hopes of winning over Wallace supporters in both the South and the large industrial states of the North. If Nixon did pursue such a strategy, Humphrey expected that moderate Republicans would vote Democratic, just as they had in 1964. If Nixon did not move to the right, he would likely lose several pivotal states and Humphrey would emerge victorious. Attacking Wallace, then, only helped Nixon. Humphrey would thus target his Republican opponent. As for northern blue-collar Democrats who might vote for Wallace because of racial matters, Humphrey would try to win their backing by stressing economic issues, as he and Johnson had four years earlier.[25]

The vice president wasted little time employing this strategy. Arguing that most Americans urgently wanted something done about crime, several of Humphrey's aides recommended that he make a strong law and order speech. Voters still saw the vice president as lacking firmness and strength, they reported. Humphrey, though, held to the theme he had outlined that spring. Vowing to make the campaign "a referendum on human rights and opportunity in America," he stressed that the country faced "a dangerous election, a hazardous national choice" in which it would either "turn backward into a continually increasing polarizing of the nation and a widening spiral of fear . . . or . . . continue to go forward into a new day of justice and order." Though the vice president denounced Wallace for "[owing] his political existence to the fears and hates aroused by [the race] issue," he concentrated his fire on Nixon. The GOP nominee, Humphrey conceded, was "a fair and just man," but Nixon had nonetheless "chosen . . . to join forces with the most reactionary elements in American society." Rather than celebrating "the tradition of Lincoln," Nixon was "openly competing with Mr. Wallace for the votes of people who at very best want to put the brakes on our progress toward full opportunity." Whereas Nixon and Wallace talked almost exclusively about the effects of crime and how they would use the law to stop it, Humphrey continued to link poverty and crime. Informed that Nixon wanted to double the conviction rate, Humphrey replied that his Republican opponent needed to show some interest in "doubling our efforts in housing, doubling our efforts in trying to help little children, doubling our efforts in trying to train the jobless." Similarly, Humphrey tried to convince a group of union members that "America is not going to be a better country just because you build a new jail."[26]

Such an appeal, Humphrey quickly learned, was getting him nowhere, especially among blue-collar workers. Polls revealed that for the first time in more than thirty years organized labor was failing to give a majority of its support to the Democratic presidential candidate. An August survey of one Illinois union had found Wallace with 315 votes, Nixon with 33, and Humphrey with just 15. Likewise, Wallace had 80 percent of the votes of a UAW union in New Jersey. Humphrey was still in front among union members outside the South, but only by seven percentage points. Greatly alarmed by this development, the vice president wanted some influential labor leaders to travel with him at all times and union bosses to expose the antilabor record of Wallace. Humphrey knew that his problems among union members required more than cosmetic changes, however. Social issues involving crime, housing, education, and race had taken precedence over economic concerns, and he had to find a way to reverse that. Humphrey believed that union members, whom he called "the backbone of the Democratic vote," were drifting to Nixon and Wallace because they felt that "Great Society programs [were] only oriented to the black man and to the poorest of the poor." In their zeal to fight poverty, Humphrey suggested, Democrats had lost touch with middle-income whites. He diagnosed their opposition to antipoverty efforts as stemming more from a feeling of being ignored than from racism or anger over programs that had failed to live up to expectations. At the same time, he insisted that they would remain Democrats if the party's urban, medical, and educational proposals could be made relevant to them and if he could assure them he did not tolerate violence. "There isn't any doubt that this matter will win or lose the election," he privately observed.[27]

Humphrey attempted to win these voters back by releasing in mid-September an eighty-four-point program to fight crime. Much of it was similar to what he had outlined in June. "The Rap Browns, the Stokely Carmichaels—extremists of the left and of the right—will not have their way and we will not allow them to terrorize or stampede Americans," he vowed. According to the Humphrey campaign, soaring crime rates were attributable to growing expectations among the poor, the burgeoning youth population, increased crowding in urban areas, and new methods of reporting crimes. The centerpiece of Humphrey's plan to solve this problem was increased federal aid to cities so that they could hire more police officers, boost their pay, and improve their training and equipment. Other proposals included reorganizing the Justice Department to better coordinate federal anticrime efforts, speeding up the creation of regional criminal justice centers, improving relations between African Americans and the police, and placing greater stress on rehabilitation of criminals. Altogether, aides estimated, the anticrime measures would cost the federal government nearly one billion dollars annually.[28]

Humphrey had presented a far more detailed anticrime plan than either of his opponents, yet it availed him little. Law and order was never as significant a concern among voters as Vietnam, but it was the one area where a wide array of Americans wanted increased government activity. The repeated attempts by Wallace and Nixon to blame the enormous increase in crime on the Great Society undoubtedly helped explain a mid-September Gallup poll showing Nixon with 43 percent of the vote, Humphrey with 31 percent, and Wallace with 19 percent. Former North Carolina governor Terry Sanford urged Humphrey to propose a series of one-on-one debates with Wallace in the South, but the vice president was focusing on Nixon. Humphrey tried to draw Nixon into a specific discussion on crime and poverty, but Nixon refused to take the bait. More troubling was the failure of Humphrey's anticrime message to register with voters. "I don't think there's any realization in this country of where HH stands on law and order," lamented Humphrey's campaign director. "There is no doubt," a pollster commented at a campaign staff meeting, "that Humphrey's soft image in the area of law and order is hurting us more than anything else." The vice president's aides knew that he could not move to the right of Nixon or Wallace on this issue, but many wanted him to place less emphasis on social justice and more on fighting crime. Some advised that these matters be addressed in separate speeches. Others worried that doing so would alienate liberals, who saw "law and order" as a code phrase for racism and believed that Humphrey was already talking too much about it. The vice president still had not found the right balance between order and justice and was thus in danger of being deserted by both conservative and liberal Democrats.[29]

Humphrey had set his sights on Nixon during the early weeks of the campaign, but by the end of September the only gap that had been narrowed was the one between Wallace and him. Humphrey now led the former Alabama governor by only seven percentage points. AFL-CIO chief George Meany warned that Wallace had strong support among the union's members and that 1.1 million of them had recently registered to vote. "The white backlash is much greater than anyone is willing to admit," commented a union leader. Union backing for Wallace, columnists Rowland Evans and Robert Novak reported, was burgeoning into "a full fledged political revolution." This was disastrous news for Humphrey, who had counted on Wallace taking votes from Nixon. The vice president had to win the blue-collar vote to overtake Nixon in several large northern industrial states, and doing so meant confronting Wallace directly. Humphrey promptly launched a blistering attack on the former Alabama governor during a swing through the Midwest. The former governor was a "racist" whose law and order theme was "the greatest hoax in American history," he charged, because crime in Alabama had risen faster than the national average during Wallace's administration. Humphrey also hoped to rally union members by calling attention to economic conditions in Alabama. "In Wallaceland, the worker finds low wages, low unemployment benefits, the lowest workmen's compensation in the country, unemployment rates above the national average, and the highest sales tax in the country," he reminded them. Meanwhile, leaders of organized labor were mounting a massive literature drive aimed at the rank-and-file to hammer home Wallace's hostility to blue-collar workers and to demonstrate that voting for him would only aid Nixon, who also had done little to help unions.[30]

Organized labor was not the only part of the New Deal coalition needing Humphrey's attention. Still strapped for cash during September, the Humphrey campaign had not undertaken many voter registration drives in black neighborhoods. Later that month Humphrey went beyond his Marshall Plan for the cities and his program to promote minority entrepreneurship by proposing that all Americans be guaranteed a "new and basic right" of living above the poverty level. Humphrey's earlier proposals had stressed the role of the private sector, but to those he was now adding plans firmly rooted in New Deal liberalism. Admitting that many Great Society efforts had not always worked well, Humphrey nonetheless insisted that the War on Poverty was essential and even indicated that he would expand it. "You don't take 25,000 units of penicillin to fight infection when you need 200,000 units," he observed. "You might as well take a peppermint for all the effect that it will have on you." Employment opportunities, Humphrey suggested, would be opened up through better management of the economy, expanded job training programs, and federally funded jobs for the hard-core unemployed. Furthermore, he pledged to raise Social Security and unemployment benefits, increase welfare payments to those unable to work, and give consideration to income maintenance proposals. Such programs would obviously provide a modicum of relief to many African Americans, but many remained ill-defined. Indeed, a Humphrey adviser publicly acknowledged their limits in helping inner city residents by commenting that they would have little effect on families headed by women or those with men who worked but could not earn enough to support their family.[31]

Humphrey also faced enormous problems in Dixie. "We're losing our shirt in the South," one aide announced to the campaign staff. The Deep

South had to be conceded to Wallace, but because Nixon enjoyed big leads in several northern and western states Humphrey had to win nearly all of the Upper South and border states. Though a few of these races were close, Humphrey had his work cut out for him. Well aware of the unpopularity of Humphrey among their constituents, southern Democrats who had backed the vice president in Chicago now quickly deserted him. In Tennessee neither Governor Buford Ellington nor Senator Albert Gore had made one speech for him. Democrats running for office in North Carolina, one reporter noted, had concluded that Humphrey was "a prime carrier of a kind of political bubonic plague" and were "determined to act as if [he] did not exist." Wallace was obviously popular across Dixie, but, thanks in large part to Strom Thurmond, so was Nixon. The GOP nominee had astutely decided to leave the arch-segregationist vote to Wallace and instead seek the support of whites who were disturbed about crime and the pace of racial change. Thurmond played an integral role in this strategy. The South Carolina Republican campaigned across the region claiming that "a vote for Wallace is a vote for Humphrey." One television ad put out by Thurmond urged voters not to focus on Wallace but rather on the "unacceptable Hubert Humphrey." Another contrasted Nixon's denunciation of HEW as "overzealous" in pushing school desegregation and his support for "true freedom of choice" with Humphrey's endorsement of the Supreme Court decision earlier that year outlawing freedom of choice plans. Democratic presidential candidates had been losing ground in the South since the 1950s, and, with just a month to go until the election, Humphrey showed no signs of being able to reverse this trend.[32]

The vice president made his first foray into Dixie in early October. A coalition of African Americans and 15–20 percent of whites, he hoped, might be enough to narrowly win a few states. He again highlighted the crime rate in Alabama and the poor economic conditions facing most of the state's citizens. Rather than downplay racial matters, Humphrey offered his bluntest language of the campaign in hopes of drawing liberals and African Americans to the polls. In Knoxville he likened Wallace's candidacy to the rise of Hitler and denounced him as "an apostle of the politics of fear and the politics of racism." Humphrey turned up the heat in his efforts to paint Wallace as a hypocrite regarding law and order by rightly pointing out that while governor he had chosen not to obey certain laws (presumably he was referring to school integration laws) and that some of Wallace's managers and electors were drawn from extremist groups such as the Ku Klux Klan, the White Citizens Councils, and the John Birch Society. The vice president was only slightly gentler with Nixon. The GOP nominee was "surely no racist," Humphrey acknowledged again, but he linked Nixon with Wallace by insisting that the former was "[appealing] to the same fears, the same passions, the same frustrations which . . . could unleash in this country a torrent of unreasoning hate and opposition." Nixon, Humphrey reminded one audience, would be in debt to Thurmond, "the backwash of South Carolina politics," if the Republicans captured the White House. Declaring the Democratic Party to be "the best friend the South ever had," Humphrey, as he had in 1964, urged white southerners to vote their wallets rather than their race. "I don't recall any Republicans that have ever done anything for Georgia except Sherman, and you know what he did to it," Humphrey told one interviewer.[33]

By mid-October Humphrey's private polls showed a much closer race than had been reported. National and regional breakdowns showing big leads for Nixon had masked Humphrey's status in individual states. He trailed badly in some states but led slightly in others. Organized labor's drive for Humphrey was starting to pay dividends, and he greatly helped himself in a nationally televised address on September 30 by announcing that he would consider a bombing halt in Vietnam temporarily to pursue peace.[34]

Humphrey's slight modification of his position on the war improved his standing, but he had not yet found an effective way to deal with the crime issue. Still refusing to debate specific policies for how to deal with soaring crime rates, Nixon accused Humphrey of having "a personal attitude of indulgence and permissiveness toward the lawless" and attacked the vice president as "a do-nothing candidate" regarding crime. "I'm going to send [Nixon] some kind of talcum powder," a frustrated Humphrey responded. "He must be getting saddle sore, straddling all those issues." Most voters, meanwhile, wanted the government to take swift and decisive action to halt violence. "This issue is costing Humphrey votes," one aide lamented, "and will continue to do so unless something is done about it." Humphrey was not comfortable preaching a strong law and order message, but, conceding that something had to be done, he agreed to give a nationally televised address on the subject in mid-October. The vice president's speechwriters wrestled for several days over how to identify Humphrey with the fears of blue-collar whites without angering African Americans or ardent white liberals. The issue, Humphrey declared to the nation's voters, was not white versus black, but rather those who abided by the law versus those who did not. Vowing "no compromise" with "armed terrorist groups of any color or persuasion," he pledged to back legislation to halt "guerrilla bands and vigilantes," touted his impressive crime-fighting record while mayor of Minneapolis, outlined the most important parts of his anticrime plan, and proposed a tenfold increase in funding for the Safe Streets Act. Had he stopped there, Humphrey might have helped his candidacy among many whites. But, against the advice of several aides, he went on to link fighting crime to social justice. "Anyone who seriously believes that order can exist without liberty and justice is tragically, even dangerously, misguided," Humphrey asserted. "And anyone who tells this country, as Mr. Nixon has, that poverty and crime have little or no relationship is fooling you and himself." Declaring that that programs to provide job training, medical care, and education were "not cheap," Humphrey insisted that the nation had to pay the price because "to do less will cost more—in crime, delinquency, welfare, and lost tax dollars." A Nixon victory would represent the triumph of "the voices of bigotry and fear," Humphrey warned, and would result in the loss of "everything we have labored so hard to build."[35]

Humphrey continued to stress these themes as election day neared. Much-needed cash had begun to pour in following his pledge of a temporary bombing halt, and as a result the campaign was able to go forward with television ads. One depicted a mother wondering if her baby would grow up safely and a voice noting, "But for every jail that Mr. Nixon would build, Mr. Humphrey would also build a house. For every policeman that Mr. Wallace would hire, Mr. Humphrey would also hire a good teacher." Another commercial touted his Marshall Plan for the cities. In an ad on law and order, he also discussed his plans to fight hunger and unemployment. Though Humphrey varied the emphasis of his speeches depending upon the audience, he repeatedly called for national unity behind his goals of order and justice. He told a largely white crowd in Kansas City, "I think that people that have been deprived for a century, been denied a chance I had, not only deserve equal opportunity, they deserve a little extra help." What that meant specifically, he did not say. Humphrey acknowledged the concerns of St. Louis housewives over crime, but he reminded them that African Americans wanted strong law enforcement too. In a Connecticut union hall, with numerous Wallace supporters in attendance, Humphrey declared, "Let me tell that young man with the white face down there it isn't a black man that is going to take your job, it's a Republican administration." Wallace's record while governor, Humphrey insisted, made "Scrooge look like a social worker."[36]

Though Humphrey was rising in the polls, African Americans had only lukewarmly embraced his campaign. Just fifteen hundred people attended a rally in Watts in late October. This was more than twice the number that had seen him during the summer, but still woefully short of what was needed for him to win California. The poor turnout clearly upset Humphrey. He finally won the endorsements of Coretta Scott King and Ralph Abernathy, who believed that his televised law and order speech had been too antiblack, a few days later, but the help seemed to come too late to mobilize African American voters.[37]

Humphrey showed signs of mounting a strong challenge to Nixon during the final week of the campaign. He attracted large and enthusiastic crowds at stops in Texas and California. Wallace, meanwhile, had slipped badly because of the union publicity effort and the reckless statements of his vice presidential candidate concerning the use of nuclear weapons in Vietnam. On the eve of the election, therefore, Humphrey trailed Nixon by just two percentage points.[38]

The vice president and his staff gathered in a Minneapolis hotel suite on election night to await the returns. Early reports indicated a close race. By eleven Humphrey had moved slightly ahead. As the night wore on, however, Nixon surged in front. When reporters indicated that Nixon would likely win Ohio, Illinois, and New Jersey, Humphrey dejectedly observed, "Well, before long the American people will learn they just elected a paper mache man." The networks declared Nixon the winner at eight the following morning. The Republican nominee received 43.4 percent of the vote to 42.7 percent for Humphrey and 13.5 percent for Wallace. In the electoral college Nixon won 302 votes, Humphrey 191, and Wallace 45.[39]

Nixon's narrow margin of victory masked the extent to which white voters had repudiated the Democratic Party. By receiving almost 57 percent of the total vote between them, Nixon and Wallace had delivered a staggering blow to the New Deal coalition. Humphrey ran worse in the South than any Democrat since 1868. He lost ten of eleven southern states and received just 20 percent of the white vote. Humphrey did better in the large industrial states of the North, where he carried Michigan, New York, and Pennsylvania. Nevertheless, he lost Illinois and Ohio to Nixon. Humphrey garnered 50 percent or more of the vote in just five states; Nixon did so in fifteen. A survey of sixty urban areas across the nation showed that Humphrey had won 524,000 fewer votes in those areas than John F. Kennedy had in 1960, and a whopping 5.3 million less than Johnson had in 1964. A closer look at the urban vote in the North revealed an even more worrisome scenario for the Democrats. In several large industrial cities the percentage of mostly white precincts giving Wallace at least 15 percent of the vote stood near or above 50 percent. The former Alabama governor proved especially popular among blue-collar whites who lived near African American neighborhoods. Unlike more affluent whites, these voters could not afford to move to the suburbs and resented what they considered to be black intrusion into "their" areas.[40]

Blacks were the only segment of the New Deal coalition that remained steadfastly loyal. Humphrey received 88 percent of the black vote. Last-minute registration drives, as well as a sense that a Nixon presidency would be a disaster for them, brought many blacks to the polls. Largely on the strength of an eight percentage point increase among African American voters in the South, overall black participation dropped just one percentage point from 1964. In the North, however, black turnout was down seven percentage points largely because of dissatisfaction over Vietnam, the death of King, and poor organization by the Humphrey campaign. Had the same number of nonwhites come to the polls in 1968 as in 1964, Humphrey would have won more popular votes than Nixon.[41]

The New Deal coalition, having been broken to a considerable degree by racial politics in both the North and the South, was thus but a shell of its former self. Humphrey had overestimated white Americans' willingness to continue the War on Poverty and their sympathy for blacks. The reservoir of goodwill he had counted on to carry him to victory did not exist, at least not in 1968. White middle-class Americans had grown hostile to government efforts to aid the poor and weary of demands by African Americans that the government do more to promote equality. More important, Humphrey's loss signaled that social issues related to crime, housing, and race had supplanted economics at the core of American politics. For a generation the Democratic Party had successfully campaigned on the legacy of the New Deal's economic benefits for white southerners and northern blue-collar whites. Now, though, several years of heightened racial tensions over jobs, housing, crime, and other issues led these core constituencies to repudiate a Democratic Party they considered to be too pro–African American. Their desertion of the Democrats cannot, of course, be attributed solely to race. Nor can it be blamed upon Humphrey entirely. Nevertheless, Humphrey does bear some responsibility for his miserable showing. As the Humphrey campaign knew that spring, the election would hinge on its ability to convince blacks to come to the polls in sufficient numbers and to hold conservative Democrats tempted to vote for Nixon or Wallace. Humphrey largely failed on both counts. His proposals for economic development did not catch fire with many blacks, and his campaign, largely because of financial troubles, had done a poor job of voter registration. Humphrey, moreover, was unable to convince whites that he shared their outrage over crime. At numerous points during the campaign he went against advice to place more emphasis on order and less on justice. Every time he talked about order he immediately followed with a discussion on the need to combat poverty. Humphrey's plea for order and justice was intellectually appealing, but he and the Democrats paid a high political price for being too forthright. Finally, Humphrey did not perceive early enough the threat posed by Wallace. Humphrey mistak-

enly assumed that Nixon would move to the right to compete with the former Alabama governor. The Republican nominee deftly supported major
civil rights initiatives such as *Brown* or the Voting Rights Act in principle, but
at the same time he assured whites that he would move slowly in implementing them. Instead of attacking Nixon so heavily early on, Humphrey
would have better served the campaign by warding off Wallace's raids on the
Democratic base. As two Humphrey aides later recalled, the loss of white voters to Wallace in the urban areas of Ohio and New Jersey cost Humphrey the
overall popular vote.[42]

Years later, Supreme Court Justice Thurgood Marshall called Humphrey's
loss "a tragedy for the civil rights movement." Marshall was clearly right in
suggesting that Humphrey would have rejected the politics of hate and division practiced by Nixon once in office. Unlike either of his opponents,
Humphrey sought to unify the country. As president, he would have challenged whites to renounce the politics of hate and fear and to put up desperately needed resources to address the myriad of problems in the ghetto.
At the same time, he would have called upon African Americans to resist the
politics of violence and vengeance. On the other hand, had Humphrey won
he would have had a difficult time getting his antipoverty programs through
Congress, and no one can say for certain whether his Marshall Plan for the
cities, proposals to reduce crime, and plans to increase spending on antipoverty efforts would have alleviated much of the economic and social
problems that were besetting African Americans and poisoning relations between the races.[43]

For twenty years Humphrey had been the leading voice in Washington
fighting for civil rights. His loss meant that in just three months he would be
out of politics for the first time since the early 1940s. Humphrey, however,
still maintained he would play a role in the battle for equality. "I shall continue my personal commitment to the cause of human rights . . . and to the
betterment of man," he assured his disappointed supporters on election
night. Just how he would do so no one, not even Humphrey himself, could
say with certainty.[44]

9

Jobs and the Failed Search for an Interracial Coalition

I

On the overcast and chilly afternoon of January 20, 1969, Humphrey solemnly watched as Richard Nixon was sworn in as president. Humphrey later recalled, "I sat there and couldn't help but think, well, we came mighty close." He knew that his defeat in November meant that he would likely never occupy the Oval Office. Out of public life for the first time in twenty-three years and worried that his political career was over, he returned to Minnesota and soon began teaching at the University of Minnesota and Macalester College in Saint Paul, writing his memoirs, and giving lectures across the country.[1]

Humphrey's loss led him to think deeply about the politics of race and the future of the Democratic Party. The broad public support for civil rights that existed in 1964 and 1965 had collapsed as a result of riots, crime, and other interracial tensions. The rise of Wallace and Nixon's victory, Humphrey told a reporter, meant that the Democrats could not take the votes of middle-class whites for granted. He believed that the decline in support for the Democrats among this group partly represented an unsurprising reluctance by whites to share power with African Americans and other minorities, but he also refused to blame the party's misfortunes solely on racism. Middle-class whites felt "that most if not all of the attention of government is going to a limited group," Humphrey observed. He insisted that whites favored African Americans having good jobs and decent housing, but he also argued that they legitimately wanted to know that the government was looking out for their concerns about employment, housing, education, and safe neighborhoods. Crime and other violence only bred fear, which "[brought] out the worst in people, rather than calling forth the best." As far as Humphrey was concerned, too many wealthy liberals who lived far away from the daily racial tensions in urban areas displayed a "snobbishness" by looking down upon many whites as racists and made "too many excuses for outright violence and destruction." He contended that the Democrats needed the support of middle-class whites, who made up 65 percent of the population, if they were to win office and advance their programs to help African Americans and the poor. Humphrey sounded like Wallace in some respects, but the former vice president had not shifted with the political winds as much as it might seem. He was not calling upon his party to renounce its commitment to racial justice. Neither his condemnation of violence nor his concern for middle-class whites was new; he had expressed both regularly while vice president. Rather, Humphrey's analysis demonstrated his abiding faith in the goodness of most Americans and his hope that a broad interracial coalition could be formed once again. This would be difficult, he readily admitted, but unless the Democrats could do it they were doomed to suffer more defeats. How the party could do so, Humphrey did not say.[2]

Two unexpected developments in the summer of 1969 provided Humphrey with a chance to play a role in addressing such matters. Massachusetts Senator Edward Kennedy's accident at Chappaquiddick left the party without a leader to challenge Nixon in 1972. Moreover, Senator Eugene McCarthy of Minnesota announced that he would not seek reelection in 1970. Humphrey, who desperately longed to be back in Washington, eyed McCarthy's seat. "It's a resurrection," he proclaimed. "I'm high as a kite. I'm on the run. I'll win in a walk." He would first return to the Senate, and there await his party's call to battle Nixon again.[3]

Though Vietnam continued to be the most pressing issue facing the nation, Humphrey hoped to focus attention on Nixon's domestic policies too. He would again seek racial harmony around the theme of order and justice. "I have heard a call for leadership which will not tolerate mindless and senseless violence," he declared as he announced his candidacy before a large crowd of reporters and well-wishers in Minneapolis. "And at the same time, I have heard the voice of compassion and tolerance and justice—the true voice of our people." He attacked Nixon for his lack of attention to urban problems. "What is the program for the cities?" Humphrey asked. At the same time, he attempted to reach middle-class whites by insisting that destruction of property and other violence "cannot be condoned" and by sharply criticizing Nixon's economic policies. Unemployment, he noted, had risen alarmingly to more than 5 percent, inflation was eating away at incomes, and interest rates had climbed to their highest level in one hundred years.[4]

Humphrey made a more concerted attempt to bridge racial divisions a month later in a major address to the American Bar Association. Asserting that popular stereotypes of blue-collar whites as racists and liberals as permissive elitists were "simplistic . . . [and] far from the truth," he maintained that both groups supported antipoverty programs and favored law and order. Liberals had allowed the law and order issue to be co-opted by Wallace and the Republicans because they were late in condemning violence. Even when they did speak out, Humphrey argued, they did so "too softly and apologetically." He noted:

> Liberals above all other political types should know . . . that the first casualty of violence and disorder abroad or at home is liberalism itself. . . . But what liberals must do now is an ironical imperative: *they must show the courage to take on a popular position* when the cause is right. And I happen to think that the cause of justice and law and order is right. . . . [Liberals] must let the hard-hats, Mr. and Mrs. Middle America, know that they understand what is bugging them, and they must let America know that they too condemn crime and riots and violence and extreme social turbulence, and they scorn extremists of the left as well as the extremists of the right—the black extremists with guns and the white extremists with sheets and guns.

Though he still argued that poverty, discrimination, and unemployment contributed to crime, Humphrey now contended that liberals had to make restoration of civil peace their top priority. Only when white middle-class voters moved beyond their concern over violence would the Democrats regain their trust. Antipoverty, health care, education, and civil rights programs were urgently needed, Humphrey indicated, but he feared that "in the short run violence and crime [were] rapidly becoming a barrier to the attainment of these long-run goals." The speech, which had been written by neoconservative Ben Wattenberg, provoked the ire of many liberals. Humphrey bristled at the criticism. "I don't think I have to re-establish my liberal credentials," he groused. "I've spent a lifetime trying to point out that you can't have civil order without civil justice." Humphrey routinely stressed the compatibility between law and order and liberal policies during his vice presidency and the 1968 campaign, but critics rightly pointed out that Humphrey's willingness to give law and order a higher priority in the short term was a departure from past practice. More important, the speech also widened the gap, which had opened over the issue of Vietnam, between him and liberals who equated law and order with racism. Humphrey, who had once stood on the left of the Democratic Party, now wanted to pull liberalism back from its drift further leftward regarding crime.[5]

This split was evident in the DFL Senate primary, where he faced challenger Earl Craig. An African American professor who had worked in McCarthy's 1968 presidential campaign, Craig acknowledged Humphrey's early support for civil rights but ran newspaper ads showing Humphrey's arm-in-arm meeting with segregationist Lester Maddox in 1967 and dismissed him as representative of "a kind of unresponsive and stale liberalism" that offered only patchwork solutions. Such charges got under Humphrey's skin. It was ironic, he wrote longtime friend Eugenie Anderson, that "after a lifetime of championing the cause of the black man, I should now be faced by an opponent who is black and says that I am not sufficiently liberal. If this is a way of testing a man's character, believe me, mine is being tested." Craig proved no match for Humphrey, who crushed him in the September primary by winning 80 percent of the vote. Though Humphrey's Republican opponent in November tried to blame liberalism for urban violence, Humphrey cruised to another easy victory.[6]

II

Upon his return to Washington Humphrey quickly clashed with Nixon over several urban issues. Seeing federal antipoverty programs as little more than wasteful bureaucracies, the president wanted to shut many of them down and send the money to state or local governments in the form of federal grants. Humphrey saw federal efforts as essential and accused the president of "a basic absence of policy toward establishing equal justice and opportunity." When Nixon closed the PCOYO and shifted its functions to other departments, Humphrey warned that the nation would "pay and pay and pay in lost lives, in violence, disorder, crime, sickness, sadness, and despair." When the president impounded $1.5 billion of urban aid that Congress had appropriated, Humphrey asserted that the United States "should be charged with criminal neglect" for letting so many people live in poverty.[7]

At the same time, Humphrey introduced several measures that reflected his interest in building an interracial coalition around economic issues. Reaching back to his 1968 campaign, he offered a bill to establish a national domestic development bank. Local branches of the bank would sell stock to the public and then provide loans to state and local governments, businesses, and nonprofit organizations. Such an approach, Humphrey hoped, would provide an efficient and inexpensive way to promote urban develop-

ment. The bank would presumably enable cities to avoid the troubles asso-
ciated with the sale of municipal bonds, which had suffered greatly during
the Nixon administration's first two years in office, or with federal money,
which the president was impounding regularly and was in relatively short
supply as a result of the recession of 1970–71. Humphrey also sponsored or
co-sponsored proposals to create a national health care system, make public
works jobs available in areas of high unemployment, strengthen the EEOC
by granting it cease-and-desist powers and increasing its funding (there was
a twenty-five-thousand-case backlog and a two-year wait for the resolution
of a complaint), provide dental care for poor children, and give free school
lunches to all students regardless of family income. None of this legislation
became law.[8]

The emergence of busing further complicated Humphrey's goal of
forming an interracial coalition around economic matters. HEW estimated
that 57 percent of African American students in the North and West, and 32
percent in the South, attended overwhelmingly black schools. The continued imbalance, which was rooted in housing patterns, led the federal courts
to turn to busing, which had been used for decades to maintain segregation
in the South. This approach received the qualified endorsement of the
Supreme Court in April 1971, when it unanimously ruled in *Swann v. Char-
lotte-Mecklenburg County Schools* that busing could be used to achieve desegregation so long as it did not harm the health of the students involved. Busing presented Humphrey with a thorny moral and political problem. A
September 1971 poll revealed that just 15 percent of whites and only 45 percent of African Americans favored busing. Though many liberals in the
Democratic Party supported busing, many blue-collar whites who still lived
in central areas of the nation's cities viewed it as a threat to the stability of
their neighborhoods and their children's education. To them it provided further proof that the federal government put the concerns of African Americans ahead of their interests. A full endorsement of busing, then, would undermine Humphrey's attempt to bring blue-collar whites back into the
Democratic Party. On the other hand, how could someone who had championed *Brown* and fought to end segregation in public accommodations permit African American children to continue to attend schools where the student body was almost all black?[9]

A few weeks before schools were to open that fall, Nixon reaffirmed his
stand against busing by revealing that he had instructed HEW and the Justice Department to hold it to a minimum. The president, moreover, retreated from Justice Department plans for busing in Austin, Texas, and asked Congress to amend his $1.5 billion request for school desegregation funds to

prohibit use of any of that money for busing. Humphrey accused the Nixon administration of creating "a situation of total confusion" regarding busing. He insisted that "there can be no retreat from the effort to end the educational and cultural handicaps born by . . . children brought up in a segregated atmosphere." At the same time, however, Humphrey weakly tried to distance himself from the issue. Busing represented "only one method, and certainly not always the best solution," he claimed. "Busing has its only justification if it improves the quality of education and the equality of educational opportunity." This was a distinction without a difference, because busing almost always would improve the educational opportunities of black students. Humphrey struggled to find a way out of the dilemma by calling for school district rezoning, careful location of new schools, and greater federal aid for public education. Whether these proposals would ease racial tensions or remedy the problem of segregation was very much in doubt. Given housing patterns, new district boundaries would still likely result in some students not being able to attend their neighborhood school. Increased federal funding of education and building new schools in African American neighborhoods might have led to better educational opportunities for black students, but neither policy addressed the issue of segregation.[10]

The problems created by busing were but one of many Humphrey faced during his first year back in the Senate. Though he had offered a spirited critique of Nixon's domestic policies, his antipoverty and civil rights legislation went nowhere. Moreover, Humphrey was personally miserable much of the time. Colleagues accorded him little respect and denied his requests to return to his old seats on the powerful Appropriations and Foreign Relations Committees. The clublike atmosphere that marked the Senate during the 1950s had disappeared. Gone too were the days when Humphrey enjoyed close relationships with Senate leaders. He now seemed to be just another legislator.[11]

III

On January 10, 1972, Humphrey traveled to Philadelphia with a corps of relatives, supporters, staff members, and reporters to announce his candidacy for the Democratic presidential nomination. That the loser of the 1968 election would make another run at the White House surely surprised many Americans, but Humphrey, who had received a warm welcome as he made speeches around the country since his return to the Senate, thought himself the best man to challenge Nixon and could not resist the temptation to make one more run at the White House. As he had four years earlier, Humphrey would make the problems of the inner city central to his campaign. "A nation that developed a Marshall Plan to rebuild Europe can develop another to rebuild our neighborhoods and crime-ridden cities," he declared.[12]

Humphrey's campaign sputtered from the start due in large part to his confusing and sometimes contradictory approach to racial matters. Though the Humphrey camp desperately wanted the busing issue to disappear, it played an important role in several primaries. Humphrey rejected calls for an antibusing amendment to the federal constitution, yet he denounced busing to achieve a specific racial balance in a particular school as "absolutely ridiculous." This was a false issue, however, because no court anywhere had ordered busing to achieve a specific racial balance. Humphrey continued to endorse busing "where it will advance the quality of education of those children bused." This vague position still left many voters understandably confused about how much busing would occur. Humphrey made things worse for himself by flip-flopping on Nixon's call for a one-year moratorium on court orders to enforce busing and permanent legislative restrictions on busing. Critics rightly pointed out that it was becoming harder and harder to know just where Humphrey stood on this vital issue. The *New York Times* charged that his positions "had all the unfortunate trappings of a man who would rather be president than right." Former Cleveland mayor Carl Stokes publicly accused Humphrey of trying to "out-Wallace Wallace," while a longtime African American friend wrote him that he "never thought [he'd] live to see the day when [he'd] have to be defensive about a Humphrey statement, or position, on a civil rights issue." Humphrey continued to maintain that the way out of the busing dilemma was better enforcement of open housing laws, increased federal aid to schools, and the redrawing of district boundaries, but when reporters challenged him by pointing out that none of these had worked well, he defensively retorted, "Let's quit nit-picking. You're not going to change my mind by asking questions." Humphrey's approach to busing won him few white votes and cost him black support, as by May many African American leaders, including Coretta Scott King, Ralph Abernathy, Jesse Jackson, and Michigan representative John Conyers, had endorsed Senator George McGovern of South Dakota, who favored busing. Clearly, Humphrey still had not found a way to reconcile his commitment to racial equality with his concern for blue-collar whites.[13]

Humphrey withdrew from the race at the Democratic convention in July once it became clear that McGovern would win. Pledging to continue to fight for "justice and compassion," he ruefully looked back on a campaign that had been a miserable failure. "A lot of people that I've done a lot for didn't seem to know it," he lamented. "The young blacks are different from their parents, and they don't know too much about me." Humphrey bore much of the blame for that himself. To be sure, he won most of the African American votes cast in the primaries, yet he had waffled on busing, refused to confront George Wallace on issues such as busing and welfare, and given insufficient attention the economic development of the inner city. In some cases Humphrey suggested ridiculous proposals for helping the ghetto. Asked about taking money spent on the space program and using it to develop the cities, he told a largely white Pennsylvania audience that stood to benefit from space exploration, "The only way to clean up the ghettos is with technology, and that is coming out of the space program." Humphrey, moreover, had relied too heavily on his longtime liberal allies in the African American community. This older generation of black leaders could help him little among younger blacks. In many states Humphrey ran ads replaying parts of his 1948 convention speech. Intended to show him as a longtime defender of racial justice, such tactics gave the impression that he did not understand contemporary racial problems.[14]

As Humphrey had feared, Nixon trounced McGovern in November. The president triumphed in forty-nine states—the largest total ever—and received an astounding 60.7 percent of the vote. Though African Americans remained loyal Democrats, other members of the New Deal coalition deserted their party like passengers on a sinking ship. Indeed, 37 percent of Democrats nationwide voted for Nixon. This startling figure masked even more alarming trends among particular regions or groups. The president swept the South, where thanks to overwhelming white support he won more than 70 percent of the vote in six states. Nixon also scored impressive gains in the North. Fifty-five percent of blue-collar workers voted for the president, up from 41 percent in 1968. He also registered a seventeen percentage point increase in the votes of union family members over his total four years earlier. Nixon was the first Republican to win a majority of Catholic and blue-collar voters. The Irish, Italian, Polish, and other "ethnics" who had once been an integral part of the Democratic Party were continuing a move to the right begun in 1968. Race was not the only reason behind the decision of some Democrats to bolt to the GOP, but fears about crime, busing, and other racial tensions played a leading role.[15]

McGovern's emphasis on the poor during the campaign exacerbated Humphrey's worry that the Democrats were losing touch with middle-class whites. So too did recent reforms in the Democratic Party intended to give greater representation to women, racial minorities, and youth at the party's conventions. Humphrey expressed his concerns about the party's future at a civil rights symposium held at the Lyndon B. Johnson Library in December. Asserting that the majority of whites recognized that the battle for racial justice was not over, he added that the election results nonetheless demonstrated "that any political appeal that appears, rightly or wrongly, as favoring one group or class of people over another is going to be rejected by the American people." Humphrey maintained:

> The Democratic Party got into trouble when its internal reforms came to be perceived as establishing specific quotas that favored young people, women, and blacks over the more traditional elements of the party, particularly ethnic Americans, blue collar workers, the elderly, and elected Democratic officials. And, by the same token, I would argue that the civil rights movement got into trouble when more and more people came to see it as an effort to give blacks a special break that was afforded no other group in American society. We know this perception is wrong. But it exists, whether we like it or not.

Simple math dictated that the Democrats could not ignore middle-class whites, for African Americans and other minorities did not gain when the Democrats lost elections. "There just aren't enough blacks, Chicanos, Indians, and Puerto Ricans to form an electoral majority," Humphrey pointed out. "Overemphasis on the needs of these identifiable groups can be and has been counterproductive." But would winning the support of middle-class whites mean sacrificing the party's commitment to racial justice and fighting poverty? Humphrey thought not. He argued that the Democrats could "find common denominators—mutual needs, mutual wants, common hopes, the same fears—and use this body of accepted information as the binding that holds together a coalition of people: a coalition representing the hopes and fears of the majority." That interracial coalition, Humphrey insisted, could be rallied around the issues, of jobs, health care, education, and personal safety for all citizens, not just African Americans. Those who put racial matters such as busing above these chiefly economic concerns would be doomed to political failure, he intimated.[16]

IV

Humphrey renewed his quarrel with Nixon over urban matters when he returned to Washington in January. When the president sought to cut funding for the Model Cities program, eliminate other urban development efforts altogether, slash spending on jobs programs for youth, and impound money, Humphrey staunchly defended existing programs and offered a handful of new antipoverty measures. "A national policy of developing a healthy and hopeful people will . . . be the only thing that will save our cities," he wrote. Accusing Nixon of "domestic disengagement," Humphrey criticized the president for accepting an unemployment rate of 5.2 percent while proposing cuts of $600 million in job training and employment programs. "If you're going to dismantle every program in which there is some mismanagement, we'd be a pacifist nation," Humphrey sarcastically pointed out. "It appears that it's all right for the rich to louse up, but if you're black and poor, you mustn't make any mistake at all." Declaring that the government needed to be the "employer of first opportunity," he sponsored legislation to establish a permanent program of public service employment that would provide up to one million new jobs and job training. When Nixon sought to impound funds for a summer jobs program, Humphrey maintained that poor youth deserved the opportunity to overcome "conditions that can only breed a profound distrust" and proposed spending an additional $67.6 million on the program. Humphrey also contended that cities needed his national domestic development bank, expanded child nutrition programs, and the continuation of community action agencies, not Nixon's plans for revenue sharing or federal grants. Once again, none of Humphrey's bills became law.[17]

Meanwhile, busing continued to make trouble for Humphrey. White hostility toward busing greatly intensified as it spread throughout the North, and particularly ugly confrontations occurred in Boston during the spring of 1974. Eager to capitalize on such developments, busing opponents in Congress offered a bill to halt all busing intended to promote desegregation and forbid any attempt to alter district lines unless it could be proved that the original lines had been drawn with the intent of creating a segregated school system. If enacted, the legislation would have severely limited the powers of federal or local authorities to achieve integrated schools. The Senate defeated the proposal, but by just one vote. "It is certainly a sorry matter," Humphrey wrote Roy Wilkins, "that after so many years we should have so close a vote on such a regressive measure." Though Humphrey had opposed this effort, he still maintained that busing was a "temporary issue" and that the more important question was how to provide equal educational opportunity for all through district rezoning, new school construction in poor areas, and increased federal aid for schools.[18]

V

All Humphrey's previous urban development and antipoverty legislation paled in comparison to the measure he offered in August 1974. Joining forces with California congressman Augustus Hawkins and the Congressional Black Caucus, he introduced legislation that would guarantee employment for all citizens over sixteen years old. Modeled after the Employment Act of 1946, the measure would establish employment "at wages reflecting regional levels of compensation, statutory minimum wages, or those wages established by prevailing collective bargaining agreements, whichever is highest," as a right of all Americans over age sixteen. Individuals denied this right would be able to sue the federal government for injunctive relief and/or damages. To meet the goal of full employment, workers would first be channeled to the private sector—a result of the bill's requiring the president to submit to Congress every six months a detailed plan of fiscal and monetary policies to stimulate the economy so as to ensure adequate demand for labor. Anyone who remained unemployed would work in public service jobs identified by local governments but paid for by the federal government. Possible public service jobs included infrastructure construction and repair, fighting drug abuse, administering recreational programs, assisting the elderly, preventing juvenile delinquency, or aiding charitable or educational institutions.[19]

Humphrey believed that bold new policies were urgently needed to address a burgeoning economic crisis. "Social justice demands and economic necessity requires that every American . . . be provided with a job," he declared." The United States, he maintained, was entering a new economic era and old assumptions had to be discarded. Economic data seemed to buttress Humphrey's claim. By the early 1970s the unemployment rate was consistently more than 5 percent, whereas in the mid-1960s it had usually been between 3 and 4 percent. Contrary to prevailing economic theories, high unemployment had also been accompanied by rising inflation and sluggish economic growth. That whites were suffering from increased joblessness worried Humphrey greatly, but full employment obviously had special implications for African Americans, who had much higher rates of unemployment. In this sense the proposal represented an example of what political scientist Theda Skocpol calls "targeting within universalism." To be sure, the post–World War II boom had resulted in the substantial growth of the black middle class, but many African Americans remained largely untouched by this progress. The economic position of many blacks worsened during the late 1960s and early 1970s. Black unemployment had climbed to between 9 and 10 percent, up approximately three percentage points from a few years earlier, while the rate for African American teens had been in the 25–35 percent range. These alarming figures understated the depth of the economic crisis in black America because they did not include individuals who had given up looking for work or many African Americans who worked but made little money. The Census Bureau estimated that 30.5 percent of the labor supply in sixty poverty areas of fifty-one major cities was "subemployed" in 1970—either unemployed or making less than four thousand dollars per year. The labor force participation rate among African American males over age sixteen had decreased from 85.2 percent in 1954 to 73.6 percent in 1972. Median black family income relative to white income had increased during the late 1960s, but after reaching 62 percent in 1970 it slid below 60 percent by 1973. Whereas real black family income grew at a rate twice that for whites between 1965 and 1969, it declined .2 percent between 1970 and 1973 while real white family income grew by 6.1 percent. Finally, as Humphrey frequently pointed out, by 1970 a larger share of African Americans (more than 42 percent) were employed in jobs in the lowest-skilled categories than a decade earlier.[20]

Numerous factors accounted for the declining fortunes of many African Americans in the nation's inner cities. Most important, the economic restructuring of urban areas, especially those in the North, was well underway. Between 1940 and 1970 five million African Americans had left the South for the urban North and West, but many of the high-paying unskilled manufacturing jobs that had sustained early waves of migrants were shifting to the suburbs, the Sunbelt, or overseas. Others were being phased out due to technological developments. The result was a postindustrial economy dominated by service sector jobs that either required training most African Americans lacked or, in cases where advanced skills were not needed, paid meager wages and offered few benefits. Many inner city neighborhoods offered little paid work of any type. The economic misfortunes of urban America were not simply the result of impersonal market forces, however. Job discrimination remained an all too common part of African American life. Numerous policies by businesses and governments at the federal state and local levels, including redlining by banks and insurance companies and subsidies and tax breaks for highway construction and home ownership, helped encourage the flight of white residents and businesses to the suburbs. Finally, broad cultural transformations, such as the reshaping of gender roles and family life, and behavior choices by urban residents themselves, contributed to the worsening situation. The result was an inner-city population that was increasingly marginalized economically and socially.[21]

Humphrey-Hawkins constituted a dramatic departure from many of the ways liberalism had developed over the previous thirty years. For most of the post–World War II period liberals, including Humphrey, had concentrated on taxation and spending policies to address labor and poverty issues. They had assumed during the 1940s and 1950s that economic growth and FEPC laws would lift African Americans out of poverty. Even a New Dealer like Humphrey had become enamored with the Keynesian tax cut of 1963 as a weapon against poverty. The civil rights laws of the 1960s helped produce some economic advances for blacks, but it was clear that many difficulties remained. This realization led in part to the War on Poverty, but rather than provide direct cash assistance or employment to the poor the Johnson administration had attempted to offer education and job training to give the disadvantaged the opportunity to compete. Contrary to the Great Society assumptions that poverty resulted from personal shortcomings and that the American economy was fundamentally healthy, Humphrey stressed structural problems in the economy as the source of unemployment and proposed a major overhaul of economic policy unrivaled since the 1930s. Humphrey was now hoping to return liberalism to its roots in New Deal-style economic reform (though no New Deal program had ever gone so far as to guarantee employment). Whereas the federal government had largely separated poverty and broader economic policies during the post-1945 era, Humphrey sought to make the former an integral part of the latter. Many Democrats had favored temporary public service employment during the late 1960s, but by proposing a permanent system of public jobs Humphrey and his allies also countered the longstanding notion that such efforts were to be temporary solutions to especially severe short-term economic downturns. Humphrey's focus on jobs also differed greatly from that of many liberal activists during this period. To him "idleness was a disease," while any type of employment was "a therapy." Recalling how he worked as a caretaker of several homes while in college, he maintained, "There are streets to be cleaned. It is not beneath anybody." Humphrey lamented that unemployment compensation, though necessary, had "become a permanent kind of income maintenance program, which it wasn't ever intended to be." On the other hand, social welfare groups such as the National Welfare Rights Organization saw greater levels of public assistance as the solution to poverty. Public service jobs, in their eyes, were coercive programs that stigmatized recipients and trapped them in poverty because they gained few valuable skills or training. Finally,

Humphrey-Hawkins stood in sharp contrast to liberalism's growing emphasis on group rights and personal liberties during the early 1970s. Since the mid-1960s liberals had focused increasingly on questions of social and political rights for a wide range of previously marginalized groups, including African Americans, women, criminal defendants, immigrants, Native Americans, homosexuals, welfare recipients, and children. Questions of economic power had taken a back seat to these concerns, but now Humphrey wanted to return economics to the top of the liberal agenda.[22]

Humphrey considered unemployment to be the underlying factor in numerous social and political problems. Though high inflation worried him (he tried to assuage potential critics by announcing that his bill needed an anti-inflation provision), growing up during the Depression had convinced him that unemployment was far more devastating. "I can think of nothing more destructive for a society than to have large numbers of fellow citizens told by the economic system . . . that they are not needed," he asserted. Crime, violence, alcoholism, drugs, family dissolution, and other social maladies plaguing American cities, he contended, stemmed primarily from the lack of jobs. Humphrey also expected that guaranteeing employment for all would ease tensions between whites and African Americans and thus help forge the liberal interracial political coalition centered on economic issues that he had called for at the Johnson Library. This coalition would develop not only because violent crime, which had increased 47 percent in the previous five years, would decrease as African Americans and poor whites found work, but also because economic competition between the races would be minimized. Unless jobs were guaranteed, whites and African Americans could be pitted against one another for employment and promotions. "Without a new departure," Humphrey testified before a House subcommittee, "I fear that many of the government's so-called *affirmative* action programs will turn out to be negative."[23]

Full employment topped Humphrey's agenda when Congress reconvened in January 1975. The overall unemployment rate for December stood at 7.1 percent, while that for African Americans was 12.8 percent. Black teen unemployment had climbed to nearly 38 percent. The number of jobless African Americans had swelled by roughly 40 percent in 1974, from 890,000 to 1.3 million, and more black workers were staying unemployed for longer periods of time. According to the Urban League, counting those who had given up looking for work revealed that the real unemployment rate among blacks was 25.8 percent. Whichever figures one cited, it was hard to disagree with league director Vernon Jordan's gloomy conclusion that African Americans were suffering from "a major depression." Humphrey echoed such thoughts when he told Jesse Jackson, one hundred members of Congress, and liberal leaders who had gathered for a full employment breakfast before the start of a new session that the nation was entering "a period of economic hardship which has not been equaled since the days of the soup kitchens and the boarded up banks of the Great Depression." Insisting that "a nation which spends $100 billion each year in its military budget can give every American a good job," Humphrey called upon the audience to rally behind his proposals for full employment, a tax cut for low- and middle-income families, and a national domestic development bank.[24]

As head of Congress's Joint Economic Committee, Humphrey took his case to the public during the winter of 1975–76 by conducting hearings into the state of the economy in several cities. Nationally, unemployment had climbed to 8.5 percent; the African American unemployment rate was 13.9 percent. The head of the Chicago Urban League informed the committee that 36 percent of the city's African American population was unemployed, working part time, or too discouraged to look for work and predicted that "neither Chicago nor this country can survive the devastation that a generation of unemployed blacks . . . will inflict." An employee of the Georgia Department of Offender Rehabilitation testified that the lack of economic opportunities for African Americans had led to a "shadow economy" of thieves and drug dealers. Mayor Tom Bradley of Los Angeles painted a similarly grim picture of the lack of economic opportunity for African Americans in his city, and a UCLA economics professor vividly described the temptations of the "street economy" for young African Americans. The hearings deepened Humphrey's belief in the urgent need for full employment. The nation's urban areas, he lamented, had become plagued by "guerrilla warfare and terrorism," which made city life comparable to that of the fifteenth and sixteenth centuries, when cities had to build walls to protect residents from roving bands of thieves. Predicting that failure to address the unemployment problem would only lead to more alcoholism, drug abuse, crime, and other social ills, Humphrey argued that it was far better to pay people for a public service job than to give them unemployment or welfare checks. "I was brought up in the old fashioned school, and I consider all these modern conservatives the most radical people I have ever met in my whole life," he stated. "They just believe in handing it out. I believe in working it out."[25]

Humphrey unveiled a new version of his full employment bill in March 1976. He had privately indicated as early as the previous September that it would need to be modified if he expected to gain support in Congress, and with the presidential election approaching Humphrey hoped that it could be a central part of the Democrats' campaign. That meant wooing union support. Organized labor backed off the original bill out of fears that it was inflationary and would in the long run cost jobs. Humphrey enlisted the aid of the AFL-CIO, but only after agreeing not to include price controls, which union leaders worried would soon lead to wage controls. The revised legislation thus met the chief concerns of both labor and African Americans. The new bill differed from the original in several critical respects, however. First, it added an extensive economic planning provision that would have modeled federal economic policy along the lines of several European countries. According to Humphrey, Congress, the president, and the Federal Reserve needed to work closely together to coordinate economic policy. Even more important were the changes regarding employment. Individuals could no longer sue the federal government if they lacked a job. Full employment, which was now defined as 3 percent unemployment, would be achieved within four years of enactment. Special provisions for youth unemployment, fighting inflation, greater coordination with state and local governments, and a countercyclical aid program for distressed areas were added. "The bill begins with the idea that work and productivity are better than welfare and waste," Humphrey told the Senate. He hoped to build momentum for his new measure by celebrating the thirtieth anniversary of the Employment Act of 1946 at two-day conference in Washington attended by labor and civil rights leaders. Even with these changes, however, Humphrey-Hawkins attracted few new supporters. Just 6 senators and 110 representatives co-sponsored it.[26]

Whereas full employment advocates saw joblessness as the nation's chief economic problem, President Ford had declared inflation to be "domestic enemy number one" upon taking office in August 1974. Spurred by rising oil prices, the end of wage and price controls, growing federal budget deficits, and a poor harvest, among other factors, inflation in 1974 reached nearly 14 percent, its highest rate since the end of World War I. Accepting the Phillips curve trade-off between inflation and unemployment, administration officials feared that a public service jobs program would only exacerbate price increases. Other Republicans dismissed Humphrey-Hawkins as unrealistic by noting that quarterly unemployment rates had been below 4 percent just twice since 1948, with both periods occurring during special circumstances related to war. Conservative economist Milton Friedman described Humphrey-Hawkins as a measure whose good intentions were "exceeded only by the badness of the results it would produce." Humphrey-Hawkins would ironically decrease overall employment, Friedman maintained, because paying for public service jobs would require higher taxes, borrowing, or printing of money, all of which were detrimental to employers. Assistant Secretary of Labor William Kolberg testified that the true cost of the bill was close to fifty billion dollars, far more than the twelve billion dollars that Humphrey had estimated. Other conservatives contended that Humphrey and his allies had fundamentally misunderstood the nature of unemployment and over-sold the virtues of public service jobs. Because state and local governments would substitute federal money for local initiatives, there would be little or no net job growth, they predicted. (Economists referred to this as the "displacement effect.") Worse, in the eyes of many conservatives public service jobs would be of little use because unemployment tended to be cyclical, not structural. Most of the jobless remained unemployed for approximately two months, which was too little time for a public service job to be of much use. Other conservatives perceptively observed that public service jobs were not as easy an alternative to welfare as Humphrey had portrayed because many of the adults on welfare were disabled, senior citizens, or young women who headed households. Moving this last group into the workforce constituted an especially difficult problem because they needed day care for their children, but Humphrey-Hawkins had nothing to say on this subject. President Ford, who would veto several public works employment bills during his tenure in office, called Humphrey-Hawkins "a vast election year boondoggle" and thought it unnecessary because the economy was improving overall by the spring of 1976. Federal Reserve chair Arthur Burns labeled it "dangerous and inflationary," and Council of Economic Advisers chair Alan Greenspan charged that the measure mistakenly assumed a nonexistent level of economic forecasting and control by government and that employment did not always lead to greater productivity. (Humphrey had maintained that the way to reduce inflation was to put people to work, which would increase productivity.) The Ford administration also flatly rejected attempts by Humphrey and others to compare the 1970s with the Great Depression. Joblessness was more tolerable than in the past, it argued, because of unemployment insurance and the increased number of women and teens working. Not unsympathetic to the plight of the unemployed, the president offered temporary extensions of unemployment insurance and, in hopes of stimulating hiring, tax breaks for businesses. Humphrey blasted the latter as "pretty much what was recommended by Herbert Hoover."[27]

Conservative criticism was unsurprising, but the legislation seemed to be under attack from all quarters. Humphrey-Hawkins suffered a grave setback when numerous prominent liberal economists questioned it too. Charles Schultze of the Brookings Institution alarmingly predicted that provisions calling for those working in government jobs programs to receive "prevailing" wage rates for the area would lead to a massive shift of low-skilled workers

from the private to the public sector, thus driving up the cost of labor and leading to dramatic price increases. One liberal economist suggested that the economy would have to grow at an unprecedented 7.5 percent annual rate for three
consecutive years to reach the unemployment target, and another predicted
that the measure would result in 15 percent annual inflation by 1980. Lyndon
Johnson's top economic adviser described the bill as "great poetry . . . but not
a desirable, feasible program." Humphrey-Hawkins also drew fire from the
nonpartisan Congressional Budget Office and the Congressional Research
Service, both of which expressed fears about public service jobs leading to increased inflation. Liberal groups such as the National Organization for Women,
ADA, and various religious organizations, though still favorably disposed to the
bill as better than nothing, attacked it for retreating from the original promise
of jobs for all within a short period. Finally, Humphrey-Hawkins sparked criticism from younger, more conservative Democrats who argued that the proposal would only exacerbate anti-Washington feelings among the public. "We
make these promises and then we fail to keep them," one Democratic fresh-
man complained, "and nobody believes we will do anything that we say."[28]

Humphrey countered with a vigorous defense of his legislation. Critics
who believed that the public sector jobs should pay significantly less than
private sector employment would "turn the legislation into an exercise in
irony by increasing poverty while increasing employment." The government,
he contended, should not stand powerless while abstract market forces led to
high unemployment and created "a class whose only experience is welfare,
unemployment, and crime." The market was not simply an end in itself but
rather a means "to obtain justice." Those who were "alarmed" over the inflation rate or the budget deficit, he suggested, were ignoring the tremendous
suffering resulting from joblessness:

> Well, I wish they would take a walk with me through some of our cities.
> I'd show them something really alarming. Like the fact that the richest
> nation on this planet is willing to sacrifice the suffering of millions of
> Americans to some notion of "price stability" for the wealthy. . . . Like the
> fact that in this country of two-car garages and matching sets of lawn fur-
> niture, there are children crying from hunger and families broken by
> poverty. Like the fact that in this land of hot-lather shaving machines and
> electric can-openers, there are millions of Americans who have never
> seen the inside of a decent school or a doctor's office.[29]

Humphrey and other liberal Democrats had initially hoped to approve
the measure quickly and then make a political issue out of the certain veto

by Ford, but this plan derailed when opposition by liberal economists caused many Democrats to have second thoughts. In August wary first-term Democrats in the House voted 65–10 to ask the leadership not to bring Humphrey-Hawkins up that fall lest it be used against them in November. That his full employment bill was headed in the wrong direction was not lost on Humphrey, who felt trapped between his desire to help labor and African Americans and the criticism of many liberal economists whom he deeply respected. Schultze's testimony, he confessed to liberal economist Walter Heller, "has been damaging and has caused us a great deal of concern." Humphrey acknowledged that some of the legislation's original features had been included to rally African Americans and labor behind it. "Quite frankly, we would have had no support for this bill unless we had introduced it with the prevailing wage feature and with the less than adequate provisions on inflation," he informed Heller. "The AFL and CIO were adamant as you can well imagine, and the Black Caucus wanted everything they could possibly think of plus another ten to fifteen percent. This is understandable but it doesn't necessarily make the product [salable]." Humphrey admitted that wages for public jobs would have to be reduced and that the measure needed a better balance between employment and inflation, though he still regarded jobs as the top issue. Such a strategy risked alienating African Americans and labor, but the full-employment coalition lacked the political muscle to get the legislation through Congress.[30]

Humphrey's efforts to make full employment the centerpiece of the Democrats' 1976 campaign met with similar results. Governor Jimmy Carter of Georgia, the surprise early leader of the pack and a proponent of smaller, more efficient government, contended that a federal job guarantee would be "too expensive." Attacks on big government were "a disguised new form of racism," Humphrey countered. Such overblown rhetoric drew a sharp response from Carter, who called him a "loser." Eager to placate labor, liberals, and African Americans, the Democratic Party had included a tepid call for full employment in the party's platform, but it did not mention Humphrey-Hawkins by name. Carter, who won the nomination in July, barely mentioned Humphrey-Hawkins on his way to winning the presidency in November.[31]

VI

As Washington prepared to inaugurate a new president, Humphrey geared up for another attempt to pass his full employment measure. Unemployment had decreased slightly to 8.1 percent, still far above what he deemed acceptable. Recognizing that he had to make some further concessions to build support within his own party, he offered a substantially reworked version of his legislation. The new bill greatly weakened the federal government's role in economic planning and set targets of 3 percent unemployment by 1980 for those over age twenty and an inflation rate no greater than 5 percent annually. Youth unemployment would be reduced "as promptly as possible." Public service jobs would not be created for at least two years following the enactment of the legislation, and even then they would be "mainly in the lower ranges of skills and pay" to encourage people to find work in the private sector. The public jobs provision of the bill, moreover, was streamlined through the elimination of local employment councils that would have identified jobs and facilitated placing the unemployed in them. Liberal groups such as ADA and African American organizations worried that the legislation had become an empty symbol rather than an answer to joblessness, but Humphrey insisted that it was still better than the status quo. "This business of just relying on unemployment compensation, food stamps, and welfare as a supplement to tax cuts is not what I call a sensible long-term program," he wrote. Despite these changes, Humphrey-Hawkins had had just seventy-nine co-sponsors in the House and Senate and little prospect for gaining any more allies.[32]

Once in office, Carter hoped to avoid the measure altogether. Rather than expand federal involvement in urban and economic matters, Carter favored a greater role for the private sector and devolution of many federal programs. Humphrey-Hawkins had a few allies within the White House, notably Secretary of Labor Ray Marshall, but Secretary of the Treasury Michael Blumenthal, Budget Director Bert Lance, Council of Economic Advisers Chair Charles Schultze, and the president firmly opposed it. A goal of 3 percent unemployment within four years, Schultze still believed, risked accelerating inflation to unacceptable levels. Contending that it had already proposed an adequate public service jobs program, the administration wanted to eliminate provisions for establishing public employment jobs. It also expressed concerns that the sections dealing with economic forecasting would be expensive and that the measure would lead to confrontations between the executive branch and the Federal Reserve. "These disagreements go to the heart of the Humphrey-Hawkins bill," one administration official privately noted. "They crystallize the distance between the administration's economic views and those of the Black Caucus and other congressional liberals."[33]

Carter could not afford to ignore Humphrey-Hawkins entirely, however. Having strained relations with the liberal wing of the Democratic Party during the campaign, he needed its assistance once in office, and liberals, despite some reservations, were lining up behind the bill. Coretta Scott King and Murray Finley of the Amalgamated Textile Workers Union had formed a Full Employment Action Council, which consisted of dozens of liberal groups, to rally support for it. Likewise, Humphrey and Hawkins brought pressure on Carter in early June by submitting a resolution in which leaders of thirty-two liberal organizations, including the AFL-CIO, NAACP, Leadership Conference on Civil Rights, National Council of Negro Women, ADA, and Full Employment Action Council, called upon him to back the proposal. As far as they were concerned, Carter had done little to indicate that he considered urban issues a high priority. How the administration handled Humphrey-Hawkins, then, went well beyond the legislation itself. "We are treading on very unstable grounds politically and socially," one White House official privately wrote. "I'm getting nervous because we are going to be blasted soon for our inactivity in this area." Eager not to offend African American or other liberal groups, Carter opted to seek a compromise. Instead of 3 percent unemployment for adults within four years of enactment of the legislation, the administration proposed a target of 4.75 percent within five years for those over sixteen. It also sought to eliminate the provisions making the government the employer of last resort and to include language giving the president more leeway to fight inflation.[34]

Humphrey, meanwhile, had little to say directly about the fate of his bill. He was absent from much of the day-to-day wrangling in Washington that summer because of ill health. The cancer that had led to the removal of his bladder and prostate in the fall of 1976 had spread through his abdomen. As a result, Humphrey had to undergo extensive treatments, and then another surgery, in Minneapolis the following spring. The second operation revealed what many had feared: Humphrey was dying.[35]

The senator kept close tabs on developments in Washington as best he could. Consultations with Humphrey's staff had led the administration to think that he was more inclined than Hawkins to accept additional compromises, but talks with the bill's sponsors late that summer resulted in a stalemate. After initially giving the administration's proposals a warm reception, Humphrey and Hawkins sent back a measure incorporating few of the changes the president desired. Carter refused to back down either, but he decided not to foreclose the possibility of an agreement. Meanwhile, the jobless rate among African Americans climbed to 14.5 percent in August, equaling a post–World War II high. Black teen unemployment stood at more than 40 percent. "Everyday the urgent necessity of the passage of the Humphrey-Hawkins bill becomes more apparent to me," Humphrey wrote his co-sponsor from his bed in Minneapolis. "A balanced budget at the expense of a frustrated and unbalanced America is no answer to our problems."[36]

Another round of negotiations opened that fall after a member of Humphrey's staff indicated that the senator was willing to bargain. The president still refrained from endorsing Humphrey-Hawkins and insisted that fighting inflation was a high priority. Though the parties ironed out many of their differences during October, they disagreed about setting specific unemployment goals and giving the president the right to modify those targets when inflation threatened. Humphrey and Hawkins decided to grant the president authority to change the goals if the administration would set specific employment targets. The sponsors wanted to set a goal of 4 percent unemployment within a four- or five-year time frame. Believing this would be too inflationary, the administration was prepared to accept a 4 percent target with no time restrictions. Humphrey and Hawkins held firm, and the president soon settled on a five-year time frame. With these issues resolved, Carter announced his support for Humphrey-Hawkins in mid-November.[37]

Despite the extensive modifications of the legislation, Humphrey, who had returned to Washington in late October, gamely insisted that it had been made more workable, not weaker. The bill's affirmation of the right to a job and its targets for unemployment, Humphrey maintained, signaled that the federal government would put unemployment at the center of its economic policy making. The Congressional Black Caucus, Coretta Scott King's Full Employment Action Council, and the National Urban League also endorsed the measure.[38]

Liberal critics, however, rightly contended that Humphrey-Hawkins represented more symbol than substance. Jesse Jackson blasted Carter for trying "to get the greatest political mileage at the least economic cost." The compromise bill Humphrey introduced in December paled in comparison to earlier versions and would likely do little to ease the plight of the unemployed. Its affirmation of the "right" to a job rang hollow because sections allowing individuals to sue the government for denying that right had been eliminated. It no longer declared that fighting unemployment was more important than keeping inflation low. Not only did the new measure increase the target rate for an acceptable level of unemployment, but it also stretched out the time frame for achieving that goal and even allowed the president to modify the target. Most important, provisions authorizing a new federal jobs program for the unemployed had been stripped.[39]

Humphrey never saw what became of his legislation. On the evening of January 13, 1978, just a month after he had introduced the latest version of Humphrey-Hawkins in the Senate, he fell into a coma and died at his home in Waverly, Minnesota. Humphrey-Hawkins became law nine months later. The final draft passed the House in March essentially intact. The Senate did not approve it until the final day of the session, and then only after an inflation target had been added. Joined by Hawkins and Muriel Humphrey, who was appointed to serve the remainder of her husband's term, Carter signed the bill in late October. "I think [Humphrey's] here with us in spirit," the president solemnly observed. The ceremony symbolized the changes that had been made in the legislation, for Carter downplayed the employment issue and used the occasion instead to stress the importance of fighting inflation.[40]

It is not surprising that the Carter administration prevailed. Politically, Humphrey-Hawkins never stood a chance. The administration rightly calculated that full employment was a losing political issue for the Democrats. Humphrey and other full employment proponents were out of step with the antigovernment mood that characterized the 1970s. Vietnam, the failures of the War on Poverty, stagflation, and Watergate, among other developments, had greatly eroded American's trust and confidence in the competence of government. There simply was no groundswell of support for a massive new employment program. Jobless African Americans and whites were largely unorganized for formal participation in the political system. Unions, meanwhile, were rapidly losing political clout in the 1970s. Organized workers had dropped from near 30 percent of the labor force to near 20 percent by decade's end. Moreover, unions were largely absent from the South and West, the fastest growing parts of the country. Most voters, especially whites, were employed and thus predictably viewed inflation as a greater evil than unemployment. Contrary to Humphrey's repeated claims, full employment would have been inflationary, and middle-class suburbanites, well on their way to becoming the largest constituency in American politics, already felt squeezed by high inflation and rising taxes. They were not willing to support a party that asked them to accept even higher prices to help the less fortunate. The legislation would have required substantial government spending initially, which would have also been a difficult sell politically. Full employment also failed because Humphrey and his allies were trying to appeal to a class solidarity that did not exist. Most working-class whites felt little or no connection to the black poor. Tensions over education, housing, and crime had been developing between the races for decades in the urban North, and neither whites nor blacks would or could easily subsume them into a common alliance centered on economic concerns. Finally, chances for a strong full employment bill collapsed under the weight of the history of poverty and labor policy during the post–World War II era. Humphrey and his allies were trying to reverse three decades of policy. Choices made during the 1950s and

1960s stressed Keynesian fiscal and monetary policy as the key to economic growth and lower levels of poverty. The War on Poverty emphasized individual shortcomings of the unemployed. Thus, there had been little groundwork laid among policy makers, economists, or the public for far-reaching policies such as full employment.[41]

Humphrey-Hawkins suffered from substantive problems as well, for it was not the panacea that supporters suggested. As both liberal and conservative economists attested, full employment would not have achieved both low unemployment and low inflation simultaneously. Even stalwart liberal economist John Kenneth Galbraith, who sympathized with the bill's aims, warned Humphrey-Hawkins supporters against the "wishful economics" of thinking that there was "some undiscovered fiscal or monetary magic" to achieve low unemployment and low inflation. Humphrey mistakenly assumed that all new public service jobs would represent net additions to the overall employment picture. He posited too much faith in the government's ability to fine tune an economy that was growing ever more complex as a result of increased international trade and technological developments. In addition, the relationship between crime and joblessness was more ambiguous than he had contended. As James Q. Wilson and others have persuasively argued, people do not commit crimes simply because they are poor or unemployed. Finally, though conservative explanations of poverty underplayed forces beyond an individual's ability to control, Humphrey and his allies were guilty of economic determinism. They rightly called attention to impersonal macroeconomic trends during the post–World War II era that had contributed to urban poverty, but full employment proponents demanded too little from individuals. Poverty and other problems resulted from both economic and behavioral factors, but Humphrey talked only about the former.[42]

These considerable shortcomings, however, do not mean that full employment was without merit. Indeed, Humphrey and his liberal allies deserve credit for several accomplishments. They understood the importance of economic issues regarding questions of racial equality. Racial justice, they insisted, would not be achieved simply by eliminating segregation and securing voting rights. More important, Humphrey and his allies realized that even low-paying public service jobs represented a preferable social and economic alternative to traditional forms of welfare and that some sort of government jobs program would have to be an essential part of any meaningful welfare overhaul. They correctly maintained that neither cash payments nor economic growth alone would be enough to create stable families and healthy neighborhoods. Finally, Humphrey and his allies called attention to serious economic and social problems confronting both African Americans and whites and thus asked important questions about the effects of a new economic world on millions of Americans. Few politicians dared to broach these issues in such a direct manner.

The fight over Humphrey-Hawkins constituted a pivotal battle regarding the development of liberalism during the 1970s. The failure of Humphrey and his allies to push the Democratic Party toward race-neutral policies signaled that the identity politics that had come to the fore during the mid-1960s would continue to dominate liberal thought. The Democratic Party would, for better or worse—depending upon one's perspective—still support race-conscious policies such as affirmative action. Full employment represented an unsuccessful attempt to redirect liberalism back toward its New Deal roots in economic reform. By the 1970s liberalism had come to primarily focus on personal and group rights. The economic questions that stood at the center of political debate in the 1930s and early 1940s had long been replaced by this new agenda. Indeed, the New Deal meant relatively little to Carter or many other Democrats who came to power during the 1970s holding grave doubts about government's ability to solve large social and economic problems. The Democratic Party would thus make no new significant attempt to mitigate the effects of the market. This was understandable from a political viewpoint, but such an approach also meant that questions involving the intersection of race, class, and economic power have remained on the periphery of American politics for the last twenty years. Many factors accounted for the shift in emphasis from economic to social and political rights, but Humphrey had played a leading role. Little did he realize that by championing long overdue social and political rights he was helping to undermine his ability to fight for another cherished ideal, economic equality.[43]

Introduction

1. *Washington Post*, January 15, 1978, p. 14.

2. *Minneapolis Tribune*, January 15, 1978, p. 11; *New York Times*, January 15, 1978, pp. 1, 27; *Washington Post*, January 15, 1978, p. 13.

3. *Congressional Record*, 95th Cong., 2d sess., p. 6; *Washington Post*, January 15, 1978, p. 1; *Washington Post*, January 16, 1978, pp. 1, 13.

4. *Minneapolis Tribune*, January 16, 1978, p. 1A; *Minneapolis Tribune*, January 17, 1978, p. 6A; Solberg, *Hubert H. Humphrey*, p. 456.

5. *Minneapolis Tribune*, January 15, 1978, pp. 2B, 8B; *Washington Post*, January 15, 1978, p. 13; *Congressional Record*, 95th Cong., 2d sess., pp. 620, 1,559.

6. *Congressional Record*, 88th Cong., 1st sess., p. 14,040.

7. Lawson, "Freedom Then, Freedom Now," *American Historical Review* 96 (April 1991): 456–471.

8. Plotke, *Building a Democratic Political Order*, pp. viii–ix; Remarks by Senator Hubert H. Humphrey, December 11, 1972, box 3, 1971–1977 subject files, Hubert H. Humphrey Papers, Minnesota Historical Society, St. Paul, Minnesota. Recent studies chronicling the strength of conservative politics include Hodgson, *The World Turned Right Side Up*; Brennan, *Turning Right in the Sixties*; Carter, *The Politics of Rage*; Kazin, *The Populist Persuasion*; McGirr, "Suburban Warriors"; Diamond, "Right-Wing Movements"; Poulson, "Organizing the American Right." See also Ribuffo, "Why Is There So Much Conservatism?"

9. Edsall and Edsall, *Chain Reaction*; Sleeper, *Liberal Racism*; Dionne, *Why Americans Hate Politics*.

10. Wills, *Certain Trumpets*, p. 14.

11. Gerstle, "Race and the Myth of the Liberal Consensus"; Brinkley, "The Problem of American Conservatism"; Wills, *Certain Trumpets*, pp. 13–22.

12. Brinkley, *The End of Reform*, pp. 8–11; Patterson, *Grand Expectations*, pp. 562–592, 637–677; William Connell interview with author, August 11, 1997; Hyman Bookbinder interview with author, August 5, 1997.

13. Carter, *From George Wallace to Newt Gingrich*, pp. 40–41.

14. *Congressional Record*, 94th Cong., 1st sess., p. 33,985.

Prologue

1. *New York Times*, June 1, 1964, p. 57; *Minneapolis Tribune*, June 2, 1964, p. 20. "My Childhood" also aired in Washington, D.C., Los Angeles, Sacramento, Kansas City, and Peoria.

2. Eisele, *Almost to the Presidency*, pp. 13–16.

3. Frances Howard Oral History, Hubert H. Humphrey Oral History Project, Minnesota Historical Society, St. Paul, Minnesota; *Atlantic Monthly* (November 1966), pp. 83–84; Humphrey, *The Education of a Public Man*, p. 35.

4. Hubert Humphrey to Winthrop Griffith, May 16, 1962, box 1, personal and family files, HP; *Link*, November 1974, pp. 29–31.

5. Solberg, *Hubert H. Humphrey*, pp. 44–49; Eisele, *Almost to the Presidency*, pp. 21–23; U.S. Congress, *Thirtieth Anniversary*, p. 56.

6. Solberg, *Hubert H. Humphrey*, p. 45; Howard Oral History; Eisele, *Almost to the Presidency*, p. 25.

7. Arthur Naftalin interview with author, December 28, 1993; Solberg, *Hubert H. Humphrey*, pp. 66–72.

8. Humphrey, *Education of a Public Man*, pp. 65–66; Charles Hyneman Oral History, Hubert H. Humphrey Oral History Project; Cecil Newman interview by Charles MacDonald, n.d., box 1, autobiography files (AF), HP; Charles Hyneman and Hubert Humphrey interview by Norm Sherman, March 11, 1969, box 1, AF, HP.

9. Hubert Humphrey, *The Political Philosophy of the New Deal* (Baton Rouge: Louisiana State University Press, 1970), pp. 12–102.

10. Solberg, *Hubert H. Humphrey*, pp. 86–87; Eisele, *Almost to the Presidency*, pp. 53–55; interview of Hubert Humphrey by Norm Sherman, September, 1969, box 2, AF, HP; Newman interview; *Minneapolis Spokesman*, May 7, 1943, p. 1.

11. Eisele, *Almost to the Presidency*, pp. 52–54; *Minneapolis Spokesman*, May 7, 1943, p. 1; *Minneapolis Spokesman*, June 4, 1943, p. 4; *Minneapolis Spokesman*, June 11, 1943, p. 4; Newman interview; Speech by Hubert H. Humphrey, May 27, 1943, box 1, speech files (SPF), HP; Solberg, *Hubert H. Humphrey*, p. 88–91.

12. J. I. Jaffe to Hubert Humphrey, November 25, 1943, Harry Vermes to Hubert Humphrey, January 11, 1944, L. M. Cohen to Hubert Humphrey, January 31, 1944, all in box 16, personal and family files, HP; Speech by Hubert Humphrey, April 28, 1944, box 1, SPF, HP.

13. Arthur Naftalin interview with author, December 28, 1993; *Minneapolis Spokesman*, April 14, 1944, p. 3; *Minneapolis Spokesman*, December 15, 1944, p. 1; *Minneapolis Spokesman*, December 22, 1944, p. 8.

14. Jonas Schwartz to Hubert Humphrey, March 24, 1944, box 16, personal and family files, HP; Ed Ryan Oral History, Hubert H. Humphrey Oral History Project; *Minneapolis Tribune*, March 24, 1944, p. 11; Carl Zietlow to Hubert Humphrey, November 1, 1944, box 1, mayoralty files (MF), HP.

15. Solberg, *Hubert H. Humphrey*, pp. 99–102.

1. Race and Reform in Minneapolis

1. Report, March 26, 1945, box 17, Jewish Community Relations Council of Minneapolis Papers (JCRCP), Minnesota Historical Society, St. Paul, Minnesota.

2. *Minneapolis Tribune*, March 27, 1945, p. 9. In January 1945 a Jewish teen suffered a broken tooth after simply acknowledging that he was Jewish. A year earlier two Jewish teens had been beaten up by youths who announced afterward, "We're beating them up because they're dirty Jews." During a school holiday in 1943 several brawls between Jews and non-Jews occurred around a skating rink at a park in North Minneapolis. Concerned Jewish parents reported the incidents to the police, who took no action. Report, September 1944; Report, December 1944; Report by Detective Ed Ryan, January 9, 1944; all in box 17, JCRCP; Report, December 1941, box 16, JCRCP.

3. Press release, April 2, 1945, box 24, MF, HP. In 1943 alone Fisk University tallied 242 incidents in 47 cities, including enormously destructive riots in Harlem and Detroit. See Dalfiume, "The 'Forgotten Years,' "; Sitkoff, "Racial Militancy"; Capeci and Wilkerson, *Layered Violence*.

4. Radio speech, June 9, 1945; Radio speech, May 1, 1945; both in box 1, speech files (SPF), HP; Statement in Reference to the Establishment of a Fair Employment Practices Commission in the City of Minneapolis, n.d., box 24, MF, HP; *Minneapolis Spokesman*, March 16, 1945, p. 9; *Minneapolis Spokesman*, June 8, 1945, p. 4; interview of Cecil Newman by Charles MacDonald, n.d., box 1, autobiography files, (AF), HP; Henry Piper to Hubert Humphrey, June 24, 1945, box 2, MF, HP.

5. *Minneapolis Tribune*, June 12, 1945, pp. 1, 7.

6. *Minneapolis Tribune*, June 12, 1945, pp. 1, 7; Radio speech, April 17, 1945, box 1, SPF, HP.

7. Solberg, *Hubert H. Humphrey*, pp. 57–63; Spangler, *The Negro In Minnesota*, pp. 65–125; Governor's Interracial Commission, "The Negro Worker's Progress," pp. 12–15; David Taylor, "Blacks," in Holmquist, *They Chose Minnesota*, p. 81; Hyman Berman, "The Jews," in Holmquist, *They Chose Minnesota*, pp. 492–500.

8. Taylor, "Blacks," pp. 81–84; Report, November 18, 1943, box 17, JCRCP; Governor's Interracial Commission, "The Negro and His Home in Minnesota," pp. 52–54; Spangler, *The Negro in Minnesota*, pp. 125–132. For the experiences of blacks in other midwestern cities, see Trotter, *Black Milwaukee*; Kusmer, *A Ghetto Takes Shape*; Hirsch, *Making the Second Ghetto*; Sugrue, *The Origins of the Urban Crisis*.

9. Anthony Cassius Oral History (OH), Nellie Stone Johnson OH, Albert Allen OH, all in Twentieth-Century Radicalism in Minnesota Oral History Project, Minnesota Historical Society, St. Paul, Minnesota; Minneapolis Urban League, "Community Survey of Social and Health Work in Minneapolis, 1938," Minnesota Historical Society, St. Paul, Minnesota; Taylor, "Blacks," pp. 83–84. *Minneapolis Spokesman*, December 10, 1943, p. 1; *Minneapolis Spokesman*, March 3, 1943, p. 1; *Minneapolis Spokesman*, December 17, 1943, p. 1.

10. Taylor, "Blacks," pp. 80–87; Cassius OH; Hase, "W Gertrude Brown's Struggle for Racial Justice," pp. 118–136; Nellie Stone Johnson OH, Twentieth-Century Radicalism in Minnesota Oral History Project.

11. Dinnerstein, *Anti-Semitism in America*, p. 80; Naftalin interview with author;

Friendly, *Minnesota Rag*, pp. 46, 164; Gordon, *Jews in Transition*, p. 47; leaflets all in box 17, JCRCP; Berman, "The Jews," p. 500; Berman, "Political Anti-Semitism in Minnesota"; *Woman's Home Companion*, October 1951, pp. 33, 94–96; Report, October 10, 1939, box 16, JCRCP; Report, January 11, 1941; Report, May 19, 1941; Statement, June 17, 1942; Statement, June 18, 1942; Report, December 17, 1943; Report, March 19, 1945; all in box 17, JCRCP; Report, August 28, 1941, box 19, JCRCP; Report and Recommendations of the Evaluation Committee—1942, box 30, JCRCP; Report, February 22, 1944; Report, February 19, 1943; Gerald L. K. Smith Report, June 13, 1944; all in box 47, JCRCP; McWilliams, "Minneapolis," p. 61; *National Jewish Monthly*, March 1947, p. 235. On Smith's anti-Semitism, see Jeansonne, *Gerald L. K. Smith*, pp. 101–111; and Ribuffo, *The Old Christian Right*, pp. 167–177; *Minneapolis Tribune*, May 15, 1940, p. 12; *Minneapolis Tribune*, May 16, 1940, p. 13; Statement, n.d., box 17, JCRCP; Martin Lebedo OH, Robert Latz OH, both in Twentieth-Century Radicalism in Minnesota Oral History Project; Berman, "The Jews," pp. 495–502.

12. Inaugural Address, July 3, 1945, box 1, SPF, HP; *Minneapolis Spokesman*, July 6, 1945, p. 1. Discrimination, Humphrey privately noted, was "a most perplexing issue," which "if . . . not properly handled . . . may become increasingly worse in the years ahead." Hubert Humphrey to Charles Washington, July 25, 1945, box 3, MF, HP.

13. Genevieve Steefel to George Rundquist, April 16, 1945; Genevieve Steefel to Exploratory Committee on City-Wide Race Relations Committee, May 20, 1945; Genevieve Steefel to L. Howard Bennett, May 28, 1945; L. Howard Bennett to Genevieve Steefel, June 11, 1945; L. Howard Bennett to Genevieve Steefel, November 8, 1945; all in box 9, Genevieve Steefel Papers, Minnesota Historical Society, St. Paul, Minnesota; Naftalin interview with author; Supplemental Information on Development, Problems, and Future Outlook of the Mayor's Council on Human Relations, December 20, 1947; Arthur Naftalin to Curtis Campaigne, February 7, 1947; both in box 16, MF, HP; Sugrue, *Origins of the Urban Crisis*, p. 30; Leonard Ramburg and Glen Wallace OH, HHHOHP.

14. Helen Mudgett to Hubert Humphrey, September 29, 1945, box 9, Steefel Papers; *Minneapolis Tribune*, February 10, 1946, p. 1; *Minneapolis Spokesman*, February 15, 1946, p. 1; Nellie Stone Johnson OH, Twentieth-Century Radicalism in Minnesota Oral History Project; Walter Jackson, *Gunnar Myrdal and America's Conscience*, pp. 100–101. When the council's only African American resigned (becoming a missionary to Liberia) two months after it had been formed, Humphrey convinced *Spokesman* editor Cecil Newman to serve. Hubert Humphrey to Cecil Newman, July 17, 1946, box 16, MF, HP.

15. A Statement of Purpose, Mayor's Council on Human Relations, box 25, MF, HP; Committee Personnel for Mayor's Council on Human Relations; Minutes of Meeting, Mayor's Council on Human Relations, February 12, 1946; both in box 16, MF, HP. The council in Buffalo received an annual appropriation of $10,000 from the city. The group in Chicago had city funding totaling $60,000, while those in Cleveland and San Francisco had $25,000 and $15,000 respectively. Minutes of Meeting, Mayor's Council on Human Relations, March 6, 1946, box 16, MF, HP.

16. Mayor's Council Report, June 1, 1947; Mayor's Council on Human Relations, Projects to Establish a Sound Policy, n.d.; both in box 10, Steefel Papers; Press Re-

lease, n.d., Solomon Fineberg to Sam Scheiner, August 30, 1946; Sam Scheiner to Reuben Youngdahl, August 5, 1946; all in box 48, JCRCP; Hubert Humphrey to Will Lundquist, August 29, 1946, box 20, MF, HP. It is unclear how the violence at the Smith rally began.

17. A Report to the People of Minneapolis by the Mayor's Council on Human Relations, October 1946, box 25, MF, HP; Minutes of Meeting, Mayor's Council on Human Relations, September 4, 1946; Wilfred Leland to Arthur Stade, April 20, 1946; Minutes of Meeting, Mayor's Council on Human Relations, July 30, 1946; Minutes of Meeting, Mayor's Council on Human Relations, September 24, 1946; Comments of Critics, n.d.; Minutes of Meeting, Mayor's Council on Human Relations, July 30, 1946; all in box 16, MF, HP; *Minneapolis Tribune*, July 15, 1947, p. 11; Wilfred Leland to Minneapolis Restaurant Association, September 14, 1946, box 9, Steefel Papers; Mayor's Council on Human Relations Report, n.d.; Minutes of Meeting, Mayor's Council on Human Relations, October 6, 1947; Mayor's Council on Human Relations Projects to Establish Sound Policy, n.d.; all in box 10, Steefel Papers; Committee on Integration Techniques, Unfinished Business, December 5, 1946, box 9, Steefel Papers. The National Conference of Christians and Jews called *Neither Free Nor Equal* an "outstanding example of democracy in action." J. Roger Deas to Hubert Humphrey, November 4, 1947, box 16, MF, HP. Similarly, when the council helped organize a community effort to oppose an appearance by the racist and anti-Semitic Gerald L. K. Smith, the executive director of the Jewish Community Relations Council wrote the executive secretary that minority groups were "very proud" of the "beneficial work" undertaken by the council during its first six months of existence. Samuel Scheiner to Reuben Youngdahl, August 5, 1946, box 48, JCRCP.

18. Wilfred Leland to Real Estate Board of Minneapolis, July 1, 1946; CORE to Hubert Humphrey, July 2, 1946; Minutes of Meeting, Mayor's Council on Human Relations, July 30, 1946; Minutes of Meeting, Mayor's Council on Human Relations, August 12, 1946; Mayor's Council Report, September 1, 1947; Minutes of Meeting, Mayor's Council on Human Relations, June 16, 1947; all in box 16, MF, HP; *Minneapolis Tribune*, July 19, 1946, p. 22; Projects to Establish Sound Policy, box 10, Steefel Papers; Hubert Humphrey to Lewis Booth, June 9, 1947, box 15, MF, HP; Samuel Scheiner to Reuben Youngdahl, August 15, 1948, box 48, JCRCP.

19. Wilfred Leland to Mayor's Council on Human Relations, March 8, 1947; Hubert Humphrey to Wilfred Leland, February 25, 1947; Minutes of Meeting, Mayor's Council on Human Relations, July 8, 1946; Minutes of Meeting, Mayor's Council on Human Relations, August 16, 1948; Minutes of Meeting, Mayor's Council on Human Relations, May 17, 1948; Hubert Humphrey to Helen George, March 14, 1947; D. J. Strouse to Hubert Humphrey, March 25, 1947; all in box 16, MF, HP; Minneapolis Urban League, Twenty-Second Annual Report, March 1948, box 17, MF, HP; Cecil Newman interview by Charles MacDonald, box 1, AF, HP.

20. Minutes of Meeting, Mayor's Council on Human Relations, April 2, 1946; Minutes of Meeting, Mayor's Council on Human Relations, April 22, 1946; Minutes of Meeting, Mayor's Council on Human Relations, May 6, 1946; R. Augustine Skinner to Glen MacLean, July 21, 1947; Excerpt from Minutes of Meeting of the Mayor's Council, July 14, 1947; all in box 16, MF, HP; Minutes of Meeting, Committee on In-

tegration Techniques, May 27, 1946; Wilfred Leland to Committee on Integration Techniques, December 20, 1946; both in box 9, Steefel Papers; Cecil Newman interview by Charles MacDonald, n.d., box 1, AF, HP; Projects to Establish a Sound Policy, Mayor's Council on Human Relations, n.d., box 10, Steefel Papers.

21. Minutes of Meeting, Executive Committee of Mayor's Council on Human Relations, September 20, 1948, box 16, MF, HP.

22. Minutes of Meeting, Mayor's Council on Human Relations, March 6, 1946; Minutes of Meeting, Mayor's Council on Human Relations, September 4, 1946; Minutes of Meeting, Mayor's Council on Human Relations, September 24, 1946; Hubert Humphrey to Eva Noffziger, October 14, 1946; Emmett O' Brien to Edward Waite, October 14, 1947; Excerpts from Minutes of Meetings Related to Plan Developed by the Budget Committee for Raising the Funds Required to Meet the Two-Year Budget, n.d.; Minutes of Meeting, Executive Committee, Mayor's Council on Human Relations, October 25, 1947; Hubert Humphrey to Minneapolis City Council, March 13, 1947; Hubert Humphrey to Gael Sullivan, August 27, 1947; Wilfred Leland to Hubert Humphrey, October 29, 1947; Hubert Humphrey to Jack Jorgenson, November 26, 1947; Hubert Humphrey to Robert Wishart, November 26, 1947; Hubert Humphrey to George Phillips, January 19, 1948; Hubert Humphrey to Robert Wishart, January 20, 1948; Donald Dayton to Hubert Humphrey, March 10, 1948; Gideon Seymour to Emmett O' Brien, March 11, 1948; Hubert Humphrey to George Phillips, May 11, 1948; Hubert Humphrey to Toby Cook, May 12, 1948; Hubert Humphrey to Peter Olson, June 4, 1948; Hubert Humphrey to Frank Fager, June 4, 1948; all in box 16, MF, HP; *Minneapolis Tribune*, October 4, 1946, p. 17; *Minneapolis Tribune*, December 29, 1946, p. 6; Minutes of Meeting, Mayor's Council on Human Relations, August 26, 1947; Wilfred Leland to Reuben Youngdahl, October 14, 1947; Minutes of Meeting, Mayor's Council on Human Relations, October 31, 1947; all in box 10, Steefel Papers.

23. *Congress Weekly*, March 5, 1948, pp. 43–45; Community Self-Survey of Human Relations, June 1, 1947, box 3, JCRCP; Minutes of Meeting, Mayor's Council on Human Relations, March 6, 1946; Report to the Mayor's Council on Human Relations on a Possible Structure of Community Organization for the Self-Survey, n.d.; both in box 16, MF, HP; *Minneapolis Tribune*, October 8, 1946, p. 17; *Minneapolis Tribune*, November 8, 1947, p. 10; *Minneapolis Star*, December 23, 1946, p. 1; Jackson, *Gunnar Myrdal and America's Conscience*, pp. 94–98. One council member later recalled why the group chose to do the survey, "We had some vague ideas about doing something [to combat racism], but even if we had known exactly what needed to be done we wouldn't have known how to go about doing it." *Woman's Home Companion*, November, 1951, p. 94. The *Spokesman* acknowledged doubts in the African American community about the need "to survey the obvious," but it concluded that blacks ought to participate because whites needed to know about the lack of opportunities for many African Americans. *Minneapolis Spokesman*, February 21, 1947, p. 4.

24. *Minneapolis Tribune*, November 12, 1946, p. 13; Minutes of Meeting, Mayor's Council on Human Relations, November 25, 1946; Mayor's Council on Human Relations—Program for 1947, Status of Community Self-Survey, March 7, 1947; Oliver Perry to Hubert Humphrey, January 30, 1947; all in box 16, MF, HP; Wilfred Le-

land to Charles Johnson, May 18, 1945, box 9, Steefel Papers. Surveys had been done in San Francisco, Pittsburgh, and Kalamazoo, Michigan. B. W. Lambert, Comparison of Different Types of Self-Surveys, n.d., box 3, JCRCP. The delay occurred in part because a few council members questioned whether the survey, which had been intended only for African Americans, could be applied to Jews. The problems of blacks and Jews were not unrelated, of course, but nor were they exactly the same. Johnson, however, urged the council to include Jews in the study, and the Minnesota Jewish Council contributed $2,500 to the survey. Genevieve Steefel to Charles Johnson, May 24, 1946; Wilfred Leland to Charles Johnson, May 18, 1946; Conference on Community Self-Survey, June 19, 1946; Charles Johnson to Genevieve Steefel, June 5, 1946; all in box 9, Steefel Papers; Pascha Goldberg to Bradshaw Mintener, January 20, 1947, box 16, MF, HP. Leaders of the survey included a lawyer from Pillsbury Company, the chair of the board at a leading hospital, the dean of the University of Minnesota graduate school, a legislative representative from a railroad union, and a vice president from Honeywell.

25. Minutes of Meeting, Mayor's Council on Human Relations, February 3, 1947; Mayor's Council on Human Relations, Program for 1947; Instructions—Schedule for Family and Home; Instructions for Employee Interviews; Instructions for Business Establishment; all in box 16, MF, HP; Community Self-Survey of Human Relations, June 1, 1947, box 3, JCRCP. Participation among businesses, the head of the survey plausibly speculated, was lower than leaders had hoped because many establishments feared that information about minority employment would be turned over to the city FEPC, which had been created in January 1947. In some cases survey leaders had to promise that information obtained would not be used against businesses, unions, or individuals in any way. Minutes of Meeting, Steering Committee of Self-Survey, March 17, 1947, box 10, Steefel Papers. The survey opened the eyes of many volunteers to the difficulties of minority life in Minneapolis. One woman commented, "I have never met an educated Negro until this thing started." Another observed, "When I learned how little income they had and how they had to scrape to make ends meet, it actually made me angry." *Woman's Home Companion,* October, 1951, p. 94.

26. Summary of the Findings and Recommendations of the Self-Survey, box 3, JCRCP; Summary of the Findings of the Industry-Labor Committee of the Community Self-Survey; Report of the Social Welfare Agencies Committee; Report of the Health and Hospitals Committee; all in box 1, Amos Deinard Files, Minneapolis Fair Employment Practices Committee Papers (MFEPCP), Minnesota Historical Society, St. Paul, Minnesota; *Minneapolis Tribune,* November 30, 1948, p. 1. The survey committees also offered policy recommendations. Often these were vague calls for increased education of the public, but some were more concrete. The Housing Committee raised the idea of securing better housing for minorities through the use of public funds. The Industry and Labor Committee urged businesses and unions to provide more job training, while the Social Welfare Agencies Committee suggested that agencies should open up leadership positions to minorities and meet with leaders of minority groups to discuss ways to make their services available to all. The Education Committee recommended increased intercultural education in the public

schools. Survey leaders had debated including law enforcement and public information services, but budgetary and staff issues prevented these areas from being investigated. Minutes of Meeting, Mayor's Council on Human Relations, March 31, 1947,
box 16, MF, HP.

27. Hubert Humphrey to C. Capron, February 11, 1947; Minutes of Meeting,
Mayor's Council on Human Relations, January 6, 1947; both in box 16, MF, HP; *Minneapolis Tribune*, March 30, 1948, p. 3; *Minneapolis Spokesman*, December 3, 1948, p. 1.

28. Hubert Humphrey to Mrs. Allen Bruce, December 6, 1945, box 1, MF, HP;
The Campaign for an FEPC Ordinance in Minneapolis, box 1, MFEPCP. On the
state and federal FEPCs of the 1940s, see Ruchames, *Race, Jobs, and Politics*, pp.
165–180; Jack Greenberg, *Race Relations and American Law* (New York: Columbia
University Press, 1959); Paul Norgren and Samuel Hill, *Toward Fair Employment* (New
York: Columbia University Press, 1964); Berger, *Equality by Statute*; Reed, *Seedtime for
the Modern Civil Rights Movement*.

29. Hubert Humphrey to Minneapolis City Council, January 22, 1946, box 15,
MF, HP; Jonas Schwartz to Hubert Humphrey, January 2, 1946; Hubert Humphrey
to Jonas Schwartz, January 7, 1946; Hubert Humphrey to Grace Langley, February
26, 1946; all in box 4, MF, HP; *Minneapolis Spokesman*, January 4, 1946, p. 1; *Minneapolis
Spokesman*, February 8, 1946, p. 1; *Minneapolis Spokesman*, February 15, 1946, p. 1.

30. Minutes of Meeting, Mayor's Council on Human Relations, March 6, 1946;
Minutes of Meeting, Mayor's Council on Human Relations, March 19, 1946; both in
box 16, MF, HP; Hy Edelman and Douglas Hall to City Council, March 5, 1946; History of Adoption of the Ordinance and Operation of the Commission, n.d.; Douglas
Hall to J. W. Straiton, July 2, 1946; all in box 15, MF, HP; Campaign for an FEPC Ordinance in Minneapolis, box 1, MFEPCP; *Minneapolis Tribune*, October 4, 1946, p. 17.
Chicago and Milwaukee had passed fair employment laws, but neither city had a
commission for enforcement. Chicago's law did not provide for imprisonment, but
violators faced up to a $200 fine. Milwaukee's merely stipulated a $10 fine or five days
in jail. Clarence Mitchell of the NAACP addressed a pro-FEPC rally in February and
pointed out how African Americans around the nation were losing jobs they had ac-
quired during the war. *Minneapolis Tribune*, February 15, 1946, p. 13. The need for an
employment law was great. According to an Urban League report released in the
spring of 1946, only fifty-seven of three hundred companies responding to a survey
said that they had hired African Americans "without any pressure" from human rights
groups. *Minneapolis Tribune*, March 15, 1946, p. 20.

31. *Minneapolis Tribune*, January 3, 1947, p. 5; *Minneapolis Tribune*, January 31, 1947,
p. 9; *Minneapolis Spokesman*, February 7, 1947, p. 1; The Campaign for a Fair Employ-
ment Practices Ordinance in Minneapolis; Action by Mayor's Council on Human
Relations on Minneapolis FEPC Ordinance; both in box 1, MFEPCP; History of the
Adoption of the Ordinance and Operations of the Commission, n.d., box 15, MF,
HP; *Proceedings of the City Council of Minneapolis, July 1946 to July 1947*, City Hall
Archives, Minneapolis, Minnesota, pp. 662–690; Hubert Humphrey to Douglas Hall,
March 5, 1947, box 16, MF, HP. Humphrey, who was in New York at the time of the
vote, sent a telegram to the council urging adoption of the measure. Hubert Hum-
phrey to Eric Hoyer, January 31, 1947, box 15, MF, HP.

32. *Minneapolis Tribune*, February 16, 1947, p. 1; Wilfred Leland to Hubert Humphrey, February 17, 1947; Wilfred Leland to Hubert Humphrey, n.d.; William Seabron to Hubert Humphrey, February 22, 1947; Albert Allen and Curtis Chivers to Hubert Humphrey, n.d.; Hubert Humphrey to Charles Smith, March 7, 1947; Robert Wishart to Hubert Humphrey, February 5, 1947; Arthur Naftalin to Hubert Humphrey, March 7, 1947; all in box 15, MF, HP; Hubert Humphrey to Minneapolis City Council, May 2, 1947, box 2, MFEPCP; *Minneapolis Spokesman*, May 2, 1947, p. 1; *New York Times*, May 25, 1947, p. 39; Southern, *Gunnar Myrdal and Black-White Relations*, p. 225. Some members of the African American community thought that the black attorney appointed to the commission was too conservative. It is unclear why Humphrey chose him over other African American candidates. William Seabron to Hubert Humphrey, February 22, 1947, box 15, MF, HP.

33. Cecil Newman interview by Charles MacDonald, n.d., box 1, AF, HP; Radio Speech, May 11, 1947; Radio Speech, June 3, 1947; both in box 1, SF, HP; Solberg, *Hubert H. Humphrey*, p. 109; *Minneapolis Spokesman*, May 9, 1947, p. 4; *Minneapolis Tribune*, January 7, 1947, p. 22; *Minneapolis Tribune*, March 18, 1947, p. 1.

34. FEPC, Report on Operations, June 1947–October 1949, box 1, MFEPCP; Minutes of Meeting, FEPC, February 12, 1948; Minutes of Meeting, May 20, 1948; Minutes of Meeting, August 19, 1948; Minutes of Meeting, FEPC, September 21, 1948; Presentation of Fair Employment Practice Policy to an Employee Group, n.d.; all in box 1, Amos Deinard Files, MFEPCP.

35. William Seabron to George Jensen, August 20, 1947; Rose Moses-F. W. Woolworth Case, May 27, 1947; Complaint of Discrimination, August 18, 1947; all in box 2, MFEPCP; U.S. Congress, Senate Subcommittee on Labor and Public Welfare, *Antidiscrimination in Employment*, p. 444; Report on 1947 Operations, n.d.; Minutes of Meeting, FEPC, May 20, 1948; Minutes of Meeting, FEPC, July 20, 1948; Minutes of Meeting, FEPC, October 25, 1948; all in box 1, Amos Deinard Files, MFEPCP; Report on Operations, June 1947–October 1949, box 1, MFEPCP.

36. History and Aims of the Joint Committee for Equal Opportunity, August 27, 1951; Letter to the presidents of the forty-four organizations comprising the Joint Committee for Employment Opportunity, November 16, 1948; both in box 13, Minneapolis Central Labor Union Papers, Minnesota Historical Society, St. Paul, Minnesota; Mrs. John Gruner to George Dayton, October 10, 1947, box 10, Steefel Papers; Hubert Humphrey to Donald Dayton, January 26, 1948; Margaret Howard to Hubert Humphrey, March 10, 1948; both in box 16, MF, HP; Taylor, "Blacks," p. 84.

37. FEPC, Report of Operations, June 1, 1947 to October 31, 1949, box 1, MFEPCP; Minneapolis Urban League, Twenty-Second Annual Report, March 16, 1948, box 16, MF, HP; *Minneapolis Spokesman*, November 25, 1949, p. 4. Similarly, the industrial secretary of the Urban League commented in July 1948, "We have placed Negroes in a number of industries never before open to them. But these are individual placements. There is no normal movement of Negroes into all fields of employment yet." *Minneapolis Tribune*, July 12, 1948, p. 19. The Communist Party in Minneapolis charged that FEPC had made little difference for many blacks and in 1947 and 1948 undertook a vigorous campaign to promote hiring of black teachers by Minneapolis schools. As of 1947 there was only one black teacher in the system. *Min-*

neapolis Spokesman, September 12, 1947, p. 1; Wilfred Leland to Morris Robinson, September 23, 1947, box 16, MF, HP; Carl Ross OH, Twentieth-Century Radicalism in Minnesota Oral History Project, flyer, "Labor Must Save FEPC," n.d., box 1, Samuel Davis Papers, Minnesota Historical Society, St. Paul, Minnesota.

38. FEPC, Report of Operations, June 1, 1947, to October 31, 1949, box 1, MFEPCP; Wilfred Leland to Harry Baron, August 20, 1948, box 15, MF, HP; Minutes of Meeting, FEPC, February 26, 1948; Minutes of Meeting, FEPC, May 20, 1948; Minutes of Meeting, FEPC, June 10, 1948; Minutes of Meeting, FEPC, September 21, 1948; Minutes of Meeting, FEPC, September 28, 1948; all in box 1, Amos Deinard Files, MFEPCP. The criteria for resolution of cases underwent a significant change in 1948. Cases could be satisfactorily adjusted either by hiring the individual making the complaint or, if that particular individual were not qualified, by employing someone else in a similar position. Companies thus had to prove that they would hire minorities. Procedures for Handling Complaints, March 18, 1948, box 1, MFEPCP; Criteria for Disposition of Cases, n.d., box 1, Amos Deinard Files, MFEPCP.

39. U.S. Congress, House Subcommittee of the Committee on Education and Labor, *Hearings on Federal Fair Employment Practice Act*, p. 96; Hubert Humphrey to Minnesota House Labor Committee, April 2, 1947, box 15, MF, HP. Similarly, Humphrey inflated the FEPC's record when he publicly wrote in the fall of 1948, "Examination of policy turned into examination of conscience, and the little barriers that can exist inside even a democratic city began to crumble away." *Survey Graphic*, October 1948, p. 421.

40. *Minneapolis Spokesman*, July 27, 1945, pp. 1–2. In 1941 an officer berated a Jew who had illegally parked by commenting, "Hitler should come over here into this country and clean out the Jews. The Jews are responsible for this present war. The Jews break the laws of this country . . . and if I had my way about it I'd wipe them all out of this country." Mr. Valene to Samuel Scheiner, December 2, 1941, box 17, JCRCP.

41. *Minneapolis Spokesman*, August 3, 1945, p. 1; *Minneapolis Spokesman*, September 7, 1945, pp. 1, 6; Cecil Newman interview with Charles MacDonald, n.d., box 1, AF, HP; Summary of Dreamland Cafe Incident, n.d.; Re: Dreamland Cafe Incident; both in box 1, Davis Papers.

42. Hubert Humphrey to Glen MacLean, July 21, 1947; Glen MacLean and Hubert Humphrey to Minneapolis Police Officers, August 1947; R. Augustine Skinner to Glen MacLean, July 21, 1947; Glen MacLean to Hubert Humphrey, August 1, 1947; R. Augustine Skinner, Curtis Chivers, and James Perlman to Hubert Humphrey, August 2, 1947; Hubert Humphrey to R. Augustine Skinner, August 5, 1947; all in box 16, MF, HP; Hubert Humphrey to Dining Car Workers, October 25, 1948; Hubert Humphrey to Ed Ryan, November 20, 1945; both in box 20, MF, HP; Cecil Newman to Hubert Humphrey, March 11, 1948, box 4, MF, HP.

43. Minutes of Meeting, Mayor's Council on Human Relations, March 6, 1946; Minutes of Meeting, Mayor's Council on Human Relations, April 2, 1946; Minutes of Meeting, Mayor's Council on Human Relations, April 11, 1946; Report on Sessions with Chief Kluchesky, April 11, 1946; Minutes of Meeting, Mayor's Council on

Human Relations, May 6, 1946; Sam Scheiner to Hubert Humphrey, May 13, 1946; Minutes of Meeting, Mayor's Council on Human Relations, August 26, 1946; Minutes of Meeting, Mayor's Council on Human Relations, September 4, 1946; all in box 16, MF, HP; American Council on Race Relations Report, May 16, 1946, box 47, Philleo Nash Papers, Harry Truman Library (TL), Independence, Missouri; *Minneapolis Tribune*, April 10, 1946, p. 9; *Minneapolis Tribune*, July 6, 1946, p. 10; *Saturday Evening Post*, December 28, 1946, p. 82; Projects to Establish a Sound Policy, n.d., box 10, Steefel Papers.

44. Agenda, Mayor's Council on Human Relations, September 20, 1948; Minutes of Meeting, Mayor's Council on Human Relations, October 25, 1948; both in box 16, MF, HP; Provisional Report of City Government Policy Committee, n.d., box 20, MF, HP. In December 1946, for instance, police used excessive force in arresting a black conscientious objector who was distributing pacifist literature downtown. *Minneapolis Spokesman*, December 20, 1946, p. 3. Nearly two years later an officer used offensive language toward a black man after he had complained about a restaurant's inordinate delay in serving him. G. W. MacLean to Mayor's Council on Human Relations, November 4, 1948, box 20, MF, HP.

45. Arthur Naftalin interview with author; *Woman's Home Companion*, October 1951, p. 97; *Minneapolis Tribune*, November 23, 1949, p. 16; *Minneapolis Spokesman*, November 16, 1951, pp. 1–2.

46. Southern, *Gunnar Myrdal and Black-White Relations*, p. 69; William Simms to Guichard Parris, December 30, 1947, box 16, MF, HP. In addition to appointing the two African Americans who served on the Mayor's Council on Human Relations and the FEPC, Humphrey named African Americans to three other committees he had created. These included the Mayor's Emergency Housing Committee, the Mayor's Law Enforcement Committee, the Mayor's Traffic Safety Committee, and the Mayor's Youth Welfare Committee.

47. *Minneapolis Spokesman*, May 9, 1947, p. 4; *Minneapolis Spokesman*, October 10, 1947, p. 2; *Woman's Home Companion*, October 1951, p. 97; Hubert H. Humphrey OH, Moorland-Spingarn Research Center, Howard University; *Congressional Record*, 81st Cong., 2d sess., p. A3,206; Minneapolis Urban League, Twenty-Second Annual Report, March 16, 1948, box 16, MF, HP.

48. Schulman, *Lyndon B. Johnson and American Liberalism*, pp. 36–42; Southern, *Gunnar Myrdal and Black-White Relations*, pp. 10–45; Kellogg, "Civil Rights Consciousness in the 1940s"; Jackson, *Gunnar Myrdal and America's Conscience*, pp. 100–106, 270–283; Wills, *Certain Trumpets*, pp. 11–22. Humphrey called *An American Dilemma* an "outstanding" work that proposed "a big challenge to the American people." U.S. Congress, Senate Subcommittee on Labor and Public Welfare, *Antidiscrimination in Employment*, p. 429.

49. Gary Gerstle, "The Protean Character of American Liberalism." On liberals' views of the public, see also Lasch, *The True and Only Heaven*, pp. 412–475.

50. Jackson, *Gunnar Myrdal and America's Conscience*, pp. 233–237.

51. *New Republic*, June 16, 1947, pp. 14–16; *New Republic*, October 18, 1948, p. 8; *Survey Graphic*, June 1948, pp. 293–296.

2. Into the National Arena

1. Minutes of Steering Committee of Community Self-Survey, March 17, 1947, box 10, Steefel Papers; Hubert Humphrey to Members of Mayor's Council on Human Relations, February 19, 1948; Hubert Humphrey to Wilfred Leland, February 25, 1948; J. Mitchell Garrsion to Hubert Humphrey, February 6, 1948; all in box 16, MF, HP.

2. Gillon, *Politics and Vision*, pp. 16–28; Solberg, *Hubert H. Humphrey*, p. 115; Hubert Humphrey to Members of Mayor's Council on Human Relations, February 19, 1948; Joseph Lohman to Hubert Humphrey, September 17, 1948; box 16, MF, HP. On civil rights during the New Deal, see Sitkoff, *A New Deal for Blacks*; Weiss, *Farewell to the Party of Lincoln*.

3. The Almost American Game, n.d., Report of Conference to Promote Democratic Participation in Bowling, n.d.; Olga Madar to Hubert Humphrey, March 11, 1947; Arthur Naftalin to Hubert Humphrey, March 20, 1947; Hubert Humphrey to Olga Madar, March 26, 1947; A Handbook for Area Committees for Fair Play in Bowling, n.d.; all in box 16, MF, HP; Report of Conference to Promote Democratic Participation in Bowling, April 1, 1947; Why All Americans Should be Able to Bowl in ABC, n.d.; both in box 1, UAW Recreation Department Papers, Walter Reuther Library, Wayne State University Archives, Detroit, Michigan. Civil rights groups such as the Congress of Racial Equality (CORE) had worked since the early 1940s with mixed results to end discrimination in public spaces such as restaurants, stores, and places of recreation in the North. See Meier and Rudwick, *CORE*. With more than one million members and 1,350 local chapters, the ABC was the largest sports organization in the world. Bowling, moreover, was growing rapidly. The number of teams sanctioned by the ABC more than doubled between 1930 and 1946. Representatives from the *Chicago Defender*, the Anti-Defamation League of B'nai B'rith, the National Recreation Association, and the Japanese-American Citizens' League, among others, attended the Chicago meeting.

4. *Minneapolis Spokesman*, September 19, 1947, p. 1; *Arrowhead Bowling News*, December 12, 1947, p. 1; Minutes of Minneapolis Area Committee for Fair Play in Bowling, n.d.; Hubert Humphrey to Members of the National Committee for Fair Play in Bowling, October 29, 1947; Hubert Humphrey to Charles Johnson, December 11, 1947; all in box 16, MF, HP; Hubert Humphrey to William Oliver, November 12, 1947, box 3, William Oliver Papers, Reuther Library. UAW leaders such as Reuther were committed to civil rights, but race divided many union members. Some local branches maintained separate seniority lists or job classifications for whites and blacks, while others forbade blacks from joining. Boyle, *The UAW and the Heyday of American Liberalism*, pp. 15–16.

5. William Oliver to Hubert Humphrey, March 24, 1948; Hubert Humphrey to William Oliver, April 5, 1948; Frank Baker to Hubert Humphrey, March 10, 1948; Betty Hicks to Hubert Humphrey, March 10, 1948; Day Letter, April 12, 1948; Why All Americans Should be Allowed to Bowl in ABC, n.d.; William Oliver to Hubert Humphrey, April 20, 1948; all in box 16, MF, HP; Buffalo Committee for Fair Play in Bowling News, January 23, 1948, box 1, UAW Recreation Department Papers; Olga Madar to Walter Reuther, January 9, 1948; Hubert Humphrey to Betty Hicks, March

22, 1948; Bulletin, National Committee for Fair Play in Bowling, n.d.; all in box 1, UAW Recreation Department Papers; Report of American Council on Race Relations, April 1948, box 1, Department of Civil Rights files, AFL-CIO Papers, George Meany Archives, Silver Spring, Maryland. *Minneapolis Spokesman,* April 9, 1948, p. 6; Minutes of Meeting, Minneapolis Area Committee for Fair Play in Bowling, n.d.; William Oliver to Hubert Humphrey, December 10, 1948; both in box 3, Oliver Papers; *Minneapolis Tribune,* May 13, 1950, p. 1. A teachers' strike prevented Humphrey from attending, but he sent his secretary to join three other NCFPB members in making the group's case before the ABC.

6. Reed, *Seedtime for the Modern Civil Rights Movement,* pp. 11–17, 140–160, 340–343; U.S. Congress, Senate Subcommittee on Labor and Public Welfare, *Antidiscrimination in Employment,* pp. 429–447; Lawson, *Running for Freedom,* p. 13. Because an effort the previous year had failed, liberals softened their legislation by adding requirements that conciliatory methods be used before legal means were pursued.

7. Berman, *The Politics of Civil Rights in the Truman Administration,* pp. 43–70; McCullough, *Truman,* pp. 588–589; *Minneapolis Spokesman,* November 7, 1947, p. 1. Though no staunch believer in racial equality, the president believed that the Constitution required him to prevent racial violence and promote equal opportunity. He abhorred the blinding by police of a black South Carolina serviceman who had just been discharged from the army, the savage murder of two black couples in July 1946 by a white mob in Georgia, and the dumping of black veterans from a truck in Mississippi. In December 1946 he appointed a committee of prominent businessmen, academics, lawyers, and labor and religious leaders to study the problem of racial violence.

8. McCullough, *Truman,* pp. 586–587; *Minneapolis Spokesman,* February 6, 1948, p. 1; *New York Times,* January 19, 1948, p. 1. Wallace favored anti–poll tax, antilynching, and FEPC legislation. In a November 1947 memo Truman aide Clark Clifford outlined a strategy for the president's reelection that included making "new and real" efforts to keep African Americans from voting Republican. Blacks, Clifford reported, were "cynical, hardboiled traders" on the verge of shifting back to the Republicans out of frustration with the obstructionism of southern Democrats over civil rights legislation. The South, Clifford predicted, was "safely Democratic" and could be "safely ignored." Clark Clifford to Harry Truman, November 19, 1947, box 23, Clark Clifford Papers, TL.

9. Garson, *The Democratic Party and the Politics of Sectionalism,* pp. 218–261; *Congressional Record,* 80th Cong., 2d sess., p. 1,120; *Newsweek,* February 16, 1948, pp. 24–25; *Washington Times-Herald,* February 20, 1948, p. 1; *New York Herald-Tribune,* February 4, 1948, p. 1.

10. McCullough, *Truman,* p. 608; Hubert Humphrey to Max Lerner, March 22, 1948, box 28, MF, HP; Hubert Humphrey to James Loeb, March 24, 1948, series II, box 238, ADA Papers, State Historical Society of Wisconsin, Madison, Wisconsin; Hubert Humphrey to Walter White, July 7, 1948, box 28, MF, HP. Getting rid of the rebellious southerners and the Wallace forces would be "a tremendous shot-in-the-arm" for the Democrats, Humphrey wrote, because it would enable labor to assume a much stronger role in party affairs. *Progressive,* April, 1948, p. 5.

11. James Loeb to ADA Executive Committee, March 16, 1948, series II, box 238, ADA Papers; James Loeb to Hubert Humphrey, April 14, 1948, series V, box 47, ADA Papers; Gillon, *Politics and Vision*, pp. 33–41. ADA leaders had rightly appraised the political threat to liberal Democrats, for in late March the NAACP issued a statement announcing that African Americans would vote only for candidates who supported the Truman civil rights program. Declaration of Negro Voters, March 27, 1948, box 1235, office files, Harry Truman Papers (TP), TL.

12. Solberg, *Hubert H. Humphrey*, p. 111–123; Cohen, *Undefeated*, p. 133; Senate Candidacy Speech, April 23, 1948, box 2, Senate files, (SF) HP; *Minneapolis Spokesman*, April 30, 1948, p. 1. In announcing his candidacy Humphrey urged "action on civil rights that guarantees equality of opportunity." Ball, in contrast, had once favored an FEPC with enforcement provisions but now supported one that would be merely educational.

13. James Loeb to Hubert Humphrey, April 14, 1948; James Loeb to Frank Mc-Culloch, April 24, 1948; Frank McCulloch to Jacob Arvey, May 4, 1948; all in series V, box 47, ADA Papers; Hubert Humphrey to William O' Dwyer, April 29, 1948; Jacob Arvey to Hubert Humphrey, May 7, 1948; both in series II, box 29, ADA Papers; Hubert Humphrey to Herbert Lehman, file 404d, June 10, 1948, Herbert Lehman Papers, Columbia University, New York, NY; Hubert Humphrey to Emily Taft Douglas, June 10, 1948, box 25, MF, HP; Hubert Humphrey to William O'Dwyer, June 9, 1948, box 28, MF, HP; Garson, *The Democratic Party and the Politics of Sectionalism*, pp. 266–267.

14. Hubert Humphrey to William O'Dwyer, June 9, 1948, box 28, MF, HP; Herbert Lehman to Hubert Humphrey, June 15, 1948, file 404d, Lehman Papers; Press Release, July 5, 1948, box 28, MF, HP; *New York Times*, July 5, 1948, p. 1.

15. Democratic National Committee Press Release, June 14, 1948, box 14, DNC Papers, TL; Schlesinger, *A History of American Presidential Elections*, p. 3,041.

16. Statement by Twenty-One Negro Organizations, July 8, 1948, box 26, MF, HP; *Philadelphia Inquirer*, July 9, 1948, pp. 1, 9; *Washington Post*, July 9, 1948, p. 1; *New York Star*, July 11, 1948, p. 1.

17. *Baltimore Sun*, July 11, 1948, p. 1; *Washington Daily News*, July 12, 1948, p. 1; *Washington Times-Herald*, July 10, 1948, p. 1; *New York Star*, July 11, 1948, p. 1.

18. *New York Herald-Tribune*, July 11, 1948, p. 1; *New York Star*, July 11, 1948, pp. 1, 4.

19. *New York Star*, July 12, 1948, p. 1; *Washington Post*, July 13, 1948, p. 1.

20. *Baltimore Sun*, July 14, 1948, p. 1; *Minneapolis Tribune*, July 14, 1948, pp. 1, 2. The two-thirds rule, which had been eliminated in 1936, required a candidate to receive two-thirds of the votes of the convention to win the nomination. The rule aided the South, which could withhold its support from a candidate to extract concessions from him on particular issues.

21. During Civil Rights Discussion, n.d., box 26, MF, HP; *Baltimore Sun*, July 14, 1948, p. 1; Chester Bowles to Walter White, July 22, 1948, series II, box A225, NAACP Papers, Library of Congress, Washington, D.C. *Minneapolis Tribune*, July 14, 1948, pp. 1, 2. Even if southerners did leave, Humphrey thought that the party would be stronger because of it. The Republicans had expressed approval for "enactment and just enforcement" of federal legislation dealing with lynching and employment op-

portunity. They had also gone on record against segregation in the armed services and the poll tax and in favor of equal educational opportunity.

22. During Civil Rights Discussion, n.d., box 26, MF, HP; *Washington Post*, July 14, 1948, pp. 1, 4.

23. Joseph Rauh Oral History, HHHOHP.

24. Humphrey, *The Education of a Public Man*, p. 113; Solberg, *Hubert H. Humphrey*, p. 16; Rauh OH, HHHOHP; *Minneapolis Tribune*, July 4, 1948, p. 1. Polls in Minnesota showed Humphrey leading Ball 46–38 percent.

25. Rauh OH, HHHOHP; Hubert Humphrey to Norm Sherman, May 8, 1974, box 2, AF, HP; Andrew Biemiller Oral History, HHHOHP; Solberg, *Hubert H. Humphrey*, p. 16.

26. Brown, *Democracy at Work*, pp. 184–189; McCullough, *Truman*, p. 636; *Minneapolis Tribune*, July 15, 1948, pp. 1, 4; Biemiller OH, William Shore OH, Rauh OH, all in HHHOHP; *New York Herald-Tribune*, July 15, 1948, p. 1.

27. Hubert Humphrey Speaks Out on Human Rights, box 25, MF, HP.

28. Ibid.

29. Ibid.

30. *Washington Post*, July 15, 1948, p. 1; Griffith, *Humphrey*, p. 156; *Minneapolis Tribune*, July 15, 1948, p. 1; McCullough, *Truman*, p. 640.

31. *Minneapolis Tribune*, July 15, 1948, p. 1; *Washington Star*, July 15, 1948, p. 1; Brown, *Democracy at Work*, pp. 202–210; *New York Star*, July 15, 1948, p. 1; *New York Times*, July 15, 1948 p, 1, 22; *Philadelphia Inquirer*, July 15, 1948, p. 1; *New York Herald-Tribune*, July 15, 1948 p. 1.

32. Brown, *Democracy at Work*, p. 304; *Philadelphia Inquirer*, July 15, 1948, p. 1. Truman continued to keep his distance from the liberal civil rights plank. He only referred to civil rights once during his acceptance speech and that was to charge the Republicans with hypocrisy on this issue.

33. NAACP Press Release, July 15, 1948, series II, box A225, NAACP Papers; *Broadcasting*, July 19, 1948, p. 72; *Washington Post*, July 15, 1948, p. 1; *Chicago Defender*, July 24, 1948, p. 4; *Minneapolis Spokesman*, July 16, 1948, p. 1; *Minneapolis Tribune*, July 18, 1948, p. 1.

34. Cohodas, *Strom Thurmond and the Politics of Southern Change*, pp. 174–176; Garson, *The Democratic Party and the Politics of Secession*, pp. 283–303. On September 2 a Roper poll showed Truman trailing Dewey by thirteen percentage points. A month later George Gallup reported that Dewey led Truman by seven percentage points. Just days before the election Gallup found Dewey ahead by five percentage points. *New York Herald-Tribune*, September 9, 1948, p. 1; Gallup, *The Gallup Poll*, pp. 761, 766.

35. *Minneapolis Tribune*, July 19, 1948, p. 2; Hubert Humphrey to Joseph Clark, July 30, 1948, box 25, MF, HP; Chester Bowles to Walter White, July 22, 1948, series II, box A225, NAACP Papers; Hubert Humphrey to Chester Bowles, July 28, 1948, box 26, MF, HP.

36. *Louisville Courier-Journal*, November 6, 1948, p. 7; *Saturday Evening Post*, October 1, 1949, p. 120; *Minneapolis Spokesman*, November 5, 1948, p. 1.

37. Solberg, *Hubert H. Humphrey*, pp. 124–129; *Minneapolis Tribune*, November 3, 1948, pp. 1, 2.

38. Hubert Humphrey to Harry Truman, November 4, 1948, president's personal file 4232, TP, TL.

39. Sitkoff, "Harry Truman and the Election of 1948," p. 615.

40. *Louisville Courier-Journal*, November 6, 1948, p. 7; *Minneapolis Tribune*, December 3, 1948, p. 6; *Minneapolis Tribune*, November 4, 1948, pp. 1, 9.

3. FEPC: Stalemate in the Senate

1. *Minneapolis Tribune*, January 4, 1949, p. 2; Eisele, *Almost to the Presidency*, p. 87; *Saturday Evening Post*, October 1, 1949, p. 122; *New York Times*, January 2, 1949, p. 41; *Minneapolis Tribune*, January 2, 1949, p. 1; *Time*, January 17, 1949, pp. 13–15.

2. Humphrey, *Education*, p. 126; Solberg, *Hubert H. Humphrey*, p. 136; Cohen, *Undefeated*, p. 154. To be sure, Humphrey also received a seat on the more influential Labor and Welfare Committee, yet few thought he could cause trouble in a body that included Robert Taft, the influential Ohio Republican who authored the Taft–Hartley labor law, which Humphrey had campaigned against vigorously in the fall.

3. *Saint Paul Pioneer Press*, January 14, 1949, p. 3; Statement by Hubert H. Humphrey, January 13, 1949, series II, box 53, ADA Papers; *Minneapolis Spokesman*, May 16, 1952, p. 4; Humphrey, *Beyond Civil Rights*, pp. 64–65; Humphrey OH, Howard University; *Survey Graphic*, October 1948, pp. 419–422; *University of Chicago Roundtable*, February 6, 1949, box 36, Nash Papers, TL; *American Mercury*, January 1949, p. 18; Bartley, *The New South*, pp. 10–63; Sullivan, *Days of Hope*, pp. 193–220; Sosna, *In Search of the Silent South*, pp. 140–171. During the New Deal and World War II, the South's industrial capacity increased by 40 percent. Approximately $4.4 billion was spent on war plants in the South. Bloom, *Class, Race, and the Civil Rights Movement*, pp. 65–66. In the 1940s organized labor in the South enjoyed some success in bring blacks and whites together in the battle for economic justice. Moreover, the number of registered black voters in the South increased substantially in the 1940s. In 1940 there were just 250,000 registered African Americans (5 percent of eligible total), but by 1952 there were over 1 million (20 percent of the eligible population). Korstad and Lichtenstein, "Opportunities Found and Lost"; Bartley and Graham, *Southern Politics and the Second Reconstruction*, p. 25. Similarly, during the late 1940s the Supreme Court had invalidated the white primary, struck down a Virginia law requiring segregation on buses moving across state lines, outlawed restrictive covenants, and ruled that unions could not forbid blacks from joining and still claim to represent them. Garson, *The Democratic Party and the Politics of Sectionalism*, pp. 175–185. On the conservative coalition in Congress see Patterson, *Congressional Conservatism and the New Deal*.

4. *Pittsburgh Courier*, November 13, 1948, p. 1; *Chicago Defender*, January 1, 1949, p. 6; Truman, *Public Papers of the Presidents*, p. 6; McCoy and Ruetten, *Quest and Response*, pp. 156–157.

5. Humphrey, "The Senate on Trial"; McCoy and Ruetten, *Quest and Response*, p. 173; Minutes of Meeting, March 14, 1949, box 625, Senate Files (SF), HP; *University of Chicago Roundtable*, February 6, 1949, box 36, Nash Papers, TL; *American Mercury*, January, 1949, p. 18; *Chicago Defender*, March 5, 1949, pp. 1, 2; Key, *Southern Politics*, pp. 644–675; Sitkoff, *A New Deal for Blacks*, pp. 281–295; Zangrando, *The NAACP*

Crusade Against Lynching, pp. 98–165; On previous cloture attempts, average attendance in the Senate was just eighty-three members. Southern Democrats thus needed to pick up only five votes to maintain a filibuster.

6. A. Philip Randolph to Harry Truman, January 28, 1949, box 1510, official files,
TP; Walter White to Harry Truman, January 25, 1949, box 1510, official files, TP; *New
York Times*, January 26, 1949, p. 6; *New York Times*, February 1, 1948, p. 28; Berman, *The
Politics of Civil Rights During the Truman Administration*, pp. 143–151; Walter White to
Branch Presidents, February 21, 1949, box 60, J. Howard McGrath Papers, TL; *Chica-
go Defender*, February 19, 1949, p. 1; McCoy and Ruetten, *Quest and Response*, pp.
173–178; *Minneapolis Tribune*, March 13, 1949, p. 1; *Congressional Record*, 81st Cong., 1st
sess., p. 2.612; Walter White to Hubert Humphrey, March 15, 1949, series II, box A415,
NAACP Papers; *New York Times*, March 15, 1949, pp. 1, 3; *Saint Paul Pioneer Press*,
March 16, 1949, p. 1; *Saint Paul Pioneer Press*, March 17, 1949, p. 1; *Saint Paul Pioneer
Press*, March 19, 1949, p. 1; *Minneapolis Tribune*, March 17, 1949, pp. 1, 16; Minutes of
Meeting, March 14, 1949, box 625, SF, HP; Hubert Humphrey to Frank Paskowitz,
August 12, 1949, series III, box 29, ADA Papers; *Congressional Record*, 81st Cong., 1st
sess., p. 2,418, A3,236. Following the vote, Humphrey challenged his colleagues to
pledge to remain in session until the legislation promised in the civil rights planks of
the Democratic and Republican platforms was brought to a vote. Few responded to
Humphrey's appeal.

7. *Congressional Record*, 81st Cong., 1st sess., p. 3,153, 5,291; William Seabron to
Hubert Humphrey, May 9, 1949, box 1, William Seabron Papers, Reuther Library;
Minneapolis Tribune, March 26, 1949, p. 1; *Chicago Defender*, April 9, 1949, pp. 1, 2; *Saint
Paul Pioneer Press*, March 26, 1949, p. 1; *New York Times*, May 3, 1949, p. 18; *Minneapolis Tribune*, April 21, 1949, p. 5; *New York Times*, April 15, 1949, p. 15; *Congressional Record*,
81st Cong., 1st sess., p. 5,478; McCoy and Ruetten *Quest and Response*, pp. 184–185.
Liberal Republicans sought to preserve their civil rights credentials by sponsoring an
antilynching bill of their own. Unlike the Republican bill, Humphrey's measure did
not require evidence of a conspiracy to deprive a victim of civil rights. Humphrey's
legislation also set up machinery for civil damages against local governments where
lynchings occur and provided for a maximum fine of $10,000 and twenty years in
prison for those who performed the deed. Humphrey would not accept the Republican legislation because he and the NAACP regarded it as too weak. Thanks to
the Republicans, Humphrey found himself in a difficult position on civil rights matters several weeks after the rules fight. Two conservative Republican senators who
had regularly opposed civil rights legislation presented an antisegregation amendment to a public housing bill they hoped to defeat. To support the amendment meant
a southern filibuster and thus loss of a bill that would benefit thousands of people.
Humphrey voted to defeat the amendment, and the housing bill soon passed. A
month later another Republican sincerely offered an antisegregation amendment to
a measure providing federal money for school construction. Once again, Humphrey
sided with the majority, as the Senate defeated the antisegregation amendment and
then approved the school legislation. Humphrey might have defended his position
by simply highlighting the tremendous need for schools across the nation and noting that the issue had divided African Americans, but he weakly insisted that he had

cast a pro–civil rights vote because "ignorance breeds intolerance." How segregated schools would promote tolerance, he did not say.

8. Stephen Spingarn to Clark Clifford, March 21, 1949, box 3, Clark Clifford Files, TP; Stephen Spingarn to Clark Clifford, March 29, 1949, box 3, Clark Clifford Files, TP; Watson, *Lion in the Lobby*, pp. 170, 179–180.

9. U.S. Department of Commerce, *Historical Statistics of the United States*, p. 135; U.S. House of Representatives, Subcommittee on Education and Labor, *Federal Fair Employment Practice Act*, pp. 482–485.

10. *New York Times*, May 25, 1949, p. 1; U.S. House of Representatives, Subcommittee on Education and Labor, *Federal Fair Employment Practice Act*, pp. 93–106; *Saint Paul Pioneer Press*, May 8, 1949, pp. 1, 2; *Minneapolis Tribune*, May 11, 1949, p. 1; *Minneapolis Tribune*, May 25, 1949, p. 17; FEPC, 1949, series II, box A259, NAACP Papers; Watson, *Lion in the Lobby*, pp. 179–180; Washington *Post*, June 6, 1949, p. 1; *Saint Paul Pioneer Press*, July 13, 1949, p. 8. McCoy and Ruetten, *Quest and Response*, p. 186; *Minneapolis Tribune*, September 22, 1949, p. 2; *Minneapolis Tribune*, September 29, 1949, p. 3; Berman, *The Politics of Civil Rights During the Truman Administration*, p. 163; *Washington Daily News*, October 3, 1949, p. 3; Hubert Humphrey to Wilfred Leland, October 3, 1949, box 5, Max Kampelman Papers, Minnesota Historical Society, St. Paul, Minn.; Hamby, *Man of the People*, p. 493; Gallup, *The Gallup Poll*, pp. 834, 860. By October Truman had just a 51 percent approval rating, down six percentage points from July. Blacks were greatly disappointed over the failure to amend the filibuster rule or pass legislation. Roy Wilkins reported that there had been a "considerable change in the mood of colored people" since the beginning of the year. Likewise, the NAACP passed a resolution identifying Truman and Congress as sharing responsibility for the "betrayal" of the wishes of the electorate. Roy Wilkins to David Niles, June 20, 1949, box 482, president's personal files, TP.

11. McCoy and Ruetten, *Quest and Response*, p. 151; Humphrey OH, Howard University; Hubert Humphrey to Guy Mason, May 9, 1949, box 1, A. Philip Randolph Papers, Library of Congress, Washington, D.C.; Hubert Humphrey to Norman Elson, October 19, 1949, box 5, Kampelman Papers; *Minneapolis Spokesman*, July 29, 1949, p. 1; *Minneapolis Spokesman*, October 28, 1949, p. 1.

12. Solberg, *Hubert H. Humphrey*, pp. 138–139; Eisele, *Almost to the Presidency*, p. 93.

13. Statement of Policy and Objectives, NAACP Civil Rights Committee, October 15, 1949, series II, box H7, NAACP Papers; Roy Wilkins to Harry Truman, February 8, 1950, box 267, official files, TP; Truman, *Public Papers of the Presidents*, pp. 9–10; Hubert Humphrey to Herbert Mitgang, November 2, 1949, box 5, Kampelman Papers; *Chicago Defender*, January 21, 1950, p. 3; Roy Wilkins to David Niles, January 13, 1950, box 739, general files, TP; Excerpts from Address by Senator Hubert H. Humphrey, New York City-Wide FEPC Rally, January 31, 1950; box 2, SPF, HP; *New York Times*, February 8, 1950, p. 18; *Minneapolis Tribune*, February 19, 1950, p. 4; *Minneapolis Tribune*, February 24, 1950, p. 2; *New York Times*, April 14, 1950, p. 1; *Chicago Defender*, April 22, 1950, pp. 1, 2. Similarly, the *Chicago Defender* angrily suggested that the Democrats had simply offered "more promises and few accomplishments." *Chicago Defender*, March 11, 1950, p. 6.

14. Berman, *The Politics of Civil Rights During the Truman Administration*, pp.

172–174; *Congressional Record*, 81st Cong., 2d sess., pp. 6,605–6,606, 6,614–6,627, 7,201.

15. Hubert Humphrey to Wilfred Leland, February 8, 1951, box 5, Kampelman Papers; *Minneapolis Tribune*, May 18, 1950, p. 4; *Congressional Record*, 81st Cong., 2d sess., pp. 7,103, 7,145–7,151, 7,201; The following day Humphrey called Russell Long of Louisiana to order after he claimed that FEPC proponents were bowing to "professional agitators."

16. Stephen Spingarn, Memorandum on FEPC, May 16, 1950, box 1510, official files, TP; Situation Report Re Senate Cloture Vote on FEPC, May 18, 1940, box 6, Phileo Nash Files, TP; *New York Times*, May 20, 1950, p. 8; *Congressional Record*, 81st Cong., 2d sess., pp. 6,457, 7,307; Roy Wilkins to Herbert Lehman, May 24, 1950, File 937, Lehman Papers; Roy Wilkins to Walter White, May 23, 1950, series II, box 408, NAACP Papers; Phileo Nash to Stephen Spingarn, June 21, 1950. box 6, Phileo Nash Files, TP; Charles Murphy and Stephen Spingarn to Harry Truman, July 3, 1950, box 6, Phileo Nash Files, TP; Scott Lucas to Hubert Humphrey, June 15, 1950, box 625, SF, HP; *New York Times*, July 9, 1950, p. 37; *Minneapolis Tribune*, July 13, 1950, p. 2; National Council for a Permanent FEPC Newsletter, May 19, 1950, box 6, Phileo Nash Files, TP; Gallup, *Gallup Poll*, pp. 903, 925. Truman had an approval rating of 37 percent in April. It climbed to 43 percent in September.

17. Berman, *The Politics of Civil Rights During the Truman Administration*, pp. 180–185; Evans and Novak, *Lyndon B. Johnson and the Exercise of Power*, pp. 39–43; Fite, *Richard B. Russell, Jr.*, p. 266; *Congressional Record*, 82d Cong., 1st sess., p. 450. Truman, *Public Papers of the Presidents*, p. 12; *Congressional Record*, 82d Cong., 1st sess., p. 2,843.

18. Hubert Humphrey to Harry Truman, January 12, 1951, box 17, Phileo Nash Files, TP; Clarence Mitchell to Irving Ives, January 19, 1951, box 2, SF, HP; McCoy and Ruetten, *Quest and Response*, p. 269. Hubert Humphrey to Cecil Newman, March 19, 1951, box 5, Kampelman Papers; Berman, *The Politics of Civil Rights During the Truman Administration*, pp. 186–188; *Chicago Defender*, June 2, 1951, pp. 1–2. In March the Senate defeated an amendment offered by Humphrey and other liberals to protect black soldiers from violence. The loss disturbed Humphrey so much that he wrote Majority Leader McFarland that he was "thoroughly persuaded that if the uncompromising attitude toward civil rights continues, the . . . Republican Party will capture the Congress in 1952." Hubert Humphrey to Ernest McFarland, March 15, 1951, box 5, Kampelman Papers.

19. *Congressional Record*, 82d Cong., 1st sess., pp. 7,015–7,022.

20. *Washington Post*, December 4, 1951, p. 1; *Chicago Defender*, December 15, 1951, p. 3; *New York Times*, December 4, 1951, p. 26.

21. *New York Herald-Tribune*, September 15, 1951, p. 1; *Minneapolis Tribune*, November 2, 1951, p. 5; *New York Times*, November 13, 1951, p. 1; *New York Herald-Tribune*, November 13, 1951, p. 1; *Chicago Tribune*, November 4, 1951, p. 6; *Washington Star*, November 9, 1951, p. 6; *New York Herald Tribune*, September 15, 1951, p. 8. Among the governors opposing Truman were Fielding Wright of Mississippi, Herman Talmadge of Georgia, John Battle of Virginia, and James Byrnes of South Carolina.

22. *Minneapolis Spokesman*, November 23, 1951, p. 1; Gallup, *The Gallup Poll*, pp. 1,007–1,022. Polls showed several possible Republican nominees routing the presi-

dent in 1952. On November 16, Gallup released a poll indicating that Eisenhower lead Truman 64 percent to 28 percent. The next day, a poll showed Earl Warren ahead of Truman 55 percent to 33 percent.

23. Frank Spencer to Hubert Humphrey, February 8, 1951, box 3, SF, HP; Hubert Humphrey to Aubrey Williams, January 2, 1952, box 3, SF, HP; Jonathan Daniels to Hubert Humphrey, November 27, 1951, box 3, SF, HP; John Bolt Culbertson to Hubert Humphrey, January 1, 1952, box 3, SF, HP; Hubert Humphrey to John Bolt Culbertson, January 29, 1952, box 3, SF, HP; *Louisville Courier-Journal*, November 27, 1951, p. 6; Max Kampelman to R. C. Jacobson, November 30, 1951, box 5, Kampelman Papers. Humphrey's search for common ground with the South was not as misguided as may first appear. To be sure, Byrd and numerous other southerners regularly stirred up racist sentiment. But, in the pre-*Brown* era, there were several economically liberal and, for the South, racially moderate politicians who enjoyed success. These included Jim Folsom, John Sparkman, and Lister Hill in Alabama, Lyndon Johnson in Texas, W. Kerr Scott in North Carolina, Sid McMath and J. William Fulbright in Arkansas, Albert Gore and Estes Kefauver in Tennessee. See Bartley and Graham, *Southern Politics and the Second Reconstruction*, pp. 24–50; Black, *Southern Governors and Civil Rights*, pp. 29–47. By 1951 twelve southern cities had passed antimask or anti–cross burning laws. *Congressional Record*, 82d Cong., 1st sess., p. 7,021.

24. Max Kampelman to Loren Miller, November 28, 1951, box 3, SF, HP; Max Kampelman to Charles Murphy, November 29, 1951, box 3, SF, HP; Max Kampelman to Walter White, November 27, 1951, series II, box A318, NAACP Papers; *Minneapolis Tribune*, November 22, 1951, p. 5; *Washington Post*, December 14, 1951, p. 5; *Tampa Tribune*, November 27, 1951; *Savannah Morning News*, December 5, 1951, p. 6; *Minneapolis Star*, December 18, 1951, p. 20. Liberal editor Jonathan Daniels wrote Humphrey that his letter was "a notable attempt" to avoid the "hot-tempered" debate that usually surrounded racial issues. Predictably, other editors were not so favorably disposed. One paper told Humphrey to "keep his nasty nose and noisy voice out of the home affairs of the South," while others blasted him as "intolerant" and "intemperate."

25. *Washington Star*, December 14, 1951, p. 6; Hays, *A Southern Moderate Speaks*, p. 67; Hubert Humphrey to C. A. Scott, December 28, 1951, box 5, Kampelman Papers.

26. Berman, *The Politics of Civil Rights During the Truman Administration*, p. 196; U.S. Senate, Subcommittee on Labor and Labor-Management Relations, *Discrimination and Full Utilization of Manpower Resources*, pp. 1–20; *New York Times*, April 8, 1952, p. 1; *New Republic*, July 21, 1952, pp. 14–15; Press Release, U.S. Senate, Committee on Labor and Public Welfare, Subcommittee on Labor and Labor-Management Relations, June 24, 1952, box 322, SF, HP; *Washington Post*, May 7, 1952, p. 8. Likewise, attempts by Humphrey to pass antilynching legislation came to naught.

27. Speech at ADA Convention, May 17, 1952, box 3, SPF, HP; Excerpts from Address by Senator Hubert H. Humphrey, February 17, 1952, series II, box A318, NAACP Papers; *Saint Paul Dispatch*, March 19, 1952, p. 20; Minutes of Convention Strategy Meeting, May 20, 1952, box 549, SF, HP; Max Kampelman to Eugenie Anderson, July 2, 1952, box 549, SF, HP; Lazarowitz, *Years in Exile*, p. 37; *Minneapolis Spokesman*, March 14, 1952, p. 1. Hubert Humphrey to Theodore Christman, July 14,

1952. box 549, SF, HP; Hubert Humphrey to Herchel Laskowitz, March 6, 1952, box 549, SF, HP; Hubert Humphrey to Ione Hunt, May 9, 1952, box 549, SF, HP; U.S. Department of Commerce, *Historical Statistics of the United States*, part 1, pp. 23–27. Between 1940 and 1950 hundreds of thousands of African Americans left the South to find jobs in the war plants of the North and West. During this decade the black population increased by 66.9 percent in Illinois, 112.5 percent in Michigan, 60.8 percent New York, 51.3 percent in Ohio, and a whopping 272 percent in California. Humphrey stated in February, "Some of the leaders of my political party are now urging harmony. Their yardstick for harmony is to gloss over or retreat from the proclaimed platform outlining our objectives in the field of civil rights legislation. This is not harmony. This is capitulation, surrender." Among those calling for harmony were DNC Chair Frank McKinney, Platform Committee Chair John McCormack, House Speaker Sam Rayburn, and Massachusetts Governor Paul Dever, who was to be the keynote speaker at the convention.

28. Hubert Humphrey to J. G. Ricketts, March 19, 1952, box 549, SF, HP; Brooks Hays Memorandum, n.d., 564, SF, HP.

29. Hubert Humphrey to Ione Hunt, May 9, 1952, box 549, SF, HP. One adviser counseled that Humphrey should avoid being linked too closely to ADA and was "interested to see any ideas that might be developed on how we can show that HH is really the man to 'unite' the Party." Arthur Naftalin to HH, Max, and Bill, May 1, 1952, box 549, SF, HP.

30. *Newsweek*, July 28, 1952, p. 20; *U.S. News and World Report*, August 1, 1952, p. 36; *Time*, July 28, 1952, pp. 7–8; Greene, *The Crusade*, p. 62; Parmet, *The Democrats*, pp. 123–124; *New York Herald-Tribune*, July 21, 1952, p. 13.

31. *Minneapolis Tribune*, July 20, 1952, p. 1; Schlesinger, *A History of American Presidential Elections*, p. 3,238.

32. Martin, *Civil Rights and the Crisis of Liberalism*, pp. 109–110; *Washington Post*, July 25, 1952, p. 2; *Minneapolis Tribune*, July 21, 1952, pp. 3–4; *Newsweek*, July 28, 1952, p. 20; *U.S. News and World Report*, August 1, 1952, p. 36; *Time*, July 28, 1952, pp. 7–8; Greene, *The Crusade*, p. 62; Parmet, *The Democrats*, pp. 123–124; David, Moos, and Goldman, *Presidential Nominating Politics in 1952*, p. 106; Hubert Humphrey to Vincentia Martin, August 13, 1952, box 549, SF, HP; Herbert Lehman to Hubert Humphrey, September 9, 1952, file 404c, Lehman Papers. Lehman wrote Humphrey, "I recall with much interest the night meeting in which you and I . . . were deeply concerned with the wisdom of the strategy in connection with the proposed loyalty oath. I think history has demonstrated that our concern at the time was justified." Humphrey also noted two weeks after the convention, "It was my opinion that this serious problem could have been met in other ways." Hubert Humphrey to Bill Magie, August 14, 1952, box 549, SF, HP. Eisenhower was immensely popular across the country. By the end of July fifty-four southern newspapers had endorsed the war hero or indicated that they would. If the former general ran well in the South, he would be difficult to beat. Parmet, *Eisenhower and the American Crusades*, p. 108.

33. *Washington Post*, July 21, 1952, p. 5; *New York Herald-Tribune*, July 21, 1952, pp. 1–2; Arnold Aronson to delegates of the 1952 Democratic Convention, n.d., box E11, LCCR Papers, Library of Congress, Washington, D.C.; Brooks Hays Memorandum,

n.d., box 564, SF, HP; Lazarowitz, *Years in Exile*, p. 43; Statement by Hubert Humphrey on the Democratic Party and Its Candidates, August 11, 1952, box 549, SF, HP; *Congressional Quarterly*, August 8, 1952, p. 826; Walter Reuther to Hubert Humphrey, July 29, 1952, box 549, SF, HP; press release, series II, box A225, NAACP Papers. Pointing to the antifilibuster clause, Humphrey announced that the platform "represents a victory for all those who believe in liberal democracy." *Washington Post*, July 26, 1952, p. 7. Senator Herbert Lehman of New York was the sole liberal on a platform committee dominated by moderates. Party officials had deliberately kept Humphrey off the committee in hopes of avoiding a repeat of 1948.

34. Greene, *The Crusade*. pp. 159–161; Fontenoy, *Estes Kefauver*, p. 223; Martin, *Civil Rights and the Crisis of Liberalism*, pp. 106–111. Humphrey was not the only liberal from 1948 who favored harmony in 1952. A month after the convention, ADA activist Joe Rauh wrote Humphrey that the "dignity and decisiveness" of Stevenson's nomination "was due in no small measure to your pumping sense into a large number of heads in the wee hours of Friday morning." Joe Rauh to Hubert Humphrey, September 5, 1952, box 549, SF, HP; Similarly, Jacob Arvey, who had backed Humphrey's floor fight in 1948, wrote Humphrey, "You were a conciliator rather than a stubborn protagonist. You were a compromiser rather than a fanatical last ditch crusader. You fought for the things you believed right yet were willing to weigh them in relation to other considerations." Jacob Arvey to Hubert Humphrey, September 8, 1952, box 549, SF, HP; *Minneapolis Tribune*, July 27, 1952, p. 1; Statement by Hubert Humphrey on the Democratic Party and Its Candidates, August 11, 1952, box 549, SF, HP. White commented, "It will be difficult if not impossible to see Negro voters and other civil rights advocates support a nominee whose voting record has been one of consistent opposition to the civil rights objectives of the Democratic Party." Similarly, New York congressman Adam Clayton Powell remarked that Sparkman meant "sheer political death" for the Democrats.

35. Martin, *Civil Rights and the Crisis of Liberalism*, pp. 114–115; *Minneapolis Spokesman*, October 24, 1952, p. 1; Max Kampelman to Adlai Stevenson, August 7, 1952, box 550, SF, HP; DNC Publicity Division to Max Kampelman, October 18, 1952, box 550, SF, HP; Burk, *The Eisenhower Administration*, pp. 15–20. In October Senator Harry Byrd of Virginia blasted the Democratic platform and announced he would not support Stevenson because he favored Humphrey's FEPC bill and majority cloture in the Senate. Byrd's decision brought a sharp response from Humphrey, who held Stevenson up as the civil rights candidate. "Senator Byrd's unbridled attacks on the Democratic Party and its standard-bearer completes the cycle and brings into the open the unholy alliance of all the major Dixiecrat leaders with the Republican Party in an open conspiracy against civil rights and other humanitarian and social legislation," Humphrey remarked.

36. On the rightward drift of the Democratic Party during the 1940s, see Brinkley, *The End of Reform*; Wolfe, *America's Impasse*; and Gillon, *Politics and Vision*.

37. U.S. Department of Commerce, *Historical Statistics of the United States*, p. 135; Sugrue, *Origins of the Urban Crisis*, pp. 4–8; Stern, "Poverty and Family Composition Since 1940," pp. 222–224. In 1950 the proportion of black householders who worked full time was 45 percent, twelve percentage points below the white rate. In 1949 black

full-time workers were three times as likely as white workers not to earn a living wage. Only 13 percent of fully employed whites lived in poverty, but 50 percent of fully employed blacks did.

38. Hubert Humphrey to J. G. Ricketts, March 19, 1952; Hubert Humphrey to Theodore Christman, July 14, 1952; Hubert Humphrey to Ione Hunt, May 9, 1952; Max Kampelman to Clarence Berdahl, October 9, 1951; all in box 549, SF, HP; Eisele, *Almost to the Presidency*, pp. 90–95; Griffith, *Humphrey*, pp. 182–196; Cohen, *Undefeated*, p. 163; Hubert Humphrey to Ione Hunt, May 9, 1952, box 549, SF, HP.

4. Desegregation, Voting Rights, and the Elusive Search for Consensus

1. *Newsweek*, January 5, 1953, p. 11; *Time*, January 5, 1953, p. 11; Burk, *The Eisenhower Administration*, pp. 17–18.

2. Clarence Mitchell to Everett Dirksen, January 9, 1953, Working Papers, Everett Dirksen Papers, Everett Dirksen Congressional Research Center, Pekin, Ill.; Joe Rauh OH I, Lyndon Baines Johnson Library (LBJL), Austin, Tex.; Clarence Mitchell to Walter White, December 22, 1952, series II, box A9, NAACP Papers; LCCR to Cooperating Organizations, December 23, 1952, box 8, Department of Legislation files, AFL–CIO Papers; Memo, January 1953, box 30, Paul and Claire Sifton Papers, Library of Congress, Washington, D.C.; *New York Times*, January 4, 1953, pp. 1, 64; *New York Times*, January 8, 1953, p. 1; Boyle, *The UAW and the Heyday of American Liberalism*, pp. 111–112; Hubert Humphrey to R. D. Stickney, January 8, 1953, box 92, SF, HP. Humphrey's argument about drafting new rules had been developed by Joseph Rauh and other liberal leaders interested in civil rights. Southern Democrats predictably voted against Humphrey, while Taft had used threats of poor committee assignments to obtain Republican votes against the attempt. Just fourteen Democrats, five Republicans, and one independent sided with Humphrey.

3. *Congressional Record*, 83d Cong., 1st sess., p. 325; Hubert Humphrey to Richard Russell, January 26, 1953, box 92, SF, HP; Hubert Humphrey to Spessard Holland, January 26, 1953, box 92, SF, HP; Hubert Humphrey to Thomas Stokes, January 23, 1953, box 104, SF, HP. Humphrey's package included legislation to make lynching a federal crime, outlaw the poll tax, create a civil rights division in the Justice Department, eliminate certain forms of discrimination in interstate transportation, protect voting rights, amend existing civil rights statutes, create a Joint Congressional Committee on Civil Rights, and strengthen laws relating to involuntary servitude. He approached Attorney General Herbert Brownell about his bill to create a civil rights division in the Justice Department and increase the number of FBI personnel to investigate civil rights violations. Since the bill had slim chance of passing, Humphrey inquired whether Brownell could achieve these objectives through executive action. He did not mind if the Republicans received the political credit. "I am tired of having civil rights remain a political football," he wrote. Hubert Humphrey to Herbert Brownell, February 24, 1953, box 92, SF, HP.

4. U.S. Senate, Subcommittee on Labor and Labor-Management Relations, *State and Municipal Fair Employment Legislation*, pp. 1–20; U.S. Senate, Subcommittee on Labor and Labor-Management Relations, *Employment and Economic Status of Negroes in the United States*, pp. 9–19; Press Release, November 20, 1952, series II, box A256,

NAACP Papers; Press Release, November 24, 1952, series II, box A256, NAACP Papers; *Congressional Record*, 83d Cong., 1st sess., pp. 325, 395–409; Hubert Humphrey to Herbert Lehman, January 5, 1953, file 404c, Lehman Papers; Hubert Humphrey to Max Kampelman, January 8, 1953, box 104, SF, HP; Hubert Humphrey to Thomas Stokes, January 23, 1953, box 104, SF, HP; *Washington Post*, January 26, 1953, p. 1.

5. U.S. Congress, Senate Subcommittee on Civil Rights, Committee on Labor and Public Welfare, *Antidiscrimination in Employment*, pp. 76–79; Hubert Humphrey to Leo Bohanon, March 9, 1954, box 104, SF, HP; Hubert Humphrey to Abbott Washburn, January 22, 1954, box 104, SF, HP; Clarence Mitchell to Roy Wilkins, November 29, 1954, box 104, SF, HP. The armed forces operated some educational facilities, but local officials managed others with state funds. Humphrey, who had monitored desegregation of military units shortly after coming to the Senate, had become involved with the school issue a year earlier, when a woman informed him of Jim Crow schools at a base in Texas. Pentagon officials initially told Humphrey that the school was beyond federal control, and he had decided to drop the matter. Lobbyist Clarence Mitchell of the NAACP, however, reminded him that Truman had once vetoed school legislation because it required segregation at all base schools. Humphrey and the NAACP secured from Pentagon and Office of Education officials a pledge to end segregated schools on all military posts if they could legally do so. Eisenhower announced in March 1953 that segregation in federally controlled schools would be eliminated by fall and that military officials would work with local authorities to achieve the same policy in locally run schools. Two months later Humphrey kept pressure on the executive branch by requesting a progress report from Department of Health, Education, and Welfare (HEW) Secretary Oveta Culp Hobby. A Texan who was no staunch advocate of equality, Hobby replied that little could be done, given local control of education. The administration completed its retreat when, as school opened that fall, the Department of Defense revealed that it would wait until 1955 to end segregation in locally supported base schools. "There is no reason why [desegregation] cannot take place on every military post within the jurisdiction of the United States," an irate Humphrey wrote the president. *Minneapolis Spokesman*, March 9, 1951, p. 4; *New York Times*, March 8, 1951, p. 15; Hubert Humphrey to Anna Rosenberg, March 7, 1951, box 5, Kampelman Papers; Hubert Humphrey to Anna Rosenberg, March 3, 1952; Anna Rosenberg to Hubert Humphrey, June 16, 1952; Hubert Humphrey to Oveta Culp Hobby, May 4, 1953; Oveta Culp Hobby to Hubert Humphrey, May 18, 1953; Hubert Humphrey to Dwight Eisenhower, September 23, 1953; all in box 92, SF, HP; Recent Highlights in the NAACP Campaign Against Segregation in Schools on Military Posts, series II, box A649, NAACP Papers; Nichols *Breakthrough on the Color Front*, pp, 194–196; Burk, *The Eisenhower Administration*, pp. 28–32. The school issue was not the first time Humphrey had become involved in military matters. Pointing to numerous incidents of violence against black soldiers, he had sponsored an anti-lynching amendment to a draft extension bill in 1950. *Chicago Defender*, July 1, 1950, p. 4. A year later, he brought pressure on the army to end racial designation on soldiers' orders and sponsored an amendment to make killing or assaulting a member of the armed forces a federal offense. *New York Herald Tribune*, March 8, 1951,

p. 6; *Chicago Defender*, March 10, 1951, pp. 1, 2. He privately arranged to have Secretary of Defense George Marshall report to him and a group of liberal senators on the military's progress in desegregating its forces. *Progressive*, May 1951, pp. 21–23. Humphrey also received numerous complaints from African Americans in the armed forces regarding unequal treatment. He regularly took the issue up with Defense Department Officials. John Hannah to Hubert Humphrey, June 1, 1953; John Hannah to Hubert Humphrey, August 14, 1953; both in box 92, SF, HP; Hubert Humphrey to Charles Thomas, July 15, 1955, box 116, SF, HP.

6. Kluger, *Simple Justice*, pp. 700–708; Statement by Hubert H. Humphrey on Supreme Court's Desegregation Decision, box 104, SF, HP.

7. *Minneapolis Spokesman*, October 29, 1954, p. 5; Herb Waters to Earle Clements, October 25, 1954, box 552, SF, HP; Solberg, *Hubert H. Humphrey*, p. 168. Humphrey's campaign solicited endorsements from Allen Ellender of Louisiana, John Stennis of Mississippi, and Albert Gore of Tennessee. It is unclear whether Gore or Ellender responded to the request. Stennis was unable to give Humphrey an endorsement because he received the request too late, but he would have been "more than glad" to give "a very warm and strong telegram of endorsement." Humphrey won the election by 162,000 votes. John Stennis to Hubert Humphrey, October 30, 1954, box 552, SF, HP; Hubert Humphrey to Doris Kirkpatrick, May 13, 1955, box 89, SF, HP; Richard Bolling Oral History I, LBJL; Rauh OH I, LBJL; Booth Mooney Oral History II, LBJL; Stephen Mitchell to Hubert Humphrey, September 9, 1954, box 563, SF, HP; Abraham Holtzman, "The Loyalty Pledge Controversy in the Democratic Party," box 92, Mitchell Papers, TL; Agenda for Special Rules Committee Meeting, December 3, 1954, box 24, Mitchell Papers, TL; *New Orleans Times-Picayune*, December 4, 1954, pp. 1, 3; Hubert Humphrey to Frank Morrison, December 16, 1954, box 563, SF, HP; *New York Amsterdam News*, December 18, 1954, p. 6; Cecil Newman to Hubert Humphrey, n.d., box 117, SF, HP; Transcript of Meeting, Special Advisory Committee on Rules for the 1956 Democratic National Convention, April 16, 1955, box 117, DNC Papers, John F. Kennedy Library (JFKL), Boston, Mass.; Hubert Humphrey to James Doyle, April 27, 1955, box 563, SF, HP. One liberal member of the DNC wrote that he was bothered by liberal support for "party leaders' genuflections to the Dixiecrats." Similarly, a black reporter wrote that the committee's decision, as well as Humphrey's repeated emphasis on his Civil Rights Commission bill, signaled that "the Democratic Party [had] quietly entombed civil rights in order to win back the Dixiecrats." *Chicago Defender*, January 1, 1955, p. 9.

8. Clarence Mitchell to Roy Wilkins, November 29, 1954, box 104, SF, HP; Brock, *Americans for Democratic Action*, p. 157; *Chicago Defender*, January 29, 1955, p. 9; Roy Wilkins and Arnold Aronson to Hubert Humphrey, December 22, 1954, box 117, SF, HP; Hubert Humphrey to Edward Donahue, January 31, 1955, box 117, SF, HP; Rauh OH I, LBJL.; Hubert Humphrey to Walter White, January 13, 1955; Walter White to Hubert Humphrey, January 28, 1955; Hubert Humphrey to Walter White, February 8, 1955; all in series II, box A196, NAACP Papers. Chances for success on the first day were "dim," NAACP leaders admitted, but they nonetheless expected that an attempt would be made.

9. Griffith, *Humphrey*, pp. 213–214; Solberg, *Hubert H. Humphrey*, pp. 160–164;

Dallek, *Lone Star Rising*, pp. 424–425; Harry McPherson OH I, LBJL. Humphrey recalled, years later, "It's fair to say that Lyndon Johnson did more to bring me into those more social relationships with the conservative members of the Democratic Party than any other person in the Congress." Hubert H. Humphrey OH I, LBJL.

10. Hubert Humphrey to Walter White, February 8, 1955, series II, box A196, NAACP Papers; Hubert Humphrey to Cecil Newman, January 18, 1955, box 117, SF, HP; Hubert Humphrey to Allen Ellender, February 15, 1955, series II, box A318, NAACP Papers. Polls showed that few citizens in regarded desegregation as an important issue facing the nation. In January 1955 just 4 percent of the public identified desegregation as the most important problem facing the nation. By July that total had not changed. Gallup, *Gallup Poll*, pp. 1,300, 1,345. Hubert Humphrey to Earle Clements, January 20, 1955; Hubert Humphrey to Dale Harris, May 2, 1955; both in box 118, SF, HP; Roy Wilkins to Herbert Lehman, April 20, 1955, series II, box A267, NAACP Papers; Hubert Humphrey to Lister Hill, March 14, 1955; Hubert Humphrey to Paul Butler, March 14, 1955; both in box 560, SF, HP; Burk, *The Eisenhower Administration*, pp. 148–149; Hubert Humphrey to Adlai Stevenson, July 8, 1955, box 561, SF, HP; Hubert Humphrey to Adlai Stevenson, July 23, 1955, box 561, SF, HP. The school issue was a thorny matter that divided African American leaders. Congressman Adam Clayton Powell of New York sponsored the antisegregation amendment, yet William Dawson of Illinois opposed it.

11. *Saint Paul Pioneer Press*, April 18, 1955, p. 1; Hubert Humphrey to Roy Wilkins, April 22, 1955, series II, box A318, NAACP Papers; Roy Wilkins to Max Kampelman, April 28, 1955; Roy Wilkins to Hubert Humphrey, April 28, 1955; Hubert Humphrey to Roy Wilkins, May 5, 1955; all in series II, box A318, NAACP Papers. Wilkins had also criticized Humphrey in March. Humphrey responded, "I will take a back seat [to] no one here in the Congress on the issue of civil rights. . . . Let's stay on the same ball team, Roy. This is no time for those of us of kindred spirit and similar objectives to part and divide. . . . Very frankly, Roy, if the people who are deeply concerned about civil rights and civil liberties are going to swing brick bats at everyone who doesn't hew to the line as some self-appointed political puritans draw it, then our cause is hopeless. I deeply resent having anyone try to discipline my thinking in terms of slavishly following a policy or line that someone else charts." Hubert Humphrey to Roy Wilkins, March 31, 1955, box 117, SF, HP.

12. *New York Times*, May 26, 1955, p. 15; *New York Times*, June 1, 1955, pp. 1, 26; Hubert Humphrey to Paul Butler, June 1, 1955, box 560, SF, HP; Hubert Humphrey to Paul Butler, August 16, 1955, box 441, DNC Papers, JFKL. Humphrey commented on the Court's decision, "I had expected more, much more in the way of detailed programming for the end of segregation."

13. McMillen, *The Citizens' Council*, pp. 207–235; Bartley, *The Rise of Massive Resistance*, pp. 77–82. Humphrey called the minister's death "outrageous" and noted that he was "ashamed to know that such a terrible deed could happen in [the United States]." He informed Wilkins he would be happy to prod the FBI or the Justice Department to become involved. Hubert Humphrey to Roy Wilkins, June 1, 1955, box 561, SF, HP. As far as Humphrey was concerned, the Till case demonstrated the need to make lynching a federal crime. "These states that cry loudest for 'states' rights,' "

he observed, "continue to prove to the nation that only the federal government can protect the rights of individuals in some areas." Hubert Humphrey to Edith Davis, October 24, 1955, box 117, SF, HP.

14. Hubert Humphrey to Richard Bolling, January 12, 1956, box 127, SF, HP; Andrew Biemiller to Boris Shiskin, February 3, 1956, box 8, Department of Legislation files, AFL-CIO Papers; Hubert Humphrey to Cecil Newman, February 8, 1956, box 560, SF, HP; Hubert Humphrey to Paul Butler, February 7, 1956, box 441, DNC Papers, JFKL; Hubert Humphrey to Thomas Hennings, April 6, 1956, folder 5385, Thomas Hennings Papers, Western Historical Collection, University of Missouri, Columbia, Mo.

15. *Congressional Record*, 84th Cong., 2d sess., pp. 4,459–4,461, 4,463; *Fresno Bee*, March 13, 1956, p. 1; Hubert Humphrey to Clement Wright, April 10, 1956, box 127, SF, HP. The grim prospects for civil rights legislation took an additional turn for the worse in March, when James Eastland became head of the Senate Judiciary Committee, which was responsible for nearly all civil rights bills. Humphrey informed Johnson of "trouble brewing in [the] liberal ranks" over the appointment and asked the majority leader to name Lehman to fill another vacancy on the committee. Johnson ignored him. The majority leader apparently tricked Humphrey and the liberals in the Eastland affair. Humphrey was in Minnesota at the time of the announcement, but he reported that he "had the assurance from the Senate leadership that the Eastland appointment would not come before us until the following week." Even if liberals had been present to voice their opposition, Humphrey lamented, the "Sacred Cow" of the seniority system would have assured the Mississippian of the position. Eastland wielded considerable power, Humphrey admitted, but he could be overcome if four Republicans joined four Democrats to support his legislation. *Minneapolis Spokesman*, March 9, 1956, p. 1; Hubert Humphrey to Mrs. F. L. Renaud, April 12, 1956; Hubert Humphrey to William Langer, April 6, 1956; Hubert Humphrey to Cecil Newman, April 5, 1956; all in box 127, SF, HP; Hubert Humphrey to Thomas Hennings, April 6, 1956, folder 5385, Hennings Papers; Hubert Humphrey to Lyndon Johnson, February 28, 1956, box 130, SF, HP. The NAACP continued to demand the inclusion of an antisegregation amendment that denied funds to any district that had not completely integrated. Humphrey regarded this as "a rather abrupt and unwise decision," which would not only sink the school bill but would also fail to give districts a fair chance to comply with *Brown*. He approached Johnson with an amendment that would deny federal money to states or locales only when a federal court had found there had been unacceptable progress toward integration or when a district had announced that it had no intention to integrate at all. Humphrey hoped that this approach would ease tensions because it presumed innocence until proven guilty. Hubert Humphrey to Cecil Newman, February 8, 1956; Hubert Humphrey to himself, March 19, 1956; Hubert Humphrey to Lyndon Johnson, May 26, 1956; all in box 560, SF, HP; Roy Wilkins to Hubert Humphrey, May 14, 1956, box 128, SF, HP; Civil Rights in the 84th Congress, box 8, Department of Legislation files, AFL-CIO Papers; Hubert Humphrey to Thomas McEnroe, April 9, 1956, box 127, SF, HP.

16. Lawson, *Black Ballots*, pp. 141–153; Graham, *The Civil Rights Era*, p. 34.

17. *Congressional Record*, 84th Cong., 2d sess., p. 15,497; U.S. Senate, Committee

on the Judiciary, *Civil Rights Proposals*, pp. 72–73; Hubert Humphrey to Roy Wilkins, May 5, 1956, box 127, SF, HP.

18. Hubert Humphrey to Lyndon Johnson, June 29, 1956, box 127, SF, HP; Hubert Humphrey to J. L. Markham, July 2, 1956, box 89, SF, HP; Minutes of Meeting, Democratic Policy Committee, June 27, 1956, box 364, Lyndon Johnson Senate Papers, LBJL; Dallek, *Lone Star Rising*, pp. 497–98; Douglas, *In the Fullness of Time*, pp. 281–283; Rauh OH I, LBJL; Hubert Humphrey to Cecil Newman, August 4, 1956, box 127, SF, HP; Boyle, *UAW and Heyday of American Liberalism*, pp. 108–124. The failure to enact civil rights and other liberal legislation angered UAW lobbyist Paul Sifton. "By the end of the 84th Congress, this sapping of liberal strength had amounted to collapse," he wrote his colleagues in Detroit. Paul Sifton to Roy Reuther, August 23, 1956, box 30, Sifton Papers. Noting that Humphrey had "certainly had a rough year," Johnson thanked Humphrey for his loyalty to the Democratic Party and his practical approach to problems. He wrote: "During the past few years, we have had the rise of a school of liberal philosophy in this Country which holds that words are more important than deeds. As a liberal, you have breasted this current and clung fast to the position that there is nothing incompatible with liberalism and achievement. I know this has cost you in terms of some of your personal relationships with others. But it has also given you a unique status in the life of our Country—a status which means that you will be on the scene as a national leader long after the others are forgotten." Lyndon Johnson to Hubert Humphrey, September 18, 1956, box 91, Lyndon Johnson Senate Papers.

19. Sundquist, *Dynamics of the Party System*, p. 279; Thomson and Shattuck, *The 1956 Presidential Campaign*, p. 92; Excerpts from a Speech by Roy Wilkins, July 1, 1956, series II, box A245, NAACP Papers; Joe Rauh to Hubert Humphrey, July 10, 1956, box 13, Rauh Papers; *New York Herald-Tribune*, August 8, 1956, p. 7.

20. Hubert Humphrey to Joe Rauh, July 14, 1956, box 560, SF, HP; Hubert Humphrey to John McCormack, August 4, 1956, box 563, SF, HP.

21. Solberg, *Hubert H. Humphrey*, p. 172; Humphrey, *Education*, pp. 187–189. Stevenson denied ever promising Humphrey the vice presidential nomination.

22. *Chicago Tribune*, August 10, 1956, p. 3; *New York Times*, August 13, 1956, p. 13; Transcript, "Face the Nation," August 12, 1956, box 562, SF, HP; Robert Nathan, Some Observations and Highlights on the Democratic National Convention in Chicago, August 16, 1956, box 29, Joseph Rauh Papers, Library of Congress, Washington, D.C.; *Minneapolis Tribune*, August 14, 1956, p. 2; *Minneapolis Tribune*, August 11, 1956, p. 5.

23. *Chicago Defender*, August 25, 1956, p. 2; NAACP Disappointed Over Democrats' Civil Rights Plank, series II, box A65, NAACP Papers; *Minneapolis Tribune*, August 17, 1956, p. 6.

24. *Minneapolis Tribune*, August 17, 1956, p. 2; *Washington Post*, August 16, 1956, p. 9; Boyle, *UAW and the Heyday of American Liberalism*, p. 125.

25. *Progressive*, December 1958, pp. 19–22; *Chicago Tribune*, August 16, 1956, p. 6; Boyle, *UAW and the Heyday of American Liberalism*, pp. 125–126; Hubert Humphrey to Joe Rauh, September 19, 1956, box 44, Rauh Papers. A member of ADA summed up the thoughts of many liberals by noting that he had been "sorry to see the way

[Humphrey had] turned out with respect to the civil rights fight." Robert Nathan, *Some Observations and Highlights*, n.d., box 29, Rauh Papers. Similarly, UAW lobbyist Paul Sifton believed that Humphrey had "crossed the Mason-Dixon line" and was delighted at Johnson's failure to help Humphrey. Claire Sifton to Tony Sifton, August 23, 1956, box 6, Sifton Papers. It is unclear what Johnson said to Humphrey that night, but the following day he helped give Texas's votes to Tennessee Senator Albert Gore on the first ballot and John F. Kennedy on the second. Boyle, *The UAW and the Heyday of American Liberalism*, pp. 125–126.

26. Schlesinger, *History of American Presidential Elections*, p. 3,445; Moon, "The Negro Vote and the Presidential Election of 1956"; Burk, *Eisenhower Administration and Black Civil Rights*, p. 170; *Crisis*, December 1956, pp. 614–615; Republican National Committee, 1956 Elections, political files, Dirksen Papers; Roy Wilkins to Hubert Humphrey, December 4, 1956, series II, box A171, NAACP Papers; Bolling, *House Out of Order*, p. 182. Eisenhower received the majority of African American ballots in ten northern cities and in twelve southern cities where blacks had solidly backed the Democrats in 1952. He also cut into Democratic margins in the African American areas of Chicago, Detroit, St. Louis, Baltimore, Harlem, and Kansas City. The GOP appealed to African Americans on the grounds that they could expect nothing from a party that included staunch civil rights opponents such as James Eastland. Humphrey countered by noting that Eastland could be overridden if just four Republican members of the Senate Judiciary Committee voted for civil rights measures. The Republicans in Congress, he charged, engaged in "a program of blocking and obstructing" civil rights bills. Reminding black voters of the gains under FDR and Truman and how the Republicans had backed efforts to tighten the filibuster rule in 1949, Humphrey blasted Eisenhower for "[failing] to use the power and prestige of his high office to create a climate for peaceful integration" and pointed out that the president had waited three years before submitting civil rights legislation. *Minneapolis Spokesman*, November 9, 1956, p. 1; Radio Speech, November 3, 1956, box 6, SPF, HP.

27. Bartley, *Rise of Massive Resistance*, pp. 131–215; Ambrose, *Eisenhower*, p. 336; McMillen, *White Citizens' Councils*, pp. 224–225; Morris, *The Origins of the Civil Rights Movement*, pp. 31–33.

28. Democratic Declaration of 1957, box 30, Office of the President Papers, George Meany files, 1952–1960, AFL-CIO Papers; Hubert Humphrey to Drew Pearson, December 31, 1956, box 136, SF, HP; Roy Wilkins to Hubert Humphrey, October 5, 1956, series III, box A65, NAACP Papers; Hubert Humphrey to Roy Wilkins, October 16, 1956, series III, box A65, NAACP Papers; Roy Wilkins to Thomas Hennings, folder 3334, Hennings Papers; Hubert Humphrey and Paul Douglas to Clifford Case, November 21, 1956, box 141, SF, HP; Hubert Humphrey and Paul Douglas to Clinton Anderson, November 20, 1956, box 1077, Clinton Anderson Papers, Library of Congress, Washington, D.C.

29. Hubert Humphrey to J. L. Markham, January 23, 1957, box 89, SF, HP; *New York Times*, January 3, 1957, p. 1; *Congressional Record*, 85th Cong., 1st sess., pp. 167–168; Hubert Humphrey to Howard Scott, January 17, 1957, box 141, SF, HP; Hubert Humphrey to Walter Reuther, January 22, 1957, box 136, SF, HP; Shuman,

"Senate Rules and the Civil Rights Bill," pp. 957–959. To bolster the chances for victory, Humphrey met with Vice President Richard Nixon in hopes of obtaining a parliamentary ruling in support of his position. Nixon agreed, but his decision was nonbinding.

30. Hubert Humphrey to Paul Ziffren, January 28, 1957, box 136, SF, HP; Hubert Humphrey to Thomas Hennings, February 13, 1957, box 144, SF, HP; Hubert Humphrey to Walter Reuther, January 22, 1957, box 136, SF, HP; *Congressional Record*, 85th Cong., 1st sess., pp. 343–365, p. 11, 689; Hubert Humphrey to Ruth Maney, March 27, 1957, box 136, SF, HP; U.S. Congress, Senate Subcommittee on Constitutional Rights, *Civil Rights, 1957*, pp. 164–165.

31. Hubert Humphrey to Stewart Alsop, July 20, 1957, box 136, SF, HP; Lawson, *Black Ballots*, pp. 153–166; Hubert Humphrey to Joe Rauh, January 15, 1957, series V, box 14, ADA Papers; Civil Rights in the 85th Cong., 1st sess., December 31, 1957, box 456, Emanuel Celler Papers, Library of Congress, Washington, D.C.; George Reedy to Michael Gillette, June 2, 1982, in George Reedy OH, LBJL. Humphrey and the liberals, along with GOP help, put the House bill on the Senate calendar by invoking little-used Rule XIV, thus avoiding Eastland's Judiciary Committee. Three weeks later the Senate voted to take up the measure.

32. Ware, "The National Association for the Advancement of Colored People," p. 94; *New York Times*, June 21, 1957, p. 1; *Congressional Record*, 85th Cong., 1st sess., pp. 9,785–9,806, 10,771–10,774; *Minneapolis Spokesman*, July 12, 1957, pp. 1, 4; *New York Times*, July 17, 1957, pp. 1, 14; Shuman, "Senate Rules and the Civil Rights Bill," pp. 968–969; *Washington Post*, July 12, 1956; *New York Times*, July 14, 1957, p. 3; Eisenhower, *Public Papers of the Presidents*, pp. 521, 547; *Time*, August 12, 1957, p. 25; *New York Times*, July 18, 1957, pp. 1, 13; *Washington Post*, July 24, 1957, p. 10; Hubert Humphrey to J. L. Markham, July 23, 1957, box 89, SF, HP.

33. Dallek, *Lone Star Rising* pp. 520–521; Harry McPherson Oral History I, LBJL; Evans and Novak, *Lyndon B. Johnson and the Exercise of Power*, p. 132; Memorandum, George Reedy to Lyndon Johnson, n.d., box 404, Lyndon Johnson Papers, Senate files, LBJL: Memorandum, George Reedy to Lyndon Johnson, n.d., box 408, Lyndon Johnson Senate Papers, LBJL; George Reedy to Lyndon Johnson, December 3, 1956, box 567, Lyndon Johnson Senate Papers, LBJL; Rauh OH I, LBJL; George Reedy to Michael Gillette, June 2, 1982, in George Reedy OH, LBJL; Ware, "The National Association for the Advancement of Colored People," p. 116; *Congressional Record*, 85th Cong., 1st sess., p. 12,429, 13,120; *Washington Post*, July 19, 1957, p. 10–11; *Saint Louis Post-Dispatch*, July 18, 1957, pp. 1, 5; Roy Wilkins to Hubert Humphrey, July 19, 1957, box 136, SF, HP; *Newsweek*, July 29, 1957, pp. 23–24; *Saint Louis Post-Dispatch*, July 19, 1957, pp. 1, 4; *New York Times*, July 21, 1957, p. 1, 37; Howard Shuman Oral History, JFKL; *New York Times*, July 25, 1957, p. 1; Hubert Humphrey to L. Howard Bennett, August 12, 1957, box 136, SF, HP.

34. *Congressional Record*, 85th Cong., 1st sess., pp. 5,988, 10,773; *Saint Louis Post-Dispatch*, July 26, 1957, pp. 1, 4; Lawson, *Black Ballots*, p. 171.

35. *Congressional Record*, 85th Cong., 1st sess., pp. 13,119, 13,851; Transcript, "Face the Nation," July 28, 1957, box 136, SF, HP; Hubert Humphrey to Harry Frederickson, July 11, 1957, box 84, SF, HP; *New Leader*, April 29, 1957, pp. 16–18; Carl Auer-

bach to Hubert Humphrey, June 16, 1957, box 136, SF, HP; Carl Auerbach to Joe Rauh, box 26, Rauh Papers; George Reedy OH, LBJL; Hubert Humphrey OH I, LBJL; *New York Times*, August 3, 1957, p. 6; Carl Auerbach interview with author, March 14, 1997; Auerbach came to Washington in July at Humphrey's request and met almost daily with Humphrey regarding the status of the jury amendment. Humphrey and Johnson also conferred regularly. Republican civil rights proponents cogently argued that even under Auerbach's plan registrars could face a jury trial by refusing to register African Americans until after an election had already occurred. Labor leaders welcomed the jury amendment's call for jury trials for contempt proceedings. For decades unions had wanted to eliminate injunctions and replace them with jury trials in labor cases. Northern liberals sympathetic to unions were thus in the awkward position of having to defend jury trials for labor cases but not for civil rights cases. Johnson also rallied western Democrats to his side by persuading the southerners to vote with the westerners on a public power bill of great interest to them. Lawson, *Black Ballots*, pp. 188–192; Carl Auerbach OH, HHHOHP.

36. *New York Times*, August 8, 1957, p. 1; Hubert Humphrey to Stuart Alsop, July 20, 1957, Hubert Humphrey to L. Howard Bennett, August 12, 1957, Hubert Humphrey to J. S. Smith, August 7, 1957, box 136, SF, HP; Hubert Humphrey to Cecil Newman, August 13, 1957, Hubert Humphrey to J. S. Smith, August 7, 1957, all in box 136, SF, HP; Hubert Humphrey to Anton Thompson, August 17, 1957, box 89, SF, HP; Julius Edelstein to Herbert Lehman, August 9, 1957, file 221–537, Lehman Papers; *New York Times*, August 10, 1957, p. 16; Reedy OH, LBJL; *Washington Post*, August 13, 1957, p. 1; *Saint Louis Post-Dispatch*, August 24, 1957, p. 1; Memorandum on the Civil Rights Bill, August 13, 1957, box 456, Emanuel Celler Papers, Library of Congress, Washington, D.C.; Boyle, *The UAW and the Heyday of American Liberalism*, p. 134.

37. Burk, *The Eisenhower Administration*, pp. 174–181; Eisenhower, *Public Papers of the President*, pp. 640–641; Parmet, *The Democrats*, p. 154; Lazarowitz, *Years in Exile,* pp. 139–144; *New York Times*, September 16, 1957, pp. 1, 21. This was not the first time that Humphrey had blasted Eisenhower for his failure to become involved in the school desegregation crisis. In 1956 he declared, "The power of the presidency should be used positively and firmly to supplant defiance with compliance throughout America. . . . The president is in a unique position to influence public behavior favorably on the issue of desegregation. I regret to say that President Eisenhower, however well-meaning, has not exhibited the kind of leadership which the situation requires." *Minneapolis Spokesman*, June 8, 1956, p. 6.

38. Burk, *The Eisenhower Administration*, pp. 182–186; Hubert Humphrey to E. B. Girdley, November 1, 1957; Hubert Humphrey to Allen Stuart, October 14, 1957; Hubert Humphrey to Richard Rubischko, October 24, 1957; Hubert Humphrey to Clyde Nessom, December 19, 1957; Hubert Humphrey to W. F. Vatthauser, October 29, 1957; Hubert Humphrey to Allen Cain, October 1, 1957; all in box 136, SF, HP. At one unknown point during the long and turbulent history of school desegregation during the late 1950s, Humphrey called upon the federal government to consider taking over local schools if necessary. Statement, n.d., box 650, SF, HP. Humphrey also blasted the administration for its record in promoting economic opportunity. The President's Committee on Government Contracts, he pointed out, had never can-

celed or denied a contract due to employment discrimination. *Congressional Record*, 85th Cong., 1st sess., p. 370.

39. *Congressional Record*, 85th Cong., 2d sess., pp. 8,239–8,240, A5,871.

40. *Congressional Record*, 85th Cong., 2d sess., pp. 1,417–1,418, 1,890–1,899. As the 1958 session ended, Humphrey had to fight a rearguard battle to protect the authority of the Supreme Court. Conservative Republicans and southern Democrats had proposed several bills that would impede the struggle for civil rights in the South. Thanks to some clever parliamentary maneuvering by Johnson, the measures were defeated. Harry McPherson OH IV, LBJL; McPherson, *A Political Education*, pp. 133–134; Murphy, *Congress and the Court*, pp. 197–217; Hubert Humphrey Oral History III, LBJL; Watson, *Lion in the Lobby*, pp. 412–414.

41. Rauh OH I, LBJL; Statement of Senators Case, Douglas, Humphrey, and Javits, September 23, 1958, series III, box A65, NAACP Papers; *New York Times*, September 23, 1958, p. 27; Hubert Humphrey and Paul Douglas to Newly Elected Democratic Senate Candidates, November 10, 1958, box 44, Department of Legislation files, AFL-CIO Papers; Sundquist, *Politics and Policy*, p. 239; Lazarowitz, *Years in Exile*, p. 133; Rauh OH I, LBJL; Roy Wilkins to Hubert Humphrey, January 15, 1958, series III, box A65, NAACP Papers; Hubert Humphrey to Roy Wilkins, January 16, 1958, series III, box A65, NAACP Papers; *Congressional Record*, 86th Cong., 1st sess., p. 1,383; Berman, *A Bill Becomes a Law*, p. 8; Lawson, *Black Ballots*, p. 222; Remarks Prepared for Delivery to the 50th Anniversary Convention of the National Association for the Advancement of Colored People, July 15, 1959, box 420, SF, HP. Rule XXII was amended slightly when the Senate approved Johnson's proposal to allow cloture by two-thirds of those senators present and voting. Johnson was able to rally support for his plan and erode backing for majority cloture by promising newly elected senators favorable committee assignments if they voted with him. Roy Wilkins rightly pointed out that such a change was largely cosmetic, since all senators would likely be present for a civil rights vote. Humphrey, who had written all Senate candidates urging them to vote for majority cloture, regretfully informed Wilkins that the new rule fell "far short of what we had hoped and worked so hard for."

42. U.S. Commission on Civil Rights, *Report of the U.S. Commission on Civil Rights, 1959*, pp. 59–145; *Congressional Record*, 86th Cong., 1st sess., p. 18,581, 18,879; *New York Times*, September 12, 1959, pp. 1, 22; Berman, *A Bill Becomes a Law*, p. 32; Hubert Humphrey to Roy Wilkins, September 22, 1959, series III, box A171, NAACP Papers. When the executive branch received at least nine complaints from an area claiming civil rights violations, the Civil Rights Commission would investigate. If the allegations proved true, the president would appoint a federal employee in the area to serve as a registrar.

43. U.S. Senate, Committee on Rules and Administration, *Hearings on Federal Registrars*, pp. 110–112; Berman, *A Bill Becomes a Law*, pp. 44–45; Lawson, *Black Ballots*, pp. 224–233; Burk, *The Eisenhower Administration*, pp. 243–249. The referee plan would grant the attorney general authority to obtain an injunction against individuals who discriminated against potential voters. If discrimination were widespread, the federal government could ask a court to hold that a "pattern" existed in the area under question. Upon ruling in the government's favor, the court would appoint a

referee, who would gather evidence regarding the voting qualifications of the individuals filing the charges. After finding that the voters met state requirements, the judge would assign the referee to watch the polling place to ensure that voting proceeded smoothly.

44. *Congressional Record*, 86th Cong., 2d sess., pp. 4,259–4,262, 4,911, 5,177, 6,428–6,429, 7,810; Roy Wilkins to Stuart Symington, September 3, 1959, box 22, Stuart Symington Papers, Western Historical Collection, Columbia, Mo.; U.S. Senate, Committee on Rules and Administration, *Hearings on Federal Registrars*, p. 112; Press Release, January 21, 1960, series III, box A171, NAACP Papers; Press Release, March 14, 1960, Rauh Papers; *Minneapolis Tribune*, March 21, 1960, p. 2; Lawson, *Black Ballots*, pp. 234–247; Berman, *A Bill Becomes a Law*. pp. 67–69; Notes on Legislative Leadership Meeting, box 1, Dwight Eisenhower files, Dirksen Papers; Dallek, *Lone Star Rising*, pp. 562–565; Minutes of Meeting, Democratic Policy Committee, March 29, 1960, box 364, Lyndon Johnson Senate files, LBJL; *New York Times*, April 9, 1960, pp. 1, 15.

45. L. Howard Bennett to Hubert Humphrey, July 31, 1959, box 567, SF, HP; *New York Times*, January 15, 1960, p. 12; Press Release, January 25, 1960, box 10, SPF, HP; *New York Times*, February 15, 1960, p. 11; *Chicago Defender*, March 1, 1960, p. 11.

46. Carson, *In Struggle*, pp. 9–14; *Chicago Defender*, March 16, 1960, p. 7.

47. Gerald Heany OH, HHHOHP; *Milwaukee Journal*, April 6, 1960, p. 13; *Minneapolis Tribune*, April 7, 1960, pp. 1,9; White, *The Making of the President, 1960*, pp. 91–96; Karl Rolvaag to Sam Rizzo, December 23, 1959, box 1, Wisconsin for Humphrey Committee Papers, State Historical Society of Wisconsin, Madison, Wis.; Hubert Humphrey to Joe Rauh, December 28, 1959, box 715, SF, HP; James Weschler to Hubert Humphrey, January 28, 1960; Joe Rauh to Marvin Rosenberg, March 7, 1960; James Weschler to Hubert Humphrey, January 28, 1960; Hubert Humphrey to Joe Rauh, April 18, 1960; all in box 18, Rauh Papers; Frank Reeves Oral History, JFKL; Frank Reeves to Hubert Humphrey, February 8, 1960, box 19, Rauh Papers; *Minneapolis Tribune*, February 7, 1960, pp. 1, 8; Brauer, *John F. Kennedy and the Second Reconstruction*, pp. 1–29; *Milwaukee Journal*, March 24, 1960, pp. 1, 12; *New York Times*, March 21, 1960, p. 12; Senator Hubert Humphrey for President—Newsletter Number Two, n.d., box 106, Nash Papers; Hubert Humphrey to William Black, February 16, 1960, box 567, SF, HP; *Milwaukee Journal*, March 15, 1960, p. 1; *Milwaukee Journal*, March 21, 1960, p. 16; Press Release, March 21, 1960, box 1028, Pre-Presidential Papers, JFKL; *Minneapolis Tribune*, March 10, 1960, pp. 1, 5; *Milwaukee Journal*, March 28, 1960, p. 11; Hubert Humphrey to Bob Barrie, April 26, 1960; Hubert Humphrey Press Release, May 9, 1960; Harry Ernst to William Connell, n.d.; all in box 575, SF, HP; *New York Times*, April 22, 1960, pp. 16, 17; *Charleston Gazette*, May 5, 1960, pp. 11–12; interview between Drew Pearson, Jack Anderson, and Hubert Humphrey, April 22, 1960, box 3, personal and family files, HP; Fleming, *Kennedy vs. Humphrey*, pp. 149–150; J. Raymond Depaulo Oral History, JFKL; William Jacobs Oral History, JFKL; Frank Reeves Oral History, JFKL; John Amos Oral History, JFKL; Stuart Calhoun Oral History, JFKL; Eisele, *Almost to the Presidency*, p. 148.

48. James Sundquist Oral History, JFKL; Schlesinger, *A History of American Presidential Elections*, pp. 3,508–3,510; *Saint Louis Post-Dispatch*, July 13, 1960, pp. 1, 14; Hu-

bert Humphrey, Human Rights for All, box 10, SPF, HP; Press Release, July 12, 1960, series III, box 246, NAACP Papers.

49. *Minneapolis Tribune*, July 11, 1960, pp. 1, 3; *New York Times*, July 11, 1960, p. 20; *Chicago Defender*, July 12, 1960, p. 12; *New York Times*, July 10, 1960, p. 47; Schlesinger, *A Thousand Days*, p. 40; Solberg, *Hubert H. Humphrey*, pp. 212–213; *Minneapolis Tribune*, June 28, 1960, p. 4; *Minneapolis Tribune*, June 29, 1960, pp. 7, 9; *New York Times*, June 28, 1960, p. 30; *New York Times*, June 30, 1960, p. 12; *New York Times*, July 12, 1960, p. 22. In June the Kennedy camp had sent signals to liberals, who favored Humphrey for the vice presidential nomination, that the Massachusetts senator wanted a midwestern liberal as his running mate. Kennedy even raised the possibility in a meeting with Humphrey, but it is unclear whether Humphrey ever thought he had a good chance. Brauer, *John F. Kennedy*, pp. 37–38, Dallek, *Lone Star Rising*, p. 573; White, *The Making of the President, 1960*, pp. 172–177; Joe Rauh Oral History II, LBJL.

50. *New York Times*, October 9, 1960, p. 7; *New York Times*, October 12, 1960, pp. 1, 32; Press Release, October 12, 1960, box 144, DNC Papers, JFKL; Boris Shiskin to George Meany, October 17, 1960, box 26, Office of the President Papers, AFL-CIO Papers; Report to Senator Kennedy from the National Conference on Constitutional Rights and American Freedom, series III, box A171, NAACP Papers.

51. Branch, *Parting the Waters*, pp. 357–365; Hubert Humphrey to Lyndon Johnson, October 26, 1960; Hubert Humphrey to James Rowe, n.d.; both in box 372, Lyndon Johnson Senate Papers; Hubert Humphrey to Roy Wilkins, October 27, 1960, box 6, Roy Wilkins Papers, Library of Congress, Washington, D.C.; Hubert Humphrey to Roy Wilkins, November 4, 1960, box 586, SF, HP.

52. Eisele, *Almost to the Presidency*, p. 157; Schlesinger, *A Thousand Days*, p. 930; Brauer, *John F. Kennedy*, pp. 45–60.

53. Stern, *Calculating Visions*, pp. 40–42; Schlesinger, *A Thousand Days*, pp. 931–935; Graham, *The Civil Rights Era*, pp. 31–41; Sundquist, *Politics and Policy*, pp. 254–260; Harris Wofford, Memorandum to President-Elect Kennedy on Civil Rights—1961, box 1071, Pre-Presidential Papers, JFKL. The need for FEPC, Wofford wrote, was "slight." Paul Douglas, Hubert Humphrey, and Joseph Clark to Stuart Symington, October 20, 1960, box 22, Symington Papers; *Congressional Record*, 87th Cong., 1st sess., p. 75; *New York Times*, January 3, 1961, p. 19; *New York Times*, January 12, 1961, pp. 1, 19; Joe Rauh, The Effort to Obtain a New Senate Rule XXII at the Opening of a New Congress, December 1960, series III, box A65, NAACP Papers; Douglas, *In the Fullness of Time*, p. 195. The pro–civil rights forces went down to defeat 50–46. Humphrey took some comfort in the close vote, but conceded that "progress [was] all to slow." Hubert Humphrey to Roy Wilkins, February 1, 1961, box 7, SF, HP.

54. Brauer, *John F. Kennedy*, pp. 61–99; Hubert Humphrey to Cecil Newman, April 20, 1961, box 5, SF, HP; *Congressional Record*, 87th Cong., 1st sess., p. 3,472–3,477, 5,810–5,813. Several of Humphrey's black friends and former aides received government jobs, including Frank Reeves (special assistant to the president), Carl Rowan (deputy assistant secretary of state for public affairs) and Eddie Waters (assistant protocol chief in the State Department).

55. *Congressional Record*, 87th Cong., 1st sess., pp. 855–856, 3,443, 3,477, 4,720, 7,929; *New York Times*, February 24, 1961, pp. 1, 14; Memorandum, February 6, 1961,

box 6, Wilkins Papers; *New York Times*, July 10, 1961, p. 21; Martin Luther King Oral History, JFKL; Stern, *Calculating Visions*, p. 45; Statement by Roy Wilkins on the White House Attitude Towards Civil Rights Legislation, May 10, 1961, series III, box A72, NAACP Papers; Harris Wofford to John F. Kennedy, May 22, 1961, box 360, White House central files (WHCF), JFKL; *New York Times*, August 31, 1961, p. 14. When the White House simply indicated that the president did not think it was a propitious time to push for civil rights, Roy Wilkins called the president's approach "mistaken and regrettable," while other civil rights leaders also expressed their disappointment. The Republican civil rights package included Title III, indefinite extension of the Civil Rights Commission, completion of the sixth grade as proof of literacy for voting registration, and financial and technical assistance to desegregating school districts. Humphrey's legislation consisted of FEPC, an end to discrimination in interstate transportation, antilynching, protection of members of the armed forces, and an extension of the Civil Rights Commission. Even the extension of the Civil Rights Commission was not what civil rights leaders had expected. They had anticipated that its functions would be broadened and strengthened. Privately, Humphrey expressed concern that Kennedy had been "very late" in giving his support to liberals' efforts to extend the commission. Humphrey to Jack, May 31, 1961, box 185, SF, HP.

56. Branch, *Parting the Waters*, pp. 412–485; Sitkoff, *The Struggle for Black Equality*, pp. 101–111.

57. *New York Times*, May 22, 1961, pp. 1, 26; *New York Times*, May 23, 1961, pp. 1, 30; Burke Marshall to Hubert Humphrey, June 30, 1961, Jack to Senator, July 5, 1961, both in box 510, SF, HP; Hubert Humphrey to John Stennis, July 5, 1961, box 510, SF, HP; Hubert Humphrey to James Eastland, July 5, 1961, box 570, SF, HP; Chafe, *The Unfinished Journey*, p. 209. Privately, Humphrey approached Mississippi Senators John Stennis and James Eastland and expressed concern for the safety of the arrested students, though his staff informed him that there was little the federal government could do since Title III had not been enacted.

58. U.S. Commission on Civil Rights, *Voting: 1961*, pp. 29–37; *Congressional Record*, 87th Cong., 2d sess., p. 7,916; Brauer, *John F. Kennedy*, pp. 132–133.

59. *Congressional Record*, 87th Cong., 2d sess., pp. 3,876, 4,176; Press Release, January 30, 1962, Republican Congressional Leadership files, Dirksen Papers; U.S. Senate, Subcommittee on Constitutional Rights, *Literacy Tests and Voter Requirements in Federal and State Elections*, pp. 472–473; Stern, *Calculating Visions*, pp. 74–75. The vote proved the continued existence of southern Democrat-Republican cooperation on civil rights issues. Thirty southern and western Democrats joined twenty-three Republicans to block cloture.

60. Branch, *Parting the Waters*, pp. 524–561, 603–632, 647–672; *New York Times*, August 2, 1962, pp. 1, 15; Sitkoff, *Struggle for Black Equality*, pp. 124–126; *New York Times*, October 2, 1962, pp. 1, 24; *Congressional Record*, 87th Cong., 2d sess., pp. 21,033, 22, 119; Hubert Humphrey to Joe Rauh, November 16, 1962, box 19, Rauh Papers.

61. Philip Hart and Hubert Humphrey to Edward Kennedy, November 29, 1962, box 241, SF, HP; Hubert Humphrey to Clinton Anderson, October 11, 1962, box 7, SF, HP; *Minneapolis Tribune*, January 16, 1963, p. 3; *New York Times*, January 16, 1963,

pp. 1, 8; Chronology of Filibuster Fight, n.d., box 43, Rauh Papers; Joe Rauh to John F. Kennedy, December 7, 1962, box 482, WHCF, JFKL; *Minneapolis Tribune*, February 1, 1963, pp. 1, 8; *New York Times*, February 8, 1963, pp. 1, 6; Hubert Humphrey to Clarence Mitchell, February 12, 1963, box 220, SF, HP; Newsletter from Senator Hubert Humphrey, February 1963, series III, box A171, NAACP Papers.

62. Hubert Humphrey, Philip Hart, Joseph Clark, Harrison Williams, Paul Douglas, and Claire Engle to the President, January 8, 1963, box 362, WHCF, JFKL; Brauer, *John F. Kennedy*, p. 221–228; Graham, *Civil Rights Era*, p. 70; *Congressional Record*, 88th Cong., 1st sess., pp. 4,847–4,848; Hubert Humphrey to John Sherman Cooper, January 29, 1963, box 218, SF, HP; Watson, *Lion in the Lobby*, p. 544; Hubert Humphrey to John Bailey, February 16, 1963, box 191, WHCF, JFKL; John Stewart to author, March 28, 1997, in author's possession.

63. *Nation*, March, 1963, pp. 260; Sitkoff, *Struggle for Black Equality*, pp. 127–138; Branch, *Parting the Waters*, pp. 756–802. The violence in Birmingham was followed by violence in Chicago, Philadelphia, Savannah, and Cambridge, Md. Hundreds of peaceful protests occurred as well.

64. Hubert Humphrey to Jay Phillips, May 10, 1963, box 218, SF, HP; Brauer, *John F. Kennedy*, pp. 233–249; *Minneapolis Tribune*, May 12, 1963, pp. 1, 6; *New York Times*, May 13, 1963, p. 25; Hubert Humphrey to Charles Platt, May 28, 1963; Hubert Humphrey to Robert Gavin, June 3, 1963; Hubert Humphrey to Jerry Anderson, June 7, 1963; Hubert Humphrey to Morris Ernst, July 3, 1963; Hubert Humphrey to R. E. Comstock, May 27, 1963; all in box 218, SF, HP; Whalen and Whalen, *The Longest Debate*, p. 19. In the ten weeks following Birmingham there were 758 demonstrations with 13,786 people arrested in 75 southern cities alone.

65. Hubert Humphrey, Philip Hart, et. al. to John F. Kennedy, May 15, 1963, box 218, SF, HP; Memorandum, n.d., box 241, SF, HP; John Stewart to Senator, n.d., box 241, SF, HP. Kennedy held the meetings early that summer, seeing a total of more than 1600 influential leaders.

66. Branch, *Parting the Waters*, pp. 800–807; Kennedy, *Public Papers of the Presidents*, pp. 468–471; Brauer, *John F. Kennedy*, pp. 258–267; Memorandum, n.d., box 241, SF, HP; Norbert Schlei Oral History, JFKL.

67. *Congressional Record*, 88th Cong., 1st sess., pp. 11,096–11,172; Labor Views on Administration's Civil Rights Package, June 10, 1963, box 9, Department of Legislation files, AFL-CIO Papers; Graham, *Civil Rights Era*, pp. 83–87; Sitkoff, *Struggle for Black Equality*, pp. 151–158.

68. Stern, "Poverty and Family Composition Since 1940," pp. 237–238; Carnoy, *Faded Dreams*, pp. 14–16; U.S. Senate, Subcommittee on Manpower, *Equal Employment Opportunity*, pp. 135–139; *Congressional Record*, 88th Cong., 1st sess., pp. 11, 165, 13,242–13,249. During the 1950s numerous northern cities lost hundreds of thousands of manufacturing jobs as companies automated, opened new facilities elsewhere, or reduced employment for other reasons. See Sugrue, *Origins of the Urban Crisis*, pp. 128–146.

69. *Congressional Record*, 88th Cong., 1st sess., pp. 14,039–14,040; Collins, *The Business Response to Keynes*, pp. 178–184; Weir, "The Federal Government and Un-

employment," pp. 172–174. Moreover, as Weir notes, administrative incoherence in the Labor Department and tensions between it and state-based agencies and their allies on Capitol Hill also made a massive new government jobs program unlikely.

70. U.S. Senate, Subcommittee on Manpower, *Equal Employment Opportunity*, p. 94; *Congressional Record*, 88th Cong., 1st sess., pp. 11, 743, 13,242–13,245; Hubert Humphrey to Friend, August 1, 1963, series III, box A147, NAACP Papers; Graham, *Civil Rights Era*, pp. 111–117; John Stewart to Berl Bernhard, January 2, 1963, box 218, SF, HP; U.S. Commission on Civil Rights, *Employment: 1961*, pp. 157–164; Hubert Humphrey to John Stewart, June 12, 1963, box 1, William Connell Papers, Minnesota Historical Society, St. Paul, Minn. African Americans who left the South for life in northern cities, Humphrey thought, suffered high unemployment partly because "they [had] no mechanical aptitude, actually no work habits that fit into industrial life where promptness on the job and being able to keep up the pace of fast-moving [machinery] is required." Given these circumstances, Humphrey insisted that any job training program had to include educational efforts "about urban living and the adjustments which would come to any individual in an urban situation."

71. Sitkoff, *Struggle for Black Equality*, pp. 159–160; Brauer, *John F. Kennedy*, pp. 273–274; Hubert Humphrey to Martin Luther King, n.d., box 185, SF, HP. Even after plans for the march were being made, Humphrey held to his belief that the morning events include meetings between citizens and state congressional delegations. The program of speakers and music at the Lincoln Memorial was scheduled for the afternoon. A meeting between elected officials and citizens, he noted, would show legislators the depth of support for civil rights legislation and, Humphrey believed, provide a "constructive alternative" that would help avoid "serious problems that might arise." Hubert Humphrey to Stephen Currier, August 12, 1963, series III, box A228, NAACP Papers.

72. *Congressional Record*, 88th Cong., 1st sess., pp. 16, 115–16,116; Branch, *Parting the Waters*, pp. 880–883; Hubert Humphrey to Martin Luther King, September 5, 1963, box 218, SF, HP; *Minneapolis Tribune*, August 29, 1963, pp. 1, 6.

73. Branch, *Parting the Waters*, pp. 892–895; Hubert Humphrey, Philip Hart, Thomas Kuchel, and Jacob Javits to the President, September 17, 1963, box 366, WHCF, JFKL; *Congressional Record*, 88th Cong., 1st sess., pp. 17,204–17,206, 17, 471.

74. John Field to Hubert Humphrey, October 17, 1963, box 1, Connell Papers; *Congressional Record*, 88th Cong., 1st sess., p. 19,743.

75. Hubert Humphrey to Rodney Jacobson, March 14, 1956, box 18, SF, HP; Hubert Humphrey to Stewart Alsop, July 20, 1957, box 136, SF, HP. Humphrey noted, "I must say that Senator [Lister] Hill [Alabama] is about as fine a liberal as I have known, except on the issue of civil rights. . . . He has voted with labor almost one-hundred percent, and so has Sparkman. So has Senator Long, Senator Olin Johnston of South Carolina, Senator Scott Kerr of North Carolina, and others." Letter, John Stewart to author, March 28, 1997, in author's possession.

76. Burner, *Making Peace with the 60s*, pp. 33–36.

77. Johnson, *Public Papers of the Presidents*, p. 9; Whalen and Whalen, *Longest Debate*, p. 78.

5. A Moment of Triumph: The 1964 Civil Rights Act

1. Press Release, January 18, 1964, box 16, Marquis Childs Papers, State Historical Society of Wisconsin, Madison, Wis.

2. Whalen and Whalen, *Longest Debate*, p. 136; Hubert Humphrey OH III, LBJL; Memorandum, n.d., box 241, SF, HP.

3. Garrow, *Bearing the Cross*, p. 302; Hubert Humphrey to Doris Fleeson, February 27, 1964, box 742, SF, HP.

4. Whalen and Whalen, *Longest Debate*, pp. 109–121; Graham, *Civil Rights Era*, pp. 133–139; Stephen Horn, Periodic Log Maintained During the Discussions Concerning the Passage of the Civil Rights Act of 1964 (Horn Log), p. 20, Library of Congress, Washington, D.C. Other provisions of the measure included a requirement that states gather voting statistics for House races since 1960 (Title VIII), a section on Judicial appeal (Title IX), the creation of a Community Relations Service (Title X), and a miscellaneous section (Title XI).

5. Horn Log, pp. 5–6, 26, 38; Loevy, *To End All Segregation*, p. 134–137; Press Conference, February 20, 1964, Republican Congressional Leadership Series, Dirksen Papers; Hubert Humphrey Oral History III, LBJL; *Washington Star*, February 27, 1964, p. 15. Humphrey's Republican allies included Kenneth Keating (New York), Jacob Javits (New York), Leverett Saltonsall (Massachusetts), Clifford Case (New Jersey), and J. Glenn Beall (Maryland). Among his Democratic colleagues, Humphrey needed the help of senators such as Alan Bible (Nevada), Howard Cannon (Nevada), J. Howard Edmondson (Oklahoma), Carl Hayden (Arizona), Mike Monroney (Oklahoma), and Daniel Inouye (Hawaii). As for the GOP, he had to have Frank Carlson (Kansas), Roman Hruska (Nebraska), James Pearson (Kansas), Bourke Hickenlooper (Iowa), and Jack Miller (Iowa).

6. Horn Log, pp. 24–26a; Watson, *Lion in the Lobby*, p. 602; Mike Manatos to Larry O' Brien, February 17, 1964, box 21, White House Aides Files, Harry McPherson, LBJL; Horn Log, p. 13; Memo, February 25, 1964, series III, box A72, NAACP Papers; Whalen and Whalen, *Longest Debate*, pp. 139–140; *Washington Post*, February 24, 1964, p. 1. To help drum up support for cloture, Humphrey decided that the Senate had to dispose of a cotton and wheat bill before it addressed civil rights. Considering civil rights before the farm legislation, he reasoned, meant that senators from states such as Iowa, Nebraska, and Kansas might make concessions on the civil rights bill to silence the filibuster that was blocking the farm legislation, which was of greater interest to most of their constituents. Others disagreed. Mitchell worried that the farm bill would cause an unnecessary delay, while the Johnson administration hoped to use it as a carrot to persuade the southerners to end their filibuster. Some pro–civil rights Republicans publicly criticized Humphrey for putting "cotton before people." Humphrey persuaded Johnson and Senate leaders, however, and the Senate approved the farm bill on Friday, March 6. The path was now clear to take up civil rights the following Monday.

7. Loevy, *To End All Segregation*, pp. 168–172; *Congressional Record*, 88th Cong., 2d sess., p. 3,717; Graham, *Civil Rights Era*, p. 144. Transcript, *Meet the Press*, March 8, 1964 (Washington, D.C.: Merkle, 1964), pp. 1–3; Hubert Humphrey OH III, LBJL. House bill was introduced on February 17. Nine days later, after the Senate had passed

Kennedy's tax cut, Mansfield moved to place the civil rights legislation directly on the calendar instead of the following customary procedure of sending it to the Judiciary Committee. Outraged southern Democrats demanded that the bill receive a full committee hearing. Still under the direction of James Eastland of Mississippi, the Judiciary Committee had held only eight days of hearings on the bill in 1963, during which it had heard from just one witness, Attorney General Robert F. Kennedy. As far as Humphrey was concerned, the dozens of hearings on FEPC, voting, and other civil rights bills that had been held since he had joined the Senate provided more than enough information about this legislation. "There has been no lack of hearings," he argued. "There has been a lack of action." In fact, he pointed out, only one of 121 civil rights bills had ever been reported out of the Judiciary Committee in the previous decade, and even that had occurred only because of specific instructions from the full Senate. Like Humphrey, a majority of the Senate was exasperated with southern delaying tactics and voted to place the bill directly on the Senate calendar.

8. Loevy, *To End all Segregation*, pp. 160–161; Fite, *Richard B. Russell*, pp. 409–414; *Congressional Record*, 88th Cong., 2d sess., pp. 4,745–4,754; Whalen and Whalen, *Longest Debate*, p. 125.

9. *Congressional Record*, 88th Cong., 2d sess., pp. 4,999–5,000, 5,092, 5,999–6,010, 6,549.

10. Hubert Humphrey to Stuart Symington, March 2, 1964, box 16, Symington Papers; Whalen and Whalen, *Longest Debate*, p. 144; Memorandum, n.d., box 241, SF, HP; *Congressional Quarterly Weekly Report*, March 20, 1964, p. 549; *Congressional Record*, 88th Cong., 2d sess., pp. 5,042–5,046; *Washington Post*, March 13, 1964, p. 13; Horn Log, p. 31a. Humphrey agreed to let the LCCR representative sit in on the meetings twice a week.

11. Memorandum, n.d., box 241, SF, HP; Horn Log, p. 31a; Hubert Humphrey to Bob Barrie, John Stewart, and Bill Connell,, February 29, 1964, box 594, SF, HP; Findlay, "The Churches and the Civil Rights Act of 1964," p. 82. Similarly, Humphrey wrote the president about persuading the networks to do television specials on the civil rights debate. This was critical, he indicated, to the drive for cloture. "For example," Humphrey noted, "if we could get people like Lawrence Welk, the Beverly Hillbillies, Jimmy Dean, and some Republican-oriented entertainers like Bob Hope or John Wayne, it would appeal to [midwestern senators'] constituents. Then I would get people like Reuben Youngdahl, who is the pastor of the largest Lutheran church in America, perhaps Billy Graham, Bishop [Sheen], and . . . really make a concerted effort to convince the midwesterner that anyone who is against voting for cloture is against civil rights, morality, motherhood, virtue, God, and country." Hubert Humphrey to Lyndon Johnson, March 18, 1964, box 241, SF, HP.

12. *Congressional Record*, 88th Cong., 2d sess., pp. 5,422–5,424; *New York Times*, March 21, 1964, p. 14; Horn Log, pp. 48, 65; *Washington Post*, March 15, 1964, pp, 1, 4; *Washington Post*, March 22, 1964, p, 9; *Washington Post*, March 23, 1964, p. 6.

13. Whalen and Whalen, *Longest Debate*, p. 147; *Congressional Record*, 88th Cong., 2d sess., p. 6,455; Horn Log, pp. 24, 51–52; Loevy, *To End All Segregation,* p. 179.

14. Whalen and Whalen, *Longest Debate*, pp. 149–150; *Congressional Record*, 88th Cong., 2d sess., pp. 6,528–6,552.

15. *Newsweek*, April 13, 1964, pp. 26–31.

16. Whalen and Whalen, *Longest Debate*, pp. 152–160; *Washington Post*, April 8, 1964, p. 3; Horn Log, pp. 79–94; Memorandum, n.d., box 241, SF, HP.

17. Hubert Humphrey to Clinton Anderson, April 3, 1964, box 688, Anderson Papers; Hubert Humphrey to Stuart Symington, April 3, 1964, box 16, Symington Papers; Arnold Aronson to Cooperating Organizations, April 13, 1964, series III, box A206, NAACP Papers; Loevy, *To End All Segregation*, p. 191; Whalen and Whalen, *Longest Debate*, p. 158; Watson, *Lion in the Lobby*, p. 608.

18. *Congressional Quarterly Weekly Report*, April 10, 1964, pp. 687–688; Lesher, *George Wallace*, pp. 282–285; White, *The Making of the President, 1964*, p. 234; *Washington Post*, April 9, 1964, p. 1.

19. Garrow, *Bearing the Cross*, p. 319; *Time*, April 24, 1964, p. 18; *New York Times*, April 15, 1964, p. 38; *New York Times*, April 16, 1964, pp. 1, 24, Horn Log, p. 90; *Congressional Quarterly Weekly Report*, April 17, 1964, p. 717. The leaders of the NAACP, National Urban League, and other civil rights groups urged orderly nonviolent demonstrations, and the national leaders of CORE suspended the chapter. Similarly, civil rights leader Bayard Rustin worried that the stall-in would hurt chances for a strong bill. King, though, was privately chagrined at Humphrey and Kuchel's statement. He commented, "Frankly, I have gotten a little fed-up with the lectures we are receiving from the white power structure, even when it comes from such tried-and-true friends as Humphrey and Kuchel, Javits and Keating." King wanted the movement to continue direct action protests even though whites in the North might oppose such tactics. Garrow, *Bearing the Cross*, pp. 322–323; Anderson, *Bayard Rustin*, p. 272.

20. Horn Log, p. 87; Hubert Humphrey to Clinton Anderson, April 9, 1964, box 689, Anderson Papers; *Congressional Record*, 88th Cong., 2d sess., p. 8,914. On the floor of the Senate Humphrey responded to a challenge that the bill would lead to quotas, "If the senator can find in Title VII . . . any language which provides that an employer will have to hire on the basis of percentage or quota related to color, race, religion, or national origin, I will start eating the pages one after another, because it is not in there." *Congressional Record*, 88th Cong., 2d sess. p. 7,420; *Washington Post*, April 10, 1964, p. 2; *Washington Post*, April 12, 1964, p. 2; *Washington Post*, April 17, 1964, p. 2; Horn Log, p. 128.

21. Horn Log, p. 86; John Stewart Diary, April 21, 1964, box 241, SF, HP; Gallup, *Gallup Poll*, pp. 1,827, 1,863; MacNeil, *Dirksen*, p. 231. A poll of February 2, 1964 showed 61 percent approval for the bill, up from 47 percent in July, 1963. Seventy-one percent whites outside the South favored it.

22. Loevy, *To End All Segregation*, pp. 248–250; Horn Log, pp. 128–192; *Washington Post*, April 28, 1964, p. 6. Several Democrats were growing upset at Dirksen's ability to set the agenda. "I don't know," one commented, "whether my opponent is Russell or Dirksen."

23. Whalen and Whalen, *Longest Debate*, pp. 164–166; Loevy, *To End All Segregation*, p. 202; *Congressional Record*, 88th Cong., 2d sess., p. 9,535; *New York Times*, April 29, 1964, pp. 1, 29; Memorandum, n.d., box 241, SF, HP; Findlay, "The Churches and the Civil Rights Act of 1964," p. 82.

24. John Stewart Diary (Stewart Diary), April 21, 1964 and April 29, 1964, box 241, SF, HP; Horn Log, p. 130.

25. Stewart Diary, April 21, 1964, April 29, 1964, and April 30, 1964, box 241, SF, HP; Horn Log, pp. 140–142.

26. Horn Log, pp. 94, 147; *Los Angeles Times*, May 1, 1964, pp. 1, 28; *New York Times*, May 1, 1964, pp. 1, 16.

27. Stewart Diary, May 5, 1964, box 241, SF, HP; Horn Log, p. 159. Liberal Democrats were furious with Humphrey for conducting the meetings in Dirksen's office. "You're the manager of the bill. We're the majority party. Why don't you call Dirksen to your office?" they asked. Humphrey replied, "I don't care where we meet Dirksen. We can meet him in a nightclub, in the bottom of a mine, or in a manhole. It doesn't make any difference to me." Humphrey OH III, LBJL.

28. Loevy, *To End All Segregation*, pp. 250–252; Horn Log, p. 140; Stewart Diary, May 6, 1964, box 241, SF, HP; *Congressional Record*, 88th Cong., 2d sess., p. 10, 213; *New York Times*, May 12, 1964, p. 28.

29. Roy Wilkins to Hubert Humphrey, May 8, 1964, series III, box A67, NAACP Papers; Watson, *Lion in the Lobby*, pp. 597–613; Horn Log, p. 161; Hubert Humphrey to Walter Reuther, May 8, 1964, box 225, SF, HP; Hubert Humphrey to Walter Reuther, May 15, 1964, box 410, Reuther Papers; *Washington Post,* May 11, 1964, p. 1; Garrow, *Bearing the Cross*, p. 325.

30. Stewart Diary, May 13, 1964, box 241, SF, HP; Horn Log, p. 177; *New York Times*, May 14, 1964, pp. 1, 28; Griffith, *Humphrey*, p. 282; Graham, *Civil Rights Era*, pp. 147–148; Minutes, Joint Republican Congressional Leaders Meeting, June 2, 1964, Republican Congressional Leadership Files, Dirksen Papers; *Congressional Quarterly Weekly Report*, June 19, 1964, p. 1,206. Dirksen and other northern legislators wanted to keep federal civil rights enforcement confined largely to the South, and thus the "pattern or practice" phrase was inserted to deflect attention from discrimination in the North, which many assumed was more isolated than that in the South. Second, northern leaders believed that the myriad of state and local FEPCs would adequately address employment problems in the North. See Hill, "Black Workers, Organized Labor, and Title VII," pp. 263–273. Among those still listed as doubtful for cloture were Wallace Bennett (R–Utah), Alan Bible (D–Nevada), Howard Cannon (D–Nevada), Norris Cotton (R–New Hampshire), Carl Curtis (R–Nebraska), Roman Hruska (R–Nebraska), Len Jordan (R–Idaho), Edwin Mechem (R–New Mexico), Karl Mundt (R–South Dakota), Millard Simpson (R–Wyoming), John Williams (R–Delaware), Ralph Yarborough (D–Texas), and Milton Young (R–North Dakota). Still considered possible for cloture were Dirksen, George Aiken (R–Vermont), Frank Carlson (R–Kansas), Edward Long (D–Missouri), Jack Miller (R–Iowa), James Pearson (R–Kansas), Frank Lausch (D–Ohio), and Norris Cotton (R–New Hampshire).

31. Horn Log, pp. 168–177; *Christian Science Monitor*, May 12, 1964, p. 1; *New York Times*, May 13, 1964, p. 1; *Congressional Record*, 88th Cong., 2d sess., p. 10, 616; *Washington Post*, May 12, 1964, pp. 1, 5.

32. Stewart Diary, May 19, 1964, box 241, SF, HP; *New York Times*, May 20, 1964, pp. 1, 34.; Memorandum, n.d., box 241, SF, HP; *Congressional Record*, 88th Cong., 2d

sess., pp. 11,847, 11,936, 12, 715–12,724; Whalen and Whalen, *Longest Debate*, p. 190; *Washington Post,* May 24, 1964, p. 6. After a long and sometimes heated debate, civil rights proponents had agreed to follow the lead of a federal circuit court which had recently struck down busing in Gary, Indiana by concluding that the Constitution forbade segregation but did not require integration.

33. Stewart Diary, n.d., box 241, SF, HP; Memorandum, n.d., box 241, SF, HP; Whalen and Whalen, *Longest Debate*, pp. 190–192; Loevy, *To End All Segregation*, p. 275. Humphrey knew what Hickenlooper was doing since one of the senators attending the Iowan's gatherings reported to him. Hickenlooper's amendments included a revised jury trial plan, restricting Title VII to employers with more than one hundred employees, and removing all provisions dealing with assistance for school desegregation.

34. Memorandum, n.d., box 241, SF, HP.

35. Memorandum, n.d., box 241, SF, HP; Whalen and Whalen, *Longest Debate*, pp. 196–197; Loevy, *To End All Segregation*, p. 282; *Congressional Record*, 88th Cong., 2d sess., p. 13, 310; *New York Times*, June 11, 1964, pp. 1, 21; *Time*, June 19, 1964, pp. 15–18.

36. *New York Times*, June 11, 1964, pp. 1, 21; Whalen and Whalen, *Longest Debate*, pp. 199–200; *Washington Post*, June 11, 1964, p. 9; *New York Post*, June 11, 1964, p. 7. Johnson helped nail down the votes of a few western Democrats. Humphrey had little time to savor the victory, however. With the Senate operating under cloture, each member had up to one hour to speak about the bill. Within minutes after the roll call North Carolina Democrat Sam Ervin offered an amendment to prevent the federal government from trying someone who had been accused of violating the law but had been found innocent by a state court. The Senate passed it, but the amendment did not become part of the legislation, because of a miscount of the original tally followed by a parliamentary maneuver by a southern senator that unintentionally prevented the amendment from being reconsidered. Following this narrow escape for Humphrey and his allies, the Senate defeated a proposal to remove Title VI from the bill and then recessed. Humphrey met that afternoon with Justice Department officials, civil rights lobbyists, and pro–civil rights colleagues to hatch plans to counter future southern amendments, but the gathering adjourned without a firm agreement about what to do. Some pro–civil rights leaders urged quick rejection of all amendments in an effort to pass the legislation as soon as possible. Recommending a more cautious approach, Humphrey suggested that such a strategy could backfire by leading to retribution on an amendment they wanted to defeat. He was especially concerned about amendments to Title VI. The southerners' feelings, he maintained, had to be taken into account even though cloture had been achieved. Stewart Diary, n.d., box 241, SF, HP; Hubert Humphrey to Walter Reuther, June 11, 1963, box 410, Reuther Papers.

37. Stewart Diary, n.d., box 241, SF, HP; *Congressional Record*, 88th Cong., 2d sess., pp. 13, 504, 13, 724. The testing amendment was originally rejected 49–38. Humphrey considered it redundant and unnecessary. Several days later, sponsor John Tower of Texas modified it slightly and the Senate approved it on a voice vote. While the southerners' amendments were being considered, Humphrey turned his attention to implementation of the bill. He pressed Johnson to call a White House civil rights

conference at which southern and African American leaders would discuss racial problems. Johnson refused. He also suggested a governor's conference in each state and that the U.S. Conference of Mayors hold a general session regarding racial issues. *Minneapolis Tribune*, June 15, 1964, pp. 1, 9; *Minneapolis Tribune*, June 16, 1964, p. 34.

38. Loevy, *To End All Segregation*, pp. 299–302; Stewart Diary, n.d., box 241, SF, HP; Humphrey, *Education of a Public Man*, p. 285.

39. *Congressional Record*, 88th Cong., 2d sess., pp. 14,443–14,444.

40. *New York Times*, June 20, 1964, pp. 1, 10; Humphrey, *Education of a Public Man*, p. 285; Griffith, *Humphrey*, pp. 284–285; *Washington Post*, June 20, 1964, pp. 1, 12; Hubert Humphrey to James Reston, June 20, 1964, box 726, SF, HP.

41. *Minneapolis Tribune*, June 21, 1964, pp. 1, 10.

42. *New York Times*, July 3, 1964, pp. 1, 9; *Minneapolis Tribune*, June 20, 1964, p. 3; Johnson, *A White House Diary*, p. 174.

43. Title VI would indeed prove to be an important tool in subsequent decades, but its effectiveness was far less than many civil rights advocates had expected. See Halpern, *On the Limits of the Law.*

44. *Minneapolis Star*, June 23, 1964, pp. 1, 8; *San Francisco Chronicle*, June 23, 1964, p. 5; *Minneapolis Tribune*, June 12, 1964, p. 4; *Washington Post*, June 20, 1964, p. 10; Arnold Aronson to Hubert Humphrey, June 24, 1964, box A3, LCCR Papers; Humphrey, *Education*, p. 284. Regarding Russsell's strategy, Humphrey commented a month later, "The biggest mistake [the southerners] made was to go for broke. . . . If they had called up amendments in the beginning, when we didn't know how things would turn out, there is no question that they could have made serious inroads on this bill." *Reporter*, July 16, 1964, p. 23.

45. *Congressional Record*, 88th Cong., 2d sess., pp. 13,312–13,315.

46. Edsall and Edsall, *Chain Reaction*, p. 37; Gallup, *The Gallup Poll*, pp. 1,884, 1,888–1,891. A June 10 poll asked respondents whom they would vote for if two candidates were alike in every way except civil rights. Sixty percent said they'd vote for the pro–civil rights candidate, compared to just 25 percent for the anti–civil rights candidate. Similarly, in an early July presidential trial heat, Johnson led Goldwater 77–18 percent and Richard Nixon 70–27 percent.

6. Preserving the New Deal Coalition: The Politics of Race in 1964

1. Faber, *The Road to the White House*, pp. 144–146; *U.S. News and World Report*, August 3, 1964, p. 22–23; *Time*, August 7, 1964, pp. 17–18; *Minneapolis Tribune*, August 4, 1964, p. 1; *New York Times*, August 12, 1964, p. 22; Additional racial violence occurred in Toledo (July 23), St. Louis (July 25), and Centreville, Illinois (July 25). *U.S. News and World Report*, August 10, 1964, pp. 24–25; *Congressional Record*, 88th Cong., 2d sess., pp. 16,384–85, 16,957–58.

3. *Newsweek*, August 3, 1964, p. 15; *Time*, July 31, 1964, p. 9; *U.S. News and World Report*, August 3, 1964, p. 15; *Time*, July 31, 1964, p. 9; *U.S. News and World Report*, August 3, 1964, p. 27; *New York Times*, July 25, 1964, p. 1; *Nation*, August 10, 1964, p. 41; Gallup, *The Gallup Poll*, p. 1, 890, 1, 896. Shortly after the New York riot, four leading civil rights organizations, including the NAACP and the SCLC, issued a joint statement calling for a "broad curtailment" of mass demonstrations. African Ameri-

cans, they suggested, needed to devote their time to political organizing to keep Barry Goldwater from becoming president. CORE and SNCC refused to go along. *New York Times*, July 31, 1964, p. 1; *Washington Post*, August 17, 1964, p. 1. Overall, 60 percent of Americans still approved of Johnson's handling of civil rights, while 54 percent supported the 1964 Civil Rights Act.

5. White, *Making of the President, 1964*, p. 202–217; Brennan, *Turning Right*, pp. 47–81; Transcript, *Face the Nation*, pp. 293–294. Humphrey met with Clarence Mitchell just after the New York riot to discuss its implications. The media, Mitchell pointed out, contributed to the escalating tensions by constantly asking African American leaders if a riot were about to break loose. Racial justice would be better served if the press focused on the progress that had occurred and highlighted the vast majority of African Americans who took no part in the violence, the NAACP lobbyist argued. Humphrey agreed with his longtime ally and asked the Johnson administration to approach the television networks about this matter. Hubert Humphrey to Jack Valenti, August 5, 1964, Ex HU 2, box 3, WHCF, LBJL; Hubert Humphrey to himself, August 4, 1964, Ex HU 2, box 3, WHCF, LBJL.

6. Solberg, *Hubert H. Humphrey*, pp. 240–245; Gallup, *The Gallup Poll*, pp. 1,888–1,891; *New York Times*, July 31, 1964, pp. 1, 8; *New Republic*, August 8, 1964, pp, 3, 4; *Washington Post*, August 6, 1964, pp, 3–4. During the spring Humphrey's backers had privately lined up meetings with labor, business, and political leaders to round up support for Humphrey as the Democratic vice presidential nominee. They also sent out material favorable to Humphrey to party leaders across the country. *New York Times*, August 27, 1964, p. 22. Following the New York riot, William Connell approached James Rowe, a Johnson adviser who also happened to be a close friend of Humphrey's, in hopes of heading off any anti-Humphrey sentiment that might have been brewing in the administration. The Democrats, Connell wrote, could not "win over any of the haters" and thus had to stand on their record. They needed to confront the backlash directly by firmly supporting law and order, defending the civil rights bill, and assuring workers that they were against hiring quotas. Connell did not specifically urge the administration to select Humphrey, but the implication was clear. William Connell to James Rowe, July 24, 1964, box 595, SF, HP; William Connell to John Stewart, July 20, 1964, box 7, Connell Papers; Hubert Humphrey to Harry Golden, August 11, 1964, box 1046, Vice-Presidential Files (VPF), HP; Hubert Humphrey to Ralph McGill, August 5, 1964, box 726, SF, HP; *Minneapolis Tribune*, August 17, 1964, p. 19. Between 1950 and 1962 the GOP went from two seats in the House of Representatives to eleven. Whereas it had drawn only one-sixth to one-fourth of the southern vote between 1932 and 1948, Eisenhower had won 37 percent in 1952 and 49 percent in 1956. Nixon had captured 46 percent in 1960. *Commentary*, August 1964, p. 24. Southern party leaders instead favored more moderate northerners such as Senators Thomas Dodd of Connecticut or Eugene McCarthy of Minnesota.

7. Dittmer, *Local People*, pp. 273–286, 290; Nicolaus Mills, *Like a Holy Crusade*, pp. 136–145; Carson, *In Struggle*, pp. 123–124; *Time*, September 4, 1964, p. 31; *New York Times*, August 16, 1964, p. 1. Democratic politicians were not the only ones looking for some sort of compromise that would hold the party together. In early August Martin Luther King told Johnson assistant Lee White that he hoped for a compro-

mise that would keep southern resistance in check and maintain African American morale. King, White reported to the president, was having a harder time trying to hold down violence and fully expected Goldwater to capitalize on the white backlash. Lee White to Lyndon Johnson, August 13, 1964, box 81, EX PL 1/ST 24, WHCF, LBJL. Prominent southern Democrats who were absent included Senators Harry Byrd of Virginia, Richard Russell and Herman Talmadge of Georgia, Russell Long and Allen Ellender of Louisiana, John Stennis and James Eastland of Mississippi, and John Sparkman and Lister Hill of Alabama. One-third of the South's Democratic governors were also absent. Governors who had announced their support for Goldwater included Paul Johnson of Mississippi, Orval Faubus of Arkansas, and George Wallace of Alabama.

8. Interview of Joseph Rauh, Anne Romaine Files (Romaine Files), State Historical Society of Wisconsin, Madison, Wis. On the violence aimed at civil rights workers in Mississippi during the summer of 1964, see Belknap, *Federal Law and Southern Order*, pp. 128–158; Cagin and Dray, *We Are Not Afraid*; McAdam, *Freedom Summer*.

9. *Washington Post*, August 19, 1964, pp. 1, 6; *Minneapolis Tribune*, August 26, 1964, pp. 1, 3; Rauh interview, Romaine Files; Rauh OH III, LBJL.

10. *New York Times*, August 23, 1964, pp. 1, 81; Carson, *In Struggle*, p. 125; *Washington Post*, August 23, 1964, pp. 1, 24, 26; Sitkoff, *Struggle for Black Equality*, pp. 180–182.

11. Hubert Humphrey to Eugenie Anderson, August 22, 1964, box 1, personal and family files, HP; William Connell to Staff, August 22, 1964, box 1, Connell Papers; Goldberg, *Barry Goldwater*, pp. 196–208. On Democratic fears of Goldwater, see *Washington Post*, August 23, 1964, p. 21; Brennan, *Turning Right*, pp. 50–59, 90–95. Humphrey was not alone in worrying that Goldwater would be a tough opponent for Johnson in 1964, as many of Johnson's advisers feared that the Arizona senator had a chance to stage an upset. Similarly, the Kennedy administration had been keeping close tabs on arch-conservative organizations such as the John Birch Society in the early 1960s.

12. Transcript, *Meet the Press*, August 23, 1964, pp. 12–14; Rauh interview, Romaine Files; Mills, *Like a Holy Crusade*, pp. 150–151; Rauh OH III, LBJL; Gillon, *The Democrats' Dilemma*, pp. 71–73; *Washington Post*, August 22, 1964, pp. 1, 4.

13. Rauh interview, Romaine Files; *Washington Post*, August 25, 1964, pp. 1, 10; *New York Times*, August 24, 1964, p. 17; interview of Ed King, Romaine Files; interview of Fannie Lou Hamer, Romaine Files; *Minneapolis Tribune*, August 25, 1964, p. 2.

14. Freedom Summer Reviewed: The Mississippi Freedom Democratic Party and the Atlantic City Convention, November 1, 1979, box 1, Mississippi Freedom Summer Reviewed: A Fifteen Year Perspective on Progress in Race Relations, 1964–1979, State Historical Society, Madison, Wis.; Rauh interview, Romaine Files; *Washington Post*, August 25, 1964, pp. 1, 10.

15. Gillon, *The Democrats' Dilemma*, p. 73; *Washington Post*, August 26, 1964, pp. 1, 6, 10; *New York Times*, August 26, 1964, pp. 1, 28; *Washington Post*, September 5, 1964, p. 9; Boyle, *UAW and the Heyday of American Liberalism*, p. 195.

16. Bayard Rustin OH, LBJL; *Washington Post*, September 5, 1964, p. 9; Anderson, *Bayard Rustin*, p. 278. Roy Wilkins and James Farmer also supported the administration compromise.

17. Rauh interview, Romaine Files; interview of Ella Baker by Anne Romaine, Romaine Files.

18. Aaron Henry OH, LBJL; King interview, Romaine Files; Freedom Summer Reviewed, box 1, Mississippi Freedom Summer Reviewed Papers.

19. Interview of King, Romaine Files; Dittmer, *Local People*, pp. 295–297; Freedom Summer Reviewed, box 1, Mississippi's Freedom Summer Reviewed Papers. Intense pressure from the Johnson administration was critical in eroding MFDP support in the Credentials Committee. The administration let members of the committee know that they would pay a high price for backing the MFDP. One woman was told that her husband would not receive a judgeship. Another member learned that there would be no poverty program in his district. A businessman was informed that his firm would lose a government contract. It is doubtful that the MFDP delegates would have accepted any slight modification of the two at-large seats, such as the four-half-seat idea. Leaders may have found the proposal somewhat appealing, but most of the delegates were not impressed. Dittmer, *New York Times*, August 26, 1964, p. 28; Mills, *Like a Holy Crusade*, p. 160.

21. Forman, *The Making of Black Revolutionaries*, pp. 392–395; Carson, *In Struggle*, p. 128; Dittmer, *Local People*, pp. 300–302; interview of Hamer, Romaine Files; Freedom Summer Reviewed, box 1, Mississippi's Freedom Summer Reviewed Papers.

22. Norman Sherman interview with author, June 2, 1997.

23. Solberg, *Hubert H. Humphrey*, pp. 246–256; Evans and Novak, *Lyndon Baines Johnson and the Exercise of Power*, p. 459; White, *The Making of the President, 1964*, p. 286; Eisele, *Almost to the Presidency*, p. 215; Goodwin, *Remembering America*, p. 300; *New York Times*, August 25, 1964, p. 23. Exactly when Johnson made up his mind and when Humphrey learned he was the choice is unclear. Goodwin, an administration speechwriter, is "almost certain" that Johnson had decided upon Humphrey well before the convention but ensured that Humphrey would be the last to know to add drama to the process and make Humphrey all the more grateful. Circumstantial evidence raises the possibility that Humphrey knew he was the nominee before the MFDP affair was resolved. On Monday, August 24, phone lines that could accommodate up to eighteen new phones were installed in Humphrey's summer home in Minnesota. The phone company told inquisitive reporters that it was doing this "just in case" Humphrey were selected.

24. New York Times, August 27, 1964, pp. 1, 22–23; *Minneapolis Tribune*, August 27, 1964, pp. 1, 2; *Washington Post*, August 26, 1964, p. 8; Humphrey, *Los Angeles Times*, August 27, 1964, p. 1; *New York Times*, August 28, 1964, p. 15; *New York Times*, August 27, 1964, p. 21; *Atlanta Constitution*, August 28, 1964, pp. 1, 15; *Minneapolis Tribune*, August 28, 1964, pp. 1, 9; *New York Times*, August 28, 1964, p. 13. According to the *Charleston News and Courier*, the choice of Humphrey was "the crowing insult to southern Democrats," who "now see the party of their fathers in the hands of their worst enemies." *Charleston News and Courier*, August 28, 1964, p. 8.

26. *Minneapolis Tribune*, August 28, 1964, p. 3; Goldberg, *Barry Goldwater*, pp. 186–193. There was little, if any, scuffling over the civil rights plank in 1964. The Democrats affirmed the Civil Rights Act as "the greatest civil rights measure in the history of the American people." The party was against racial discrimination, but it was

also "equally firm in opposing any policy of quotas or 'discrimination in reverse.'" *New York Times*, August 23, 1964, pp, 1, 81.

27. Faber, *Road to the White House*, pp. 156–157; *U.S. News and World Report*, September 7, 1964, p. 30.

28. Hubert Humphrey to Virginia Kelly, August 31, 1964, box 726, SF, HP; Solberg, *Hubert H. Humphrey*, pp. 258–259; *Washington Post*, September 1, 1964, p. 2; *Los Angeles Times*, September 18, 1964, p. 21; *New York Times*, September 19, 1964, p. 14; *Time*, September 25, 1964, p. 22; *Arkansas Gazette*, September 19, 1964, pp. 1, 2; Transcript, Press Conference, September 18, 1964, box 14, SPF, HP; *Washington Post*, September 19, 1964, p. 4; *Washington Post*, September 23, 1964, p. 21; *Minneapolis Tribune*, September 18, 1964, p. 3; *Houston Post*, September 18, 1964, pp, 1, 10; *Minneapolis Tribune*, September 21, 1964, p. 10.

30. *Memphis Commercial Appeal*, September 27, 1964, p. 1; *New York Times*, September 27, 1964, p. 65; *New York Times*, September 28, 1964, p. 12; *Minneapolis Tribune*, September 27, 1964, p. 13; *New York Times*, September 30, 1964, p. 23; *Atlanta Constitution*, September 30, 1964, pp. 1, 13; Transcript, Press Conference, September 29, 1964, box 14, SPF, HP; Transcript, Speech by Humphrey, September 29, 1964, box 14, SPF, HP; *Minneapolis Tribune*, September 30, 1964, p. 16; *Time*, October 9, 1964, p. 25; *New York Times*, October 9, 1964, p. 25. The pamphlet was prepared for use in Washington, D.C., but Republican officials ordered a quick halt to its distribution in light of Humphrey's charges.

31. *New York Times*, September 19, 1964, p. 14; Fite, *Richard B. Russell, Jr.*, pp. 420–421; *Minneapolis Tribune*, April 13, 1968, p. 1; *Raleigh News and Observer*, March 1, 1967, p. 1; Ed McCormack to Hubert Humphrey, October 15, 1964, box 1046, VP Files, HP.

32. Cohodas, *Strom Thurmond and the Politics of Southern Change*, p. 361; Charles Roche to Cliff Carter, September 24, 1964, PL/ST 10, box 42, WHCF, LBJL; Ralph McGill to Lyndon Johnson, September 30, 1964, PL 2, box 84, WHCF, LBJL. Small-town whites, McGill reported, were in an "ugly mood." The Atlanta editor discussed this with Humphrey during his visit to Georgia and reported the problem to the president. Unions, Humphrey noted, were developing plans to counter the Republican misinformation campaign, but there were so few in the South that their impact would be minimal.

33. Luther Hodges to Lyndon Johnson, August 10, 1964, Buford Ellington to Lyndon Johnson, August 10, 1964, both in box 77, confidential files, WHCF, LBJL; *New York Times*, August 24, 1964, p. 17; *Washington Post*, August 30, 1964, p. E1. Hodges recommended that Johnson make a statement, perhaps in his acceptance speech at Atlantic City, that there would be no "redistribution" of jobs. Johnson made no such remark at the convention. *New York Times*, August 28, 1964, p. 12; *Commentary*, August, 1964, pp. 28–32.

34. *Washington Post*, September 8, 1964, p. 8; *New York Times*, September 8, 1964, p. 17. The White House worried greatly about the effects of misinformation regarding the Civil Rights Act. Johnson called for an aggressive campaign to set the record straight. In late September Senate Democrats took to the floor to clarify the issue. The administration also prepared a pamphlet for distribution to union members

telling exactly what the Civil Rights Act did and did not do. Lee White to Lyndon Johnson, September 28, 1964, Ex HU 2, box 3, WHCF, LBJL.

35. Faber, *Road to the White House*, pp. 162–180; *Minneapolis Tribune*, September 11, 1964, p. 22; *New York Times*, April 2, 1964, p. 20; Goldberg, *Barry Goldwater*, pp. 218–225. A *Chicago Sun-Times* poll of steel workers in July had showed them favoring Johnson 53–47 percent, a remarkably narrow margin. White, *The Making of the President, 1964*, p. 235.

36. *Chicago Defender*, September 5, 1964, p. 6; *New York Times*, September 12, 1964, p. 10; *Washington Post*, September 13, 1964, p. 4; *Denver Post*, September 13, 1964, pp. 1, 3; *Washington Post*, September 14, 1964, p. 4; *New York Times*, September 12, 1964, p. 10; *New York Times*, September 14, 1964, p. 27; *Washington Post*, September 24, 1964, p. 2; Transcript, *Meet the Press,* September 20, 1964, pp. 6–10. In Evansville, Indiana reporters asked Humphrey if he thought Goldwater was turning race against race. Humphrey replied, "I feel that some of the remarks of Senator Goldwater, such as 'civil rights breeds violence and hatred and bitterness, and are an invitation to disorder, to lawlessness,' that is a most unfortunate statement on the part of a presidential candidate, and he ought not to say it. Furthermore, I feel that his flirtation with the Birchites is the kind of activity which can only lead to doubts as to the desire for national unity on his part." UAW Washington Report, September 28, 1964, box 7, Sifton Papers.

37. *New York Times*, September 15, 1964, p. 1; *Meet the Press,* September 20, 1964, p. 10; Goldberg, *Barry Goldwater*, p. 230.

38. *Minneapolis Tribune*, September 26, 1964, p. 3; *New York Times*, September 26, 1964, p. 12.

39. White, *The Making of the President, 1964*, p. 300; Gallup, *The Gallup Poll*, pp. 1,902–1,904. A September 18 poll found Goldwater ahead of Johnson in the South 47–46 percent.

40. Faber, *Road to the White House*, pp. 230–231; *New York Times*, October 27, 1964, p. 1; *Minneapolis Tribune*, November 1, 1964, pp. 1, 8; *New York Times*, October 3, 1964, p. 14; Goldberg, *Barry Goldwater*, p. 230. Race receded as a campaign issue as the electorate focused more attention on international affairs. In a July poll 47 percent of the public declared racial issues as the number one concern facing the nation, but in mid-October only 35 percent did.

41. *Philadelphia Inquirer*, October 10, 1964, pp. 1, 7; *New York Times*, October 21, 1964, p. 31; *New York Times*, October 29, 1964, p. 22; *Washington Post*, October 29, 1964, p. 24. The only potential roadblock to victory, the Humphrey campaign staff believed, was a domestic or international crisis. When CORE leader James Farmer announced in late October that he might bring an out-of-town group to mostly white Prince George's County, Virginia to tear down a fence that prevented African Americans from entering a shopping center, the Humphrey campaign made plans to contact Joe Rauh to try to get him to head off Farmer. It is unknown whether they were in touch with Rauh. Notes of Humphrey staff meeting, October 21, 1964, box 604, SF, HP.

42. *Minneapolis Tribune*, November 4, 1964, p. 3; Goldberg, *Barry Goldwater*, pp. 232–235.

43. Scammon, *America Votes, 1964*, pp. 124–318; *Congressional Quarterly*, November 13, 1964, p. 2,675; White, *The Making of the President, 1964*, p. 383.

44. Black and Black, *The Vital South*, pp. 202–209; White, *The Making of the President, 1964*, p. 383; Stern, *Calculating Visions*, pp. 210–211. Alabama elected five Republicans to the House of Representatives, while Georgia and Mississippi sent their first Republicans to the House in the twentieth century.

45. *New York Times*, October 27, 1964, p. 31; White, *The Making of the President, 1964*, p. 305; Solberg, *Hubert H. Humphrey*, p. 263; Notes of Humphrey staff meeting, October 21, 1964, box 604, SF, HP.

7. Civil Rights Enforcement and the Assaults on Liberalism

1. *Washington Post*, January 21, 1965, pp. 1–3, 7.

2. Humphrey, *War on Poverty*, p. 105; U.S. Department of Commerce, *Historical Statistics of the United States*, pp. 56, 135, 303, 380–382; Humphrey, *War on Poverty*, pp. 19–30, 53–63, 96, 160–168; Katz, *The Undeserving Poor*, pp. 16–23. It is difficult to identify exact rates for African Americans, since the federal government counted all minorities as "nonwhite." However, African Americans did make up the overwhelming majority of nonwhites during the period under examination here. The unemployment rate only revealed part of the picture, for it failed to account for the many more nonwhites than whites who were only employed part-time or were not even in the labor force. Nonwhites, moreover, were dropping out of the labor force at a faster rate than whites. This problem was especially acute among teenagers. In 1950 56 percent of nonwhite teenage males were in the labor force, but in 1964 only 37.7 percent were. This compared to 50.3 percent and 41 percent for white teens, respectively. Ross, "The Negro in the American Economy," pp. 24–25. Twenty-two million jobs would be eliminated between 1960 and 1970, largely because of automation, Humphrey pointed out, at the same time that maturing baby boomers would be entering the labor market. He rejected conservative economist Milton Friedman's call for a "negative income tax" that would guarantee everyone a minimum income. Though such a proposal would comprise only 2 percent of the federal budget, Humphrey believed firmly that the answer was to create meaningful jobs for all, even if job training, education, and other programs cost more than Friedman's proposal.

3. Solberg, *Hubert H. Humphrey*, pp. 264–265; Graham, *Civil Rights Era*, pp. 27–73; Harry McPherson OH V, LBJL; Eisele, *Almost to the Presidency*, pp. 224–226.

4. Nicholas Katzenbach to Hubert Humphrey, November 23, 1964, box 34, Burke Marshall Papers, JFKL; Graham, *Civil Rights Era*, pp. 160–161; Clarence Mitchell to Roy Wilkins, November 17, 1964, series III, box A332, NAACP Papers; *New York Times*, December 11, 1964, pp. 1, 31; Lee White to Clarence Mitchell, December 14, 1964, box 349, Ex FG 440, WHCF, LBJL; Lyndon Johnson to Hubert Humphrey, December 2, 1964, box 346, Ex FG 440, WHCF, LBJL. Humphrey found Katzenbach's idea so exciting that he persuaded Clarence Mitchell of the NAACP to write Johnson on his behalf. Mitchell was all too happy to oblige, for he also worried about duplication and feared that the president might accept the Chamber of Commerce's recommendation to place Secretary of Commerce Luther Hodges, the former North Carolina governor and a man of moderate racial views, in charge of enforcing the

1964 Civil Rights Act. Having Humphrey take an active role in civil rights, Mitchell noted to his boss Roy Wilkins, would "permit a good working relationship" between the NAACP and the administration. Clarence Mitchell to Roy Wilkins, December 11, 1964, series III, box A332, NAACP Papers.

5. *New York Times*, December 23, 1964, p. 19; Meeting, December 15, 1964, box 821, SF, HP; Clarence Mitchell to John Stewart, December 17, 1964, box 9, Department of Legislation Files, AFL-CIO Papers; Carl Auerbach, The Organization of the Federal Civil Rights Effort, n.d., box 824, VPF, HP.

6. Hubert Humphrey to Lyndon Johnson, January 4, 1965, box 821, SF, HP; John Stewart to Bill Moyers, n.d., John Stewart to Hubert Humphrey, January 9, 1965, box 1405, VPF, HP, John Stewart to Hubert Humphrey, November 28, 1964, all in box 1405, VPF, HP; Meeting, December 15, 1964, box 821, SF, HP; A Short History of the President's Council on Equal Opportunity, box 824, VPF, HP;, box 1405, VPF, HP; Bill Moyers to Lyndon Johnson, February 3, 1965, box 4, White House Aides Files—Lee White, LBJL; *New York Times*, February 7, 1965, p. 1; Ted Van Dyk interview with author, January 13, 1997; Lyndon Johnson to Hubert Humphrey, February 5, 1965, box 3, Ex HU 2, WHCF, LBJL. Katzenbach urged Johnson to accept the vice president's plan, but some administration officials recommended assigning coordinating responsibility only to Humphrey through a personal letter. The president initially favored this more loosely based approach, but he soon was persuaded to accept Humphrey's plan. Johnson hoped that Humphrey's good standing among liberals would shield the administration from criticism in this area. Johnson also wanted to eliminate the PCEEO, which had been a source of misery for him as vice president, and the President's Committee on Equal Opportunity in Housing. He thought that establishing a formal body like the PCEO would provide necessary political cover for abolishing these agencies and offer Humphrey greater clout with recalcitrant agency heads regarding future civil rights issues.

7. Organizational Meeting, PCEO, March 3, 1965, Lawson Knott to Hubert Humphrey, March 5, 1965, both in box 824, VPF, HP; Proposed Budget and Staff Personnel, March 2, 1965, box 1406, VPF, HP; Minutes of Organizational Meeting, PCEO, March 3, 1965, box 74, Ramsey Clark Papers, LBJL; Hubert Humphrey to Lyndon Johnson, March 4, 1965, box 31, White House Aides Files—Marvin Watson, LBJL; Hubert Humphrey to Anthony Celebreeze, March 8, 1965, box 1394, VPF, HP.

8. *Washington Post*, January 29, 1965, p. 18; Arnold Aronson to Cooperating Organizations, February 2, 1965, box 1, Leadership Conference on Civil Rights Papers, State Historical Society of Wisconsin, Madison, Wis.; Hubert Humphrey to Lyndon Johnson, March 11, 1965, box 132, Unprocessed Papers (UP), HP; U.S. Commission on Civil Rights, *Survey of School Desegregation in the Southern and Border States*, pp. 19–30; U.S. Commission on Civil Rights, *Title VI*, p. 1; Orfield, *The Reconstruction of Southern Education*, pp. ix, 40–84; Wilkinson, *From Brown to Bakke*, pp. 102–104. "The object of Title VI is to eliminate discrimination, not to shut down government programs and withhold funds," Humphrey had told an audience of city and county officials in January. When districts in Georgia and South Carolina submitted desegregation plans that largely preserved the status quo, Humphrey advised the president to "seek areas of agreement whereby a direct confrontation . . . is avoided." Good work-

ing relationships with the relatively moderate governors in those states were "essential," he argued. The South Carolina proposal centered on a freedom of choice plan in which all districts would permit African Americans to choose to go to white schools if they wanted. However, HEW officials found it sorely lacking since it failed to include specific provisions to make clear to African Americans this right. Several Georgia districts attempted delay integration by submitting the wrong form. Instead of completing the form for districts that had not integrated, they presented forms intended for districts that had begun the process.

9. David Filvaroff to Hubert Humphrey, April 22, 1965, box 1387, VPF, HP; Wiley Branton to Hubert Humphrey, June 4, 1965, box 1389, VPF, HP; Hubert Humphrey to Lyndon Johnson, July 16, 1965, box 346, Ex FG 440, WHCF, LBJL; Hubert Humphrey to Lyndon Johnson, August 6, 1965, box 53, White House Aides Files—Douglas Cater, LBJL; A Short History of the President's Council on Equal Employment Opportunity, box 824, VPF, HP. The issue of integrated faculty was particularly troublesome. During Senate debate in 1964, Humphrey unequivocally asserted that such a policy was required under Title VI. Many HEW officials, however, thought that it violated Dirksen's amendment prohibiting regulation of employment practices. Orfield, *Reconstruction of Southern Education*, pp. 63–69.

10. Matusow, *The Unraveling of America*, pp. 189–190; Orfield, *Reconstruction of Southern Education*, pp. 63–72, 92–101. Here, Humphrey bore an indirect responsibility. In drafting the guidelines, HEW officials had followed the narrow interpretation of Title VI he had offered during the Senate debate over the 1964 Civil Rights Act as opposed to a broader reading by other liberals who favored forcing southern districts to end segregation within a few months. Title VI, Humphrey had explained, required desegregation, not complete and immediate integration. He had also stressed that a district following a court desegregation order would be complying with Title VI.

11. Peter Libassi to John Stewart, April 27, 1965, Summary of Agency Reports, April 27, 1965; Review of Enforcement of Federal Civil Rights Policies in Alabama, April 27, 1965; David Filvaroff to Hubert Humphrey; Wiley Branton to Hubert Humphrey, September 20, 1965; all in box 1387, VPF, HP; Hubert Humphrey to Lyndon Johnson, May 25, 1965, box 31, White House Aides Files—Marvin Watson, LBJL; Hubert Humphrey to Lyndon Johnson, August 12, 1965, box 6, White House Aides Files—Lee White, LBJL.

12. Minutes of Meeting, PCEO, May 19, 1965; Carl Auerbach, The Organization of the Federal Civil Rights Effort, n.d.; A Short History of the President's Council on Equal Opportunity, n.d.; all in box 824, VPF, HP; David Filvaroff to Hubert Humphrey, n.d.; Wiley Branton to Hubert Humphrey, July 16, 1965; both in box 1387, VPF, HP; Wiley Branton to Hubert Humphrey, June 18, 1965; Wiley Branton to Hubert Humphrey, June 25, 1965; both in box 1389, VPF, HP; Hubert Humphrey to Lyndon Johnson, July 16, 1965, box 346, FG 440, WHCF, LBJL.

13. John Stewart to Hubert Humphrey, February 3, 1965, John Stewart to Hubert Humphrey, February 18, 1965, both in box 1, Connell Papers; Hobart Taylor to Hubert Humphrey, December 2, 1964, Memo on Meeting of PCEEO, February 24, 1965, Ward McCreedy to Hobart Taylor, February 28, 1965, Hobart Taylor to Hubert

Humphrey, April 5, 1965, John Stewart to Hubert Humphrey, July 7, 1965, all in box 824, VPF, HP; F. Peter Libassi to John Stewart, February 15, 1965, Hobart Taylor to Hubert Humphrey, April 29, 1965, both in box 828, VPF, HP; Memo, February 17, 1965, box 821, VPF, HP; Hubert Humphrey to Lyndon Johnson, May 15, 1964, Hubert Humphrey to Lyndon Johnson, June 21, 1965, John Stewart to Lee White, August 23, 1965, all in box 4, White House Aides Files—Lee White, LBJL; Hubert Humphrey to Lyndon Johnson, May 26, 1965, box 31, White House Aides Files—Marvin Watson, LBJL; Wiley Branton to Hubert Humphrey, July 2, 1965, box 1389, VPF, HP; Hubert Humphrey to Lyndon Johnson, August 11, 1965, box 1387, VPF, HP. The PCEEO poor relations with government agencies, and, more important,. It could not identify contractors under its jurisdiction, lacked sufficient staff to review adequately even those which had been identified, exempted certain large contractors with substantial government business, failed to check employment policies prior to the awarding of contracts, and had made almost no headway in breaking down employment barriers in skilled craft unions. Staff Evaluation, Contract Compliance Program, May 28, 1965, box 824, VPF, HP.

14. A Short History of the President's Council on Equal Opportunity, Lawson Knott to Hubert Humphrey, March 5, 1965, both in box 824, VPF, HP; David Filvaroff to Hubert Humphrey, March 23, 1965, box 828, VPF, HP; David Filvaroff to Hubert Humphrey, May 7, 1965, David Filvaroff to Hubert Humphrey, May 21, 1965, PCEO Bulletin, June 11, 1965, all in box 1387, VPF, HP; Hubert Humphrey to Lyndon Johnson, May 15, 1965, box 4, White House Aides Files—Lee White, LBJL; Hubert Humphrey to Lyndon Johnson, September 16, 1965, box 828, VPF, HP; Graham, *Civil Rights Era*, pp. 28–42.

15. *New York Times*, March 26, 1965, p. 23; Minutes of Meeting with Mayor Ralph Locher (Cleveland), April 19, 1965, Minutes of Meeting with Mayor Robert Wagner (New York), April 23, 1965, Minutes of Meeting with Mayor John Collins (Boston), April 30, 1965, Minutes of Meeting with Martin Katz (Gary), May 3, 1965, Minutes of Meeting with Mayor Hugh Addonizio (Newark), May 4, 1965, Minutes of Meeting with Mayor John Houlihan (Oakland), May 4, 1965, Minutes of Meeting with Mayor Frank Lamb (Rochester), May 5, 1965, all in box 405, Ex FG 744, WHCF, LBJL; LeRoy Collins to Hubert Humphrey, September 3, 1965, box 1407, VPF, HP; Hubert Humphrey to Lyndon Johnson, June 10, 1965, box 3, Ex HU 2, WHCF, LBJL; The task force offered to meet with police officials and asked Washington attorney Berl Bernhard, former staff director of the Civil Rights Commission, to develop a police-community relations program for the target cities. In June, it held a conference for representatives of thirty-nine private organizations to explain its work and urge their involvement at the local level.

16. Humphrey, *The Cause is Mankind*, pp. 86–88; PCEO Employment Task Force Agenda, Recent Employment and Unemployment Trends, n.d., box 824, VPF, HP. Humphrey's concern over youth unemployment echoed that of many social scientists who warned in the late 1950s that juvenile delinquency would become a pressing social concern. See Patterson, *America's War Against Poverty*, pp. 100–101; *Congressional Record*, 85th Cong., 1st sess., pp. 989–998; *Congressional Record*, 86th Cong., 1st sess., p. 19,242 Humphrey had sponsored bills every year since 1958 to establish a

Youth Conservation Corps for troubled kids. Warning that the lack of jobs for young people was "social dynamite," Humphrey observed in 1963, "Until we solve that problem . . . we shall continue to have a social malignancy that will spread throughout our social and economic structure." *Congressional Record*, 88th Cong., 1st sess., p. 16, 345.

17. Hubert Humphrey to Lyndon Johnson, April 23, 1965, box 346, FG 440, WHCF, LBJL; Hubert Humphrey to John Stewart, February 25, 1965, box 1, Connell Papers; Hubert Humphrey to Lyndon Johnson, May 10, 1965, box 824, VPF, HP; Statement by the President to the Cabinet, May 13, 1965, box 3, Cabinet Papers, LBJL; Bill Moyers to Lyndon Johnson, May 20, 1965, box 346, Ex FG 440, WHCF, LBJL; Press Release, May 21, 1965, box 1201, VPF, HP.

18. Gelfand, "The War on Poverty," pp. 142–143; Ted Van Dyk interview with author, January 13, 1997.

19. Hubert Humphrey to Lyndon Johnson, May 25, 1965, box 825, VPF, HP; Appearance of Hubert H. Humphrey Before a Joint Meeting of the Interagency Advisory Group, May 25, 1965, box 827, VPF, HP; Transcript, Mayor's Conference, May 5, 1965, box 796, VP Files, HP; Hubert Humphrey to Lyndon Johnson, June 10, 1965, box 132, UP, HP; Hubert Humphrey to Henry Ford II, May 26, 1965, box 1201, VPF, HP; Ted Van Dyk interview with author, January 13, 1997; Hubert Humphrey to Lyndon Johnson, June 21, 1965; Hubert Humphrey to Lyndon Johnson, June 28, 1965; both in box 135, White House Aides Files—Bill Moyers, LBJL; Civil Rights Bulletin, June 23, 1965, box 1387, VPF, HP; Hubert Humphrey to Lyndon Johnson, June 30, 1965, box 346, FG 440, WHCF, LBJL.

20. Clarence Mitchell to Roy Wilkins, July 22, 1965, box 7, Wilkins Papers; *New York Times*, August 7, 1965, pp. 1, 8; Lawson, *In Pursuit of Power*, pp. 9–17; *Chicago Sun-Times*, August 7, 1965, p. 1; Garrow, *Protest at Selma*, p. 179.

21. Sitkoff, *Struggle for Black Equality*, pp. 200–202; Edsall and Edsall, *Chain Reaction*, pp. 48–50. Other incidents of urban unrest followed on the heels of Watts. On the second day of the Watts riot violence broke out in Chicago after a fire truck struck and killed an African American woman. Here, too, the National Guard had to be deployed. Yet another riot erupted on August 14 in Springfield, Massachusetts following the arrest of eighteen African Americans outside a nightclub.

22. *Washington Post*, August 17, 1965, p. 7; *Washington Post*, August 20, 1965, p. 1; *New York Times*, August 20, 1965, p. 33; Report of the White House Conference on Equal Employment Opportunity, box 8, Ex HU 2, WHCF, LBJL; Remarks of Hubert H. Humphrey, August 19, 1965, box 1, Offield Dukes Papers, Walter Reuther Library, Wayne State University, Detroit, Mi. Ironically, several days before Watts Humphrey spoke to the National Urban League and warned that "generations of prejudice, deprivation, disease, and subservience have sown among many Negroes the seeds of profound despair, apathy, indifference and distrust." *New York Times*, August 4, 1965.

23. Harry McPherson OH IV, LBJL; Hubert Humphrey to Lyndon Johnson, August 17, 1965, box 5, White House Aides Files—Lee White, LBJL; Rainwater and Yancey, *The Moynihan Report*, pp. 1–4, 33–36; Lee White to Lyndon Johnson, September 28, 1965, box 5, White House Aides Files—Lee White, LBJL; Katz, *The Un-*

deserving Poor, pp. 44–46; Carson, *In Struggle*, pp. 191–198; Lawson, *In Pursuit of Power*, p. 44; Hubert Humphrey to Daniel Patrick Moynihan, December 10, 1965, box 822, VPF, HP.

24. LeRoy Collins to Hubert Humphrey, September 3, 1965; Interim Report, Task Force on Summer Urban Problems, September 3, 1965; both in box 1407, VPF, HP; Hubert Humphrey to Lyndon Johnson, September 16, 1965, box 828, VPF, HP. Humphrey's interpretation reflected the handful of rulings by federal courts, which had given little specific guidance on the matter. *Congressional Record*, 88th Cong., 2d sess., p. 22, 337. At the time of Humphrey's memo to Johnson, HEW was in an imbroglio over de facto segregation in Chicago. Civil rights groups had filed a complaint in July alleging that the city promoted segregation and was thus in violation of Title VI. Keppel and government lawyers spent two months studying the problem, but it was clear that the administration had not thought through the issue. Keppel decided later that month to defer federal funds to the city, but an angry Johnson quickly reversed the administration's course after consulting with Mayor Richard Daley. Orfield, *Reconstruction of Southern Education*, pp. 151–207.

25. David Filvaroff to Hubert Humphrey, August 30, 1965; Wiley Branton to Hubert Humphrey, August 13, 1965, box 1387, VPF, HP; Hubert Humphrey to Marvin Watson, August 26, 1965, box 4, White House Aides Files—Lee White, LBJL; Wiley Branton to Hubert Humphrey, August 20, 1965, box 1389, VPF, HP; Solberg, *Hubert H. Humphrey*, pp. 276–277. Regarding Watts, the White House named a special task force to coordinate federal efforts in the area. The PCEO had scheduled a meeting to discuss the situation, but the White House canceled it. Likewise, PCEO staff member Wiley Branton was in Los Angeles at the time the new task force was announced. In late August the White House instructed Secretary John Gardner to notify non-complying school districts that they were facing a fund cut-off, but the PCEO, working with Commissioner of Education Francis Keppel, had sent a similar letter a few days earlier. The White House released a report in July discussing compliance with the 1964 Civil Rights Act, but the PCEO had been working on one too. The PCEO, moreover, was uncertain whether it or the White House staff had final responsibility for planning the White House Conference on Civil Rights.

26. Califano, *The Triumph and Tragedy of Lyndon Johnson*, pp. 65–66; Harry McPherson to Joe Califano, August 20, 1965, box 3, Ex HU 2, WHCF, LBJL; Ted Van Dyk interview with author, January 13, 1997; John Stewart interview with author, March 28, 1997; Nicholas Katzenbach to Lyndon Johnson, September 20 1965, box 403, Ex FG 731, WHCF, LBJL; Lee White to Lyndon Johnson, September 20, 1965, box 4, White House Aides Files—Lee White, LBJL. Johnson had been having misgivings about the PCEO ever since he created it. In May he scrawled across the bottom of a memo announcing the appointment of PCEO staff member Wiley Branton, "Don't want to be permanent—last about three months." George Reedy to Lyndon Johnson, May 3, 1965, box 346, FG 440, WHCF, LBJL. A month later he wrote to White on the bottom of a memo from Humphrey, "When does the limit on the Council on Equal Opportunity that we created run out?" Hubert Humphrey to Lyndon Johnson, June 21, 1965, box 4, White House Aides Files—Lee White, LBJL.

27. *New Leader*, October 11, 1965, pp. 3–5; Wolk, *The Presidency and Black Civil Rights*, p. 76; David Filvaroff to Hubert Humphrey, September 21, 1965, box 1389, VPF, HP; Marvin Watson to Lyndon Johnson, September 20, 1965, box 3, Ex HU 2, WHCF, LBJL; Carson, *In Struggle*, pp. 122–123, 159–161.

28. Califano, *Triumph and Tragedy*, pp. 66–67. Humphrey did not know of the president's plans, but he may have suspected that the PCEO was in some trouble with the administration. His memo to Johnson on September 16, which outlined economic and educational problems facing African Americans, reads very much like an argument that the PCEO still had a full agenda. Furthermore, on the day Johnson met with Humphrey a PCEO staff member was drafting a memo to Humphrey listing the group's accomplishments. Humphrey's customary practice throughout the year had been to pass along to the president news he received from staff members, so it is quite likely that this would have gone to Johnson too. David Filvaroff to Hubert Humphrey, September 22, 1965, box 1387, VPF, HP.

29. Joe Califano and Lee White to Lyndon Johnson, September 24, 1965, box 3, Ex HU 2, WHCF, LBJL; Califano, *Triumph and Tragedy*, p. 69; LeRoy Collins OH, LBJL; Press Release, September 24, 1965, box 5, White House Aides Files, William Sparks, LBJL; Transcript of News Conference, September 24, 1965, box 3, Ex HU 2, WHCF, LBJL; Lyndon Johnson to Hubert Humphrey, September 24, 1965, box 4, White House Aides Files—Marvin Watson, LBJL; John Stewart interview with author, March 28, 1997.

30. *New York Times*, October 17, 1965, pp. 1, 78; *New York Amsterdam News*, November 6, 1965, p. 16; *New Leader*, October 11, 1965, p. 6; John Stewart interview with author, March 28, 1997; Ted Van Dyk interview with author, January 13, 1997; Notes of Meeting of Hubert H. Humphrey, William Connell, Joseph L. Rauh, Jr., and Leon Shull, November 9, 1965; Hubert Humphrey to James Wechsler, October 20, 1965; both in box 36, Rauh Papers; Hubert Humphrey to Walter Reuther, September 28, 1965; Walter Reuther to Hubert Humphrey, October 11, 1965; both in box 370, Walter Reuther Papers, Walter Reuther Library, Detroit, Mi.

31. Wolk, *The Presidency and Black Civil Rights*, pp. 190–211.

32. Final Report to the President on the Youth Opportunity Campaign (Summer 1965), n.d., box 132, UP, HP; Employment Statistics of 16–21 Year-Old Youths, June-July-August Averages, 1964–1967, box 1205, VPF, HP; *Congressional Record*, 89th Cong., 1st sess., p. 19, 985; Wiley Branton to Hubert Humphrey, June 25, 1965, box 1389, VPF, HP; Congressional Republicans took great delight in pointing out that Humphrey's nephew had received a summer job with the U.S. Post Office.

33. Address by Hubert Humphrey, November 16, 1965, box 67, White House Conference on Civil Rights Papers, LBJL; Rainwater and Yancey, *The Moynihan Report*, pp. 246–254; *St. Louis Post-Dispatch*, November 19, 1965, pp. 1, 7; Lawson, *Pursuit of Power*, pp. 25–29; Carson, *In Struggle*, pp. 137–144; *Chicago Defender*, November 20, 1965, p. 1; Confidential Notes on the Planning Session for the White House Conference, November 23, 1965, box 5, White House Aides Files—Lee White, LBJL; Edsall and Edsall, *Chain Reaction*, p. 59; Hubert Humphrey to Joseph Califano, January 22, 1966, box 4, Ex HU 2, WHCF, LBJL; Hubert Humphrey to Lyndon Johnson, January 24, 1966, box 21, White House Aides Files—Harry McPherson; Memo, January

22, 1966, box 1029, VPF, HP; Hubert Humphrey to Lyndon Johnson, February 2, 1966, box 3, Ex HU 2, WHCF, LBJL; Douglass Cater to Lyndon Johnson, June 18, 1966, box 4, Ex HU 2, WHCF, LBJL.

34. Lyndon Johnson to Hubert Humphrey, March 2, 1966; Hubert Humphrey to Lyndon Johnson, March 31, 1966; both in box 835, VPF, HP; Roger Wilkins to John Stewart, March 15, 1966, box 21, White House Aides Files—Harry McPherson, LBJL; Report of the Task Force on Summer Domestic Programs, box 18, White House Aides Files—Harry McPherson, LBJL; Harry McPherson to Lyndon Johnson, April 4, 1966, box 51, White House Aides Files—Harry McPherson, LBJL.

35. John Stewart to Ted Van Dyk, May 12, 1966, box 835, VPF, HP; Chronology of 1966 Youth Opportunity Campaign, box 1207, VPF, HP; John Stewart to Jack Moskowitz, September 19, 1966, box 1202, VPF, HP.

36. Meier and Rudwick, *CORE*, pp. 374–415; Carson, *In Struggle*, pp. 204–205; Sitkoff, *Struggle for Black Equality*, pp. 214–215; Radosh, "From Protest to Black Power," pp. 280–281; Burner, *Making Peace with the 60s*, pp. 49–50. Carmichael had even called for African Americans to "stand up and take over" and "move on over" whites if necessary.

37. Norman Sherman interview with author, June 2, 1997; *New York Times*, June 2, 1966, p. 21; *Minneapolis Tribune*, June 1, 1966, p. 18; *Minneapolis Tribune*, June 3, 1966, p. 7; *Minneapolis Tribune*, July 7, 1966, pp. 1, 4; *Minneapolis Tribune*, July 8, 1966, p. 3; *New York Times*, July 7, 1966, pp. 1, 22; Transcript of Remarks by Vice-President Hubert H. Humphrey, July 6, 1966, series II, box 2, Aaron Henry Papers, Walter Reuther Library, Detroit, Mich.; another African American described the speech as "at best, conscious manipulating, and, at worst, stupid." Sellers, *The River of No Return*, p. 171. To help blunt the appeal of Black Power, Humphrey called for the inclusion of African American history into the larger framework of American history. Hubert Humphrey to John Stewart, August 26, 1966, box 1, Dukes Papers. Humphrey's views of Black Power mirrored those of Bayard Rustin. Anderson, *Bayard Rustin*, pp. 283–290.

38. Excerpts from an Address by the Vice President of the United States, July 18, 1966, box 1202, VPF, HP; Joint Senate-House Republican Leadership Press Conference, July 22, 1966, Republican Congressional Leadership Files, Dirksen Papers; *Baltimore Sun*, August 22, 1966, p. 4; Hubert Humphrey to Eiler Ravnholt, August 19, 1966, box 835, VPF, HP; *Report of the National Advisory Commission on Civil Disorders*, p. 38. *Birmingham Post-Herald*, July 20, 1966, p. 10; *Phoenix Gazette*, July 26, 1966, p. 12; Ted Van Dyk interview with author, January 13, 1997. Similarly, a midwestern paper accused Humphrey of "[bending] to political pressure." *Toledo Times*, July 26, 1966, p. 10. An eastern paper was only slightly more generous. It said that his "tongue obviously outran his judgment." *Pittsburgh Press*, July 20, 1966, p. 18.

39. Matusow, *Unraveling of America*, pp. 204–205; Garrow, *Bearing the Cross*, pp. 470–525; *Washington Post*, August 13, 1966, p. 4; *New York Times*, August 27, 1965, p. 16; Sundquist, *Politics and Policy*, p. 499. By September of 1966 52 percent of the public thought that Johnson was pushing integration "too fast," up from 44 percent in July. Similarly, in June 60 percent of whites outside the South said they would object to

sending their children to a school where more than half of the children were African American. Gallup, *The Gallup Poll*, p. 2,010.

40. Hubert Humphrey to Lyndon Johnson, June 9, 1966, box 18, White House Aides Files—Harry McPherson, LBJL; William Cannon to Hubert Humphrey, July 6, 1966, Hubert Humphrey to Lyndon Johnson, July 19, 1966, box 322, White House Aides Files—James Gaither, LBJL; Chronology of 1966 Youth Opportunity Campaign, box 1207, VPF, HP; Memorandum for the Vice President, July 6, 1966, box 836, VPF, HP; White House Aides Files—James Gaither, LBJL; Hubert Humphrey to Robert McNamara, August 31, 1966, box 46, Ex HU 2, WHCF, LBJL; Hubert Humphrey to Lyndon Johnson, September 1, 1966, box 46, Ex HU 2, WHCF, LBJL; Robert Perrin to Sargent Shriver, September 27, 1966, box 347, Ex FG 440, WHCF, LBJL. In March African Americans had battled Mexican-Americans in Los Angeles, while two months later a police officer shot an African American. *Report of the National Advisory Commission on Civil Disorders*, p. 38.

41. Hubert Humphrey to Lyndon Johnson, September 1, 1966, box 348, Ex FG 440, WHCF, LBJL; Press Release, July 5, 1966, box 1399, VPF, HP; John Stewart to Jack Moskowitz, September 19, 1966, box 1202, VPF, HP; Memorandum, n.d., Bill Graham to Joe Califano, November 17, 1966; both in box 322, White House Aides Files—James Gaither, LBJL; Draft of note to attendees of National Council of Negro Women Convention, November 17, 1966, box 1, Dukes Papers; Marion Barry Jr. to Ted Parrish, May 22, 1967, box 1199, VPF, HP.

42. Memo, November 30, 1966, box 84, White House Aides Files—James Gaither, LBJL; Chronology of 1966 Youth Opportunity Campaign, box 1207, VPF, HP; Hubert Humphrey to Lyndon Johnson, December 1966, Press Release, March 21, 1967; Hubert Humphrey to Lyndon Johnson, April 18, 1967; all in box 1202, VPF, HP; *New York Times*, March 6, 1967, p. 22; Bill Graham to Joseph Califano, April 11, 1967; Stan Ross and Jim Gaither to Joe Califano, April 20, 1967; both in box 8, White House Aides Files—Joseph Califano, LBJL. Califano, who blamed Humphrey for the campaign's troubles, had other ideas. Claiming only to be looking for "options" to present to Johnson, Califano opened a December meeting with the Task Force by asking who should head the 1967 undertaking. The group quickly rallied to Humphrey's defense. Humphrey found news that Johnson's chief domestic policy adviser might be looking for ways to remove him from the youth program "rather disturbing." Bill Welsh to Hubert Humphrey, December 6, 1966; Hubert Humphrey to Bill Welsh, January 14, 1967; both in box 1202, VPF, HP.

43. *Congressional Quarterly*, November 11, 1966, p. 2,773; Bill Connell to Hubert Humphrey, March 13, 1967; Hubert Humphrey to Lyndon Johnson, April 17, 1967; both in box 2, Connell Papers; *New York Times*, April 15, 1967, pp. 1, 15; Galphin, *The Riddle of Lester Maddox*, pp. 57–58, 202; Lesher, *George Wallace*, pp. 388–391; William Connell to Herrick Roth, May 24, 1967, box 1067, VPF, HP; Norman Sherman interview with author, June 2, 1997. The GOP had gained forty-seven seats in the House, three in the Senate, and eight governorships. Humphrey had been confidentially informed that several African Americans were about to be appointed to prominent positions in Georgia even though Maddox believed he could not become too

closely tied to this matter. During the same trip Humphrey spoke to at the University of Georgia, where he criticized Martin Luther King's opposition to the Vietnam War. King's stand, Humphrey suggested, would "hurt the civil rights movement." *Atlanta Constitution*, April 15, 1967, p. 1.

44. Julie to Hubert Humphrey, April 29, 1967; Hubert Humphrey to Jack Valenti, May 5, 1967; Hubert Humphrey to W. P. Gullander, May 7, 1967; Hubert Humphrey to John Herbert, May 5, 1967; all in box 1394, VPF, HP; Hubert Humphrey to Mayors, summer 1967, box 21, Ex WE 8, WHCF, LBJL: Press Release, May 24, 1967, box 1198, VPF, HP; *Washington Post*, May 19, 1967, p. 1, 16; Hubert Humphrey to Lyndon Johnson, June 8, 1967, box 21, Ex WE 8, WHCF, LBJL. Humphrey sent information to 900,000 employers, 2,700 state and local officials, hundreds of private organizations, and thousands of media outlets. He also touted the campaign in speeches at the New York Stock Exchange, the conference of the Advertising Council, and the convention of the National League of Cities.

45. John Hein to Hubert Humphrey, June 12, 1967; Fred Minzer to Hubert Humphrey, June 13, 1967; Neal Gregory to Hubert Humphrey, June 14, 1967; Minutes of Meeting of PCOYO, June 27, 1967; all in box 1206, VPF, HP; Donald Towles to Barry Bingham, June 19, 1967; Hubert Humphrey to John Kenny, July 8, 1967; Barry Bingham to Hubert Humphrey, June 21, 1967; Hubert Humphrey to Barry Bingham, June 24, 1967; Hubert Humphrey to Albert Boutwell, June 26, 1967; Hubert Humphrey to John Kenny, July 8, 1967; all in box 1202, VPF, HP; Bruce Terris to Newbold Noyes, June 20, 1967; Programs for the Nation's Underprivileged and Other Youngsters, June 27, 1967; both in box 1198, VPF, HP; *Washington Post*, June 23, 1967, p. B1; *Washington Post*, June 28, 1967, p. B3; *Washington Post*, July 2, 1967, p. 11; Hubert Humphrey to Jess Lanier, June 26, 1967, box 1394, VPF, HP; box 1198, VPF, HP; Hubert Humphrey to Lyndon Johnson, July 7, 1967, box 1199, VPF, HP.

46. Sitkoff, *Struggle for Black Equality*, pp. 203–204; Califano, *Triumph and Tragedy*, p. 210; Larry Levinson to Lyndon Johnson, July 15, 1967, box 26, Ex HU 2/ST, WHCF, LBJL: Hubert Humphrey to Lyndon Johnson, July 17, 1967, box 866, VPF, HP; *Minneapolis Tribune*, July 23, 1967, p. 12. The National Guard troops deployed by Hughes were almost all white and especially trigger happy. Unprovoked Guardsmen frequently shot at African American-owned stores and even killed three women by firing indiscriminately into a housing project. Such behavior by the Guard alarmed Humphrey, who suggested to Johnson that special efforts be undertaken to recruit more African Americans. Matusow, *Unraveling of America*, p. 362; Hubert Humphrey to Lyndon Johnson, July 21, 1967, box 866, VPF, HP.

47. Sitkoff, *Struggle for Black Equality*, p. 204; Jerome Cavanaugh OH, LBJL; Fine, *Violence in the Model City*, p. 203; William Welsh to author, July 18, 1997, letter in author's possession.

48. Thernstrom and Thernstrom, *America in Black and White*, pp. 161–164. As the Thernstroms point out, "Studies based on comprehensive urban data suggest that 'indicators of black disadvantage do not predict either the location of riots or the severity of the violence when it occurs.' "

49. Hubert Humphrey to Lyndon Johnson, July 27, 1967, box 866, VPF, HP; Hubert Humphrey to Lyndon Johnson, August 11, 1967; Hubert Humphrey to Lyndon

Johnson, August 12, 1967; Joseph Califano to Lyndon Johnson, August 16, 1967; all in box 2, Ex LG 2, WHCF, LBJL; Hubert Humphrey to Lyndon Johnson, August 23, 1967, box 187, White House Aides Files—James Gaither, LBJL; *Washington Post*, July 25, 1967, p. 5; Patterson, *America's War Against Poverty*, p. 136; Katz, *Undeserving Poor*, pp. 83–91; Willard Wirtz interview with author, February 12, 1997; William Welsh to author, July 18, 1997, letter in author's possession. Several weeks later Humphrey expressed his exaggerated faith in the level of sympathy among the public for those living in slums by naively suggesting that the political misfortunes of the War on Poverty were attributable to the fact that most citizens "just [didn't] know" about the terrible conditions in the inner city. *Congressional Record*, 90th Cong., 1st sess., p. 24,927.

50. Norman Sherman interview with author, June 2, 1997; *Congressional Record*, 90th Cong., 1st sess., pp. 24,925–24,926; *Chicago Defender*, October 28, 1967, p. 6; Hubert Humphrey to Lyndon Johnson, September 15, 1967;

8. Order and Justice: The Politics of Race in 1968

1. Humphrey, *Beyond Civil Rights*, p. 170; *Minneapolis Tribune*, April 5, 1968, pp. 1, 13; *New York Times*, April 5, 1968, pp. 1, 24; Chester, Hodgson, and Page, *An American Melodrama*, p. 17.

2. Press Release, April 5, 1968, box 105, Willard Wirtz Papers, JFKL; White, *The Making of the President, 1968*, pp. 208–209; Press Release, April 6, 1965, box 2, Dukes Papers; *Washington Post*, April 6, 1968, p. B8; *New York Times*, April 10, 1968, pp. 1, 33; Philip Zeidman OH, HHHOHP; Norman Sherman interview with the author, June 2, 1997; Ted Van Dyk interview with the author, January 13, 1997.

3. Gould, *1968*, p. 55; *Report of the National Advisory Commission on Civil Disorders*, pp. 112–113; Kurian, *Datapedia*, p. 156; Lesher, *George Wallace*, pp. 400–406; Gallup, *The Gallup Poll*, pp. 2, 108, 2,112–2,113, 2,121–2,122.

4. Lawrence O'Brien OH XXI, LBJL; Memo for the Record, April 2, 1968, box 412, UP, HP; Gallup, *The Gallup Poll*, p. 2,123; *New York Times*, April 4, 1968, p. 22; Memo, April 2, 1968, box 8, State Files, 1968 Campaign Files, HP; *Winston-Salem Journal*, April 2, 1968, p. 6; *Washington Post*, April 28, 1968, p. 10.

5. Declaration of Candidacy for Presidential Nomination, box 28, SPF, HP; *Washington Post*, April 28, 1968, pp. 1, 14; Chester, et. al., *An American Melodrama*, pp. 143–145. "I have been," Humphrey stated, "too close to the presidency to believe that the solutions are simple and the answers easy."

6. Remarks of Hubert H. Humphrey, May 1, 1968; Remarks of Hubert H. Humphrey, May 2, 1968; both in box 105, Wirtz Papers; *Minneapolis Tribune*, May 9, 1968, p. 11; *Minneapolis Tribune*, May 16, 1968, p. 20; *Washington Star*, May 9, 1968, p. 16; *Baltimore Sun*, May 15, 1968, p. 8; Chester, Hodgson, and Page, *An American Melodrama*, p. 331; *Minneapolis Tribune*, May 21, 1968, pp. 6–7; *Washington Star*, May 16, 1968, p. 8; *U.S. News and World Report*, May 20, 1968, p. 99; Gallup, *The Gallup Poll*, pp. 2, 126–2,127. Nixon led Humphrey 39–36 percent. Wallace enjoyed the support of 14 percent of those surveyed.

7. *Time*, May 3, 1968, p. 15; *New York Times*, May 3, 1968, p. 4; *Minneapolis Tribune*, May 3, 1968, p. 4; Neal Gregory to Eiler Ravnholt, May 3, 1968, box 5, State Files,

1968 Campaign Files, HP; Transcript, *Meet the Press*, April 28, 1965, p. 11; Memo for Alabama File, May 4, 1968; Tom Owen to Clarence Martin, May 13, 1968; both in box 4, State Files, 1968 Campaign Files, HP; *U.S. News and World Report*, May 27, 1968, p. 55; Lawson, *In Pursuit of Power*, pp. 14–39; Bartley and Graham, *Southern Politics and the Second Reconstruction*, pp. 110–144; Klarman, "How *Brown* Changed Race Relations," pp. 81–118; *U.S. News and World Report*, June 10, 1968, p. 43. Most southern delegate slates firmly backed Humphrey, but this was not the case in Alabama. The regular delegation, which contained just two African Americans, was evenly split between Humphrey and Wallace supporters. Fearing that pro-Humphrey delegates from Alabama might embarrass him at the Democratic convention, Wallace signaled the Humphrey camp that he would instruct his delegates not to nominate him, not to wear Wallace buttons, and to follow the rules of the convention if they attended. The vice president thus seemed to be in a strong position no matter what happened at the convention. If the Wallace delegates attended, they would likely vote for Humphrey because they despised Kennedy and McCarthy. If the Wallace delegates boycotted or walked out, Humphrey stood to gain because he had the backing of nearly all the alternate delegates. Kennedy refused to concede Alabama, however. Knowing that he could not write off the South completely because there were too few delegates to be won in the handful of northern and western primaries, Kennedy attempted to drum up support among both white party leaders and African Americans in Alabama. He invited aides of former governor John Patterson to his home in Virginia and allied himself with the fledgling National Democratic Party of Alabama, which was preparing to mount a MFDP-style challenge to the regular delegation on grounds that it discriminated. Kennedy thought he stood to benefit no matter what developed at the convention. If the National Democratic Party of Alabama were seated, Humphrey's support in the South would be weakened not just through a reduction of delegates from Alabama but also possibly as a result of a walkout by white delegates from other southern states. If the Alabama challengers lost, Kennedy hoped to erode Humphrey's support among northern African Americans and liberals by claiming that the vice president sided with racists. Humphrey, meanwhile, considered the two African American delegates as sufficient proof of an integrated party and looked to nail down the state's votes by assuring Alabama leaders that the challenge of the National Democratic Party of Alabama would be ignored. Memo, May 3, 1968; Memo, May 4, 1968; Tom Owen to Clarence Martin, May 13, 1968; Tom Owen to Clarence Martin, May 13, 1968; Clarence Martin to Fred Harris, May 14, 1968; all in box 4, State Files, 1968 Campaign Files, HP; Memo, May 15, 1968; John Hoving to Fred Harris, June 3, 1968; both in box 8, State Files, 1968 Campaign Files.

8. Solberg, *Hubert H. Humphrey*, pp. 340–341; Orville Freeman to Hubert Humphrey, June 10, 1968, box 1, Personal Political Files, 1968 Campaign Files, HP; Remarks by Hubert H. Humphrey, June 20, 1968, box 107, Wirtz Papers; Transcript of Hubert H. Humphrey Question and Answer Session, June 20, 1968, box 349, Ex FG 440, WHCF, LBJL; Hubert Humphrey to John Gardner, June 18, 1968, box 436, Reuther Papers; *New Republic*, July 13, 1968, pp. 10–12.

9. Norman Holmes to Hubert Humphrey, June 13, 1968, box 1, United Democrats for Humphrey Staff Files, 1968 Campaign Files, HP; *New Republic*, June 8, 1968;

William Connell to Hubert Humphrey, June 8, 1968; both in box 132, UP, HP; George Booker to Larry Hayes, June 11, 1968, box 7, Issues and Speech Research Files, 1968 Campaign Files, HP; Ted Van Dyk to Hubert Humphrey, June 11, 1968, box 127, UP, HP.

10. Ted Van Dyk to Hubert Humphrey, June 11, 1968, box 127, UP, HP; William Connell to Hubert Humphrey, June 8, 1968, box 132, UP, HP; Garrow, *Bearing the Cross*, pp. 582–596; Hubert Humphrey to Ralph Abernathy, June 15, 1968; Hubert Humphrey to John Gardner, June 18, 1968; both in box 436, Reuther Papers; *New York Times*, June 16, 1968, p. 44; *Washington Post*, June 20, 1968, pp. 1, 8; *Minneapolis Tribune*, June 23, 1968, p. 8.

11. Remarks of Vice President Hubert H. Humphrey, July 2, 1968, box 96, Clark Papers, LBJL; *Washington Post*, July 2, 1968, pp. 1, 2. The idea for an Urban Development Bank had been developed by Johnson administration officials in 1966 and 1967. There were several potential problems with it. Rather than increase overall investment in the inner city, the bank might simply substitute its loans for private loans. Politicians at the federal, state, and local level might divert funds to pet projects that were not in the inner city. Finally, a similar organization which had been privately created by Robert Kennedy in the Bedford-Stuyvesant neighborhood of New York had a negligible impact due to conflicts with antipoverty agencies, the refusal of many businesses to build there, and political fighting among the representatives of the poor who served as the bank's directors. Proposal for a Federal Urban Development Bank, box 7, Issues and Speech Research Files, 1968 Campaign Files, HP; Memo for Joseph Califano, n.d., box 85, White House Aides Files—Joseph Califano; Bill Welsh to Bob Nathan, July 3, 1968, box 2, Issues and Speech Research Files, 1968 Campaign Files, HP; Robert Wallace to Robert Nathan, September 25, 1968, box 5, Task Force Files, 1968 Campaign Files, HP.

12. Press Release, July 21, 1968, box 96, Clark Papers, LBJL; *New York Times*, July 21, 1968, p. 47; Ambrose, *Nixon*, p. 125. The vice president had approached five federal departments in January about this issue and asked them to prepare a report that became the basis for his proposals. Hubert Humphrey to James Reynolds, January 29, 1968, Memo for the Vice President, February 8, 1968; Memo for the Vice President, February 14, 1968; Harry McPherson to Hubert Humphrey, March 4, 1968; Howard Samuels to Hubert Humphrey, March 5, 1968; Status Report on Federal Agency Efforts to Increase Minority Entrepreneurship; Bruce Terris to Hubert Humphrey, March 6, 1968; Hubert Humphrey to James Reynolds, March 7, 1968; all in box 1398, VPF, HP; *New York Times*, July 21, 1968, p. 47.

13. *New Republic*, July 13, 1968, pp. 10–12.

14. Marshall Loeb to John Stewart, July 8, 1968, box 1, United Democrats for Humphrey Staff Files, 1968 Campaign Files, HP; Memo, May 4, 1968, box 2, Dukes Papers; *New York Times*, July 28, 1968, pp. 1, 53; *New York Times*, July 29, 1968, pp. 1, 23; *Washington Post*, July 30, 1968, p. 2; *Wall Street Journal*, July 31, 1968, pp. 1, 18; Ofield Dukes to Bob Short, July 16, 1968; Clarence Mitchell III to Hubert Humphrey, July 18, 1968; both in box 1, Correspondence Subject Files, 1968 Campaign Files, HP; *Los Angeles Sentinel*, August 1, 1968, pp. 1A, 7C; Ofield Dukes to John Stewart, July 22, 1968, Ofield Dukes to Ted Van Dyk, July 24, 1968, both in box 2, Dukes Papers. The

Humphrey campaign was also making a secret effort, with the aide of singer Frank Sinatra, to open communication with the Black Panthers in Watts. George Carroll to Hubert Humphrey, June 25, 1968; George Carroll to Hubert Humphrey, July 9, 1968; both in box 4, William Connell and Eiler Ravnholt Files, 1968 Campaign Files, HP. Ads reminding voters of Humphrey's 1967 meeting with Lester Maddox appeared in several African American newspapers that summer. They were sponsored by a pro-McCarthy group of blacks. *Los Angeles Sentinel*, July 11, 1968, p. B11.

15. Ambrose, *Nixon*, pp. 169–171; White, *The Making of the President, 1968*, pp. 224–256; Carter, *The Politics of Rage*, p. 331; *Minneapolis Star*, August 16, 1968, pp. 1, 4; *Minneapolis Star*, August 17, 1968, p. 1. HEW had issued guidelines in 1968 requiring the elimination of dual school systems in the South. Orfield, *Reconstruction of Southern Education*, p. 339.

16. W. Henry Walker to John Hoving, June 28, 1968; John Hoving to Walter Mondale, Fred Harris, and Bob McCandless, June 29, 1968; John Hoving to Bill Welsh, Bob McCandless, and Walter Mondale, July 2, 1968; Hubert Humphrey to Richard Hughes, July 2, 1968; all in box 10, Issues and Speech Research Files, 1968 Campaign Files, HP; *New York Times*, August 12, 1968, p. 24.

17. Memo, June 26, 1968, box 8, State Files, 1968 Campaign Files, HP; Bill Connell to Larry O' Brien, August 14, 1968, box 1, Democratic Convention Files, 1968 Campaign Files, HP.

18. Chester, Hodgson, and Page, *An American Melodrama*, pp. 554–555; *Chicago Tribune*, August 21, 1968, p. 7; *Chicago Daily News*, August 21, 1968, pp. 1, 4; *Chicago Tribune*, August 22, 1968, pp. 1, 7.

19. Solberg, *Hubert H. Humphrey*, pp. 357–358; *Chicago Tribune*, August 21, 1968, p. 11; *Washington Post*, August 25, 1968, p. 1. In Georgia an interracial delegation of twenty African Americans and twenty-one whites disputed the seating of the regular delegation on grounds of discrimination and disloyalty. The regulars had been selected by Maddox and contained just two African Americans. Discrimination was common in Georgia politics, and Humphrey had reason to think that Maddox, who had declared his candidacy for the Democratic nomination on August 17, would probably back Wallace in November. The vice president found himself in a dilemma. He wanted to avoid offending white southern delegates any further so as not to spark a wider revolt, but he also recognized that the Georgia challengers had a good case. He thus proposed that both delegations be seated and that the Georgia vote be split between them. The challengers accepted this offer, but the Maddox forces balked. On the eve of the convention, then, Humphrey and the Democrats were still searching for a solution to the seating of Georgia and several other southern delegations. *Chicago Daily News*, August 22, 1968, pp. 1, 7; *Chicago Tribune*, August 23, 1968, pp. 1, 7; *New York Times*, August 27, 1968, pp. 1, 27; Joseph Rauh OH III, LBJL; Chester, Hodgson, and Page, *An American Melodrama*, pp. 556–558.

20. Solberg, *Hubert H. Humphrey*, pp. 358–359; Bill Connell to Hubert Humphrey, July 19, 1968, box 132, UP, HP; Lawrence O' Brien OH XXIII, LBJL; *Washington Daily News*, August 22, 1968, p. 4; Chester, Hodgson, and Page, *An American Melodrama*, p. 558; *New York Times*, August 28, 1967, p. 24.

21. Chester, Hodgson, and Page, *An American Melodrama*, pp. 556–557; Lawrence

O'Brien OH XXIII, LBJL; *New York Times*, August 28, 1968, pp. 1, 31, 33. Humphrey's inclination to please and his intense desire to be president had caused him to over-estimate the strength of the southern delegations. Before the convention he was just 62 votes shy of the nomination without the support of Connally's Texas delegation and the five southern favorite son states. *New York Times*, August 25, 1968, pp. 1, 72.

22. White, *The Making of the President, 1968*, pp. 293–304; *Chicago Tribune*, August 29, 1968, p. 1; *New York Times*, August 29, 1968, p. 20.

23. Solberg, *Hubert H. Humphrey*, pp. 366–367; Black and Black, *The Vital South*, pp. 113–114.

24. Acceptance speech of Hubert H. Humphrey, August 29, 1968, box 2, Dukes Papers.

25. Voter Opinion on Campaign Issues, August, 1968, box 7, Connell Papers; Hubert Humphrey to Lawrence O'Brien, September 5, 1968, box 1, Personal Political File, 1968 Campaign Files, HP; *Charlotte Observer*, September 8, 1968, p. 3B; *Washington Star*, September 11, 1968, p. 8; *New York Times*, September 1, 1968, pp. 1, 36; Memorandum on the Wallace Impact, n.d., box 3, Candidate Files, 1968 Campaign Files, HP; Gallup, *The Gallup Poll*, p. 2,155; Ted Van Dyk interview with author, January 13, 1997.

26. Speech to B'nai B'rith, September 8, 1968, box 81, Symington Papers; Orville Freeman OH, LBJL; Lawrence O'Brien OH XXV, LBJL; *New York Times*, September 14, 1968, pp. 1, 16; Remarks of Hubert H. Humphrey September 13, 1968, box 31, SPF, HP; John Stewart interview with author, March 28, 1997; *Minneapolis Tribune*, September 12, 1968, p. 4; Lesher, *George Wallace*, pp. 404–424; Wicker, *One of Us*, pp. 360–362; Ambrose, *Nixon*, p. 180.

27. Fred Panzer to Lyndon Johnson, September 11, 1968, box 7, Connell Papers; Memo, August 8, 1968, box 435, Reuther Papers; Lesher, *George Wallace*, pp. 412–413; *New York Times*, September 15, 1968, pp. 1, 76; Hubert Humphrey to Lawrence O'Brien, September 15, 1968; Hubert Humphrey to Orville Freeman, September 18, 1968; both in box 1, Personal Political Files, 1968 Campaign Files, HP. Humphrey noted, "It isn't that [the blue-collar worker] is against the black or the poor. In fact, he would like to help. But he just feels that everybody in government has forgotten him. Yet he pays the taxes and his kids fight the war."

28. *Minneapolis Tribune*, September 17, 1968, pp. 1, 6; Report of Task Force on Order and Justice, September 16, 1968, box 96, Clark Papers, LBJL. Humphrey wrote, "Those who imply that continued rioting and disruption will lead to social progress are very wrong; such behavior leads instead to hardening resistance to progress, and to repression." Humphrey, *Beyond Civil Rights*, p. 134.

29. Campaign Policy Committee Minutes, September 18, 1968; Ed Cubberley to Lawrence O'Brien, September 19, 1968; Memo, September 21, 1968; Evron Kirkpatrick to Orville Freeman, September 27, 1968; all in box 2, Lawrence O'Brien Files, 1968 Campaign Files, HP; Speech of Hubert H. Humphrey at Louisville, September 20, 1968, box 31, SPF, HP; Wicker, *One of Us*, p. 367; Gallup, *The Gallup Poll*, p. 2,159; Ted Van Dyk interview with author, January 13, 1997.

30. *Washington Post*, September 30, 1968, p. 21; *Fortune*, October, 1968, p. 227; Gallup, *The Gallup Poll*, p. 2,162; *Milwaukee Journal*, September 24, 1968, p. 2; *Min-*

neapolis Tribune, September 24, 1968, p. 2; Remarks of Hubert H. Humphrey to Labor Leaders, September 13, 1968, box 31, SPF, HP; Campaign Policy Committee Minutes, September 27, 1968; Evron Kirkpatrick to Orville Freeman, September 27, 1968; Campaign Policy Committee Minutes, September 25, 1968; all in box 2, Lawrence O'Brien Files, HP; Gerald Hursh to Orville Freeman, September 27, 1968, box 7, Connell Papers; Boyle, *UAW and the Heyday of American Liberalism*, p. 254. At the end of the month Gallup reported that Nixon had 43 percent of the vote, Humphrey 28 percent, and Wallace 21 percent. Meany, the Humphrey campaign, and others may have overestimated Wallace's strength among union members. Much of his support came from middle-class and wealthy suburbanites. Pollster Lou Harris, moreover, found that only 16 percent of union members outside the South backed Wallace. Chester, Hodgson, and Page, *An American Melodrama*, pp. 706–710.

31. Campaign Policy Committee Minutes, September 20, 1968; Campaign Policy Committee Minutes, September 25, 1968; both in box 2, Lawrence O'Brien Files, 1968 Campaign Files, HP; Edward Brice to Ofield Dukes, September 16, 1968, box 1214, VP Files, HP; A New Day—An Adequate Income for Every American, September 30, 1968, box 5, Task Force Files, 1968 Campaign Files, HP; *Michigan Chronicle*, September 28, 1968, p. 5; *Minneapolis Tribune*, September 30, 1968, p. 2. Pictures of Humphrey and Lester Maddox, moreover, were being distributed in African American communities and among white liberals. Memo, September 20, 1968, box 370, Reuther Papers. Humphrey also signaled his commitment to New Deal liberalism by indicating that he would consider maintaining part of the surtax Johnson had passed to finance the war in Vietnam and use the money for antipoverty efforts in urban areas. Humphrey was vague on just how much he would spend on fighting poverty, but he indicated that the surtax and the expected increase in tax revenues would leave about $30 billion for tax cuts, revenue sharing, and urban renewal. "Frankly," he stated, "when I see the amount of housing that needs to be rebuilt in our ghettos . . . and when I see the vast job we still have ahead of us to overcome poverty . . . it is clear to me that there are great areas in which the federal government is *not* spending too much." *Fortune*, October, 1968, p. 231; *Business Week*, September 28, 1968, pp. 130–131.

32. Campaign Policy Committee Minutes, September 27, 1968; Ed Cubberley to Lawrence O'Brien, September 30, 1968; all in box 2, Lawrence O'Brien Files, 1968 Campaign Files, HP; Campaign Policy Committee Minutes, October 5, 1968, box 118, Wirtz Papers; William Connell to Campaign Policy Committee, September 20, 1968, box 132, UP, HP; *Milwaukee Journal*, September 29, 1968, p. 12; *Charlotte Observer*, September 8, 1968, p. 3B; *Minneapolis Tribune*, September 13, 1968, p. 2; Dent, *The Prodigal South Returns to Power*, pp. 87–114; Wilkinson, *From Brown to Bakke*, p. 116.

33. Transcript of Television Interview, Nashville, Tennessee, October 1, 1968; Address by Hubert H. Humphrey, October 1, 1968; Transcript of Television Interview, Charlotte, North Carolina, October 2, 1968; all in box 32, SPF, HP; *Minneapolis Tribune*, October 2, 1968, pp. 1, 6; *Minneapolis Tribune*, October 3, 1968, pp. 1, 8; *New York Times*, October 2, 1968, pp. 1, 27; Carter, *The Politics of Rage,* pp. 295–343. Humphrey received an enthusiastic reception in Charlotte. "I haven't seen anything like it since the Roosevelt days," reported Terry Sanford of North Carolina.

34. White, *The Making of the President, 1968*, pp. 334–355; Campaign Policy Committee Minutes, October 5, 1968, box 118, Wirtz Papers; The Presidential Election of 1968, October 4, 1968, box 90, Ex PL 2, WHCF, LBJL.

35. Evron Kirkpatrick to Orville Freeman, September 27, 1968; Ed Cubberley to Lawrence O' Brien, September 30 1968; Ed Cubberley to Lawrence O' Brien, October 10, 1968; both in box 2, Lawrence O' Brien Files, 1968 Campaign Files, HP; A Survey of the Presidential Race in Illinois, box 4, State Files, 1968 Campaign Files, HP; Gerald Hursh to Orville Freeman, September 27, 1968, box 7, Connell Papers; Evron Kirkpatrick to Orville Freeman, October 4, 1968, box 1, Personal Political Files, HP; Wicker, *One of Us*, p. 361; *Newsweek*, October 7, 1968, pp. 29–30; Television Address by Hubert H. Humphrey, October 12, 1968, box 32, SPF, HP; *New York Times*, October 13, 1968, pp. 1, 76; Ambrose, *Nixon*, pp. 180–202; *New York Times*, October 14, 1968, p. 33; *New York Times*, October 15, 1968, p. 34; *New York Times*, October 30, 1968, p. 25; Solberg, *Hubert H. Humphrey*, p. 388; Ted Van Dyk interview with author, January 13, 1997; Norman Sherman interview with author, June 2, 1997; John Stewart interview with author, March 28, 1997.

36. *New York Times Magazine*, October 13, 1968, pp. 45–47; Transcript of Television Ad on Marshall Plan for Cities; Transcript of Television Ad on Civil Order; both in box 3, Issues and Speech Research Files, 1968 Campaign Files, HP; Remarks of Vice President Humphrey to International Brotherhood of Electrical Workers, October 17, 1968; Remarks of Vice President Hubert H. Humphrey to Negro Ministers, October 17 1968; both in box 32, SPF, HP; *Minneapolis Tribune*, October 16, 1968, p. 2; *Minneapolis Tribune*, October 17, 1968, p. 3; *New York Times*, October 16, 1968, pp. 1, 31; *New York Times*, October 19, 1968, p. 20; *Minneapolis Tribune*, October 23, 1968, p. 10; *New York Times*, October 29, 1968, pp. 1, 33; *New York Times*, October 16, 1968, p. 1. Humphrey was calling for an "affirmative action" that took into account race in targeting anti-poverty, educational, and other government programs. Humphrey argued that in the "short term," which he left undefined, Americans had to go beyond the ideal of a colorless society to bring African Americans to a similar socioeconomic level as whites. Humphrey, *Beyond Civil Rights*, p. 144.

37. *Los Angeles Times*, October 25, 1968, p. 3; *New York Times*, October 25, 1968, p. 27; *New York Times*, October 30, 1968, p. 25; *New York Times*, October 14, 1968, p. 33; *New York Times*, October 15, 1968, p. 34; *New York Times*, October 30, 1968, p. 25; Solberg, *Hubert H. Humphrey*, p. 388.

38. Lawrence O' Brien OH X, LBJL; Lesher, *George Wallace*, pp. 425–426; Gallup, *The Gallup Poll*, p. 2,168; John Stewart interview with author, March 28, 1997.

39. Lawrence O' Brien OH XXVI, LBJL; Ambrose, *Nixon*, pp. 219–220; Ted Van Dyk OH, HHHOHP.

40. Black and Black, *Vital South*, p. 113, 302; White, *The Making of the President, 1968*, pp. 396–401; *Congressional Quarterly Weekly Report*, December 6, 1968, p. 3,229; Chester, Hodgson, and Page, *An American Melodrama*, pp. 748- 763; Bureau of the Census, *Statistical Abstract of the United States*, p. 369; Lubell, *The Hidden Crisis in American Politics*, pp. 89–139. In Newark's largely white North and East wards, Kennedy had won 68 percent of the vote in 1960, but Humphrey received only 48 percent in 1968. Similarly, in the Chicago neighborhoods where Martin Luther King had

demonstrated for open housing in 1966, Kennedy had won 66 percent of the vote in 1960 but Humphrey only 42 percent eight years later.

41. Walters, *Black Presidential Politics in America*, pp. 31–32. The African American participation rate was 57.6 percent in 1968, compared to 58.5 percent in 1964. The rate for the country as a whole was slightly more than 60 percent. Turnout in several large northern cities with large black populations was lower than it had been in 1960, however. In New York it was down by 479,000 voters. In Chicago 241,000 fewer people voted, while in Pittsburgh 247,000 fewer did. In Detroit 137,000 fewer voters went to the polls.

42. Lubell, *The Hidden Crisis in American Politics*, pp. 100–134; John Stewart interview with author, March 28, 1997; Ted Van Dyk interview with author, January 13, 1997; Norman Sherman interview with author, June 2, 1997.

43. Rowan, *Dream Makers, Dream Breakers*, p. 352; John Stewart interview with author, March 28, 1997. On the role of race in the Republicans' electoral successes since 1968, see Carter, *From George Wallace to Newt Gingrich*.

44. *Minneapolis Tribune*, November 7, 1968, pp. 1, 12.

9. Jobs and the Failed Search for an Interracial Coalition

1. Eisele, *Almost to the Presidency*, p. 421; Solberg, *Hubert H. Humphrey*, pp. 412–416; *Washington Post*, January 21, 1969, pp. 1, 8, 16.

2. *U.S. News and World Report*, November 24, 1969, pp. 57–58.

3. Solberg, *Hubert H. Humphrey*, pp. 416–418; Eisele, *Almost to the Presidency*, p. 428.

4. Hubert H. Humphrey—Announcement Statement, June 13, 1970, box 1, 1970 Campaign Files, HP; *Minneapolis Tribune*, June 14, 1970, p. 1.

5. Remarks of Hubert H. Humphrey to American Bar Association, August 11, 1970, box 1, 1970 Campaign Files, HP. On the resentment of many white Democrats over crime, see Rieder, *Canarsie*, pp. 57–94; *New Republic*, September 19, 1970, pp. 18–19; *Minneapolis Tribune*, August 13, 1970, p. 10. The speech reflected the thesis of *The Real Majority*, which Wattenberg had coauthored with Richard Scammon.

6. *Minneapolis Tribune*, July 12, 1970, p. 4B; Hubert Humphrey to Eugenie Anderson, July 3, 1970, box 6, 1970 Campaign Files, HP; *Minneapolis Tribune*, September 17, 1970, p. 24; *New York Times*, October 1, 1970, p. 23; *Minneapolis Tribune*, September 11, 1970, p. 19; *Minneapolis Tribune*, September 27, 1970, p. 7; Solberg, *Hubert H. Humphrey*, p. 420.

7. *Congressional Record*, 92d Cong., 1st sess., pp. 6,211–6,212, 9,719–9,721, 17, 759, 33,282–33,283; Hubert Humphrey to Bayard Rustin, July 20, 1971, box 2, 1971 Legislative Files, HP. Likewise, Humphrey blasted Nixon's decision to impound $800 million for urban renewal, housing, and mass transit as "totally indefensible" and urged the president to provide more money for minority entrepreneurship.

8. *Congressional Record*, 92d Cong., 1st sess., pp. 268, 2,408, 9,869, 17,062–17,063, 22,011, 33,282; 33,581, 46,106; Hubert Humphrey to James Tate, May 21, 1971; Hubert Humphrey to Paula Hollinger, June 7, 1971; both in box 3, 1971 Legislative Files, HP. Under Humphrey's plan, the bank would have an initial capitalization of $3.5 billion raised through the sale of public stock. To lure investors, dividends on the stock would be tax exempt. There was, Humphrey noted, a "staggering backlog" of public

construction applications to the federal government—nine hundred urban renewal projects worth $2.75 billion and $560 million in public housing projects. Seventy-five percent of nonwhite children under the age of fifteen had never been to a dentist, Humphrey pointed out. Humphrey also kept watch on voter registration efforts in Mississippi. Upon hearing reports that blacks were having difficulty registering, he wrote the attorney general urging him to remedy the problem immediately. Hubert Humphrey to John Mitchell, August 25, 1971, box 2, 1971 Legislative Files, HP.

9. Wilkinson, *From Brown to Bakke,* pp. 135–194; Gallup, *The Gallup Poll,* p. 2,323; Edsall and Edsall, *Chain Reaction,* pp. 87–88.

10. Parmet, *Richard Nixon and His America,* pp. 595–596; Ambrose, *Nixon,* pp. 460–461; statement by Senator Hubert H. Humphrey on School Busing, n.d., box 3, 1971–1977 Subject Files, HP; *Congressional Record,* 92d Cong., 1st sess., p. 33, 283.

11. Solberg, *Hubert H. Humphrey,* pp. 423–424.

12. Announcement of Candidacy, January 10, 1972, box 68, Department of Legislation Files, AFL-CIO Papers; *Washington Post,* January 11, 1972, p. 10; *New York Times,* January 11, 1972, pp. 1, 9, 22; Eisele, *Almost to the Presidency,* p. 428.

13. *Minneapolis Tribune,* February 17, 1972, p. 16B, *Minneapolis Tribune,* February 19, 1972, pp. 1, 7; Press Release, February 15, 1972, box 3, 1971–1977 Subject Files, HP; *Congressional Record,* 92d Cong., 1st sess., pp. 6,274–6,276; *National Journal,* April 15, 1972, p. 630; Press Release, March 17, 1972, box 23, 1972 Campaign Files, HP; *Minneapolis Tribune,* February 25, 1972, pp. 1, 14; *Minneapolis Tribune,* February 26, 1972, p. 4; *Minneapolis Tribune,* March 1, 1972, pp. 1, 13; Hubert Humphrey to Stephanie Laskin, March 30, 1972, box 3, 1972 Legislative Files, HP; *New York Times,* March 18, 1972, pp. 1, 14; Press Release, March 20, 1972, box 2, Dukes Papers; *New York Times,* March 23, 1972, p. 42; Carter, *Politics of Rage,* p. 425; *Minneapolis Tribune,* March 23, 1972, pp. 1, 6; Ofield Dukes to Max Kampelman, April 12, 1972, box 5, Dukes Papers; Frank Reeves to Hubert Humphrey, April 18, 1972, box 3, 1972 Legislative Files, HP; Memo, Leadership Conference on Civil Rights to Participating Organizations, March 28, 1972, box 23, 1972 Campaign Files, HP; Edsall and Edsall, *Chain Reaction,* p. 89; *Minneapolis Tribune,* February 25, 1972, pp. 1, 14; *Minneapolis Tribune,* February 26, 1972, p. 4; *Minneapolis Tribune,* March 1, 1972, pp. 1, 13; *Minneapolis Tribune,* March 18, 1972, pp. 1, 7; *Minneapolis Tribune,* March 19, 1972, p. 1; *National Journal,* April 15, 1972, p. 633–634; *Minneapolis Tribune,* April 30, 1972, p. 2; *New York Times,* April 30, 1972, p. 44; *New York Times,* May 3, 1972, pp., 1, 32; *New York Times,* May 4, 1972, pp. 1, 31. Reporter Carl Rowan, meanwhile, raised doubts about "some of the strategy [Humphrey had] employed in recent weeks." Carl Rowan to Hubert Humphrey, April 19, 1972, box 1, 1972 Legislative Files, HP; *New York Times,* March 17, 1972, p. 16; *New York Times,* March 24, 1972, p. 22; *New York Times,* April 6, 1972, pp. 1, 30.

14. *New York Times,* July 12, 1972, pp. 1, 21; *New York Times Magazine,* May 28, 1972, p. 16.

15. White, *The Making of the President, 1972,* pp. 340–345; Ambrose, *Nixon,* p. 651; Wicker, *One of Us,* p. 685.

16. Remarks of Hubert H. Humphrey, December 11, 1972, box 3, 1971–1977 Subject Files, HP. Humphrey had sounded similar themes during the fall campaign. In October he warned that "the Democratic Party cannot win without having the

working families in support of its ticket." Similarly, he feared that the party "will look like it is a special interest party" if it only represented college campuses and racial minorities. *U.S. News and World Report*, October 2, 1972, pp. 26–27. The new rules required proportional representation of African Americans, women, youth, and other groups at the convention based upon the percentage of total party membership for each constituency. If 10 percent of registered Democrats were black, then 10 percent of the delegates at the convention would be black. This shifted power from traditional leaders and constituencies, such as blue-collar males, to more liberal, better-educated reformers who resented the old party leaders. Whereas voters in the mid-1950s detected no great difference between the two parties' stands on racial matters, 59 percent of the public identified the Democrats as the party most likely to aid minorities. Only 27 percent of the public thought so about the Republicans. The Democrats' platform, moreover, contained separate planks on the rights of the poor, Native Americans, mentally retarded, disabled, women, and children. The platform gave little attention to white middle-class concerns about jobs or crime. Edsall and Edsall, *Chain Reaction*, p. 95, 150.

17. Hubert Humphrey to James Hutchison, March 14, 1973, box 2, 1973 Legislative Files, HP; *Minneapolis Tribune*, March 7, 1973, pp. 1, 12; *New York Times*, March 7, 1973, p. 21; *Congressional Record*, 93d Cong., 1st sess., pp. 6,517, 7,831, 13,504, 14,915, 25,715; *New York Times*, September 13, 1973, pp. 1, 20; *New York Times*, September 25, 1973, p. 19; Press Release, February 5, 1972, box 14, 1971–1978 Subject Files, HP. Nixon's impoundment of federal funds so angered Humphrey that he accused the president of hypocrisy. "When you believe in law and order," he observed, "you ought to believe in it for yourself too." Humphrey also introduced a resolution calling for $14 billion in new spending on employment, health care, and education. Half the money would come from reductions in military spending, the other half from the elimination of certain tax preferences for wealthy Americans. Alarmed that the jobless rate among African American teens stood at 38.6 percent at the end of 1972, Humphrey joined twenty-six other senators in urging Nixon to support a summer jobs program for youth of all races. Three weeks later the president announced that $354 million would be available for youth employment. The vast majority of the money, however, would come out of the appropriation for the Emergency Employment Act, which created jobs for unemployed adults. Humphrey charged Nixon with proposing an "unconscionable" trade-off that would force local leaders to choose between parents and their children in the dispensing of federal money. But that was not all. Even if all the money went to youth, Nixon's plan provided for 36,000 fewer jobs than the previous summer. Congress eventually appropriated $44 million for the Neighborhood Youth Corps initiative, but Nixon vetoed the bill containing this funding.

18. Lukas, *Common Ground*, pp. 219–220; *Congressional Record*, 93d Cong., 2d sess., pp. 14,922, 15,073; Hubert Humphrey to Roy Wilkins, July 8, 1974, box 3, 1974 Legislative Files, HP.

19. *Congressional Record*, 93d Cong., 2d sess., pp. 29,785–29,789. On the Employment Act of 1946, see Bailey, *Congress Makes a Law*, pp. 13–75, 82–131; Collins, *The*

Business Response to Keynes, pp. 90–107; Brinkley, *The End of Reform,* pp. 227–264. Many Democrats had favored public service jobs as early as 1971, but none had introduced a plan as broad as Humphrey-Hawkins. See Weir, *Politics and Jobs,* p. 117.

20. Kurian, *Datapedia,* p. 76; *Congressional Record,* 93d Cong., 2d sess., pp. 21,278–21,279, 29,786–29,789, 34,589–34,950; *Nation,* February 5, 1977, p. 139; Levison, *The Full Employment Alternative,* pp. 15–50; Al Saunders OH, HHHOHP; Skocpol, "Targeting Within Universalism"; Ginsburg, *Full Employment and Public Policy,* p. 37; Charles Hirschmann, "Minorities in the Labor Market," p. 71; Carnoy, *Faded Dreams,* pp. 13–33; *Wall Street Journal,* July 24, 1974, p. 8; Press Release, September 29, 1972, box 3, 1971–1978 Subject Files, HP.

21. Jones, "Southern Diaspora," p. 46; Kusmer, "African Americans in the City Since World War II," pp. 458–504; Sugrue, *Origins of the Urban Crisis,* pp. 215–235; Katz, *Improving Poor People,* pp. 77–79; Trotter, "Blacks in the Urban North," pp. 56–80; Wilson, *The Truly Disadvantaged,* pp. 20–62, 125–139; Peterson, "The Urban Underclass and the Poverty Paradox"; Jencks, *Rethinking Social Policy,* pp. 134–142; Katz, "Reframing the Debate," pp. 443–452.

22. Skocpol, "The Limits of the New Deal System," pp. 301–303; Skocpol, "Brother, Can You Spare a Job?"; Wolfe, *America's Impasse,* pp. 25–67; Patterson, *America's Struggle Against Poverty,* pp. 135–140, 187; Wilson, "Social Policy and Minority Groups," pp. 232–234; Weir, Orloff, and Skocpol, "The Future of Social Policy in the United States," p. 425; Weir, *Politics and Jobs,* pp. 116–119; Mead, *The New Politics of Poverty,* pp. 187–192; U.S. Congress, Joint Economic Committee, *Youth Unemployment,* pp. 27–31; Edsall and Edsall, *Chain Reaction,* pp. 107–112; Tim Barnicle interview with author, May 27, 1997.

23. *Congressional Record,* 93d Cong., 2d sess., p. 29,785–29,789, 33,177, 34,589; U.S. House of Representatives, Subcommittee on Equal Opportunities, *Equal Opportunity and Full Employment Act of 1976,* pp. 24–38.

24. Remarks by Hubert H. Humphrey at Congressional Breakfast for Full Employment, January 15, 1975, box 40, SPF, HP; *Congressional Record,* 94th Cong., 1st sess., pp. 298–299, 4, 554, 4,833, 5,363, 8,755, 11,926, 20,072–20,078, 24,774, 33,526–33,529; *Congressional Record,* 93d Cong., 2d sess., pp. 29,785–29,789; *Minneapolis Tribune,* July 29, 1975, p. 2; Schantz and Schmidt, "Politics and Policy," p. 2; National Urban League, "Quarterly Economic Report on the Black Worker," March 1975, box 5, WHCF, Subject File LA/2, Gerald R. Ford Library (FL), Ann Arbor, Michigan. While Congress examined Humphrey's full employment measure, he gave his immediate attention to several other antipoverty and racial matters. He sponsored or supported legislation to expand the WIC program, which provided food for poor children and mothers, to give every child attending a school or day care program at least one free meal a day, to create 1.1 million summer jobs for disadvantaged youth, and to extend the Voting Rights Act. Once again, however, busing proved to be the most controversial racial issue. In September the Senate adopted an amendment to an appropriations bill that prohibited HEW from using federal funds to require school districts to bus students to achieve desegregation unless ordered to do so by a federal court. Because most busing occurred under court direction, the amendment

was unlikely to have any great effect. Nevertheless, it represented an important symbolic victory for busing opponents because it was the strongest antibusing statement the Senate had ever approved. Several northern Democrats who had customarily supported busing, moreover, reversed themselves. Humphrey joined a small bipartisan group that opposed the effort. Afterward, a disappointed Humphrey observed, "The message is that the Senate, the last bastion of civil rights support, has now joined the president and the House in opposing desegregation of towns and cities across the North and West. The message is that future efforts are unnecessary and illegitimate and perhaps existing southern desegregation can be rolled back." Though he had fought the antibusing effort, Humphrey continued to stress that equal educational opportunity was more important than busing. Busing was obviously unpopular with voters, but there was more than political expediency behind Humphrey's stand. By 1975 there were growing signs that busing's effectiveness as a tool in producing integrated schools was minimal. Whites were moving to the suburbs in part to escape busing, and the Supreme Court had forbidden transporting students from suburbs to cities in its 1974 decision in *Milliken v. Bradley*. Some studies even suggested that African Americans students did not benefit from integrated schools as much as busing proponents had anticipated. The answer to the gap in educational opportunity between the races, Humphrey still argued, was a vastly increased federal role in education that would end "the unconscionable inequality" by which the merits of a child's education depended upon the wealth of the surrounding community. Accordingly, he sponsored legislation to provide federal aid to areas that reduced or eliminated property taxes or whose school districts were deeply in debt. (Many big city districts were in debt.) The measure died in committee. William Connell to Hubert Humphrey, September 17, 1975; Gary Orfield to Hubert Humphrey, September 24, 1975, both in box 3, 1971–1977 Subject Files, HP; *Minneapolis Tribune*, September 25, 1975, p. 11; *Congressional Quarterly*, September 27, 1975, pp. 2,034–2,037; *Congressional Quarterly*, October 18, 1975, pp. 2,227–2,232; *Congressional Record*, 94th Cong., 1st sess., pp. 5,304–5,306; Wilkinson, *From Brown to Bakke*, pp. 165–182, 216–249.

25. U.S. Congress, Joint Economic Committee, *National Economic Planning*, pp. 193–194; U.S. Congress, Joint Economic Committee, *Jobs and Prices in Chicago*, pp. 2–27; U.S. Congress, Joint Economic Committee, *Jobs and Prices in Atlanta*, pp. 84–98; U.S. Congress, Joint Economic Committee, *Jobs and Prices in the West Coast Region*, pp. 2–24, 180–181; U.S. Department of Labor, *Monthly Labor Review, July 1976*, p. 74.

26. Tim Barnicle to David Broder, September 16, 1975, box 2, 1975 Legislative Files, HP; *Congressional Record*, 94th Cong., 2d sess., pp. 6,613–6,621; *Congressional Quarterly Weekly Report*, December 6, 1975, p. 2,629; *Congressional Quarterly Weekly Report*, May 15, 1976, pp. 1,171–1,175; *Minneapolis Tribune*, February 16, 1976, pp. 1, 4; *National Journal*, December 10, 1977, p. 1,930; *New York Times*, March 14, 1976, pp. 1, 28; *New York Times*, March 24, 1976, pp. 55, 67.

27. Stein, *Presidential Economics*, pp. 209–215; Porter, *Presidential Decisionmaking*, p. 101; Greene, *The Presidency of Gerald R. Ford*, pp. 72–77; Reichley, *Conservatives in an Age of Change*, pp. 384–391; *National Journal*, June 12, 1976, p. 813; Bill Diefenderfer to James Cannon, May 4, 1976, box 58, James Cannon Files, Domestic Policy Council

Papers, FL; L. William Seidman to Gerald R. Ford, n.d., box 11, James Cannon Files, Domestic Policy Council Papers; Roger Porter to William Rhatican and William Greener, August 10, 1976, box 71, L. William Seidman Files, Office of Economic Affairs Papers; Barry Chiswick to Alan Greenspan, March 16, 1975, box 146, Council of Economic Advisers Papers, Fla.; Herbert Perritt to Roger Porter, March 25, 1976, box 30, L. William Seidman Files, Office of Economic Affairs Papers, Fla.; Alan Greenspan to L. William Seidman, June 26, 1975, box 109, L. William Seidman Files, Office of Economic Affairs Papers, Fla.; Paul W. MacAvoy to Economic Policy Board, June 23, 1976, box 8, Council of Economic Advisers Records, Fla.; testimony by Alan Greenspan before the Subcommittee on Manpower, Compensation, and Health and Safety, Committee on Education and Labor, April 14, 1976, box 31, L. William Seidman Files, Office of Economic Affairs Papers; Press Release, May 29, 1975, box 25, White House Records Office, Legislation Case Files, Fla.; Press Release, February 13, 1976, box 40, White House Records Office, Legislation Case Files, FL; L. William Seidman to Robert T. Hartmann, John O. Marsh, James M. Cannon, and Max Freidersdorf, May 10, 1976, box 71, L. William Seidman Files, Office of Economic Affairs Papers, Fla.; James T. Lynn to Gerald R. Ford, June 10, 1976, box 27, Presidential Handwriting File, Fla.; Levison, *The Full Employment Alternative*, pp. 15–29; U.S. Congress, Joint Economic Committee, *Jobs and Prices in Chicago*, pp. 48–52; Schantz and Schmidt, "Politics and Policy," pp. 28–29; *New York Times*, January 20, 1976, p. 19. Republicans privately worried that they would suffer politically for their opposition to Humphrey-Hawkins. Being against the bill made them appear to be against jobs, House Republicans indicated. Thus many joined an effort by New York representative Jack Kemp to stimulate hiring in the private sector through targeted tax policies. William F. Gorog to Economic Policy Board, April 30, 1976, box 184. L. William Siedman Files, Office of Economic Affairs Papers.

28. *New York Times*, March 14, 1976, pp. 1, 28; *New York Times*, April 14, 1976, p. 65; *New York Times*, April 27, 1976, p. 20; *Congressional Quarterly*, May 15, 1976, p. 1,174; *New York Times*, May 4, 1976, pp. 55, 59; *Congressional Digest*, June, 1976, pp. 179–183; *Minneapolis Tribune*, June 4, 1976, p. 6; *Business Week*, May 31, 1976, p. 66; *Newsweek*, May 31, 1976, pp. 57–58; *New York Times*, April 14, 1976, p. 65; *Washington Post*, May 27, 1976, p. 27; *Baltimore Sun*, May 21, 1976, p. 1; Charles Schultze interview with author, March 7, 1997; U.S. Congress, House of Representatives Subcommittee on Manpower, Compensation, and Health and Safety, *Full Employment and Balanced Growth Act of 1976*, pp. 705–718, 800–837; Congressional Research Service, "The Economic Impact of a Federal Program to Achieve 3 Percent Unemployment"; U.S. Congress, House of Representatives Subcommittee on Manpower, Compensation, and Health and Safety, *Full Employment and Balanced Growth Act of 1976*, pp. 489–506.

29. Press Release, May 25, 1976, box 14, 1971–1977 Subject Files, HP; Remarks of Senator Hubert H. Humphrey to the American Jewish Committee, May 14, 1976, box 42, SPF, HP; *Minneapolis Tribune*, May 26, 1976, pp. 1, 5; *Congressional Record*, 94th Cong., 2d sess., pp. 17,710–17,711, 23,938.

30. *Business Week*, June 14, 1976, pp. 25–26; Hubert Humphrey to Walter Heller, August 6, 1976, box 2, 1976 Legislative Files, HP; Walter Heller to Brock Adams, July

21, 1976, box 2, 1976 Legislative Files, HP; *Congressional Quarterly Weekly Report*, August 21, 1976, pp. 2,278; Walter Heller OH, HHHOHP.

31. *New York Times*, April 1, 1976, pp. 1, 22; *New York Times*, May 5, 1976, p. 24; Jerry Jasinowski to Hubert Humphrey, May 19, 1976, box 2, 1976 Legislative Files, HP; *Minneapolis Tribune*, March 25, 1976, p. 8; *Newsweek*, April 12, 1976, p. 29; *Minneapolis Tribune*, May 19, 1976, p. 2; *New York Times*, May 19, 1976, p. 46; *Newsweek*, May 31, 1976, pp. 57–58; *New York Times*, July 14, 1976, pp. 1, 16; *Congressional Quarterly Weekly Report*, August 21, 1976, p. 2,278. Carter endorsed Humphrey-Hawkins in April after he had made a politically explosive remark about "black intrusion" into white neighborhoods. Carter added that he was not opposed to neighborhoods who wanted to maintain their "ethnic purity" and that he would not use government deliberately to integrate neighborhoods. *New York Times*, April 7, 1976, pp. 1, 23; *Congressional Quarterly Weekly Report*, May 21, 1977, p. 967; *Washington Post*, September 9, 1976, p. 1.

32. *Congressional Record*, 95th Cong., 1st sess., pp. 579–589, 773–774, 10,168, 12,220; Hubert Humphrey to Walter Heller, January 23, 1977, box 2, 1977–1978 Legislative Files, HP; U.S. Department of Labor, *Monthly Labor Review, March 1977*, p. 94; *New York Times*, January 19, 1977, p. 14; Leon Shull to Hubert Humphrey, March 8, 1977; Hubert Humphrey to Leon Shull, April 8, 1977; both in box 6, 1977–1978 Legislative Files, HP. Humphrey also introduced legislation to provide jobs and training programs for youth. Pointing out that 55 percent of those arrested in 1975 were under age twenty-five, he described unemployed youth as "a lethal social cancer." He declared, "There is no way that we can reduce or eliminate crime in this country until we solve the problem of youth unemployment."

33. Augustus Hawkins to Charles Schultze, May 11, 1977, Charles Schultze to James Carter, May 23, 1977; Stuart Eizenstat to James Carter, May 24, 1977; W. Michael Blumenthal to James Carter, June 2, 1977; all in box 221, Stuart Eizenstat Files, Domestic Policy Staff Files, James E. Carter Library (CL), Atlanta, Ga.; Dumbrell, *The Carter Presidency*, p. 100; Fink, "Fragile Alliance," pp. 790–794; Thomas Sugrue, "Carter's Urban Policy Crisis," unpublished paper. The Federal Reserve had similar worries about a loss of its independence. Arthur Burns to Carl Perkins, March 21, 1977, Arthur Burns Papers, Fla.

34. Press Release, June 12 1977, box 14, 1971–1977 Subject Files, HP; Bert Lance to James Carter, May 31, 1977; Stuart Eizenstat to James Carter, June 4, 1977; Michael Blumenthal to James Carter, June 6, 1977; Stuart Eizenstat to James Carter, June 6, 1977; Hubert Humphrey and Augustus Hawkins to James Carter, June 9, 1977; An Action Resolution Calling for Prompt Enactment of the Full Employment and Balanced Growth Act of 1977; Valerie Pinson to Charles Schultze, June 30, 1977; Bert Carp, Bill Johnston, and Bill Spring to Stuart Eizenstat, July 12, 1977; Lyle Gramley to Charles Schultze, July 12, 1977; all in box 221, Stuart Eizenstat Files, Domestic Policy Staff Files, CL; Ofield Dukes to Hubert Humphrey, July 21, 1977, box 2, Correspondence Files, 1971–1978, HP; *New York Times*, June 28, 1977, p. 12; Hubert Humphrey to Augustus Hawkins, September 13, 1977, box 6, 1977–1978 Legislative Files, HP. At the NACCP annual convention in June, the chair of the board of directors attacked Carter for not supporting Humphrey-Hawkins.

35. Solberg, *Hubert H. Humphrey*, p. 453–455.

36. Rick Hutcheson to James Carter, June 11, 1977, box 2, LA 2, WHCF, CL; Charles Schultze to James Carter, June 22, 1977, Dan Brill, et. al., to Mike Blumenthal, August 19, 1977, Bill Springer et al., to Stuart Eizenstat and Charles Schultze, September 1, 1977, all in box 221, Stuart Eizenstat Files, Domestic Policy Staff Files, CL; *New York Times*, September 8, 1977, p. 16; Solberg, *Hubert H. Humphrey*, pp. 448–449.

37. Lyle Gramley and William Spring to Michael Blumenthal et al., September 23, 1977; Lyle Gramley to Charles Shultze, September 26, 1977; Bert Carp and Bill Spring to Stuart Eizenstat, September 29, 1977; Hubert Humphrey and Augustus Hawkins to James Carter, October 4, 1977; Stuart Eizenstat and Charles Schultze to James Carter, October 6, 1977; Stuart Eizenstat and Charles Schultze to James Carter, October 19, 1977; all in box 221, Stuart Eizenstat Files, Domestic Policy Staff Files, CL; Memorandum, September 27, 1977; Bert Carp and Bill Spring to Stuart Eizenstat, October 7, 1977; both in box 222, Stuart Eizenstat Files, Domestic Policy Staff Files, CL; *Minneapolis Tribune*, November 15, 1977, p. 1; Kaufman, *The Presidency of James Earl Carter, Jr.*, pp. 110–111; Tim Barnicle interview with author, May 27, 1997.

38. Press Release, November 14, 1977, box 14, 1971–1977 Subject Files, HP; *Congressional Record*, 95th Cong., 1st sess., pp. 38,507–38,515; *Washington Post*, December 4, 1977, p. C7; *New York Times*, November 23, 1977, section IV, p. 9; New York *Amsterdam News*, November 26, 1977, p. 6.

39. *Congressional Record*, 95th Cong., 1st sess., pp. 38,507–38.514, *Washington Post*, December 4, 1977, p. C7; Summary of the Major Provisions in the Compromise Humphrey-Hawkins Bill, December 28, 1977, box 14, 1971–1977 Subject Files, HP; *New York Times*, November 15, 1977, pp. 1, 24; *New York Times*, November 20, 1977, section III, pp. 1, 4; *Chicago Defender*, November 17, 1977, p. 4. One union member commented, "When you are a midwife helping to bring a baby into the world, you don't say 'rotten fish' the minute it is delivered."

40. Solberg, *Hubert H. Humphrey*, p. 456; Fink, "Fragile Alliance," pp. 791–793; *New York Times*, October 29, 1978, p. 1; *Washington Post*, October 28, 1978, p. 9.

41. Edsall and Edsall, *Chain Reaction*, pp. 116–171; Ferguson and Rogers, *Right Turn*, pp. 63–64. On the lack of class solidarity between working-class whites and African Americans, see Lubell, *The Hidden Crisis in American Politics*, pp. 89–139; Rieder, *Canarsie*, pp. 1–132; Pollster George Gallup regularly asked Americans what they thought was the nation's most important problem. During the mid-1970s unemployment almost always finished a distant second to "high cost of living" or inflation. Gallup, *The Gallup Poll*, pp. 415, 443, 490, 534, 655, 760. 913, 960, 1,040, 1,219; Skocpol, "The Limits of the New Deal System, " pp. 300–302; Skocpol, "Brother, Can You Spare a Job?," pp. 229–235; Weir, *Politics and Jobs*, pp. 131–138.

42. Wilson, *Thinking About Crime*, p. 143; DiIulio, "The Impact of Inner City Crime," pp. 28–46; Greenstone, "Culture, Rationality, and the Underclass"; Jencks, *Rethinking Social Policy*, pp. 19, 112–142; Wilson and Cook, "Unemployment and Crime"; *Congressional Record*, 94th Cong., 2d sess., p. 16,416. Humphrey went so far as to declare in 1976 that a 1.4 percent rise in unemployment in 1970 was "directly

responsible" for 1,740 additional homicides. The study Humphrey used to make such a claim, Wilson and Cook cogently argue, suffered from flaws in data and methods. On structural causes of urban poverty during the 1970s, see Katz, "Reframing the 'Underclass' Debate," pp. 440–477, and Wilson, *The Truly Disadvantaged*.

43. Brinkley, *The End of Reform,* pp. 6–11; Leuchtenburg, *In the Shadow of FDR,* pp. 179–183.

Manuscript Collections

City Hall Archives, Minneapolis, Minn.
Proceedings of the City Council of Minneapolis, 1945–1947
Columbia University, New York, N.Y.
Herbert Lehman Papers
Everett Dirksen Congressional Research Center, Pekin, Ill.
Everett Dirksen Papers
George Meany Memorial Archives, Silver Spring, Md.
AFL-CIO Papers
Gerald Ford Library, Ann Arbor, Mich.
Arthur Burns Papers
Council of Economic Advisers Files
Domestic Policy Council Files
Office of Economic Affairs Papers
Presidential Handwriting File
White House Central Files
White House Records Office Files
Harry S. Truman Library, Independence, Mo.
Clark Clifford Papers
Democratic National Committee Papers
J. Howard McGrath Papers
Stephen Mitchell Papers
Phileo Nash Papers
Harry Truman Papers
James E. Carter Library, Atlanta, Ga.
Domestic Policy Staff Files
White House Central Files
John F. Kennedy Library, Boston, Mass.
Burke Marshall Papers

John F. Kennedy Pre-Presidential Papers
Democratic National Committee Papers
White House Central Files
Willard Wirtz Papers
Library of Congress, Washington, D.C.
A. Philip Randolph Papers
Clinton Anderson Papers
Emanuel Celler Papers
Leadership Conference on Civil Rights Papers
NAACP Papers
Paul and Claire Sifton Papers
Joseph Rauh Papers
Roy Wilkins Papers
Stephen Horn Papers
Lyndon Johnson Library, Austin, Tex.
Cabinet Papers
Democratic National Committee Papers
Lyndon Johnson Senate Papers
Ramsey Clark Papers
White House Aides Files
Bill Moyers
Douglas Cater
Harry McPherson
James Gaither
Joseph Califano
Lee White
Marvin Watson
William Sparks
White House Central Files
White House Conference on Civil Rights Papers
Minnesota Historical Society, Saint Paul, Minn.
Genevieve Steefel Papers
Hubert H. Humphrey Papers
Jewish Community Relations Council of Minneapolis Papers
Max Kampelman Papers
Minneapolis Central Labor Union Papers
Minneapolis Fair Employment Practices Committee Papers
Samuel Davis Papers
William Connell Papers
State Historical Society of Wisconsin, Madison, Wis.
Americans for Democratic Action Papers
Anne Romaine Files
Leadership Conference on Civil Rights Papers
Marquis Childs Papers
Mississippi Freedom Summer Reviewed Papers

Wisconsin for Humphrey Committee Papers
Walter Reuther Library, Detroit, Mich.
Aaron Henry Papers
Ofield Dukes Papers
UAW Recreation Department Papers
William Oliver Papers
William Seabron Papers
Western Historical Collection, Columbia, Mo.
Stuart Symington Papers
Thomas Hennings Papers

Newspapers and Periodicals

American Mercury
Arrowhead Bowling News
Atlanta Constitution
Baltimore Sun
Birmingham Post-Herald
Broadcasting
Business Week
Charleston Gazette
Charlotte Observer
Chicago Daily News
Chicago Defender
Chicago Sun-Times
Chicago Tribune
Christian Science Monitor
Congressional Quarterly Weekly Report
Congressional Record
Congress Weekly
Denver Post
Fortune
Fresno Bee
Jackson Clarion-Ledger
Lawrence Eagle-Tribune
Los Angeles Sentinel
Los Angeles Times
Louisville Courier Journal
Memphis Commercial Appeal
Milwaukee Journal
Minneapolis Tribune
Minneapolis Spokesman
Nation
National Jewish Monthly
National Journal
New Leader

New Orleans Times-Picayune
Newsweek
New York Amsterdam News
New York Herald Tribune
New York Star
New York Times
New Republic
Philadelphia Inquirer
Pittsburgh Courier
Pittsburgh Press
Phoenix Gazette
Progressive
Raleigh News and Observer
Saint Louis Post-Dispatch
Saint Paul Dispatch
Saint Paul Pioneer Press
San Francisco Chronicle
Saturday Evening Post
Savannah Morning News
Survey Graphic
Tampa Tribune
Time
Toledo Times
U.S. News and World Report
Washington Afro-American
Washington Daily News
Washington Post
Washington Star
Washington Times-Herald
Winston-Salem Journal
Woman's Home Companion

Government Publications

Bureau of the Census. *Statistical Abstract of the United States.* Washington, D.C.: GPO, 1970.

Congressional Research Service, "The Economic Impact of a Federal Program to Achieve 3 Percent Unemployment by the End of 1976." Washington, D.C.: Library of Congress, 1976.

Eisenhower, Dwight D. *Public Papers of the Presidents: Dwight D. Eisenhower, 1957.* Washington, D.C.: GPO, 1957.

Governor's Interracial Commission of Minnesota. "The Negro and His Home in Minnesota." St. Paul: Minnesota GPO, 1947.

Governor's Interracial Commission of Minnesota. "The Negro Worker's Progress in Minnesota." St. Paul: Minnesota GPO, 1949.

Johnson, Lyndon B. *Public Papers of the Presidents of the United States: Lyndon B. Johnson, 1963–1964.* Washington, D.C.: GPO, 1964.

Kennedy, John F. *Public Papers of the Presidents of the United States: John F. Kennedy, 1963.* Washington, D.C.: GPO, 1963.

Truman, Harry S. *Public Papers of the Presidents of the United States: Harry S. Truman, 1949.* Washington, D.C.: GPO, 1964.

Truman, Harry S. *Public Papers of the Presidents of the United States: Harry S. Truman, 1950.* Washington, D.C.: GPO, 1965.

Truman, Harry S. *Public Papers of the Presidents of the United States: Harry S. Truman, 1951.* Washington, D. C.: GPO, 1965.

U.S. Commission on Civil Rights. *Employment: 1961 Commission on Civil Rights Report.* Washington, D.C.: GPO, 1961.

U.S. Commission on Civil Rights. *Report of the U.S. Commission on Civil Rights, 1959.* Washington, D.C.: GPO, 1959.

U.S. Commission on Civil Rights. *Survey of School Desegregation in the Southern and Border States, 1965–1966.* Washington, D.C.: GPO, 1966.

U.S. Commission on Civil Rights. *Title VI: One Year After.* Washington, D.C.: GPO, 1966.

U.S. Commission on Civil Rights. *Voting: 1961 Commission on Civil Rights Report.* Washington, D.C.: GPO, 1962.

U.S. Congress. House Subcommittee of Committee on Education and Labor, *Hearings on Federal Fair Employment Practice Act.* 81st Cong., 1st sess. Washington, D.C.: GPO, 1949.

U.S. Congress. House of Representatives Subcommittee on Equal Opportunities. *Equal Opportunity and Full Employment Act of 1976.* 93d Cong., 2d sess. Washington, D.C.: GPO, 1974.

U.S. Congress. House of Representatives Subcommittee on Manpower, Compensation, and Health and Safety, Committee on Education and Labor. *Full Employment and Balanced Growth Act of 1976.* 94th Cong., 2d sess. Washington, D.C.: GPO, 1976).

U.S. Congress. Joint Economic Committee. *Jobs and Prices in Atlanta.* 94th Cong., 1st sess. Washington, D.C.: GPO, 1976.

U.S. Congress. Joint Economic Committee. *Jobs and Prices in Chicago.* 94th Cong., 1st sess. Washington, D.C.: GPO, 1976.

U.S. Congress. Joint Economic Committee. *Jobs and Prices in the West Coast Region.* 94th Cong., 1st sess. Washington, D.C.: U.S. GPO, 1976.

U.S. Congress. Joint Economic Committee. *National Economic Planning, Balanced Growth, and Full Employment.* 94th Cong., 1st sess. Washington, D.C.: GPO, 1976.

U.S. Congress. Joint Economic Committee. *Thirtieth Anniversary of the Full Employment Act of 1946—A National Conference on Full Employment.* 94th Cong., 2d sess. Washington, D.C.: U.S. GPO, 1976.

U.S. Congress. Joint Economic Committee. *Youth Unemployment.* 94th Cong., 2d sess. Washington, D.C.: GPO, 1977.

U.S. Congress. Senate Committee on the Judiciary. *Civil Rights Proposals.* 84th Cong., 2d sess. Washington, D.C.: GPO, 1956.

U.S. Congress. Senate Committee on Rules and Administration. *Hearings on Federal Registrars.* 86th Cong., 2d sess. Washington, D.C.: GPO, 1960.

U.S. Congress. Senate Subcommittee on Civil Rights. *Antidiscrimination in Employment.* 83d Cong., 2d sess. Washington, D.C.: GPO, 1954.

U.S. Congress. Senate Subcommittee on Constitutional Rights. Committee on the Judiciary. *Civil Rights, 1957.* 85th Cong., 1st sess. Washington, D.C.: GPO, 1957.

U.S. Congress. Senate Subcommittee on Constitutional Rights. Committee on the Judiciary. *Literacy Tests and Voter Requirements in Federal and State Elections.* 87th Cong., 2d sess. Washington, D.C.: GPO, 1962.

U.S. Congress. Senate Subcommittee on Employment, Poverty, and Migratory Labor. Committee on Labor and Public Welfare, *Full Employment and Balanced Growth Act of 1976,* 94th Cong., 2d sess. Washington, D.C.: GPO, 1976.

U.S. Congress. Senate Subcommittee on Labor and Labor-Management Relations. *Discrimination and Full Utilization of Manpower Resources.* 82d Cong., 2d sess. Washington, D.C.: GPO, 1952.

U.S. Congress. Senate Subcommittee on Labor and Labor-Management Relations. *Employment and Economic Status of Negroes in the United States.* 83d Cong., 1st sess. Washington, D.C.: GPO, 1953.

U.S. Congress. Senate Subcommittee on Labor and Labor-Management Relations. *State and Municipal Fair Employment Legislation.* 83d Cong., 1st sess. Washington, D.C.: GPO, 1953.

U.S. Congress. Senate Subcommittee on Labor and Public Welfare. *Antidiscrimination in Employment.* 80th Cong., 1st sess. Washington, D.C.: GPO, 1947.

U.S. Congress. Senate Subcommittee on Manpower. *Equal Employment Opportunity.* 88th Cong., 1st sess. Washington, D.C.: GPO, 1963.

U.S. Congress. Senate Subcommittee of the Committee on Labor and Public Welfare. *Antidiscrimination in Employment.* 80th Cong., 1st sess. Washington, D.C.: GPO, 1947.

U.S. Department of Commerce. *Historical Statistics of the United States: Colonial Times to 1970.* Washington, D.C.: GPO, 1975.

U.S. Department of Labor. *Monthly Labor Review, July 1976.* Washington, D.C.: GPO, 1976.

U.S. Department of Labor. *Monthly Labor Review, March 1977.* Washington, D.C.: GPO, 1977.

Books

Ambrose, Stephen. *Eisenhower: The President.* New York: Simon and Schuster, 1983.

— *Nixon: The Triumph of a Politician.* New York: Simon and Schuster, 1987.

Anderson, Jervis. *Bayard Rustin: Troubles I've Seen.* New York: HarperCollins, 1995.

Bailey, Stephen Kemp. *Congress Makes a Law: The Story Behind the Employment Act of 1946.* New York: Columbia University Press, 1946.

Bartley, Numan. *The New South, 1945–1980.* Baton Rouge: Louisiana State University Press, 1995.

— *The Rise of Massive Resistance: Race and Politics in the South During the 1950s.* Baton Rouge: Louisiana State University Press, 1969.

Bartley, Numan, and Hugh Graham. *Southern Politics and the Second Reconstruction.* Baltimore: Johns Hopkins University Press, 1975.

Belknap, Michael. *Federal Law and Southern Order: Racial Violence and Constitutional Conflict in the Post-Brown South.* Athens: University of Georgia Press, 1995.

Berger, Morroe. *Equality by Statute: The Revolution in Civil Rights.* Garden City, N.Y.: Doubleday, 1967.

Berman, Daniel. *A Bill Becomes a Law: The Civil Rights Act of 1960.* New York: Macmillan, 1962.

Berman, William. *The Politics of Civil Rights in the Truman Administration.* Columbus: Ohio State University Press, 1970.

Black, Earl. *Southern Governors and Civil Rights: Racial Segregation as a Campaign Issue in the Second Reconstruction.* Cambridge: Harvard University Press, 1976.

Black, Earl, and Merle Black. *The Vital South: How Presidents Are Elected.* Cambridge: Harvard University Press, 1992.

Bloom, Jack. *Class, Race, and the Civil Rights Movement.* Bloomington: Indiana University Press, 1987.

Bolling, Richard. *House Out of Order.* New York: Dutton, 1965.

Boyle, Kevin. *The UAW and the Heyday of American Liberalism, 1945–1968.* Ithaca: Cornell University Press, 1995.

Branch, Taylor. *Parting the Waters: America in the King Years, 1954–1963.* New York: Simon and Schuster, 1988.

Brauer, Carl. *John F. Kennedy and the Second Reconstruction.* New York: Columbia University Press, 1977.

Brennan, Mary. *Turning Right in the Sixties: The Conservative Capture of the GOP.* Chapel Hill: University of North Carolina Press, 1995.

Brinkley, Alan. *The End of Reform: New Deal Liberalism in Recession and War.* New York: Knopf, 1995.

Brock, Clifton. *Americans for Democratic Action: Its Role in National Politics.* Washington, D.C.: Public Affairs Press, 1962.

Brown, Edgar, ed. *Democracy at Work: Being the Official Report of the 1948 Democratic National Convention.* Philadelphia: Local Democratic Political Committee of Pennsylvania, 1948.

Burk, Robert. *The Eisenhower Administration and Black Civil Rights.* Knoxville: University of Tennessee Press, 1984.

Burner, David. *Making Peace with the 60s.* Princeton: Princeton University Press, 1996.

Cagin, Seth, and Philip Dray. *We Are Not Afraid: The Story of Goodman, Schwerner, and Chaney and the Civil Rights Campaign for Mississippi.* New York: Macmillan, 1988.

Califano, Joseph. *The Triumph and Tragedy of Lyndon B. Johnson.* New York: Simon and Schuster, 1991.

Capeci, Dominic, Jr., and Martha Wilkerson, *Layered Violence: The Detroit Rioters of 1943.* Jackson: University of Missipppi Press, 1991.

Carnoy, Martin. *Faded Dreams: The Politics and Economics of Race in America.* Cambridge: Cambridge University Press, 1994.

Carson, Clayborne. *In Struggle: SNCC and the Black Awakening of the 1960s.* Cambridge: Harvard University Press, 1981.

Carter, Dan. *From George Wallace to Newt Gingrich: Race in the Conservative Counterrevolution, 1963–1994.* Baton Rouge: Louisiana State University Press, 1996.

— *The Politics of Rage: George Wallace, the Origins of the New Conservatism, and the Transformation of American Politics.* New York: Simon and Schuster, 1995.

Chafe, William. *The Unfinished Journey: America Since World War II.* New York: Oxford University Press, 1986.

Chester, Lewis, Godfrey Hodgson, and Bruce Page. *An American Melodrama: The Presidential Campaign of 1968.* New York: Viking, 1969.

Cohen, Dan. *Undefeated: The Life of Hubert H. Humphrey.* Minneapolis: Lerner, 1978.

Cohodas, Nadine. *Strom Thurmond and the Politics of Southern Change.* New York: Simon and Schuster, 1993.

Collins, Robert. *The Business Response to Keynes, 1929–1964.* New York: Columbia University Press, 1981.

Dallek, Robert. *Lone Star Rising.* New York; Oxford University Press, 1992.

David, Paul, Malcolm Moos, and Ralph Goldman. *Presidential Nominating Politics in 1952: The National Story.* Baltimore: Johns Hopkins University Press, 1954.

Dent, Harry. *The Prodigal South Returns to Power.* New York: Wiley, 1978.

Dinnerstein, Leonard. *Anti-Semitism in America.* New York: Oxford University Press, 1994.

Dionne, E. J. *Why Americans Hate Politics.* New York: Simon and Schuster, 1991.

Dittmer, John. *Local People: The Struggle for Civil Rights in Mississippi.* Champaign: University of Illinois Press, 1994.

Douglas, Paul. *In the Fullness of Time: The Memoirs of Paul H. Douglas.* New York: Harcourt, Brace, and Jovanovich, 1972.

Dumbrell, John. *The Carter Presidency: A Reevaluation.* New York: Manchester University Press, 1993.

Edsall, Thomas and Mary Edsall. *Chain Reaction: The Impact of Race, Rights, and Taxes on American Politics.* New York: Norton, 1991.

Eisele, Albert. *Almost to the Presidency: A Biography of Two American Politicians.* Blue Earth: Piper, 1972.

Evans, Rowland, and Robert Novak. *Lyndon B. Johnson and the Exercise of Power.* New York: New American Library, 1966.

Faber, Harold, ed. *The Road to the White House: The Story of the 1964 Election.* New York: McGraw-Hill, 1965.

Face the Nation, 1964. New York: Holt, Rinehart, and Winston, 1972.

Ferguson, Thomas, and Joel Rogers, *Right Turn: The Decline of the Democrats and the Future of American Politics.* New York: Hill and Wang, 1986.

Fine, Sidney. *Violence in the Model City: The Cavanaugh Administration, Race Relations, and the Detroit Riots of 1967.* Ann Arbor: University of Michigan Press, 1989.

Fite, Gilbert. *Richard B. Russell, Jr.: Senator from Georgia.* Chapel Hill: University of North Carolina Press, 1991.

Fleming, Dan Jr. *Kennedy vs. Humphrey, West Virginia, 1960: The Pivotal Battle for the Democratic Presidential Nomination.* Jefferson: McFarland, 1992.

Fontenoy, Charles. *Estes Kefauver: A Biography*. Knoxville: University of Tennessee Press, 1980.

Forman, James. *The Making of Black Revolutionaries*. New York: Macmillan, 1972.

Friendly, Fred. *Minnesota Rag*. New York: Random House, 1981.

Galphin, Bruce. *The Riddle of Lester Maddox*. Atlanta: Camelot, 1968.

Gallup, George. *The Gallup Poll: Public Opinion, 1935–1971*. New York: Random House, 1972.

Garfinkel, Herbert. *When Negroes March*. New York: Atheneum, 1969.

Garrow, David. *Bearing the Cross: Martin Luther King, Jr. and the Southern Christian Leadership Conference*. New York: William Morrow, 1986.

— *Protest at Selma: Martin Luther King and the Voting Rights Act of 1965*. New Haven: Yale University Press, 1978.

Garson, Robert A. *The Democratic Party and the Politics of Sectionalism, 1941–1948*. Baton Rouge: Louisiana State University Press, 1974.

Gillon, Steven M. *The Democrats' Dilemma: Walter Mondale and the Liberal Legacy*. New York: Columbia University Press, 1992.

— *Politics and Vision: The ADA and American Liberalism, 1947–1985*. New York: Oxford University Press, 1987.

Ginsburg, Helen. *Full Employment and Public Policy: The United States and Sweden*. Lexington: Heath, 1983.

Goldberg, Robert A. *Barry Goldwater*. New Haven: Yale University Press, 1995.

Goodwin, Richard. *Remembering America: A Voice from the Sixties*. Boston: Little, Brown, 1988.

Gordon, Albert. *Jews in Transition*. Minneapolis: University of Minnesota Press, 1949.

Gould, Lewis. *1968: The Election that Changed America*. Chicago: Ivan Dee, 1993.

Graham, Hugh. *The Civil Rights Era: Origins and Development of National Policy, 1960–1972*. New York: Oxford University Press, 1990.

Greene, John. *The Crusade: The Presidential Election of 1952*. New York: University Press of America, 1985.

Greene, John Robert. *The Presidency of Gerald R. Ford*. Lawrence: University Press of Kansas, 1995.

Griffith, Winthrop. *Humphrey: A Candid Biography*. New York: William Morrow, 1965.

Halpern, Stephen. *On the Limits of the Law: The Ironic Legacy of Title VI of the 1964 Civil Rights Act*. Baltimore: Johns Hopkins University Press, 1995.

Hamby, Alonzo. *Man of the People: A Life of Harry S. Truman*. New York: Oxford University Press, 1995.

Hays, Brooks. *A Southern Moderate Speaks*. Chapel Hill: University of North Carolina Press, 1959.

Hirsch, Arnold R. *Making the Second Ghetto: Race and Housing in Chicago, 1940–1960*. Cambridge: Cambridge University Press, 1983.

Hodgson, Godfrey. *The World Turned Right Side Up: A History of Conservative Ascendancy in America*. New York: Houghton Mifflin, 1996.

Holmquist, June, ed. *They Chose Minnesota*. Saint Paul: Minnesota Historical Society Press, 1981.

Humphrey, Hubert H. *Beyond Civil Rights*. New York: Random House, 1968.

— *The Cause Is Mankind.* New York: Praeger 1964.

— *The Education of a Public Man.* New York: Doubleday, 1976.

— *The Political Philosophy of the New Deal.* Baton Rouge: Louisiana State University Press, 1970.

— *War on Poverty.* New York: McGraw-Hill, 1964.

Jackson, Walter. *Gunnar Myrdal and America's Conscience: Social Engineering and Racial Liberalism, 1938–1987.* Chapel Hill: University of North Carolina Press, 1990.

Jeansonne, Glen. *Gerald L. K. Smith: Minister of Hate.* New Haven: Yale University Press, 1988.

Jencks, Christopher. *Rethinking Social Policy: Race, Poverty, and the Underclass.* Cambridge: Harvard University Press, 1992.

Johnson, Lady Bird. *A White House Diary.* New York: Holt, Rinehart, and Winston, 1970.

Katz, Michael B. *Improving Poor People: The Welfare State, the "Underclass," and Urban Schools as History.* Princeton: Princeton University Press, 1995.

— *The Undeserving Poor: From the War on Poverty to the War on Welfare.* New York: Pantheon, 1989.

Kaufman, Burton. *The Presidency of James Earl Carter, Jr.* Lawrence: University of Kansas Press, 1993.

Kazin, Michael. *The Populist Persuasion.* New York: Basic, 1995.

Key, V. O. *Southern Politics in State and Nation.* New York: Knopf, 1949.

Kluger, Richard. *Simple Justice: The History of Brown v. Board of Education.* New York: Knopf, 1976.

Kurian, George Thomas, ed. *Datapedia of the United States, 1790–2000.* Lanham: Bernan, 1995.

Kusmer, Kenneth. *A Ghetto Takes Shape: Black Cleveland, 1870–1930.* Urbana: University of Illinois Press, 1976.

Lasch, Christopher. *The True and Only Heaven: Progress and Its Critics.* New York: Norton, 1991.

Lawson, Steven. *Black Ballots: Voting Rights in the South, 1944–1969.* New York: Columbia University Press, 1976.

— *In Pursuit of Power: Southern Blacks and Electoral Politics, 1965–1982.* New York: Columbia University Press, 1985.

— *Running for Freedom.* Philadelphia: Temple University Press, 1991.

Lazarowitz, Arlene. *Years in Exile: The Liberal Democrats, 1950–1959.* New York: Garland, 1988.

Lesher, Stephen. *George Wallace: American Populist.* New York: Addison-Wesley, 1994.

Leuchtenburg, William E. *In the Shadow of FDR: From Harry Truman to Ronald Reagan.* Ithaca: Cornell University Press, 1983.

Levison, Andrew. *The Full Employment Alternative.* New York: Coward, McCann, and Geoghega, 1980.

Loevy, Robert. *To End All Segregation: The Politics of the Passage of the 1964 Civil Rights Act.* Lanham: University Press of America, 1990.

Lubell, Samuel. *The Hidden Crisis in American Politics.* New York: Norton, 1970.

Lukas, J. Anthony. *Common Ground: A Turbulent Decade in the Lives of Three American Families.* New York: Vintage, 1986.

McAdam, Doug. *Freedom Summer.* New York: Oxford University Press, 1988.

McCoy, Donald, and David Ruetten, *Quest and Response: Minority Rights and the Truman Administration.* Lawrence: University Press of Kansas, 1973.

McCullough, David. *Truman.* New York: Simon and Schuster, 1992.

McMillen, Neil. *The Citizens' Council: Organized Resistance to the Second Reconstruction, 1954–1964.* Urbana: University of Illinois Press, 1971.

MacNeil, Neil. *Dirksen: Portrait of a Public Man.* New York: World, 1970.

McPherson, Harry. *A Political Education.* Boston: Little, Brown, 1972.

Martin, John F. *Civil Rights and the Crisis of Liberalism: The Democratic Party, 1945–1976.* Boulder: Westview, 1979.

Matusow, Allen. *The Unraveling of America: A History of Liberalism in the 1960s.* New York: Harper, 1984.

Mead, Lawrence. *The New Politics of Poverty.* New York: Basic, 1992.

Meet the Press, 1964. Washington, D.C.: Merkle, 1965.

Meet the Press, 1968. Washington, D.C.: Merkle, 1968.

Meier, August, and Elliott Rudwick. *CORE: A Study in the Civil Rights Movement, 1942–1968.* New York: Oxford University Press, 1973.

Menefee, Seldon. *Assignment U.S.A..* New York: Reynal and Hitchcock, 1943.

Mills, Nicholaus. *Like a Holy Crusade: Mississippi, 1964: The Turning Point of the Civil Rights Movement in America.* Chicago: Ivan Dee, 1992.

Morris, Aldon. *The Origins of the Civil Rights Movement.* New York: Macmillan, 1984.

Murphy, Walter. *Congress and the Court.* Chicago: University of Chicago Press, 1962.

Nichols, Lee. *Breakthrough on the Color Front.* New York: Random House, 1954.

Norgern, Paul, and Samuel Hill. *Toward Fair Employment.* New York: Columbia University Press, 1964.

Orfield, Gary. *The Reconstruction of Southern Education: The Schools and the 1964 Civil Rights Act.* New York: Wiley, 1969.

Parmet, Herbert. *The Democrats: The Years Since FDR.* New York: Macmillan, 1976.

—— *Eisenhower and the American Crusades.* New York: Macmillan, 1972.

—— *Richard Nixon and His America.* Boston: Little, Brown, 1990.

Patterson, James. *America's War Against Poverty, 1900–1980.* Cambridge: Harvard University Press, 1981.

—— *Congressional Conservatism and the New Deal: The Growth of the Conservative Coalition in Congress, 1933–1939* Lexington: University of Kentucky Press, 1967.

—— *Grand Expectations: The United States, 1945–1974.* New York: Oxford University Press, 1996.

Plotke, David. *Building a Democratic Political Order: Reshaping American Liberalism in the 1930s and 1940s.* Cambridge: Cambridge University Press, 1996.

Porter, Roger. *Presidential Decisionmaking: The Economic Policy Board.* Cambridge: Harvard University Press.

Rainwater, Lee, and William Yancey. *The Moynihan Report and the Politics of Controversy.* Cambridge: MIT Press, 1967.

Reed, Merl. *Seedtime for the Modern Civil Rights Movement: The President's Committee on Fair Employment Practices, 1941–1946.* Baton Rouge: Louisiana State University Press, 1991.

Reichley, A. James. *Conservatives in an Age of Change: The Nixon and Ford Administrations.* Washington, D.C.: Brookings Institute, 1981.

Report of the National Advisory Commission on Civil Disorders. New York: Bantam, 1968.

Ribuffo, Leo. *The Old Christian Right: The Protestant Far Right from the Great Depression to the Cold War.* Philadelphia: Temple University Press, 1983.

Rieder, Jonathan. *Canarsie: The Jews and Italians of Brooklyn Against Liberalism.* Cambridge: Harvard University Press, 1985.

Rowan, Carl. *Dream Makers, Dream Breakers: The World of Justice Thurgood Marshall.* Boston: Little, Brown, 1993.

Ruchames, Louis. *Race, Jobs, and Politics: The Story of FEPC.* New York: Columbia University Press, 1953.

Scammon, Richard, ed. *America Votes, 1964.* Washington, D.C.: Congressional Quarterly Press, 1966.

Schlesinger, Arthur. *A Thousand Days: John F. Kennedy in the White House.* Boston: Houghton-Mifflin, 1965.

Schlesinger, Arthur, ed. *A History of American Presidential Elections, 1789–1968.* New York: McGraw-Hill, 1971.

Schulman, Bruce J. *Lyndon B. Johnson and American Liberalism.* New York: Bedford, 1995.

Sellers, Cleveland. *The River of No Return: An Autobiography of a Black Militant and the Life and Death of SNCC.* New York: Morrow, 1973.

Sitkoff, Harvard. *A New Deal for Blacks.* New York: Oxford, 1978.

— *The Struggle for Black Equality.* New York: Hill and Wang, 1981.

Sleeper, Jim. *Liberal Racism.* New York: Viking, 1997.

Solberg, Carl. *Hubert H. Humphrey: A Biography.* New York: Norton, 1984.

Sosna, Morton. *In Search of the Silent South: Southern Liberals and the Race Issue.* New York: Columbia University Press, 1977.

Southern, David. *Gunnar Myrdal and Black-White Relations: The Use and Abuse of an American Dilemma, 1944–1969.* Baton Rouge: Louisiana State University Press, 1987.

Spangler, Earl. *The Negro in Minnesota.* Minneapolis: Denison, 1961.

Stein, Herbert. *Presidential Economics: The Making of Economic Policy from Roosevelt to Reagan.* Washington, D.C.: American Enterprise Institute, 1994.

Stern, Mark. *Calculating Visions: Kennedy, Johnson, and Civil Rights.* New Brunswick, N.J.: Rutgers University Press, 1992.

Sugrue, Thomas. *The Origins of the Urban Crisis: Race and Inequality in Postwar Detroit.* Princeton: Princeton University Press, 1996.

Sullivan, Patricia. *Days of Hope: Race and Democracy During the New Deal Era.* Chapel Hill: University of North Carolina Press, 1996.

Sundquist, James. *Dynamics of the Party System: Alignment and Realignment of the Political Parties in the United States.* Washington, D.C.: Brookings Institute, 1968.

— *Politics and Policy: The Eisenhower, Kennedy, and Johnson Years.* Washington, D.C.: Brookings Institute, 1968.

Thernstrom, Stephen, and Abigail Thernstrom. *America in Black and White: One Nation Indivisible, Race in Modern America.* New York: Simon and Schuster, 1997.

Thomson, Charles, and Frances Shattuck. *The 1956 Presidential Campaign.* Washington, D.C.: Brookings Institute, 1960.

Trotter, Joe. *Black Milwaukee: The Making of an Industrial Proletariat, 1915–1945.* Champaign: University of Illinois Press, 1985.

Walters, Ronald. *Black Presidential Politics in America: A Strategic Approach.* New York: State University of New York Press, 1988.

Watson, Denton. *Lion in the Lobby.* New York: William Morrow, 1990.

Weir, Margaret. *Politics and Jobs: The Boundaries of Employment Policy in the United States.* Princeton: Princeton University Press, 1992.

Weiss, Nancy. *Farewell to the Party of Lincoln.* Princeton: Princeton University Press, 1983.

— *Whitney M. Young, Jr. and the Struggle for Civil Rights.* Princeton: Princeton University Press, 1989.

Whalen, Charles, and Barbara Whalen. *The Longest Debate: A Legislative History of the 1964 Civil Rights Act.* Cabin John: Seven Locks Press, 1985.

White, Theodore. *The Making of the President, 1960.* New York: Atheneum, 1961.

— *The Making of the President, 1964.* New York: Atheneum, 1965.

— *The Making of the President, 1968.* New York: Atheneum, 1969.

— *The Making of the President, 1972.* New York: Atheneum, 1973.

Wicker, Thomas. *One of Us: Richard Nixon and the American Dream.* New York: Random House, 1991.

Wilkinson, J. Harvie. *From Brown to Bakke: The Supreme Court and School Integration, 1954–1978.* New York: Oxford University Press, 1979.

Wills, Garry. *Certain Trumpets: The Call of Leaders.* New York: Simon and Schuster, 1994.

Wilson, James Q. *Thinking About Crime.* New York: Basic, 1983.

Wilson, William Julius. *The Truly Disadvantaged: The Inner City, the Underclass, and Public Policy.* Chicago: University of Chicago Press, 1987.

Wolfe, Alan. *America's Impasse: The Rise and Fall of the Politics of Growth.* New York: Random House, 1981.

Wolk, Allan. *The Presidency and Black Civil Rights.* Rutherford: Fairleigh-Dickenson University Press, 1971.

Wynn, Neil. *The Afro-American and the Second World War.* New York: Holmes and Meier, 1976.

Zangrando, Robert. *The NAACP Crusade Against Lynching, 1909–1950.* Philadelphia: Temple University Press, 1980.

Articles and Dissertations

Auerbach, Carl. "Jury Trials and Civil Rights." *New Leader* 40 (April 29, 1957): 16–18.

Berman, Hyman. "Political Anti-Semitism in Minnesota During the Depression." *Jewish Social Studies* 28 (Summer-Fall 1976): 247–264.

Brinkley, Alan. "The Problem of American Conservatism." *American Historical Review* 99 (April 1994): 409–429.

Dalfiume, Richard A. "The 'Forgotten Years' of the Negro Revolution." *Journal of American History* 55 (June 1968): 90–106.

Diamond, Sara. "Right-Wing Movements in the United States, 1945–1992." Ph.D. diss., University of California, Berkeley, 1993.

DiIulio, John J. Jr. "The Impact of Inner City Crime." *Public Interest* 96 (Summer 1989): 28–46.

Findlay, James. "The Churches and the Civil Rights Act of 1964." *Journal of American History* 77 (June 1990): 66–92.

Fink, Gary. "Fragile Alliance: Jimmy Carter and the American Labor Movement." In Herbert Rosenbaum and Alexej Vgrinsky, eds., *The Presidency and Domestic Policies of Jimmy Carter*, pp. 783–803. Westport: Greenwood, 1994.

Finkle, Lee. "The Conservative Aims of Militant Rhetoric: Black Protest During World War II." *Journal of American History* 60 (December 1973): 692–713.

Gelfand, Mark. "The War on Poverty." In Robert A. Divine, ed., *The Johnson Years*, 1:126–154. Lawrence: University Press of Kansas, 1987.

Gerstle, Gary. "The Protean Character of American Liberalism." *American Historical Review* 99 (October 1994): 1,043–1,073.

— "Race and the Myth of the Liberal Consensus." *Journal of American History* 82 (September 1995): 579–586.

Greenstone, David. "Culture, Rationality, and the Underclass." In Christopher Jencks and Paul E. Peterson, eds., *The Urban Underclass*, pp. 399–408. Washington, D.C.: Brookings Institute, 1991.

Hase, Michiko. "W Gertrude Brown's Struggle for Racial Justice: Female Leadership and Community in Black Minneapolis, 1920–1940." Ph.D. dissertation, University of Minnesota, 1994.

Hill, Herbert. "Black Workers, Organized Labor, and Title VI of the 1964 Civil Rights Act: Legislative History and Litigation Record." In Herbert Hill and James E. Jones, eds., *Race in America: The Struggle for Equality*, pp. 263–341. Madison: University of Wisconsin Press, 1993.

Hirschmann, Charles. "Minorities in the Labor Market: Cyclical Patterns and Secular Trends in Joblessness." In Gary Sandefur and Marta Tienda, eds., *Divided Opportunities: Minorities, Poverty, and Social Policy*, pp. 63–85. New York: Plenum, 1988.

Humphrey, Hubert H. "The Senate on Trial." *American Political Science Review* 44 (September 1950): 650–660.

Jones, Jacqueline. "Southern Diaspora: Origins of the Northern 'Underclass." In Michael B. Katz, ed., *The "Underclass" Debate: Views from History*, pp. 27–54. Princeton: Princeton University Press, 1993.

Katz, Michael B. "Reframing the Debate." In Michael B. Katz, ed., *The "Underclass" Debate: Views from History*, pp. 440–477. Princeton: Princeton University Press, 1993.

Kellogg, Peter. "Civil Rights Consciousness in the 1940s." *Historian* 42 (November 1979): 18–41.

Korstad, Robert, and Nelson Lichtenstein. "Opportunities Found and Lost: Labor,

Radicals, and the Early Civil Rights Movement." *Journal of American History* 75 (December 1988): 786–811.

Klarman, Michael J. "How *Brown* Changed Race Relations: The Backlash Thesis." *Journal of American History* 81 (June 1994): 81–118.

Kusmer, Kenneth. "African Americans in the City Since World War II: From the Industrial to the Post-Industrial City." *Journal of Urban History* 21 (May 1995): 458–504.

Lawson, Steven. "Freedom Then, Freedom Now: The Historiography of the Civil Rights Movement." *American Historical Review* 96 (April 1991): 456–471.

McGirr, Lisa. "Suburban Warriors: Grass-Roots Conservatism in the 1960s." Ph.D. diss., Columbia University, 1995.

McWilliams, Carey. "Minneapolis: The Curious Twin." *Common Ground* 7 (Autumn 1946): 61–65.

Moon, Henry Lee. "The Negro Vote and the Election of 1956." *Journal of Negro Education* 26 (Summer 1957): 219–230.

Peterson, Paul E. "The Urban Underclass and the Poverty Paradox." In Christopher Jencks and Paul E. Peterson, eds., *The Urban Underclass*, pp. 3–27. Washington, D.C.: Brookings Institute, 1991.

Poulson, Neils Bjene. "Organizing the American Right, 1945–1964." Ph.D. diss., University of California, Santa Barbara, 1993.

Radosh, Ronald. "From Protest to Black Power: The Failure of Coalition Politics." In Marvin Gettleman and David Merindstein, eds., *The Great Society Reader: The Failure of American Liberalism*, pp. 278–293. New York: Random House, 1967.

Ross, Arthur. "The Negro in the American Economy." In Arthur Ross, ed., *Employment, Race, and Poverty*, pp. 3–48. New York: Harcourt, Brace, and World, 1967.

Ribuffo, Leo. "Why Is There So Much Conservatism in the United States and Why Do So Few Historians Know Anything About It?" *American Historical Review* 99 (April 1994): 438–449.

Schantz, Harvey, and Richard Schmidt. "Politics and Policy: The Humphrey-Hawkins Story." In Charles Bulmer and John Carmichael, eds., *Employment and Labor Relations Policy*, pp. 25–39. Lexington: Heath, 1980.

Shuman, Howard. "Senate Rules and the Civil Rights Bill: A Case Study." *American Political Science Review* 51 (December 1957): 955–975.

Sitkoff, Harvard. "Harry Truman and the Election of 1948: The Coming of Age of Civil Rights in American Politics." *Journal of Southern History* 37 (November 1971): 597–616.

— "Racial Militancy and Interracial Violence in the Second World War." *Journal of American History* 57 (December 1971): 661–681.

Skocpol, Theda. "Brother, Can You Spare a Job? Work and Welfare in the United States." In Theda Skocpol, ed., *Social Policy in the United States: Future Possibilities in Historical Pespective*, pp. 228–249. Princeton: Princeton University Press, 1995.

— "The Limits of the New Deal System and the Roots of Contemporary Welfare Dilemmas." In Margaret Weir, Ann Shola Orloff, and Theda Skocpol, eds., *The Politics of Social Policy in the United States*, pp. 293–312. Princeton: Princeton University Press, 1993.

— "Targeting Within Universalism: Politically Viable Policies to Combat Poverty in the United States." In Christopher Jencks and Paul E. Peterson, eds., *The Urban Underclass*, pp. 411–436. Washington, D.C.: Brookings Institute, 1991.

Stern, Mark J. "Poverty and Family Composition Since 1940." In Michael B. Katz, ed., *The "Underclass" Debate: Views from History*, pp. 220–253. Princeton: Princeton University Press, 1993.

Trotter, Joe. "Blacks in the Urban North: The 'Underclass' Question in Historical Perspective." In Michael B. Katz, ed., *The "Underclass" Debate: Views from History*, pp. 55–81. Princeton: Princeton University Press, 1993.

Ware, Gilbert. "The National Association for the Advancement of Colored People and the Civil Rights Act of 1957." Ph.D. diss., Princeton University, 1962.

Weir, Margaret. "The Federal Government and Unemployment: The Frustration of Policy Innovation from the New Deal to the Great Society." In Margaret Weir, Ann Shola Orloff, and Theda Skocpol, eds., *The Politics of Social Policy in the United States*, pp. 149–190. Princeton: Princeton University Press, 1988.

Weir, Margaret, Ann Shola Orloff, and Theda Skocpol. "The Future of Social Policy in the United States: Political Constraints and Possibilities." In Margaret Weir, Ann Shola Orloff, and Theda Skocpol, eds., *The Politics of Social Policy in the United States*, pp. 425–446. Princeton: Princeton University Press, 1993.

Wilson, James Q., and Philip J. Cook. "Unemployment and Crime—What Is the Connection?" *Public Interest* 79 (Spring 1985): 3–9.

Wilson, William Julius. "Social Policy and Minority Groups: What Might Have Been and What Might We See in the Future?" In Gary Sandefur and Marta Tienda, eds., *Divided Opportunities: Minorities and Social Policy*, pp. 231–252. New York: Plenum, 1988.

Oral Histories

Interviews Conducted by the Author

Carl Auerbach, March 14, 1997
Tim Barnicle, May 27, 1997
Hyman Bookbinder, August 5, 1997
William Connell, August 11, 1997
Arthur Naftalin, December 28, 1993
Charles Schultze, March 7, 1997
Norman Sherman, June 2, 1997
John Stewart, March 28, 1997
Ted Van Dyk, January 13, 1997
Willard Wirtz, February 12, 1997

Hubert Humphrey Oral History Project, Minnesota Historical Society, Saint Paul, Minn.

Carl Auerbach
Andrew Biemiller

Gerald Heany
Walter Heller
Frances Howard
Charles Hyneman
Neal Peterson
Leonard Ramburg and Glen Wallace
Joseph Rauh
Ed Ryan
Al Saunders
William Shore
Ted Van Dyk
Philip Zeidman

John F. Kennedy Library, Boston, Mass.
John Amos
Stuart Calhoun
Isaac Coggs
J. Raymond Depaulo
William Jacobs
Martin Luther King, Jr.
Frank Reeves
Norbert Schlei
Howard Schuman
James Sundquist

Lyndon Baines Johnson Library, Austin, Tex.
LeRoy Collins
Richard Bolling I
Orville Freeman
Aaron Henry
Hubert Humphrey I, III
Harry McPherson I, IV, V
Booth Mooney II
Lawrence O'Brien X, XXI, XXIII, XXV, XXVI
Joseph Rauh I, II, III
George Reedy
Bayard Rustin

Moorland–Spingarn Research Center, Howard University, Washington, D.C.
Hubert H. Humphrey

Twentieth-Century Radicalism in Minnesota Oral History Project, Minnesota Historical Society, St. Paul, Minn.
Albert Allen

Anthony Cassius
Nellie Stone Johnson
Robert Latz
Martin Lebedo
Carl Ross

HHH + CIVIL RTS — ASSESSMENT

"H's career shows that liberals more often than not had to
react to circumstances not of their own making and that
they usually lacked the political strength to achieve their civil
rts goals."

P. 8

COLUMBIA STUDIES IN CONTEMPORARY
AMERICAN HISTORY

William E. Luchtenberg and Alan Brinkley,
General Editors

Lawrence S. Wittner, _Rebels Against War: The American Peace Movement, 1941–1960_, 1969

Davis R. B. Ross, _Preparing for Ulysses: Politics and Veterans During World War II_, 1969

John Lewis Gaddis, _The United States and the Origins of the Cold War, 1941–1947_, 1972

George C. Herring, Jr., _Aid to Russia, 1941–1946: Strategy, Diplomacy, the Origins of the Cold War_, 1973

Alonzo L. Hamby, _Beyond the New Deal: Harry S. Truman and American Liberalism_, 1973

Richard M. Fried, _Men Against McCarthy_, 1976

Steven F. Lawson, _Black Ballots: Voting Rights in the South, 1944–1969_, 1976

Carl M. Brauer, _John F. Kennedy and the Second Reconstruction_, 1977

Maeva Marcus, _Truman and the Steel Seizure Case: The Limits of Presidential Power_, 1977

Morton Sosna, _In Search of the Silent South: Southern Liberals and the Race Issue_, 1977

Robert M. Collins, _The Business Response to Keynes, 1929–1964_, 1981

Robert M. Hathaway, _Ambiguous Partnership: Britain and America, 1944–1947_, 1981

Leonard Dinnerstein, _America and the Survivors of the Holocaust_, 1982

Lawrence S. Wittner, _American Intervention in Greece, 1943–1949_, 1982

Nancy Bernkopf Tucker, _Patterns in the Dust: Chinese-American Relations and the Recognition Controversy, 1949–1950_, 1983

Catherine A. Barnes, _Journey from Jim Crow: The Desegregation of Southern Transit_, 1983 \

Steven F. Lawson, _In Pursuit of Power: Southern Blacks and Electoral Politics, 1965–1982_, 1985

David R. Colburn, _Racial Change and Community Crisis: St. Augustine, Florida, 1877–1980_, 1985

Henry William Brands, _Cold Warriors: Eisenhower's Generation and the Making of American Foreign Policy_, 1988

Marc S. Gallicchio, _The Cold War Begins in Asia: American East Asian Policy and the Fall of the Japanese Empire_ 1988

Melanie Billings-Yun, _Decision Against War: Eisenhower and Dien Bien Phu_, 1988

Walter L. Hixson, _George F. Kennan: Cold War Iconoclast_, 1989

Robert D. Schulzinger, _Henry Kissinger: Doctor of Diplomacy_, 1989

Henry William Brands, *The Specter of Neutralism: The United States and the Emergence of the Third World, 1947–1960,* 1989

Mitchell K. Hall, *Because of Their Faith: CALCAV and Religious Opposition to the Vietnam War,* 1990

David L. Anderson, *Trapped By Success: The Eisenhower Administration and Vietnam, 1953–1961,* 1991

Steven M. Gillon, *The Democrats' Dilemma: Walter F. Mondale and the Liberal Legacy,* 1992

Wyatt C. Wells, *Economist in an Uncertain World: Arthur F. Burns and the Federal Reserve, 1970–1978,* 1994

Stuart Svonkin, *Jews Against Prejudice: American Jews and the Fight for Civil Liberties,* 1997

Doug Rossinow, *The Politics of Authenticity: Liberalism, Christianity, and the New Left in America,* 1998